Applied Supervised Learning with Python

Use scikit-learn to build predictive models from real-world datasets and prepare yourself for the future of machine learning

Benjamin Johnston and Ishita Mathur

Applied Supervised Learning with Python

Copyright © 2019 Packt Publishing

All rights reserved. No part of this book may be reproduced, stored in a retrieval system, or transmitted in any form or by any means, without the prior written permission of the publisher, except in the case of brief quotations embedded in critical articles or reviews.

Every effort has been made in the preparation of this book to ensure the accuracy of the information presented. However, the information contained in this book is sold without warranty, either express or implied. Neither the author, nor Packt Publishing, and its dealers and distributors will be held liable for any damages caused or alleged to be caused directly or indirectly by this book.

Packt Publishing has endeavored to provide trademark information about all of the companies and products mentioned in this book by the appropriate use of capitals. However, Packt Publishing cannot guarantee the accuracy of this information.

Authors: Benjamin Johnston and Ishita Mathur

Reviewer: Priyanka Das

Managing Editor: Taabish Khan

Acquisitions Editors: Aditya Date and Kunal Sawant

Production Editor: Nitesh Thakur

Editorial Board: David Barnes, Ewan Buckingham, Simon Cox, Manasa Kumar, Alex Mazonowicz, Douglas Paterson, Dominic Pereira, Shiny Poojary, Erol Staveley, Ankita Thakur, and Mohita Vyas.

First Published: April 2019

Production Reference: 1250419

ISBN: 978-1-78995-492-0

Published by Packt Publishing Ltd.

Livery Place, 35 Livery Street

Birmingham B3 2PB, UK

Table of Contents

Preface i

Python Machine Learning Toolkit 1

Introduction 2
Supervised Machine Learning 2
    When to Use Supervised Learning 4
    Why Python? 6
Jupyter Notebooks 7
    Exercise 1: Launching a Jupyter Notebook 8
    Exercise 2: Hello World 10
    Exercise 3: Order of Execution in a Jupyter Notebook 14
    Exercise 4: Advantages of Jupyter Notebooks 16
    Python Packages and Modules 18
pandas 20
    Loading Data in pandas 20
    Exercise 5: Loading and Summarizing the Titanic Dataset 22
    Exercise 6: Indexing and Selecting Data 24
    Exercise 7: Advanced Indexing and Selection 28
    pandas Methods 31
    Exercise 8: Splitting, Applying, and Combining Data Sources 35
    Lambda Functions 38
    Exercise 9: Lambda Functions 38
Data Quality Considerations 40
    Managing Missing Data 41
    Class Imbalance 46

Low Sample Size 47
Activity 1: pandas Functions 47
Summary 48

Exploratory Data Analysis and Visualization   51

Introduction 52
Exploratory Data Analysis (EDA) 52
Exercise 10: Importing Libraries for Data Exploration 54

Summary Statistics and Central Values 55
Standard Deviation 55
Percentiles 56
Exercise 11: Summary Statistics of Our Dataset 57

Missing Values 61
Finding Missing Values 62
Exercise 12: Visualizing Missing Values 63
Imputation Strategies for Missing Values 67
Exercise 13: Imputation Using pandas 68
Exercise 14: Imputation Using scikit-learn 69
Exercise 15: Imputation Using Inferred Values 70
Activity 2: Summary Statistics and Missing Values 73

Distribution of Values 74
Target Variable 74
Exercise 16: Plotting a Bar Chart 74
Categorical Data 76
Exercise 17: Datatypes for Categorical Variables 77
Exercise 18: Calculating Category Value Counts 79
Exercise 19: Plotting a Pie Chart 80
Continuous Data 81

Exercise 20: Plotting a Histogram	83
Exercise 21: Skew and Kurtosis	85
Activity 3: Visually Representing the Distribution of Values	87

Relationships within the Data 87

Relationship between Two Continuous Variables	88
Exercise 22: Plotting a Scatter Plot	89
Exercise 23: Correlation Heatmap	90
Exercise 24: Pairplot	94
Relationship between a Continuous and a Categorical Variable	96
Exercise 25: Bar Chart	96
Exercise 26: Box Plot	98
Relationship between Two Categorical Variables	101
Exercise 27: Stacked Bar Chart	101
Activity 4: Relationships Within the Data	103

Summary 104

Regression Analysis   107

Introduction 108
Regression and Classification Problems 108

Data, Models, Training, and Evaluation	108

Linear Regression 111

Exercise 28: Plotting Data with a Moving Average	112
Activity 5: Plotting Data with a Moving Average	116
Least Squares Method	117
The scikit-learn Model API	119
Exercise 29: Fitting a Linear Model Using the Least Squares Method	119
Activity 6: Linear Regression Using the Least Squares Method	124
Linear Regression with Dummy Variables	125

Exercise 30: Introducing Dummy Variables	125
Activity 7: Dummy Variables	130
Parabolic Model with Linear Regression	132
Exercise 31: Parabolic Models with Linear Regression	133
Activity 8: Other Model Types with Linear Regression	138
Generic Model Training	139
Gradient Descent	140
Exercise 32: Linear Regression with Gradient Descent	143
Exercise 33: Optimizing Gradient Descent	151
Activity 9: Gradient Descent	153
Multiple Linear Regression	154
Exercise 34: Multiple Linear Regression	155
Autoregression Models	158
Exercise 35: Creating an Autoregression Model	159
Activity 10: Autoregressors	171
Summary	172

Classification 175

Introduction	176
Linear Regression as a Classifier	176
Exercise 36: Linear Regression as a Classifier	177
Logistic Regression	182
Exercise 37: Logistic Regression as a Classifier – Two-Class Classifier	185
Exercise 38: Logistic Regression – Multiclass Classifier	191
Activity 11: Linear Regression Classifier – Two-Class Classifier	196
Activity 12: Iris Classification Using Logistic Regression	197
Classification Using K-Nearest Neighbors	198
Exercise 39: K-NN Classification	200

Exercise 40: Visualizing K-NN Boundaries 206

Activity 13: K-NN Multiclass Classifier 213

Classification Using Decision Trees 214

Exercise 41: ID3 Classification 216

Exercise 42: Iris Classification Using a CART Decision Tree 228

Summary 231

Ensemble Modeling — 233

Introduction 234

Exercise 43: Importing Modules and Preparing the Dataset 235

Overfitting and Underfitting 237

Underfitting 238

Overfitting 239

Overcoming the Problem of Underfitting and Overfitting 240

Bagging 241

Bootstrapping 241

Bootstrap Aggregation 242

Exercise 44: Using the Bagging Classifier 244

Random Forest 246

Exercise 45: Building the Ensemble Model Using Random Forest 247

Boosting 248

Adaptive Boosting 249

Exercise 46: Adaptive Boosting 250

Gradient Boosting 253

Exercise 47: GradientBoostingClassifier 254

Stacking 255

Exercise 48: Building a Stacked Model 257

Activity 14: Stacking with Standalone and Ensemble Algorithms 261
Summary 263

Model Evaluation — 265

Introduction 266
Exercise 49: Importing the Modules and Preparing Our Dataset 268

Evaluation Metrics 269
Regression 270
Exercise 50: Regression Metrics 272
Classification 273
Exercise 51: Classification Metrics 279

Splitting the Dataset 280
Hold-out Data 281
K-Fold Cross-Validation 282
Sampling 283
Exercise 52: K-Fold Cross-Validation with Stratified Sampling 284

Performance Improvement Tactics 286
Variation in Train and Test Error 286
Hyperparameter Tuning 288
Exercise 53: Hyperparameter Tuning with Random Search 291
Feature Importance 293
Exercise 54: Feature Importance Using Random Forest 293
Activity 15: Final Test Project 294

Summary 296

Appendix — 299

Index — 385

Preface

About

This section briefly introduces the authors, what this book covers, the technical skills you'll need to get started, and the hardware and software requirements required to complete all of the included activities and exercises.

About the Book

Machine learning—the ability of a machine to give correct answers based on input data—has revolutionized the way we do business. Applied Supervised Learning with Python provides a rich understanding of how you can apply machine learning techniques to your data science projects using Python. You'll explore Jupyter notebooks, a technology that's widely used in academic and commercial circles with support for running inline code.

With the help of fun examples, you'll gain experience working on the Python machine learning toolkit—from performing basic data cleaning and processing to working with a range of regression and classification algorithms. Once you've grasped the basics, you'll learn how to build and train your own models using advanced techniques such as decision trees, ensemble modeling, validation, and error metrics. You'll also learn data visualization techniques using powerful Python libraries such as Matplotlib and Seaborn.

This book also covers ensemble modeling and random forest classifiers, along with other methods for combining results from multiple models, and concludes by delving into cross-validation to test your algorithm and check how well the model works on unseen data.

By the end of this book, you'll be equipped to not only work with machine learning algorithms, but also be able to create some of your own!

About the Authors

Benjamin Johnston is a senior data scientist for one of the world's leading data-driven medtech companies and is involved in the development of innovative digital solutions throughout the entire product development pathway, from problem definition, to solution research and development, through to final deployment. He is currently completing his PhD in machine learning, specializing in image processing and deep convolutional neural networks. He has more than 10 years' experience in medical device design and development, working in a variety of technical roles and holds first-class honors bachelor's degrees in both engineering and medical science from the University of Sydney, Australia.

Ishita Mathur has worked as a data scientist for 2.5 years with product-based start-ups working with business concerns in various domains and formulating them as technical problems that can be solved using data and machine learning. Her current work at GO-JEK involves the end-to-end development of machine learning projects, by working as part of a product team on defining, prototyping, and implementing data science models within the product. She completed her masters' degree in high-performance computing with data science at the University of Edinburgh, UK, and her bachelor's degree with honors in physics at St. Stephen's College, Delhi.

Objectives

- Understand the concept of supervised learning and its applications
- Implement common supervised learning algorithms using machine learning Python libraries
- Validate models using the k-fold technique
- Build your models with decision trees to get results effortlessly
- Use ensemble modeling techniques to improve the performance of your model
- Apply a variety of metrics to compare machine learning models

Audience

Applied Supervised Learning with Python is for you if you want to gain a solid understanding of machine learning using Python. It'll help if you have some experience in any functional or object-oriented language and a basic understanding of Python libraries and expressions, such as arrays and dictionaries.

Approach

Applied Supervised Learning with Python takes a hands-on approach toward understanding supervised learning with Python. It contains multiple activities that use real-life business scenarios for you to practice and apply your new skills in a highly relevant context.

Hardware Requirements

For an optimal student experience, we recommend the following hardware configuration:

- Processor: Dual Core or better
- Memory: 4 GB RAM
- Hard disk: 10 GB available space
- Internet connection

Software Requirements

You'll also need the following software installed in advance:

- Any of the following operating systems:

    Windows 7 SP1 32/64-bit, Windows 8.1 32/64-bit, or Windows 10 32/64-bit

    Ubuntu 14.04 or later

    macOS Sierra or later

- Browser: Google Chrome or Mozilla Firefox
- Anaconda

Conventions

Code words in text, database table names, folder names, filenames, file extensions, pathnames, dummy URLs, user input, and Twitter handles are shown as follows: "This can be easily verified using Python's built-in **type** function."

A block of code is set as follows:

```
description_features = [
    'injuries_description', 'damage_description',
    'total_injuries_description', 'total_damage_description'
]
```

New terms and important words are shown in bold. Words that you see on the screen, for example, in menus or dialog boxes, appear in the text like this: "Click on the **Untitled** text and a popup will appear allowing you to rename the notebook."

Installation and Setup

Jupyter notebooks are available once you install Anaconda on your system. Anaconda can be installed for Windows systems using the steps available at https://docs.anaconda.com/anaconda/install/windows/.

For other systems, navigate to the respective installation guide from https://docs.anaconda.com/anaconda/install/.

Installing the Code Bundle

Copy the code bundle for the book to the `C:/Code` folder.

Additional Resources

The code bundle for this book is also hosted on GitHub at: https://github.com/TrainingByPackt/Applied-Supervised-Learning-with-Python.

We also have other code bundles from our rich catalog of books and videos available at https://github.com/PacktPublishing/. Check them out!

Python Machine Learning Toolkit

Learning Objectives

By the end of this chapter, you will be able to:

- Explain supervised machine learning and describe common examples of machine learning problems
- Install and load Python libraries into your development environment for use in analysis and machine learning problems
- Access and interpret the documentation of a subset of Python libraries, including the powerful pandas library
- Create an IPython Jupyter notebook and use executable code cells and markdown cells to create a dynamic report
- Load an external data source using pandas and use a variety of methods to search, filter, and compute descriptive statistics of the data
- Clean a data source of mediocre quality and gauge the potential impact of various issues within the data source

This chapter introduces supervised learning, Jupyter notebooks, and some of the most common pandas data methods.

Introduction

The study and application of machine learning and artificial intelligence has recently been the source of much interest and research in the technology and business communities. Advanced data analytics and machine learning techniques have shown great promise in advancing many sectors, such as personalized healthcare and self-driving cars, as well as in solving some of the world's greatest challenges, such as combating climate change. This book has been designed to assist you in taking advantage of the unique confluence of events in the field of data science and machine learning today. Across the globe, private enterprises and governments are realizing the value and efficiency of data-driven products and services. At the same time, reduced hardware costs and open source software solutions are significantly reducing the barriers to entry of learning and applying machine learning techniques.

Throughout this book, you will develop the skills required to identify, prepare, and build predictive models using supervised machine learning techniques in the Python programming language. The six chapters each cover one aspect of supervised learning. This chapter introduces a subset of the Python machine learning toolkit, as well as some of the things that need to be considered when loading and using data sources. This data exploration process is further explored in *Chapter 2, Exploratory Data Analysis and Visualization*, as we introduce exploratory data analysis and visualization. *Chapter 3, Regression Analysis*, and *Chapter 4, Classification*, look at two subsets of machine learning problems – regression and classification analysis – and demonstrate these techniques through examples. Finally, *Chapter 5, Ensemble Modeling*, covers ensemble networks, which use multiple predictions from different models to boost overall performance, while *Chapter 6, Model Evaluation*, covers the extremely important concepts of validation and evaluation metrics. These metrics provide a means of estimating the true performance of a model.

Supervised Machine Learning

A machine learning algorithm is commonly thought of as simply the mathematical process (or algorithm) itself, such as a neural network, deep neural network, or random forest algorithm. However, this is only a component of the overall system; firstly, we must define the problem that can be adequately solved using such techniques. Then, we must specify and procure a clean dataset that is composed of information that can be mapped from the first number space to a secondary one. Once the dataset has been designed and procured, the machine learning model can be specified and designed; for example, a single-layer neural network with 100 hidden nodes that uses a *tanh* activation function.

With the dataset and model well defined, the means of determining the exact values for the model can be specified. This is a repetitive optimization process that evaluates the output of the model against some existing data and is commonly referred to as **training**. Once training has been completed and you have your defined model, then it is good practice to evaluate it against some reference data to provide a benchmark of overall performance.

Considering this general description of a complete machine learning algorithm, the problem definition and data collection stages are often the most critical. What is the problem you are trying to solve? What outcome would you like to achieve? How are you going to achieve it? How you answer these questions will drive and define many of the subsequent decisions or model design choices. It is also in answering these questions that we will select which category of machine learning algorithms we will choose: supervised or unsupervised methods.

So, what exactly are supervised and unsupervised machine learning problems or methods? **Supervised learning** techniques center on mapping some set of information to another by providing the training process with the input information and the desired outputs, then checking its ability to provide the correct result. As an example, let's say you are the publisher of a magazine that reviews and ranks hairstyles from various time periods. Your readers frequently send you far more images of their favorite hairstyles for review than you can manually process. To save some time, you would like to automate the sorting of the hairstyles images you receive based on time periods, starting with hairstyles from the 1960s and 1980s:

Figure 1.1: Hairstyles images from different time periods

To create your hairstyles-sorting algorithm, you start by collecting a large sample of hairstyles images and manually labeling each one with its corresponding time period. Such a dataset (known as a **labeled dataset**) is the input data (hairstyles images) and the desired output information (time period) is known and recorded. This type of problem is a classic supervised learning problem; we are trying to develop an algorithm that takes a set of inputs and learns to return the answers that we have told it are correct.

When to Use Supervised Learning

Generally, if you are trying to automate or replicate an existing process, the problem is a supervised learning problem. Supervised learning techniques are both very useful and powerful, and you may have come across them or even helped create labeled datasets for them without realizing. As an example, a few years ago, Facebook introduced the ability to tag your friends in any image uploaded to the platform. To tag a friend, you would draw a square over your friend's face and then add the name of your friend to notify them of the image. Fast-forward to today and Facebook will automatically identify your friends in the image and tag them for you. This is yet another example of supervised learning. If you ever used the early tagging system and manually identified your friends in an image, you were in fact helping to create Facebook's labeled dataset. A user who uploaded an image of a person's face (the input data) and tagged the photo with the subject's name would then create the label for the dataset. As users continued to use this tagging service, a sufficiently large labeled dataset was created for the supervised learning problem. Now friend-tagging is completed automatically by Facebook, replacing the manual process with a supervised learning algorithm, as opposed to manual user input:

Figure 1.2: Tagging a friend on Facebook

One particularly timely and straightforward example of supervised learning is the training of self-driving cars. In this example, the algorithm uses the target route as determined by the GPS system, as well as on-board instrumentation, such as speed measures, the brake position, and/or a camera or **Light Detection and Ranging (LIDAR)**, for road obstacle detection as the labeled outputs of the system. During training, the algorithm samples the control inputs as provided by the human driver, such as speed, steering angle, and brake position, mapping them against the outputs of the system; thus providing the labeled dataset. This data can then be used to train the driving/navigation systems within the self-driving car or in simulation exercises.

Image-based supervised problems, while popular, are not the only examples of supervised learning problems. Supervised learning is also commonly used in the automatic analysis of text to determine whether the opinion or tone of a message is positive, negative, or neutral. Such analysis is known as **sentiment analysis** and frequently involves creating and using a labeled dataset of a series of words or statements that are manually identified as either positive, neutral, or negative. Consider these sentences: I like that movie and I hate that movie. The first sentence is clearly positive, while the second is negative. We can then decompose the words in the sentences into either positive, negative, or neutral (both positive, both negative); see the following table:

Word	Positive	Negative
I	1	1
Like	1	0
Hate	0	1
Movie	1	1

Figure 1.3: Decomposition of the words

Using sentiment analysis, a supervised learning algorithm could be created, say, using the movie database site IMDb to analyze comments posted about movies to determine whether the movie is being positively or negatively reviewed by the audience. Supervised learning methods could have other applications, such as analyzing customer complaints, automating troubleshooting calls/chat sessions, or even medical applications such as analyzing images of moles to detect abnormalities (https://www.nature.com/articles/nature21056).

This should give you a good understanding of the concept of supervised learning, as well as some examples of problems that can be solved using these techniques. While supervised learning involves training an algorithm to map the input information to corresponding known outputs, **unsupervised learning** methods, by contrast, do not utilize known outputs, either because they are not available or even known. Rather than relying on a set of manually annotated labels, unsupervised learning methods model the supplied data through specific constraints or rules designed into the training process.

Clustering analysis is a common form of unsupervised learning where a dataset is to be divided into a specified number of different groups based on the clustering process being used. In the case of k-nearest neighbors clustering, each sample from the dataset is labeled or classified in accordance with the majority vote of the k-closest points to the sample. As there are no manually identified labels, the performance of unsupervised algorithms can vary greatly with the data being used, as well as the selected parameters of the model. For example, should we use the 5 closest or 10 closest points in the majority vote of the k-closest points? The lack of known and target outputs during training leads to unsupervised methods being commonly used in exploratory analysis or in scenarios where the ground truth targets are somewhat ambiguous and are better defined by the constraints of the learning method.

We will not cover unsupervised learning in great detail in this book, but it is useful to summarize the main difference between the two methods. Supervised learning methods require ground truth labels or the *answers* for the input data, while unsupervised methods do not use such labels, and the final result is determined by the constraints applied during the training process.

Why Python?

So, why have we chosen the Python programming language for our investigation into supervised machine learning? There are a number of alternative languages available, including C++, R, and Julia. Even the Rust community is developing machine learning libraries for their up-and-coming language. There are a number of reasons why Python is the first-choice language for machine learning:

- There is great demand for developers with Python expertise in both industry and academic research.

- Python is currently one of the most popular programming languages, even reaching the number one spot in IEEE *Spectrum* magazine's survey of the top 10 programming languages (https://spectrum.ieee.org/at-work/innovation/the-2018-top-programming-languages).

- Python is an open source project, with the entire source code for the Python programming language being freely available under the GNU GPL Version 2 license. This licensing mechanism has allowed Python to be used, modified, and even extended in a number of other projects, including the Linux operating system, supporting NASA (https://www.python.org/about/success/usa/), and a plethora of other libraries and projects that have provided additional functionality, choice, and flexibility to the Python programming language. In our opinion, this flexibility is one of the key components that has made Python so popular.

- Python provides a common set of features that can be used to run a web server, a microservice on an embedded device, or to leverage the power of graphical processing units to perform precise calculations on large datasets.

- Using Python and a handful of specific libraries (or packages, as they are known in Python), an entire machine learning product can be developed–starting with exploratory data analysis, model definition, and refinement, through to API construction and deployment. All of these steps can be completed within Python to build an end-to-end solution. This is the significant advantage Python has over some of its competitors, particularly within the data science and machine learning space. While R and Julia have the advantage of being specifically designed for numerical and statistical computing, models developed in these languages typically require translation into some other language before they can be deployed in a production setting.

We hope that, through this book, you will gain an understanding of the flexibility and power of the Python programming language and will start on the path of developing end-to-end supervised learning solutions in Python. So, let's get started.

Jupyter Notebooks

One aspect of the data science development environment that distinguishes itself from other Python projects is the use of IPython Jupyter notebooks (https://jupyter.org). Jupyter notebooks provide a means of creating and sharing interactive documents with live, executable code snippets, and plots, as well as the rendering of mathematical equations through the Latex (https://www.latex-project.org) typesetting system. This section of the chapter will introduce you to Jupyter notebooks and some of their key features to ensure your development environment is correctly set up.

Throughout this book, we will make frequent reference to the documentation for each of the introduced tools/packages. The ability to effectively read and understand the documentation for each tool is extremely important. Many of the packages we will use contain so many features and implementation details that it is very difficult to memorize them all. The following documentation may come in handy for the upcoming section on Jupyter notebooks:

- The Anaconda documentation can be found at https://docs.anaconda.com.
- The Anaconda user guide can be found at https://docs.anaconda.com/anaconda/user-guide.
- The Jupyter Notebook documentation can be found at https://jupyter-notebook.readthedocs.io/en/stable/.

Exercise 1: Launching a Jupyter Notebook

In this exercise, we will launch our Jupyter notebook. Ensure you have correctly installed Anaconda with Python 3.7, as per the *Preface*:

1. There are two ways of launching a Jupyter notebook through Anaconda. The first method is to open Jupyter using the **Anaconda Navigator** application available in the **Anaconda** folder of the Windows Start menu. Click on the **Launch** button and your default internet browser will then launch at the default address, `http://localhost:8888`, and will start in a default folder path.

2. The second method is to launch Jupyter via the Anaconda prompt. To launch the Anaconda prompt, simply click on the **Anaconda Prompt** menu item, also in the Windows Start menu, and you should see a pop-up window similar to the following screenshot:

Figure 1.4: Anaconda prompt

3. Once in the Anaconda prompt, change to the desired directory using the **cd** (change directory) command. For example, to change into the **Desktop** directory for the **Packt** user, do the following:

   C:\Users\Packt> cd C:\Users\Packt\Desktop

4. Once in the desired directory, launch a Jupyter notebook using the following command:

   C:\Users\Packt> jupyter notebook

   The notebook will launch with the working directory from the one you specified earlier. This then allows you to navigate and save your notebooks in the directory of your choice as opposed to the default, which can vary between systems, but is typically your home or **My Computer** directory. Irrespective of the method of launching Jupyter, a window similar to the following will open in your default browser. If there are existing files in the directory, you should also see them here:

Figure 1.5: Jupyter notebook launch window

Exercise 2: Hello World

The *Hello World* exercise is a rite of passage, so you certainly cannot be denied that experience! So, let's print `Hello World` in a Jupyter notebook in this exercise:

1. Start by creating a new Jupyter notebook by clicking on the **New** button and selecting **Python 3**. Jupyter allows you to run different versions of Python and other languages, such as R and Julia, all in the same interface. We can also create new folders or text files here too. But for now, we will start with a Python 3 notebook:

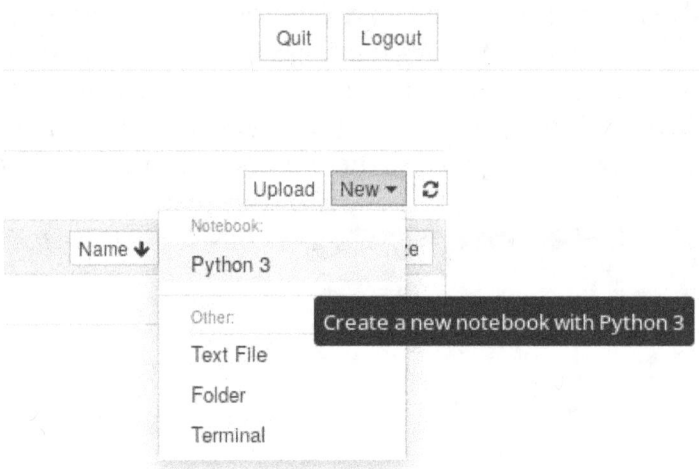

Figure 1.6: Creating a new notebook

This will launch a new Jupyter notebook in a new browser window. We will first spend some time looking over the various tools that are available in the notebook:

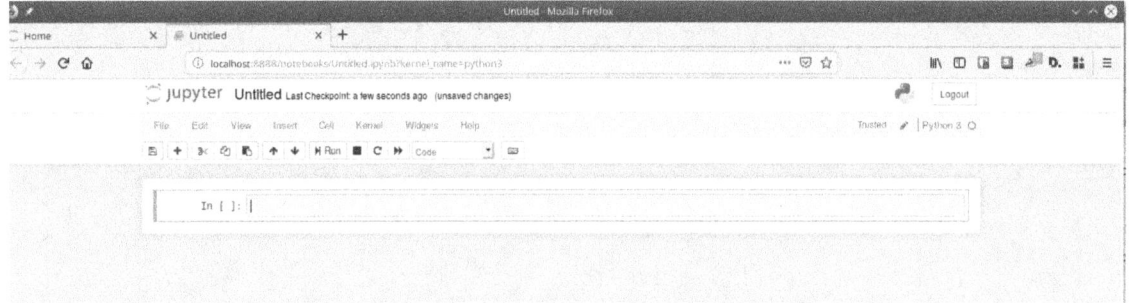

Figure 1.7: The new notebook

There are three main sections in each Jupyter notebook, as shown in the following screenshot: the title bar **(1)**, the toolbar **(2)**, and the body of the document **(3)**. Let's look at each of these components in order:

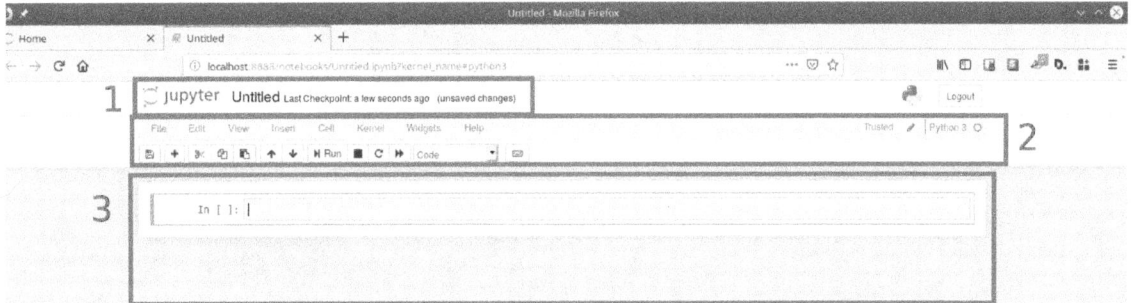

Figure 1.8: Components of the notebook

2. The title bar simply displays the name of the current Jupyter notebook and allows the notebook to be renamed. Click on the **Untitled** text and a popup will appear allowing you to rename the notebook. Enter `Hello World` and click **Rename**:

Figure 1.9: Renaming the notebook

3. For the most part, the toolbar contains all the normal functionality that you would expect. You can open, save, and make copies of—or create new—Jupyter notebooks in the **File** menu. You can search replace, copy, and cut content in the **Edit** menu and adjust the view of the document in the **View** menu. As we discuss the body of the document, we will also describe some of the other functionalities in more detail, such as the ones included in the **Insert**, **Cell**, and **Kernel** menus. One aspect of the toolbar that requires further examination is the far right-hand side, the outline of the circle on the right of Python 3.

Hover your mouse over the circle and you will see the **Kernel Idle** popup. This circle is an indicator to signify whether the Python kernel is currently processing; when processing, this circle indicator will be filled in. If you ever suspect that something is running or is not running, you can easily refer to this icon for more information. When the Python kernel is not running, you will see this:

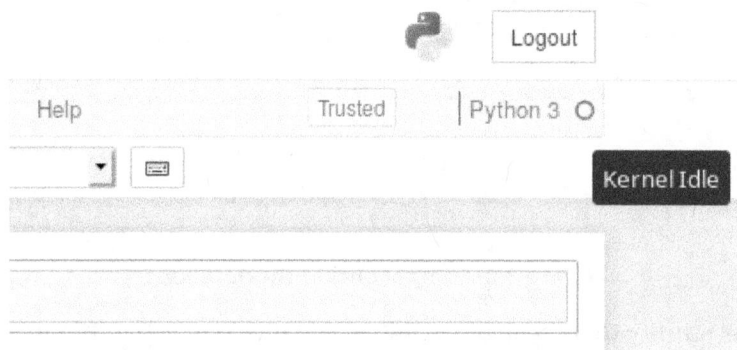

Figure 1.10: Kernel idle

When the Python kernel is running, you will see this:

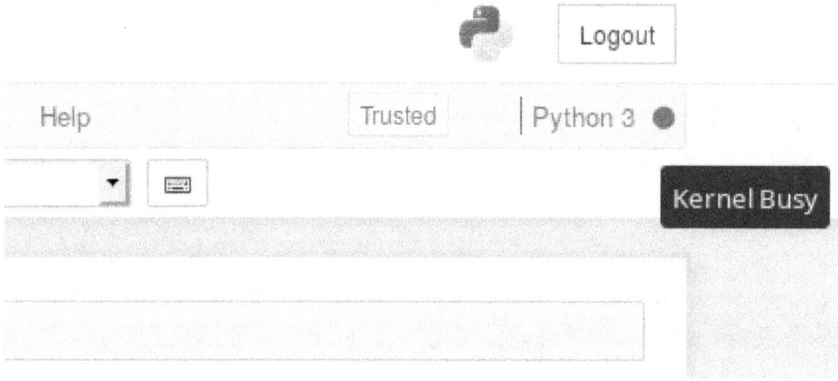

Figure 1.11: Kernel busy

4. This brings us to the body of the document, where the actual content of the notebook will be entered. Jupyter notebooks differ from standard Python scripts or modules, in that they are divided into separate executable cells. While Python scripts or modules will run the entirety of the script when executed, Jupyter notebooks can run all of the cells sequentially, or can also run them separately and in a different order if manually executed.

   Double-click on the first cell and enter the following:

   ```
   >>> print('Hello World!')
   ```

5. Click on **Run** (or use the *Ctrl + Enter* keyboard shortcut):

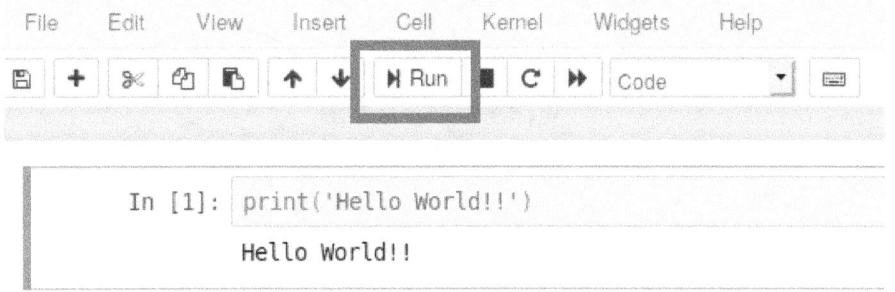

Figure 1.12: Running a cell

Congratulations! You just completed *Hello World* in a Jupyter notebook.

Exercise 3: Order of Execution in a Jupyter Notebook

In the previous exercise, notice how the **print** statement is executed under the cell. Now let's take it a little further. As mentioned earlier, Jupyter notebooks are composed of a number of separately executable cells; it is best to think of them as just blocks of code you have entered into the Python interpreter, and the code is not executed until you press the *Ctrl* + *Enter* keys. While the code is run at a different time, all of the variables and objects remain in the session within the Python kernel. Let's investigate this a little further:

1. Launch a new Jupyter notebook and then, in three separate cells, enter the code shown in the following screenshot:

    ```
    In [1]: print('Hello World!!')
            Hello World!!

    In [2]: hello_world = 'Hello World!'

    In [3]: print(hello_world)
            Hello World!
    ```

    Figure 1.13: Entering code into multiple cells

2. Click **Restart & Run All**.

    Notice that there are three executable cells, and the order of execution is shown in rectangular brackets; for example, **In [1]**, **In [2]**, and **In [3]**. Also note how the **hello_world** variable is declared (and thus executed) in the second cell and remains in memory, and thus is printed in the third cell. As we mentioned before, you can also run the cells out of order.

3. Click on the second cell, containing the declaration of **hello_world**, change the value to add a few more exclamation points, and run the cell again:

    ```
    In [1]: print('Hello World!!')
            Hello World!!

    In [4]: hello_world = 'Hello World!!!!!!!!!!!!!'

    In [3]: print(hello_world)
            Hello World!
    ```

    Figure 1.14: Changing the content of the second cell

Notice that the second cell is now the most recently executed cell (**In [4]**), and that the **print** statement after it has not been updated. To update the **print** statement, you would then need to execute the cell below it. *Warning: be careful about your order of execution.* If you are not careful, you can easily override values or declare variables in cells below their first use, as in notebooks, you no longer need to run the entire script at once. As such, it is good practice to regularly click **Kernel | Restart & Run All**. This will clear all variables from memory and run all cells from top to bottom in order. There is also the option to run all cells below or above a particular cell in the **Cell** menu:

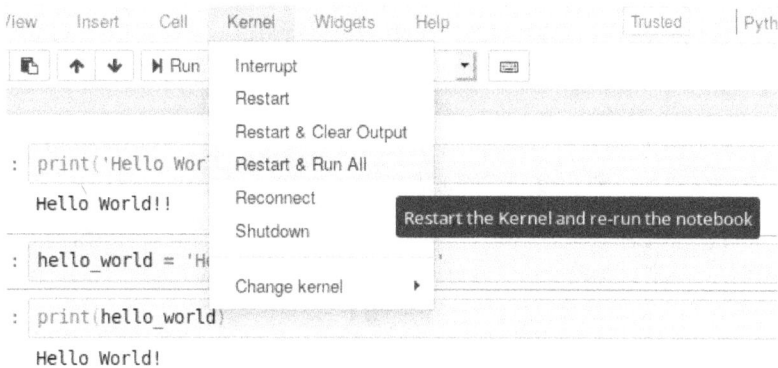

Figure 1.15: Restarting the kernel

> **Note**
>
> Write and structure your notebook cells as if you were to run them all in order, top to bottom. Use manual cell execution only for debugging/early investigation.

4. You can also move cells around using either the up/down arrows on the left of **Run** or through the **Edit** toolbar. Move the cell that prints the `hello_world` variable to above its declaration:

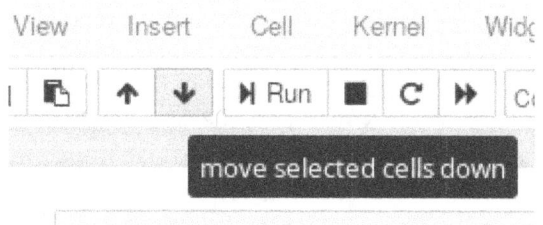

Figure 1.16: Moving cells

5. Click on **Restart & Run All** cells:

```
In [1]: print('Hello World!!')
        Hello World!!

In [2]: print(hello_world)

        NameError                                 Traceback (most recent call last)
        <ipython-input-2-51287cce4705> in <module>
        ----> 1 print(hello_world)

        NameError: name 'hello_world' is not defined

In [ ]: hello_world = 'Hello World!!!!!!!!!!!!!'
```

Figure 1.17: Variable not defined error

Notice the error reporting that the variable is not defined. This is because it is being used before its declaration. Also, notice that the cell after the error has not been executed as shown by the empty **In [ ]**.

Exercise 4: Advantages of Jupyter Notebooks

There are a number of additional features of Jupyter notebooks that make them very useful. In this exercise, we will examine some of these features:

1. Jupyter notebooks can execute commands directly within the Anaconda prompt by including an exclamation point prefix (**!**). Enter the code shown in the following screenshot and run the cell:

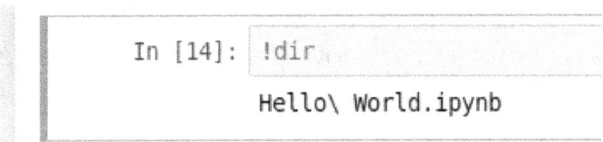

Figure 1.18: Running Anaconda commands

2. One of the best features of Jupyter notebooks is the ability to create live reports that contain executable code. Not only does this save time in preventing separate creation of reports and code, but it can also assist in communicating the exact nature of the analysis being completed. Through the use of Markdown and HTML, we can embed headings, sections, images, or even JavaScript for dynamic content.

To use Markdown in our notebook, we first need to change the cell type. First, click on the cell you want to change to Markdown, then click on the **Code** drop-down menu and select **Markdown**:

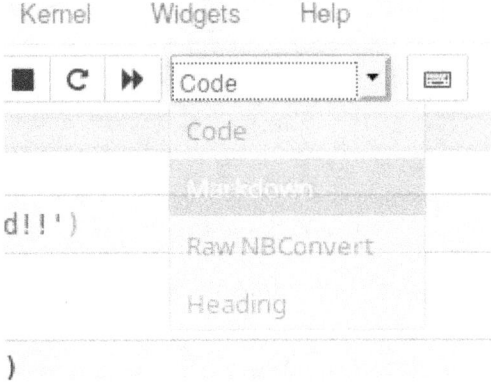

Figure 1.19: Running Anaconda commands

Notice that **In [ ]** has disappeared and the color of the box lining the cell is no longer blue.

3. You can now enter valid Markdown syntax and HTML by double-clicking in the cell and then clicking **Run** to render the markdown. Enter the syntax shown in the following screenshot and run the cell to see the output:

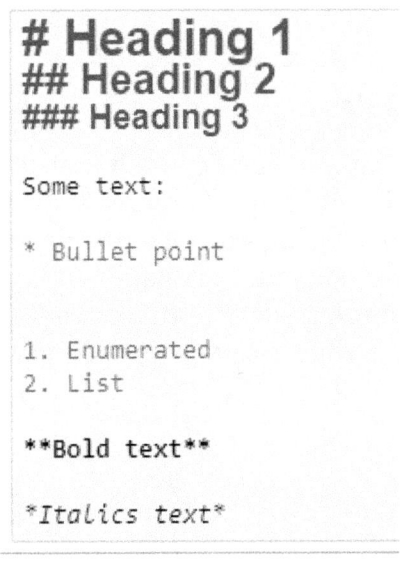

Figure 1.20: Markdown syntax

The output will be as follows:

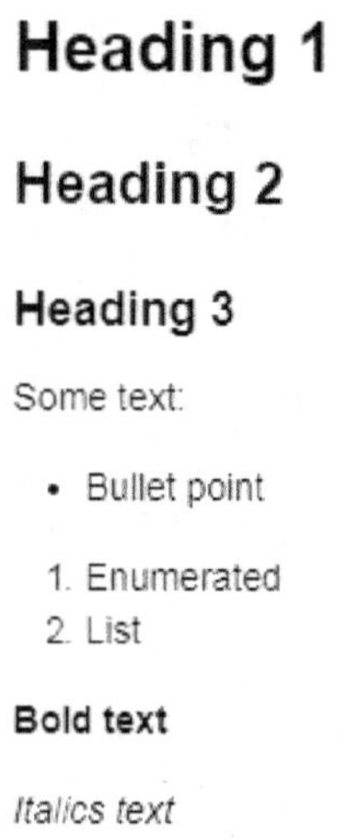

Heading 1

Heading 2

Heading 3

Some text:

- Bullet point

1. Enumerated
2. List

Bold text

Italics text

Figure 1.21: Markdown output

> **Note**
>
> For a quick reference on Markdown, refer to the `Markdown Syntax.ipynb` Jupyter notebook in the code files for this chapter.

Python Packages and Modules

While the standard features that are included in Python are certainly feature-rich, the true power of Python lies in the additional libraries (also known as packages in Python), which, thanks to open source licensing, can be easily downloaded and installed through a few simple commands. In an Anaconda installation, it is even easier as many of the most common packages come pre-built within Anaconda. You can get a complete list of the pre-installed packages in the Anaconda environment by running the following command in a notebook cell:

```
!conda list
```

In this book, we will be using the following additional Python packages:

- **NumPy** (pronounced *Num Pie* and available at https://www.numpy.org/): NumPy (short for numerical Python) is one of the core components of scientific computing in Python. NumPy provides the foundational data types from which a number of other data structures derive, including linear algebra, vectors and matrices, and key random number functionality.

- **SciPy** (pronounced *Sigh Pie* and available at https://www.scipy.org): SciPy, along with NumPy, is a core scientific computing package. SciPy provides a number of statistical tools, signal processing tools, and other functionality, such as Fourier transforms.

- **pandas** (available at https://pandas.pydata.org/): pandas is a high-performance library for loading, cleaning, analyzing, and manipulating data structures.

- **Matplotlib** (available at https://matplotlib.org/): Matplotlib is the foundational Python library for creating graphs and plots of datasets and is also the base package from which other Python plotting libraries derive. The Matplotlib API has been designed in alignment with the Matlab plotting library to facilitate an easy transition to Python.

- **Seaborn** (available at https://seaborn.pydata.org/): Seaborn is a plotting library built on top of Matplotlib, providing attractive color and line styles as well as a number of common plotting templates.

- **Scikit-learn** (available at https://scikit-learn.org/stable/): Scikit-learn is a Python machine learning library that provides a number of data mining, modeling, and analysis techniques in a simple API. Scikit-learn includes a number of machine learning algorithms out of the box, including classification, regression, and clustering techniques.

These packages form the foundation of a versatile machine learning development environment with each package contributing a key set of functionalities. As discussed, by using Anaconda, you will already have all of the required packages installed and ready for use. If you require a package that is not included in the Anaconda installation, it can be installed by simply entering and executing the following in a Jupyter notebook cell:

```
!conda install <package name>
```

As an example, if we wanted to install Seaborn, we'd run this:

```
!conda install seaborn
```

To use one of these packages in a notebook, all we need to do is import it:

```
import matplotlib
```

pandas

As mentioned before, pandas is a library for loading, cleaning, and analyzing a variety of different data structures. It is the flexibility of pandas, in addition to the sheer number of built-in features, that makes it such a powerful, popular, and useful Python package. It is also a great package to start with as, obviously, we cannot analyze any data if we do not first load it into the system. As pandas provides so much functionality, one very important skill in using the package is the ability to read and understand the documentation. Even after years of experience programming in Python and using pandas, we still refer to the documentation very frequently. The functionality within the API is so extensive that it is impossible to memorize all of the features and specifics of the implementation.

> **Note**
>
> The pandas documentation can be found at https://pandas.pydata.org/pandas-docs/stable/index.html.

Loading Data in pandas

pandas has the ability to read and write a number of different file formats and data structures, including CSV, JSON, and HDF5 files, as well as SQL and Python Pickle formats. The pandas input/output documentation can be found at https://pandas.pydata.org/pandas-docs/stable/user_guide/io.html. We will continue to look into the pandas functionality through loading data via a CSV file. The dataset we will be using for this chapter is the *Titanic: Machine Learning from Disaster* dataset, available from https://www.kaggle.com/c/Titanic/data or https://github.com/TrainingByPackt/Applied-Supervised-Learning-with-Python, which contains a roll of the guests on board the Titanic as well as their age, survival status, and number of siblings/parents. Before we get started with loading the data into Python, it is critical that we spend some time looking over the information provided for the dataset so that we can have a thorough understanding of what it contains. Download the dataset and place it in the directory you're working in.

Looking at the description for the data, we can see that we have the following fields available:

Variable	Definition	Key
survival	Survival	0 = No, 1 = Yes
pclass	Ticket class	1 = First, 2 = Second, 3 = Third
sex	Sex (male/female)	
age	Age in years	
sibsp	Number of siblings/spouses aboard the Titanic	
parch	Number of parents/children aboard the Titanic	
ticket	Ticket number	
fare	Passenger fare	
cabin	Cabin number	
embarked	Port of embarkation	C = Cherbourg, Q = Queenstown, S = Southampton

Figure 1.22: Fields in the Titanic dataset

We are also provided with some additional contextual information:

- **pclass**: This is a proxy for socio-economic status, where first class is upper, second class is middle, and third class is lower status.
- **age**: This is a fractional value if less than 1; for example, 0.25 is 3 months. If the age is estimated, it is in the form of *xx*.5.
- **sibsp**: A sibling is defined as a brother, sister, stepbrother, or stepsister, and a spouse is a husband or wife.
- **parch**: A parent is a mother or father, a child is a daughter, son, stepdaughter, or stepson. Children that traveled only with a nanny did not travel with a parent. Thus, 0 was assigned for this field.
- **embarked**: The point of embarkation is the location where the passenger boarded the ship.

Note that the information provided with the dataset does not give any context as to how the data was collected. The **survival**, **pclass**, and **embarked** fields are known as categorical variables as they are assigned to one of a fixed number of labels or categories to indicate some other information. For example, in **embarked**, the **C** label indicates that the passenger boarded the ship at Cherbourg, and the value of **1** in **survival** indicates they survived the sinking.

Exercise 5: Loading and Summarizing the Titanic Dataset

In this exercise, we will read our Titanic dataset into Python and perform a few basic summary operations on it:

1. Import the pandas package using shorthand notation, as shown in the following screenshot:

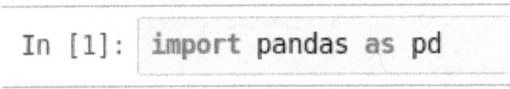

Figure 1.23: Importing the pandas package

2. Open the **titanic.csv** file by clicking on it in the Jupyter notebook home page:

Figure 1.24: Opening the CSV file

The file is a CSV file, which can be thought of as a table, where each line is a row in the table and each comma separates columns in the table. Thankfully, we don't need to work with these tables in raw text form and can load them using pandas:

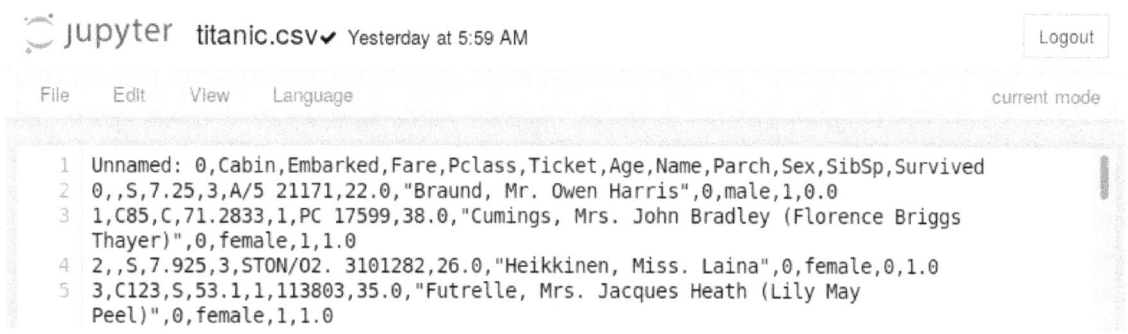

Figure 1.25: Contents of the CSV file

> **Note**
>
> Take a moment to look up the pandas documentation for the **read_csv** function at https://pandas.pydata.org/pandas-docs/stable/reference/api/pandas.read_csv.html. Note the number of different options available for loading CSV data into a pandas DataFrame.

3. In an executable Jupyter notebook cell, execute the following code to load the data from the file:

   ```
   df = pd.read_csv('Titanic.csv')
   ```

   The pandas DataFrame class provides a comprehensive set of attributes and methods that can be executed on its own contents, ranging from sorting, filtering, and grouping methods to descriptive statistics, as well as plotting and conversion.

> **Note**
>
> Open and read the documentation for pandas DataFrame objects at https://pandas.pydata.org/pandas-docs/stable/reference/frame.html.

4. Read the first five rows of data using the **head()** method of the DataFrame:

   ```
   df.head()
   ```

	Unnamed: 0	Cabin	Embarked	Fare	Pclass	Ticket	Age	Name	Parch	Sex	SibSp	Survived
0	0	NaN	S	7.2500	3	A/5 21171	22.0	Braund, Mr. Owen Harris	0	male	1	0.0
1	1	C85	C	71.2833	1	PC 17599	38.0	Cumings, Mrs. John Bradley (Florence Briggs Th...	0	female	1	1.0
2	2	NaN	S	7.9250	3	STON/O2. 3101282	26.0	Heikkinen, Miss. Laina	0	female	0	1.0
3	3	C123	S	53.1000	1	113803	35.0	Futrelle, Mrs. Jacques Heath (Lily May Peel)	0	female	1	1.0
4	4	NaN	S	8.0500	3	373450	35.0	Allen, Mr. William Henry	0	male	0	0.0

   Figure 1.26: Reading the first five rows

   In this sample, we have a visual representation of the information in the DataFrame. We can see that the data is organized in a tabular, almost spreadsheet-like structure. The different types of data are organized by columns, while each sample is organized by rows. Each row is assigned to an index value and is shown as the numbers **0** to **4** in bold on the left-hand side of the DataFrame. Each column is assigned to a label or name, as shown in bold at the top of the DataFrame.

The idea of a DataFrame as a kind of spreadsheet is a reasonable analogy; as we will see in this chapter, we can sort, filter, and perform computations on the data just as you would in a spreadsheet program. While not covered in this chapter, it is interesting to note that DataFrames also contain pivot table functionality, just like a spreadsheet (https://pandas.pydata.org/pandas-docs/stable/reference/api/pandas.pivot_table.html).

Exercise 6: Indexing and Selecting Data

Now that we have loaded some data, let's use the selection and indexing methods of the DataFrame to access some data of interest:

1. Select individual columns in a similar way to a regular dictionary, by using the labels of the columns, as shown here:

   ```
   df['Age']
   ```

```
0    22.0
1    38.0
2    26.0
3    35.0
4    35.0
5     NaN
6    54.0
7     2.0
8    27.0
```

Figure 1.27: Selecting the Age column

If there are no spaces in the column name, we can also use the dot operator. If there are spaces in the column names, we will need to use the bracket notation:

```
df.Age
```

```
0     22.0
1     38.0
2     26.0
3     35.0
4     35.0
5      NaN
6     54.0
7      2.0
8     27.0
9     14.0
10     4.0
11    58.0
```

Figure 1.28: Using the dot operator to select the Age column

2. Select multiple columns at once using bracket notation, as shown here:

```
df[['Name', 'Parch', 'Sex']]
```

	Name	Parch	Sex
0	Braund, Mr. Owen Harris	0	male
1	Cumings, Mrs. John Bradley (Florence Briggs Th...	0	female
2	Heikkinen, Miss. Laina	0	female
3	Futrelle, Mrs. Jacques Heath (Lily May Peel)	0	female
4	Allen, Mr. William Henry	0	male

Figure 1.29: Selecting multiple columns

3. Select the first row using `iloc`:

   ```
   df.iloc[0]
   ```

   ```
   Unnamed: 0                         0
   Cabin                            NaN
   Embarked                           S
   Fare                            7.25
   Pclass                             3
   Ticket                      A/5 21171
   Age                               22
   Name            Braund, Mr. Owen Harris
   Parch                              0
   Sex                             male
   SibSp                              1
   Survived                           0
   Name: 0, dtype: object
   ```

   Figure 1.30: Selecting the first row

4. Select the first three rows using `iloc`:

   ```
   df.iloc[[0,1,2]]
   ```

	Unnamed: 0	Cabin	Embarked	Fare	Pclass	Ticket	Age	Name	Parch	Sex	SibSp	Survived
0	0	NaN	S	7.2500	3	A/5 21171	22.0	Braund, Mr. Owen Harris	0	male	1	0.0
1	1	C85	C	71.2833	1	PC 17599	38.0	Cumings, Mrs. John Bradley (Florence Briggs Th...	0	female	1	1.0
2	2	NaN	S	7.9250	3	STON/O2. 3101282	26.0	Heikkinen, Miss. Laina	0	female	0	1.0

   Figure 1.31: Selecting the first three rows

5. We can also get a list of all of the available columns. Do this as shown here:

   ```
   columns = df.columns # Extract the list of columns
   print(columns)
   ```

   ```
   Index(['Unnamed: 0', 'Cabin', 'Embarked', 'Fare', 'Pclass', 'Ticket', 'Age',
          'Name', 'Parch', 'Sex', 'SibSp', 'Survived'],
         dtype='object')
   ```

   Figure 1.32: Getting all the columns

6. Use this list of columns and the standard Python slicing syntax to get columns 2, 3, and 4, and their corresponding values:

   ```
   df[columns[1:4]] # Columns 2, 3, 4
   ```

	Cabin	Embarked	Fare
0	NaN	S	7.2500
1	C85	C	71.2833
2	NaN	S	7.9250
3	C123	S	53.1000
4	NaN	S	8.0500
5	NaN	Q	8.4583
6	E46	S	51.8625
7	NaN	S	21.0750

   Figure 1.33: Getting the second, third, and fourth columns

7. Use the **len** operator to get the number of rows in the DataFrame:

   ```
   len(df)
   ```

   ```
   In [9]:  1  len(df)
   Out[9]: 1309
   ```

   Figure 1.34: Getting the number of rows

8. What if we wanted the value for the **Fare** column at row 2? There are a few different ways to do so. First, we'll try the row-centric methods. Do this as follows:

   ```
   df.iloc[2]['Fare'] # Row centric
   ```

   ```
   In [14]:  1  df.iloc[2]['Fare'] # Row centric
   Out[14]: 7.925
   ```

   Figure 1.35: Getting a particular value using the normal row-centric method

9. Try using the dot operator for the column. Do this as follows:

   df.iloc[2].Fare # Row centric

   ```
   In [15]:   1  df.iloc[2].Fare # Row centric
   Out[15]: 7.925
   ```

   Figure 1.36: Getting a particular value using the row-centric dot operator

10. Try using the column-centric method. Do this as follows:

    df['Fare'][2] # Column centric

    ```
    In [16]:   1  df['Fare'][2] # Column centric
    Out[16]: 7.925
    ```

    Figure 1.37: Getting a particular value using the normal column-centric method

11. Try the column-centric method with the dot operator. Do this as follows:

    df.Fare[2] # Column centric

    ```
    In [17]:   1  df.Fare[2] # Column centric
    Out[17]: 7.925
    ```

    Figure 1.38: Getting a particular value using the column-centric dot operator

Exercise 7: Advanced Indexing and Selection

With the basics of indexing and selection under our belt, we can turn our attention to more advanced indexing and selection. In this exercise, we will look at a few important methods for performing advanced indexing and selecting data:

1. Create a list of the passengers' names and ages for those passengers under the age of 21, as shown here:

   ```
   child_passengers = df[df.Age < 21][['Name', 'Age']]
   child_passengers.head()
   ```

	Name	Age
7	Palsson, Master. Gosta Leonard	2.0
9	Nasser, Mrs. Nicholas (Adele Achem)	14.0
10	Sandstrom, Miss. Marguerite Rut	4.0
12	Saundercock, Mr. William Henry	20.0
14	Vestrom, Miss. Hulda Amanda Adolfina	14.0

Figure 1.39: List of the passengers' names and ages for those passengers under the age of 21

2. Count how many child passengers there were, as shown here:

```
print(len(child_passengers))
```

```
In [19]:  1  print(len(child_passengers))
249
```

Figure 1.40: Count of child passengers

3. Count how many passengers were between the ages of 21 and 30. Do not use Python's **and** logical operator for this step, but rather the ampersand symbol (**&**). Do this as follows:

```
young_adult_passengers = df.loc[
    (df.Age > 21) & (df.Age < 30)
]
len(young_adult_passengers)
```

```
In [20]:  1  young_adult_passengers = df.loc[
          2      (df.Age > 21) & (df.Age < 30)
          3  ]
          4  len(young_adult_passengers)
Out[20]:  279
```

Figure 1.41: Count of passengers between the ages of 21 and 30

4. Count the passengers that were either first- or third-class ticket holders. Again, we will not use the Python logical **or** operator but rather the pipe symbol (|). Do this as follows:

```
df.loc[
    (df.Pclass == 3) | (df.Pclass ==1)
]
```

	Unnamed: 0	Cabin	Embarked	Fare	Pclass	Ticket	Age	Name	Parch	Sex	SibSp	Survived
0	0	NaN	S	7.2500	3	A/5 21171	22.0	Braund, Mr. Owen Harris	0	male	1	0.0
1	1	C85	C	71.2833	1	PC 17599	38.0	Cumings, Mrs. John Bradley (Florence Briggs Th...	0	female	1	1.0
2	2	NaN	S	7.9250	3	STON/O2. 3101282	26.0	Heikkinen, Miss. Laina	0	female	0	1.0

Figure 1.42: Count of passengers that were either first- or third-class ticket holders

5. Count the passengers who were not holders of either first- or third-class tickets. Do not simply select the second class ticket holders, but rather use the ~ symbol for the **not** logical operator. Do this as follows:

```
df.loc[
    ~((df.Pclass == 3) | (df.Pclass ==1))
]
```

	Unnamed: 0	Cabin	Embarked	Fare	Pclass	Ticket	Age	Name	Parch	Sex	SibSp	Survived
9	9	NaN	C	30.0708	2	237736	14.00	Nasser, Mrs. Nicholas (Adele Achem)	0	female	1	1.0
15	15	NaN	S	16.0000	2	248706	55.00	Hewlett, Mrs. (Mary D Kingcome)	0	female	0	1.0
17	17	NaN	S	13.0000	2	244373	NaN	Williams, Mr. Charles Eugene	0	male	0	1.0
20	20	NaN	S	26.0000	2	239865	35.00	Fynney, Mr. Joseph J	0	male	0	0.0
21	21	D56	S	13.0000	2	248698	34.00	Beesley, Mr. Lawrence	0	male	0	1.0

Figure 1.43: Count of passengers who were not holders of either first- or third-class tickets

6. We no longer need the **Unnamed: 0** column, so delete it using the **del** operator:

   ```
   del df['Unnamed: 0']
   df.head()
   ```

	Cabin	Embarked	Fare	Pclass	Ticket	Age	Name	Parch	Sex	SibSp	Survived
0	NaN	S	7.2500	3	A/5 21171	22.0	Braund, Mr. Owen Harris	0	male	1	0.0
1	C85	C	71.2833	1	PC 17599	38.0	Cumings, Mrs. John Bradley (Florence Briggs Th...	0	female	1	1.0
2	NaN	S	7.9250	3	STON/O2. 3101282	26.0	Heikkinen, Miss. Laina	0	female	0	1.0

Figure 1.44: The del operator

pandas Methods

Now that we are confident with some pandas basics, as well as some more advanced indexing and selecting tools, let's look at some other DataFrame methods. For a complete list of all methods available in a DataFrame, we can refer to the class documentation.

> **Note**
>
> The pandas documentation is available at https://pandas.pydata.org/pandas-docs/stable/reference/frame.html.

You should now know how many methods are available within a DataFrame. There are far too many to cover in detail in this chapter, so we will select a few that will give you a great start in supervised machine learning.

We have already seen the use of one method, **head()**, which provides the first five lines of the DataFrame. We can select more or less lines if we wish, by providing the number of lines as an argument, as shown here:

```
df.head(n=20) # 20 lines
df.head(n=32) # 32 lines
```

Another useful method is **describe**, which is a super-quick way of getting the descriptive statistics of the data within a DataFrame. We can see next that the sample size (count), mean, minimum, maximum, standard deviation, and 25th, 50th, and 75th percentiles are returned for all columns of numerical data in the DataFrame (note that text columns have been omitted):

```
df.describe()
```

	Fare	Pclass	Age	Parch	SibSp	Survived
count	1308.000000	1309.000000	1046.000000	1309.000000	1309.000000	891.000000
mean	33.295479	2.294882	29.881138	0.385027	0.498854	0.383838
std	51.758668	0.837836	14.413493	0.865560	1.041658	0.486592
min	0.000000	1.000000	0.170000	0.000000	0.000000	0.000000
25%	7.895800	2.000000	21.000000	0.000000	0.000000	0.000000
50%	14.454200	3.000000	28.000000	0.000000	0.000000	0.000000
75%	31.275000	3.000000	39.000000	0.000000	1.000000	1.000000
max	512.329200	3.000000	80.000000	9.000000	8.000000	1.000000

Figure 1.45: The describe method

Note that only columns of numerical data have been included within the summary. This simple command provides us with a lot of useful information; looking at the values for **count** (which counts the number of valid samples), we can see that there are 1,046 valid samples in the **Age** category, but 1,308 in **Fare**, and only 891 in **Survived**. We can see that the youngest person was 0.17 years, the average age is 29.898, and the eldest 80. The minimum fare was £0, with £33.30 the average and £512.33 the most expensive. If we look at the **Survived** column, we have 891 valid samples, with a mean of 0.38, which means about 38% survived.

We can also get these values separately for each of the columns by calling the respective methods of the DataFrame, as shown here:

```
df.count()
```

```
Cabin        295
Embarked    1307
Fare        1308
Pclass      1309
Ticket      1309
Age         1046
Name        1309
Parch       1309
Sex         1309
SibSp       1309
Survived     891
dtype: int64
```

Figure 1.46: The count method

But we have some columns that contain text data, such as **Embarked**, **Ticket**, **Name**, and **Sex**. So, what about these? How can we get some descriptive information for these columns? We can still use **describe**; we just need to pass it some more information. By default, **describe** will only include numerical columns and will compute the 25th, 50th, and 75th percentiles. But we can configure this to include text-based columns by passing the **include = 'all'** argument, as shown here:

```
df.describe(include='all')
```

	Cabin	Embarked	Fare	Pclass	Ticket	Age	Name	Parch	Sex	SibSp	Survived
count	295	1307	1308.000000	1309.000000	1309	1046.000000	1309	1309.000000	1309	1309.000000	891.000000
unique	186	3	NaN	NaN	929	NaN	1307	NaN	2	NaN	NaN
top	C23 C25 C27	S	NaN	NaN	CA. 2343	NaN	Kelly, Mr. James	NaN	male	NaN	NaN
freq	6	914	NaN	NaN	11	NaN	2	NaN	843	NaN	NaN
mean	NaN	NaN	33.295479	2.294882	NaN	29.881138	NaN	0.385027	NaN	0.498854	0.383838
std	NaN	NaN	51.758668	0.837836	NaN	14.413493	NaN	0.865560	NaN	1.041658	0.486592
min	NaN	NaN	0.000000	1.000000	NaN	0.170000	NaN	0.000000	NaN	0.000000	0.000000
25%	NaN	NaN	7.895800	2.000000	NaN	21.000000	NaN	0.000000	NaN	0.000000	0.000000
50%	NaN	NaN	14.454200	3.000000	NaN	28.000000	NaN	0.000000	NaN	0.000000	0.000000
75%	NaN	NaN	31.275000	3.000000	NaN	39.000000	NaN	0.000000	NaN	1.000000	1.000000
max	NaN	NaN	512.329200	3.000000	NaN	80.000000	NaN	9.000000	NaN	8.000000	1.000000

Figure 1.47: The describe method with text-based columns

That's better—now we have much more information. Looking at the **Cabin** column, we can see that there are 295 entries, with 186 unique values. The most common values are **C32**, **C25**, and **C27**, and they occur 6 times (from the **freq** value). Similarly, if we look at the **Embarked** column, we see that there are 1,307 entries, 3 unique values, and that the most commonly occurring value is **S** with 914 entries.

Notice the occurrence of **NaN** values in our **describe** output table. **NaN**, or **Not a Number**, values are very important within DataFrames, as they represent missing or not available data. The ability of the pandas library to read from data sources that contain missing or incomplete information is both a blessing and a curse. Many other libraries would simply fail to import or read the data file in the event of missing information, while the fact that it can be read also means that the missing data must be handled appropriately.

When looking at the output of the **describe** method, you should notice that the Jupyter notebook renders it in the same way as the original DataFrame that we read in using **read_csv**. There is a very good reason for this, as the results returned by the **describe** method are themselves a pandas DataFrame and thus possess the same methods and characteristics as the data read in from the CSV file. This can be easily verified using Python's built-in **type** function:

```
In [32]: type(df.describe(include='all'))
Out[32]: pandas.core.frame.DataFrame
```

Figure 1.48: Checking the type

Now that we have a summary of the dataset, let's dive in with a little more detail to get a better understanding of the available data.

> **Note**
>
> A comprehensive understanding of the available data is critical in any supervised learning problem. The source and type of the data, the means by which it is collected, and any errors potentially resulting from the collection process all have an effect on the performance of the final model.

Hopefully, by now, you are comfortable with using pandas to provide a high-level overview of the data. We will now spend some time looking into the data in greater detail.

Exercise 8: Splitting, Applying, and Combining Data Sources

We have already seen how we can index or select rows or columns from a DataFrame and use advanced indexing techniques to filter the available data based on specific criteria. Another handy method that allows for such selection is the **groupby** method, which provides a quick method for selecting groups of data at a time and provides additional functionality through the `DataFrameGroupBy` object:

1. Use the **groupby** method to group the data by the **Embarked** column. How many different values for **Embarked** are there? Let's see:

   ```
   embarked_grouped = df.groupby('Embarked')

   print(f'There are {len(embarked_grouped)} Embarked groups')
   ```

   ```
   In [35]:   1  embarked_grouped = df.groupby('Embarked')
              2
              3  print(f'There are {len(embarked_grouped)} Embarked groups')

   There are 3 Embarked groups
   ```

   Figure 1.49: Grouping the data by the Embarked column

2. What does the **groupby** method actually do? Let's check. Display the output of **embarked_grouped.groups**:

   ```
   embarked_grouped.groups
   ```

   ```
   {'C': Int64Index([    1,    9,   19,   26,   30,   31,   34,   36,   39,   42,
                ...
                1260, 1262, 1266, 1288, 1293, 1295, 1296, 1298, 1305, 1308],
               dtype='int64', length=270),
    'Q': Int64Index([    5,   16,   22,   28,   32,   44,   46,   47,   82,  109,
                ...
                1206, 1249, 1271, 1272, 1279, 1287, 1290, 1299, 1301, 1302],
               dtype='int64', length=123),
    'S': Int64Index([    0,    2,    3,    4,    6,    7,    8,   10,   11,   12,
                ...
                1289, 1291, 1292, 1294, 1297, 1300, 1303, 1304, 1306, 1307],
               dtype='int64', length=914)}
   ```

   Figure 1.50: Output of embarked_grouped.groups

We can see here that the three groups are **C**, **Q**, and **S**, and that **embarked_grouped.groups** is actually a dictionary where the keys are the groups. The values are the rows or indexes of the entries that belong to that group.

3. Use the **iloc** method to inspect row **1** and confirm that it belongs to embarked group **C**:

   ```
   df.iloc[1]
   ```

   ```
   Cabin                                                      C85
   Embarked                                                     C
   Fare                                                   71.2833
   Pclass                                                       1
   Ticket                                                PC 17599
   Age                                                         38
   Name        Cumings, Mrs. John Bradley (Florence Briggs Th...
   Parch                                                        0
   Sex                                                     female
   SibSp                                                        1
   Survived                                                     1
   Name: 1, dtype: object
   ```

   Figure 1.51: Inspecting row 1

4. As the groups are a dictionary, we can iterate through them and execute computations on the individual groups. Compute the mean age for each group, as shown here:

   ```
   for name, group in embarked_grouped:
       print(name, group.Age.mean())
   ```

   ```
   C 32.33216981132075
   Q 28.63
   S 29.245204603580564
   ```

   Figure 1.52: Computing the mean age for each group using iteration

5. Another option is to use the **aggregate** method, or **agg** for short, and provide it the function to apply across the columns. Use the **agg** method to determine the mean of each group:

```python
embarked_grouped.agg(np.mean)
```

	Fare	Pclass	Age	Parch	SibSp	Survived
Embarked						
C	62.336267	1.851852	32.332170	0.370370	0.400000	0.553571
Q	12.409012	2.894309	28.630000	0.113821	0.341463	0.389610
S	27.418824	2.347921	29.245205	0.426696	0.550328	0.336957

Figure 1.53: Using the agg method

So, how exactly does **agg** work and what type of functions can we pass it? Before we can answer these questions, we need to first consider the data type of each column in the DataFrame, as each column is passed through this function to produce the result we see here. Each DataFrame is comprised of a collection of columns of pandas series data, which in many ways operates just like a list. As such, any function that can take a list or a similar iterable and compute a single value as a result can be used with **agg**.

6. As an example, define a simple function that returns the first value in the column, then pass that function through to **agg**:

```python
def first_val(x):
    
    return x.values[0]


embarked_grouped.agg(first_val)
```

	Cabin	Fare	Pclass	Ticket	Age	Name	Parch	Sex	SibSp	Survived
Embarked										
C	C85	71.2833	1	PC 17599	38.0	Cumings, Mrs. John Bradley (Florence Briggs Th...	0	female	1	1.0
Q	NaN	8.4583	3	330877	NaN	Moran, Mr. James	0	male	0	0.0
S	NaN	7.2500	3	A/5 21171	22.0	Braund, Mr. Owen Harris	0	male	1	0.0

Figure 1.54: Using the agg method with a function

Lambda Functions

One common and useful way of implementing **agg** is through the use of Lambda functions.

Lambda or anonymous functions (also known as inline functions in other languages) are small, single-expression functions that can be declared and used without the need for a formal function definition via use of the `def` keyword. Lambda functions are essentially provided for convenience and aren't intended to be used for extensive periods. The standard syntax for a Lambda function is as follows (always starting with the `lambda` keyword):

```
lambda <input values>: <computation for values to be returned>
```

Exercise 9: Lambda Functions

In this exercise, we will create a Lambda function that returns the first value in a column and use it with **agg**:

1. Write the `first_val` function as a Lambda function, passed to **agg**:

   ```
   embarked_grouped.agg(lambda x: x.values[0])
   ```

Embarked	Cabin	Fare	Pclass	Ticket	Age	Name	Parch	Sex	SibSp	Survived
C	C85	71.2833	1	PC 17599	38.0	Cumings, Mrs. John Bradley (Florence Briggs Th...	0	female	1	1.0
Q	NaN	8.4583	3	330877	NaN	Moran, Mr. James	0	male	0	0.0
S	NaN	7.2500	3	A/5 21171	22.0	Braund, Mr. Owen Harris	0	male	1	0.0

   Figure 1.55: Using the agg method with a Lambda function

Obviously, we get the same result, but notice how much more convenient the Lambda function was to use, especially given the fact that it is only intended to be used briefly.

2. We can also pass multiple functions to **agg** via a list to apply the functions across the dataset. Pass the Lambda function as well as the NumPy mean and standard deviation functions, like this:

```
embarked_grouped.agg([lambda x: x.values[0], np.mean, np.std])
```

| | Fare | | | Pclass | | | Age | |
	<lambda>	mean	std	<lambda>	mean	std	<lambda>	mean
Embarked								
C	71.2833	62.336267	84.185996	1	1.851852	0.936802	38.0	32.33217
Q	8.4583	12.409012	13.616133	3	2.894309	0.380099	NaN	28.63000
S	7.2500	27.418824	37.096402	3	2.347921	0.784126	22.0	29.24520

Figure 1.56: Using the agg method with multiple Lambda functions

3. What if we wanted to apply different functions to different columns in the DataFrame? Apply **numpy.sum** to the **Fare** column and the Lambda function to the **Age** column by passing **agg** a dictionary where the keys are the columns to apply the function to and the values are the functions themselves:

```
embarked_grouped.agg({
    'Fare': np.sum,
    'Age': lambda x: x.values[0]
})
```

	Fare	Age
Embarked		
C	16830.7922	38.0
Q	1526.3085	NaN
S	25033.3862	22.0

Figure 1.57: Using the agg method with a dictionary of different columns

4. Finally, you can also execute the **groupby** method using more than one column. Provide the method with a list of the columns (**Sex** and **Embarked**) to **groupby**, like this:

```
age_embarked_grouped = df.groupby(['Sex', 'Embarked'])
age_embarked_grouped.groups
```

```
{('male',
  'S'): Int64Index([    0,    4,    6,    7,   12,   13,   17,
            23,
            ...
            1283, 1284, 1285, 1289, 1292, 1294, 1297, 1304,
            dtype='int64', length=623),
 ('female',
  'C'): Int64Index([    1,    9,   19,   31,   39,   43,   52,
           128,
            ...
            1238, 1241, 1252, 1255, 1259, 1262, 1266, 1288,
            dtype='int64', length=113),
 ('female',
  'S'): Int64Index([    2,    3,    8,   10,   11,   14,   15,
            25,
```

Figure 1.58: Using the groupby method with more than one column

Similar to when the groupings were computed by just the **Embarked** column, we can see here that a dictionary is returned where the keys are the combination of the **Sex** and **Embarked** columns returned as a tuple. The first key-value pair in the dictionary is a tuple, (`'Male'`, `'S'`), and the values correspond to the indices of rows with that specific combination. There will be a key-value pair for each combination of unique values in the **Sex** and **Embarked** columns.

Data Quality Considerations

The quality of data used in any machine learning problem, supervised or unsupervised, is critical to the performance of the final model, and should be at the forefront when planning any machine learning project. As a simple rule of thumb, if you have clean data, in sufficient quantity, with a good correlation between the input data type and the desired output, then the specifics regarding the type and details of the selected supervised learning model become significantly less important to achieve a good result.

In reality, however, this can rarely be the case. There are usually some issues regarding the quantity of available data, the quality or **signal-to-noise ratio** in the data, the correlation between the input and output, or some combination of all three factors. As such, we will use this last section of this chapter to consider some of the data quality problems that may occur and some mechanisms for addressing them. Previously, we mentioned that in any machine learning problem, having a thorough understanding of the dataset is critical if we to are construct a high-performing model. This is particularly the case when looking into data quality and attempting to address some of the issues present within the data. Without a comprehensive understanding of the dataset, additional noise or other unintended issues may be introduced during the data cleaning process leading to a further degradation of performance.

> **Note**
>
> A detailed description of the Titanic dataset and the type of data included is contained in the *Loading Data in pandas* section. If you need a quick refresher, go back and review these details now.

Managing Missing Data

As we discussed earlier, the ability of pandas to read data with missing values is both a blessing and a curse and arguably is the most common issue that needs to be managed before we can continue with developing our supervised learning model. The simplest, but not necessarily the most effective, method is to just remove or ignore those entries that are missing data. We can easily do this in pandas using the **dropna** method of the DataFrame:

```
complete_data = df.dropna()
```

There is one very significant consequence of simply dropping rows with missing data and that is we may be throwing away a lot of important information. This is highlighted very clearly in the Titanic dataset as a lot of rows contain missing data. If we were to simply ignore these rows, we would start with a sample size of 1,309 and end with a sample of 183 entries. Developing a reasonable supervised learning model with a little over 10% of the data would be very difficult indeed:

```
In [44]: len(df)
Out[44]: 1309

In [45]: len(df.dropna())
Out[45]: 183
```

Figure 1.59: Total number of rows and total number of rows with NaN values

So, with the exception of the early, explorative phase, it is rarely acceptable to simply discard all rows with invalid information. We can be a little more sophisticated about this though. Which rows are actually missing information? Is the missing information problem unique to certain columns or is it consistent throughout all columns of the dataset? We can use **aggregate** to help us here as well:

```
df.aggregate(lambda x: x.isna().sum())
```

```
Cabin       1014
Embarked       2
Fare           1
Pclass         0
Ticket         0
Age          263
Name           0
Parch          0
Sex            0
SibSp          0
Survived     418
dtype: int64
```

Figure 1.60: Using agg with a Lambda function to identify rows with NaN values

Now, this is useful! We can see that the vast majority of missing information is in the **Cabin** column, some in **Age**, and a little more in **Survived**. This is one of the first times in the data cleaning process that we may need to make an educated judgement call.

What do we want to do with the **Cabin** column? There is so much missing information here that it, in fact, may not be possible to use it in any reasonable way. We could attempt to recover the information by looking at the names, ages, and number of parents/siblings and see whether we can match some families together to provide information, but there would be a lot of uncertainty in this process. We could also simplify the column by using the level of the cabin on the ship rather than the exact cabin number, which may then correlate better with name, age, and social status. This is unfortunate as there could be a good correlation between **Cabin** and **Survived**, as perhaps those passengers in the lower decks of the ship may have had a harder time evacuating. We could examine only the rows with valid **Cabin** values to see whether there is any predictive power in the **Cabin** entry; but, for now, we will simply disregard **Cabin** as a reasonable input (or feature).

We can see that the **Embarked** and **Fare** columns only have three missing samples between them. If we decided that we needed the **Embarked** and **Fare** columns for our model, it would be a reasonable argument to simply drop these rows. We can do this using our indexing techniques, where ~ represents the **not** operation, or flipping the result (that is, where **df.Embarked** is not **NaN** and **df.Fare** is not **NaN**):

```
df_valid = df.loc[(~df.Embarked.isna()) & (~df.Fare.isna())]
```

The missing age values are a little more interesting, as there are too many rows with missing age values to just discard them. But we also have a few more options here, as we can have a little more confidence in some plausible values to fill in. The simplest option would be to simply fill in the missing age values with the mean age for the dataset:

```
df_valid[['Age']] = df_valid[['Age']].fillna(df_valid.Age.mean())
```

This is OK, but there are probably better ways of filling in the data rather than just giving all 263 people the same value. Remember, we are trying to clean up the data with the goal of maximizing the predictive power of the input features and the survival rate. Giving everyone the same value, while simple, doesn't seem too reasonable. What if we were to look at the average ages of the members of each of the classes (**Pclass**)? This may give a better estimate, as the average age reduces from class 1 through 3:

```
In [64]: df_valid.loc[df.Pclass == 1, 'Age'].mean()
Out[64]: 37.956806510096975

In [66]: df_valid.loc[df.Pclass == 2, 'Age'].mean()
Out[66]: 29.52440879717283

In [65]: df_valid.loc[df.Pclass == 3, 'Age'].mean()
Out[65]: 26.23396338788047
```

Figure 1.61: Average ages of the members of each of the classes

What if we consider sex as well as ticket class (social status)? Do the average ages differ here too? Let's find out:

```
for name, grp in df_valid.groupby(['Pclass', 'Sex']):
    print('%i' % name[0], name[1], '%0.2f' % grp['Age'].mean())
```

```
1 female 36.84
1 male 41.03
2 female 27.50
2 male 30.82
3 female 22.19
3 male 25.86
```

Figure 1.62: Average ages of the members of each sex and class

We can see here that males in all ticket classes are typically older. This combination of sex and ticket class provides much more resolution than simply filling in all missing fields with the mean age. To do this, we will use the **transform** method, which applies a function to the contents of a series or DataFrame and returns another series or DataFrame with the transformed values. This is particularly powerful when combined with the **groupby** method:

```
mean_ages = df_valid.groupby(['Pclass', 'Sex'])['Age'].\
    transform(lambda x: x.fillna(x.mean()))
df_valid.loc[:, 'Age'] = mean_ages
```

There is a lot in these two lines of code, so let's break them down into components. Let's look at the first line:

```
mean_ages = df_valid.groupby(['Pclass', 'Sex'])['Age'].\
    transform(lambda x: x.fillna(x.mean()))
```

We are already familiar with **df_valid.groupby(['Pclass', 'Sex'])['Age']**, which groups the data by ticket class and sex and returns only the **Age** column. The **lambda x: x.fillna(x.mean())** Lambda function takes the input pandas series, and fills the **NaN** values with the mean value of the series.

The second line assigns the filled values within **mean_ages** to the **Age** column. Note the use of the **loc[:, 'Age']** indexing method, which indicates that all rows within the **Age** column are to be assigned the values contained within **mean_ages**:

```
df_valid.loc[:, 'Age'] = mean_ages
```

We have described a few different ways of filling in the missing values within the **Age** column, but by no means has this been an exhaustive discussion. There are many more methods that we could use to fill the missing data: we could apply random values within one standard deviation of the mean for the grouped data, we could also look at grouping the data by sex and the number of parents/children (**Parch**) or by the number of siblings, or by ticket class, sex, and the number of parents/children. What is most important about the decisions made during this process is the end result of the prediction accuracy. We may need to try different options, rerun our models and consider the effect on the accuracy of final predictions. This is an important aspect of the process of feature engineering, that is, selecting the features or components that provide the model with the most predictive power; you will find that, during this process, you will try a few different features, run the model, look at the end result and repeat, until you are happy with the performance.

The ultimate goal of this supervised learning problem is to predict the survival of passengers on the Titanic given the information we have available. So, that means that the **Survived** column provides our labels for training. What are we going to do if we are missing 418 of the labels? If this was a project where we had control over the collection of the data and access to its origins, we would obviously correct this by recollecting or asking for the labels to be clarified. With the Titanic dataset, we do not have this ability so we must make another educated judgement call. We could try some unsupervised learning techniques to see whether there are some patterns in the survival information that we could use. However, we may not have a choice of simply ignoring these rows. The task is to predict whether a person survived or perished, not whether they may have survived. By estimating the ground truth labels, we may introduce significant noise into the dataset, reducing our ability to accurately predict survival.

Class Imbalance

Missing data is not the only problem that may be present within a dataset. Class imbalance – that is, having more of one class or classes compared to another – can be a significant problem, particularly in the case of classification problems (we'll see more on classification in *Chapter 4, Classification*), where we are trying to predict which class (or classes) a sample is from. Looking at our **Survived** column, we can see that there are far more people who perished (**Survived** equals **0**) than survived (**Survived** equals **1**) in the dataset:

```
In [71]: len(df.loc[df.Survived == 1])
Out[71]: 342

In [72]: len(df.loc[df.Survived == 0])
Out[72]: 549
```

Figure 1.63: Number of people who perished versus survived

If we don't take this class imbalance into account, the predictive power of our model could be significantly reduced as, during training, the model would simply need to guess that the person did not survive to be correct 61% (549 / (549 + 342)) of the time. If, in reality, the actual survival rate was, say, 50%, then when being applied to unseen data, our model would predict not survived too often.

There are a few options available for managing class imbalance, one of which, similar to the missing data scenario, is to randomly remove samples from the over-represented class until balance has been achieved. Again, this option is not ideal, or perhaps even appropriate, as it involves ignoring available data. A more constructive example may be to oversample the under-represented class by randomly copying samples from the under-represented class in the dataset to boost the number of samples. While removing data can lead to accuracy issues due to discarding useful information, oversampling the under-represented class can lead to being unable to predict the label of unseen data, also known as overfitting (which we will cover in *Chapter 5, Ensemble Modeling*).

Adding some random noise to the input features for oversampled data may prevent some degree of overfitting, but this is highly dependent on the dataset itself. As with missing data, it is important to check the effect of any class imbalance corrections on the overall model performance. It is relatively straightforward to copy more data into a DataFrame using the **append** method, which works in a very similar fashion to lists. If we wanted to copy the first row to the end of the DataFrame, we would do this:

```
df_oversample = df.append(df.iloc[0])
```

Low Sample Size

The field of machine learning can be considered a branch of the larger field of statistics. As such, the principles of confidence and sample size can also be applied to understand the issues with a small dataset. Recall that if we were to take measurements from a data source with high variance, then the degree of uncertainty in the measurements would also be high and more samples would be required to achieve a specified confidence in the value of the mean. The sample principles can be applied to machine learning datasets. Those datasets with a variance in the features with the most predictive power generally require more samples for reasonable performance as more confidence is also required.

There are a few techniques that can be used to compensate for a reduced sample size, such as transfer learning. However, these lie outside the scope of this book. Ultimately, though, there is only so much that can be done with a small dataset, and significant performance increases may only occur once the sample size is increased.

Activity 1: pandas Functions

In this activity, we will test ourselves on the various pandas functions we have learned about in this chapter. We will use the same Titanic dataset for this.

The steps to be performed are as follows:

1. Open a new Jupyter notebook.

2. Use pandas to load the Titanic dataset and describe the summary data for all columns.

3. We don't need the **Unnamed: 0** column. In *Exercise 7: Advanced Indexing and Selection*, we demonstrated how to remove the column using the **del** command. How else could we remove this column? Remove this column without using **del**.

4. Compute the mean, standard deviation, minimum, and maximum values for the columns of the DataFrame without using **describe**.

5. What about the 33, 66, and 99% quartiles? How would we get these values using their individual methods? Use the **quantile** method to do this (https://pandas.pydata.org/pandas-docs/stable/reference/frame.html).

6. How many passengers were from each class? Find the answer using the **groupby** method.

7. How many passengers were from each class? Find the answer by using selecting/indexing methods to count the members of each class.

    Confirm that the answers to *Step 6* and *Step 7* match.

8. Determine who the eldest passenger in third class was.

9. For a number of machine learning problems, it is very common to scale the numerical values between 0 and 1. Use the **agg** method with Lambda functions to scale the **Fare** and **Age** columns between 0 and 1.

10. There is one individual in the dataset without a listed **Fare** value, which can be found out as follows:

    ```
    df_nan_fare = df.loc[(df.Fare.isna())]
    df_nan_fare
    ```

    The output will be as follows:

	Cabin	Embarked	Fare	Pclass	Ticket	Age	Name	Parch	Sex	SibSp	Survived
1043	NaN	S	NaN	3	3701	60.5	Storey, Mr. Thomas	0	male	0	NaN

    Figure 1.64: Individual without a listed Fare value

    Replace the **NaN** value of this row in the main DataFrame with the mean **Fare** value for those corresponding with the same class and **Embarked** location using the **groupby** method.

    > **Note**
    >
    > The solution for this activity can found on page 300.

Summary

In this chapter, we introduced the concept of supervised machine learning, along with a number of use cases, including the automation of manual tasks such as identifying hairstyles from the 1960s and 1980s. In this introduction, we encountered the concept of labeled datasets and the process of mapping one information set (the input data or features) to the corresponding labels.

We took a practical approach to the process of loading and cleaning data using Jupyter notebooks and the extremely powerful pandas library. Note that this chapter has only covered a small fraction of the functionality within pandas, and that an entire book could be dedicated to the library itself. It is recommended that you become familiar with reading the pandas documentation and continue to develop your pandas skills through practice.

The final section of this chapter covered a number of data quality issues that need to be considered to develop a high-performing supervised learning model, including missing data, class imbalance, and low sample sizes. We discussed a number of options for managing such issues and emphasized the importance of checking these mitigations against the performance of the model.

In the next chapter, we will extend upon the data cleaning process that we covered and will investigate the data exploration and visualization process. Data exploration is a critical aspect of any machine learning solution, as without a comprehensive knowledge of the dataset, it would be almost impossible to model the information provided.

Exploratory Data Analysis and Visualization

Learning Objectives

By the end of the chapter, you will be able to:

- Explain the importance of data exploration and communicate the summary statistics of a dataset
- Visualize patterns in missing values in data and be able to replace null values appropriately
- Identify continuous features and categorical features
- Visualize distributions of values across individual variables
- Describe and analyze relationships between different types of variables using correlation and visualizations

This chapter takes us through how to perform exploration and analysis on a new dataset.

Introduction

Say we have a problem statement that involves predicting whether a particular earthquake caused a tsunami or not. How do we decide what model to use? What do we know about the data we have? Nothing! But if we don't know and understand our data, chances are we'll end up building a model that's not very interpretable or reliable.

When it comes to data science, it's important to have a thorough understanding of the data we're dealing with, in order to generate features that are highly informative and, consequently, to build accurate and powerful models.

In order to gain this understanding, we perform an exploratory analysis on the data to see what the data can tell us about the relationships between the features and the target variable. Getting to know our data will even help us interpret the model we build and identify ways we can improve its accuracy.

The approach we take to achieve this is to allow the data to reveal its structure or model, which helps gain some new, often unsuspected, insight into the data. Let's learn more about this approach.

Exploratory Data Analysis (EDA)

Exploratory data analysis (EDA) is defined as an approach to analyzing datasets to summarize their main characteristics, often with visual methods.

The purpose of EDA is to:

- Discover patterns within a dataset
- Spot anomalies
- Form hypotheses about the behavior of data
- Validate assumptions

Everything from basic summary statistics to complex visualizations help us gain an intuitive understanding of the data itself, which is highly important when it comes to forming new hypotheses about the data and uncovering what parameters affect the target variable. Often, discovering how the target variable varies across a single feature gives us an indication of how important a feature might be, and a variation across a combination of several features helps us come up with ideas for new informative features to engineer.

Most exploration and visualization is intended to understand the relationship between the features and the target variable. This is because we want to find out what relationships exist (or don't exist) between the data we have and the values we want to predict.

A very basic domain knowledge is usually necessary to be able to understand both the problem statement itself as well as what the data is telling us. In this chapter, we'll look at the ways we can get to know more about the data we have by analyzing the features we have.

EDA can tell us about:

- Features that are unclean, have missing values, or have outliers
- Features that are informative and are a good indicator of the target
- The kind of relationships features have with the target
- Further features that the data might need that we don't already have
- Edge cases you might need to account for separately
- Filters you might need to apply on the dataset
- The presence of incorrect or fake data points

Now that we've looked at why EDA is important and what it can tell us, let's talk about what exactly EDA involves. EDA can involve anything from looking at basic summary statistics to visualizing complex trends over multiple variables. However, even simple statistics and plots can be powerful tools, as they may reveal important facts about the data that could change our modeling perspective. When we see plots representing data, we are able to easily detect trends and patterns, compared to just raw data and numbers. These visualizations further allow us to ask questions such as "How?" and "Why?", and form hypotheses about the dataset that can be validated by further visualizations. This is a continuous process that leads to a deeper understanding of the data. This chapter will introduce you to some of the basic tools that can be used to explore any dataset while keeping in mind the ultimate problem statement.

We'll start by walking through some basic summary statistics and how to interpret them, followed by a section on finding, analyzing, and dealing with missing values. Then we'll look at univariate relationships, that is, distributions and the behavior of individual variables. This will be followed by the final section on exploring relationships between variables. In this chapter, you will be introduced to types of plots that can be used to gain a basic overview of the dataset and its features, as well as how to gain insights by creating visualizations that combine several features, and we'll then work through some examples on how they can be used.

54 | Exploratory Data Analysis and Visualization

The dataset that we will use for our exploratory analysis and visualizations has been taken from the *Significant Earthquake Database* from NOAA, available as a public dataset on Google BigQuery (`table ID: 'bigquery-public-data.noaa_significant_earthquakes.earthquakes'`). We will be using a subset of the columns available, the metadata for which is available at https://console.cloud.google.com/bigquery?project=packt-data&folder&organizationId&p=bigquery-public-data&d=noaa_significant_earthquakes&t=earthquakes&page=table, and loading it into a pandas DataFrame to perform the exploration. We'll primarily be using Matplotlib for most of our visualizations, along with Seaborn and Missingno for some. It is to be noted, however, that Seaborn merely provides a wrapper over Matplotlib's functionalities, so anything that is plotted using Seaborn can also be plotted using Matplotlib. We'll try to keep things interesting by mixing up visualizations from both libraries.

The exploration and analysis will be conducted keeping in mind a sample problem statement: *Given the data we have, we want to predict whether an earthquake caused a tsunami or not.* This will be a classification problem (more on this in *Chapter 4, Classification*) where the target variable is the `flag_tsunami` column.

Exercise 10: Importing Libraries for Data Exploration

Before we begin, let's first import the required libraries, which we will be using for most of our data manipulations and visualizations:

1. In a Jupyter notebook, import the following libraries:

   ```
   import json
   import pandas as pd
   import numpy as np
   import missingno as msno
   from sklearn.impute import SimpleImputer

   %matplotlib inline
   import matplotlib.pyplot as plt
   import seaborn as sns
   ```

   The `%matplotlib inline` command allows Jupyter to display the plots inline within the notebook itself.

2. We can also read in the metadata containing the data types for each column, which are stored in the form of a JSON file. Do this using the following command. This command opens the file in readable format and uses the `json` library to read the file into a dictionary:

   ```
   with open('dtypes.json', 'r') as jsonfile:
       dtyp = json.load(jsonfile)
   ```

Now, let's get started.

Summary Statistics and Central Values

In order to find out what our data really looks like, we use a technique known as **data profiling**. This is defined as the process of examining the data available from an existing information source (for example, a database or a file) and collecting statistics or informative summaries about that data. The goal is to make sure that you understand your data well and are able to identify any challenges that the data may pose early on in the project, which is done by summarizing the dataset and assessing its structure, content, and quality.

Data profiling includes collecting descriptive statistics and data types. Here are a few commands that are commonly used to get a summary of a dataset:

- **data.info()**: This command tells us how many non-null values there are there in each column, along with the data type of the values (non-numeric types are represented as **object** types).

- **data.describe()**: This gives us basic summary statistics for all the numerical columns in the DataFrame, such as the count of non-null values, minimum and maximum, the mean and standard deviation, and the quarter-wise percentiles for all numerical features. If there are any string-type features, it does not include a summary of those.

- **data.head()** and **data.tail()**: These commands display the first five and last five rows of the DataFrame respectively. While the previous commands give us a general idea of the dataset, it is a good idea to get a closer look at the actual data itself, which can be done using these commands.

Standard Deviation

The standard deviation represents how widespread the distribution of the values of x are.

For a set of numerical values, x_i, the standard deviation is given by:

$$\sigma = \sqrt{\frac{1}{N} \sum_{i=1}^{N} (x_i - \mu)^2}$$

Figure 2.1: Standard deviation equation

Here, σ is the standard deviation, N is the number of data points, and μ is the mean.

Say we have a set of 10 values, $x = [0,1,1,2,3,4,2,2,0,1]$. The mean, μ, will be the sum of these values, divided by 10. That is, $\mu = 1.6$:

x_i	$x_i - \mu$	$(x_i - \mu)^2$
0	-1.6	2.56
1	-0.6	0.36
1	-0.6	0.36
2	0.4	0.16
3	1.4	1.96
4	2.4	5.76
2	0.4	0.16
2	0.4	0.16
0	-1.6	2.56
1	-0.6	0.36
		SUM=14.4

Figure 2.2: Mean square values for x

Then, standard deviation = sqrt(14.4/10) = 1.2.

Percentiles

For a set of values, the nth percentile is equal to the value that is greater than n% of values in the set. For example, the 50th percentile is the value in the dataset that has as many values greater than it as it does that are less than it. Additionally, the fiftieth percentile of a dataset is also known as its median, and the twenty-fifth and seventy-fifth percentiles are also known as the lower and upper quartiles.

Say we have the same set of 10 values as earlier, $x = [0,1,1,2,3,4,2,2,0,1]$. Let's first sort this list of values. Upon sorting, we have $x = [0,0,1,1,1,2,2,2,3,4]$. To find the twenty-fifth percentile, let's first calculate the index at which the value occurs: $i = (p/100) * n)$, where $p = 25$ and $n = 10$. Then, $i = 2.5$.

Since i is not an integer, we round it up to 3 and take the third element in the list as the twenty-fifth percentile. The twenty-fifth percentile in the given list would then be 1, which is the third element in our sorted list.

Exercise 11: Summary Statistics of Our Dataset

In this exercise, we will use the summary statistics functions we read about previously to get a basic idea of our dataset:

1. Read the earthquakes data into a **data** pandas DataFrame and use the **dtyp** dictionary we read using the **json** library in the previous exercise to specify the data types of each column in the CSV:

   ```
   data = pd.read_csv('earthquake_data.csv', dtype=dtyp)
   ```

2. Use the **data.info()** function to get an overview of the dataset:

   ```
   data.info()
   ```

   The output will be as follows:

   ```
   <class 'pandas.core.frame.DataFrame'>
   RangeIndex: 6072 entries, 0 to 6071
   Data columns (total 28 columns):
   id                              6072 non-null float64
   flag_tsunami                    6072 non-null object
   year                            6072 non-null float64
   month                           5667 non-null float64
   day                             5515 non-null float64
   hour                            4044 non-null float64
   minute                          3838 non-null float64
   second                          2721 non-null float64
   focal_depth                     3120 non-null float64
   eq_primary                      4286 non-null float64
   eq_mag_mw                       1216 non-null float64
   eq_mag_ms                       2916 non-null float64
   eq_mag_mb                       1786 non-null float64
   intensity                       2748 non-null float64
   country                         6072 non-null object
   state                           308 non-null object
   location_name                   6071 non-null object
   latitude                        6018 non-null float64
   longitude                       6022 non-null float64
   region_code                     6072 non-null object
   injuries                        1169 non-null float64
   injuries_description            1349 non-null object
   damage_millions_dollars         478 non-null float64
   damage_description              4327 non-null object
   total_injuries                  1184 non-null float64
   total_injuries_description      1357 non-null object
   total_damage_millions_dollars   418 non-null float64
   total_damage_description        3148 non-null object
   dtypes: float64(19), object(9)
   memory usage: 1.3+ MB
   ```

   Figure 2.3: Overview of the dataset

3. Print the first five and last five rows of the dataset. The first five rows are printed as follows:

   data.head()

   The output will be as shown here:

	id	flag_tsunami	year	month	day	hour	minute	second	focal_depth	eq_primary	...	longitude	region_code	injur
0	338.0	No	1048.0	NaN	NaN	NaN	NaN	NaN	NaN	NaN	...	NaN	120	N
1	771.0	Tsu	1580.0	4.0	6.0	NaN	NaN	NaN	33.0	6.2	...	1.309	120	N
2	7889.0	Tsu	1757.0	7.0	15.0	NaN	NaN	NaN	NaN	NaN	...	-6.320	120	N
3	6697.0	Tsu	1500.0	NaN	NaN	NaN	NaN	NaN	NaN	NaN	...	NaN	150	N
4	6013.0	Tsu	1668.0	4.0	13.0	NaN	NaN	NaN	NaN	NaN	...	-71.050	150	N

5 rows × 28 columns

```
data.tail()
```

	id	flag_tsunami	year	month	day	hour	minute	second	focal_depth	eq_primary	...	longitude	region_code
6067	5360.0	Tsu	1993.0	8.0	8.0	8.0	34.0	24.9	59.0	7.8	...	144.801	170
6068	5009.0	No	1983.0	12.0	22.0	1.0	2.0	2.4	26.0	6.4	...	151.868	170
6069	10307.0	No	2018.0	2.0	25.0	17.0	44.0	43.0	23.0	7.5	...	142.768	170
6070	5498.0	No	1998.0	7.0	9.0	5.0	19.0	7.3	10.0	6.2	...	-28.626	130
6071	5459.0	No	1997.0	4.0	22.0	9.0	31.0	23.2	5.0	6.7	...	-60.892	90

5 rows × 28 columns

Figure 2.4: The first five rows

The last five rows are printed as follows:

   data.tail()

The output will be as shown here:

	id	flag_tsunami	year	month	day	hour	minute	second	focal_depth	eq_primary	...	longitude	region_code	injur
0	338.0	No	1048.0	NaN	NaN	NaN	NaN	NaN	NaN	NaN	...	NaN	120	N
1	771.0	Tsu	1580.0	4.0	6.0	NaN	NaN	NaN	33.0	6.2	...	1.309	120	N
2	7889.0	Tsu	1757.0	7.0	15.0	NaN	NaN	NaN	NaN	NaN	...	-6.320	120	N
3	6697.0	Tsu	1500.0	NaN	NaN	NaN	NaN	NaN	NaN	NaN	...	NaN	150	N
4	6013.0	Tsu	1668.0	4.0	13.0	NaN	NaN	NaN	NaN	NaN	...	-71.050	150	N

5 rows × 28 columns

```
data.tail()
```

	id	flag_tsunami	year	month	day	hour	minute	second	focal_depth	eq_primary	...	longitude	region_code
6067	5360.0	Tsu	1993.0	8.0	8.0	8.0	34.0	24.9	59.0	7.8	...	144.801	170
6068	5009.0	No	1983.0	12.0	22.0	1.0	2.0	2.4	26.0	6.4	...	151.868	170
6069	10307.0	No	2018.0	2.0	25.0	17.0	44.0	43.0	23.0	7.5	...	142.768	170
6070	5498.0	No	1998.0	7.0	9.0	5.0	19.0	7.3	10.0	6.2	...	-28.626	130
6071	5459.0	No	1997.0	4.0	22.0	9.0	31.0	23.2	5.0	6.7	...	-60.892	90

5 rows × 28 columns

Figure 2.5: The last five rows

We can see in these outputs that there are 28 columns, but not all of them are displayed. Only the first 10 and last 10 columns are displayed, with the ellipses representing the fact that there are columns in between that are not displayed.

4. Use **data.describe()** to find the summary statistics of the dataset. Run **data.describe().T**:

    data.describe().T

Here, **.T** indicates that we're taking a transpose of the DataFrame to which it is applied, that is, turning the columns into rows and vice versa. Applying it to the **describe()** function allows us to see the output more easily with each row in the transposed DataFrame now corresponding to the statistics for a single feature.

We should get an output like this:

	count	mean	std	min	25%	50%	75%	max
id	6072.0	4658.426219	2924.650010	1.000	2142.75000	4608.5	6475.25000	10378.000
year	6072.0	1802.307477	377.924931	-2150.000	1818.00000	1927.0	1986.00000	2018.000
month	5667.0	6.510852	3.450167	1.000	4.00000	7.0	9.00000	12.000
day	5515.0	15.734361	8.752862	1.000	8.00000	16.0	23.00000	31.000
hour	4044.0	11.308605	7.033485	0.000	5.00000	11.0	17.00000	23.000
minute	3838.0	28.855915	17.151545	0.000	14.00000	30.0	44.00000	59.000
second	2721.0	29.740243	17.132196	0.100	14.80000	29.7	44.50000	59.900
focal_depth	3120.0	41.680769	71.258782	0.000	11.00000	26.0	40.00000	675.000
eq_primary	4286.0	6.471419	1.043968	1.600	5.70000	6.5	7.30000	9.500
eq_mag_mw	1216.0	6.526562	0.937869	3.600	5.80000	6.5	7.20000	9.500
eq_mag_ms	2916.0	6.574451	0.989850	2.100	5.80000	6.6	7.30000	9.100
eq_mag_mb	1786.0	5.797592	0.716809	2.100	5.30000	5.8	6.30000	8.200
intensity	2748.0	8.325328	1.800089	2.000	7.00000	8.0	10.00000	12.000
latitude	6018.0	22.537909	22.787934	-62.877	9.87175	32.2	38.77825	73.122
longitude	6022.0	37.985633	86.726852	-179.984	-8.00000	43.3	115.50000	180.000
injuries	1169.0	2293.579127	27095.202227	1.000	10.00000	42.0	200.00000	799000.000
damage_millions_dollars	478.0	1715.606259	12157.409978	0.013	3.62500	20.9	204.35000	220000.000
total_injuries	1184.0	2510.967061	28273.298405	1.000	10.00000	42.5	200.00000	799000.000
total_damage_millions_dollars	418.0	1978.743206	12988.187606	0.010	4.31000	28.0	300.00000	220085.456

Figure 2.6: Summary statistics

Notice here that the **describe()** function only shows the statistics for columns with numerical values. This is because we cannot calculate the statistics for the columns having non-numerical values.

Missing Values

When there is no value (that is, a null value) recorded for a particular feature in a data point, we say the data is missing. Having missing values in a real dataset is inevitable; no dataset is ever perfect. However, it is important to understand why the data is missing, and if there is a factor that has affected the loss of data. Appreciating and recognizing this allows us to handle the remaining data in an appropriate manner. For example, if the data is missing randomly, then it's highly likely that the remaining data is still representative of the population. However, if the missing data is not random in nature and we assume that it is, it could bias our analysis and subsequent modeling.

Let's look at the common reasons (or mechanisms) for missing data:

- **Missing Completely at Random** (**MCAR**): Values in a dataset are said to be MCAR if there is no correlation whatsoever between the value missing and any other recorded variable or external parameter. This means that the remaining data is still representative of the population, though this is rarely the case and taking missing data to be completely random is usually an unrealistic assumption.

  For example, in a study that involves determining the reason for obesity among K12 children, MCAR is when the parents forgot to take their kids to the clinic for the study.

- **Missing at Random** (**MAR**): If the case where the data is missing is related to the data that was recorded rather than the data that was not, then the data is said to be MAR. Since it's unfeasible to statistically verify whether data is MAR, we'd have to depend on whether it's a reasonable possibility or not.

  Using the K12 study, missing data in this case is due to parents moving to a different city, hence the children had to leave the study; *missingness* has nothing to do with the study itself.

- **Missing Not at Random** (**MNAR**): Data that is neither MAR nor MCAR is said to be MNAR. This is the case of a non-ignorable non-response, that is, the value of the variable that's missing is related to the reason it is missing.

  Continuing with the example of the case study, data would be MNAR if the parents were offended by the nature of the study and did not want their children to be bullied, so they withdrew their kids from the study.

Finding Missing Values

So, now that we know why it's important to familiarize ourselves with the reasons behind why our data is missing, let's talk about how we can find these missing values in a dataset. For a pandas DataFrame, this is most commonly done using the `.isnull()` method on a DataFrame to create a mask of the null values (that is, a DataFrame of Boolean values) indicating where the null values exist—a **True** value at any position indicates a null value, while a **False** value indicates the existence of a valid value at that position.

> **Note**
>
> The `.isnull()` method can be used interchangeably with the `.isna()` method for pandas DataFrames. Both these methods do exactly the same thing—the reason there are two methods to do the same thing is because pandas DataFrames were originally based on R DataFrames, and hence have reproduced much of the syntax and ideas in the latter.

It may not be immediately obvious whether the missing data is random or not: discovering the nature of missing values across features in a dataset is possible through two common visualization techniques:

- **Nullity matrix**: This is a data-dense display that lets us quickly visualize the patterns in data completion. It gives us a quick glance at how the null values within a feature (and across features) are distributed, how many there are, and how often they appear with other features.

- **Nullity-correlation heatmap**: This heatmap visually describes the nullity relationship (or a data completeness relationship) between each pair of features, that is, it measures how strongly the presence or absence of one variable affects the presence of another.

Akin to regular correlation, nullity correlation values range from -1 to 1: the former indicating that one variable appears when the other definitely does not, and the latter indicating the simultaneous presence of both variables. A value of 0 implies that one variable having a null value has no effect on the other being null.

Exercise 12: Visualizing Missing Values

Let's analyze the nature of the missing values by first looking at the count and percentage of missing values for each feature, then plotting a nullity matrix and correlation heatmap using the `missingno` library in Python:

1. Calculate the count and percentage of missing values in each column and arrange these in decreasing order. We will use the `.isnull()` function on the DataFrame to get a mask. The count of null values in each column can then be found using the `.sum()` function over the mask DataFrame. Similarly, the fraction of null values can be found using `.mean()` over the mask DataFrame and multiplied by 100 to convert it into a percentage.

   Then, we combine the total and percentage of null values into a single DataFrame using the **pd.concat()** function, and subsequently sort the rows by percentage of missing values and print the DataFrame:

   ```
   mask = data.isnull()
   total = mask.sum()
   percent = 100*mask.mean()
   
   missing_data = pd.concat([total, percent], axis=1,join='outer',
                   keys=['count_missing', 'perc_missing'])
   missing_data.sort_values(by='perc_missing', ascending=False, inplace=True)
   missing_data
   ```

The output will be as follows:

	count_missing	perc_missing
state	5764	94.927536
total_damage_millions_dollars	5654	93.115942
damage_millions_dollars	5594	92.127800
injuries	4903	80.747694
total_injuries	4888	80.500659
eq_mag_mw	4856	79.973650
injuries_description	4723	77.783267
total_injuries_description	4715	77.651515
eq_mag_mb	4286	70.586298
second	3351	55.187747
intensity	3324	54.743083
eq_mag_ms	3156	51.976285
focal_depth	2952	48.616601
total_damage_description	2924	48.155468
minute	2234	36.791831
hour	2028	33.399209
eq_primary	1786	29.413702
damage_description	1745	28.738472
day	557	9.173254
month	405	6.669960
latitude	54	0.889328
longitude	50	0.823452
location_name	1	0.016469
id	0	0.000000
region_code	0	0.000000
flag_tsunami	0	0.000000
year	0	0.000000
country	0	0.000000

Figure 2.7: Count and percentage of missing values in each column

Here, we can see that the **state**, **total_damage_millions_dollars**, and **damage_millions_dollars** columns have over 90% missing values, which means that data for less than 10% of data points in the dataset are available for these columns. On the other hand, **year**, **flag_tsunami**, **country**, and **region_code** have no missing values.

2. Plot the nullity matrix. First, we find the list of columns that have any null values in them using the .**any()** function on the mask DataFrame from the previous step. Then, we use the **missingno** library to plot the nullity matrix for a random sample of 500 data points from our dataset, for only those columns that have missing values:

```
nullable_columns = data.columns[mask.any()].tolist()
msno.matrix(data[nullable_columns].sample(500))
plt.show()
```

The output will be as follows:

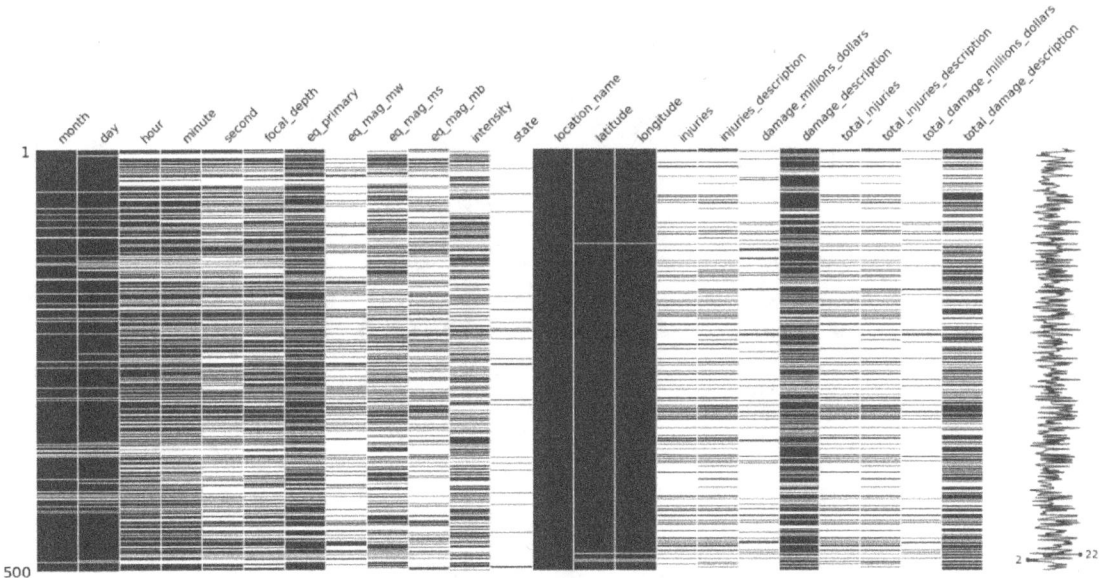

Figure 2.8: The nullity matrix

Here, black lines represent non-nullity while the white lines indicate the presence of a null value in that column. At a glance, **location_name** appears to be completely populated (we know from the previous step that there is, in fact, only one missing value in this column), while **latitude** and **longitude** seem mostly complete, but spottier.

The spark line at the right summarizes the general shape of the data completeness and points out the rows with the maximum and minimum nullity in the dataset.

3. Plot the nullity correlation heatmap. We will plot the nullity correlation heatmap using the `missingno` library for our dataset, for only those columns that have missing values:

   ```
   msno.heatmap(data[nullable_columns], figsize=(18,18))
   plt.show()
   ```

   The output will be as follows:

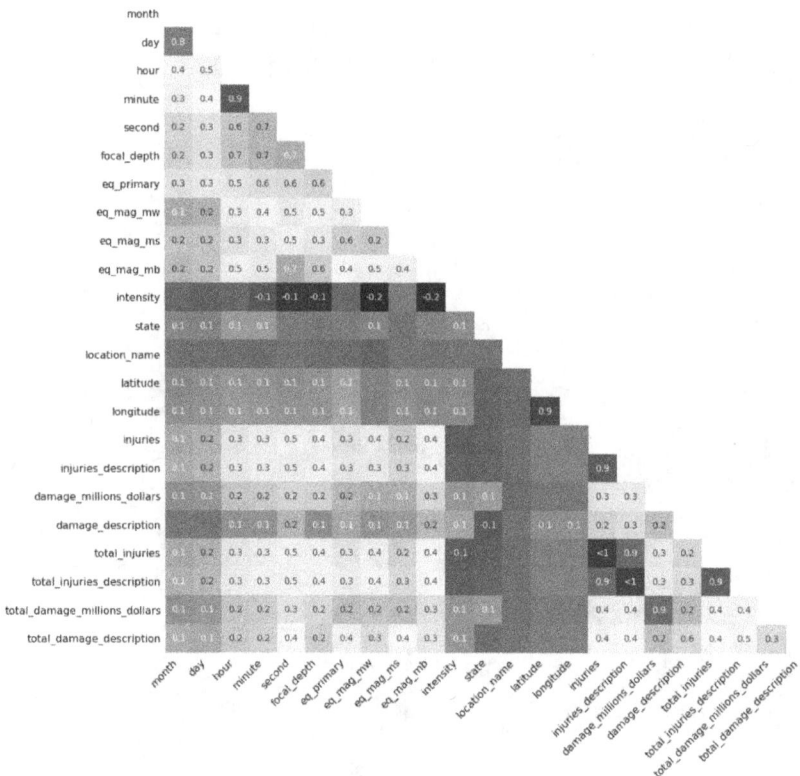

Figure 2.9: The nullity correlation heatmap

Here, we can also see some boxes labeled **<1** or **>-1**: this just means that the correlation value in those cases are close to being exactingly negative or positive, but still not quite perfectly so. We can see a value of **<1** between **injuries** and **total_injuries**, which tells us that there are a few records that have one or the other, but not both. These types of cases will require special attention—if the correlation between the values of the variables themselves is high, it means that having both is not a value and one of the two can be dropped.

Imputation Strategies for Missing Values

There are multiple ways of dealing with missing values in a column. The simplest way is to simply delete rows having missing values; however, this can result in the loss of valuable information from other columns. Another option is to impute the data, that is, replace the missing values with a valid value inferred from the known part of the data. The common ways in which this can be done are listed here:

- Create a new value that is distinct from the other values to replace the missing values in the column so as to differentiate those rows altogether. Then, use a non-linear machine learning algorithm (such as ensemble models or support vectors) that can separate the values out.
- Use an appropriate central value from the column (mean, median, or mode) to replace the missing values.
- Use a model (such as a K-nearest neighbors or a Gaussian mixture model) to learn the best value with which to replace the missing values.

Python has a few functions that are useful for replacing null values in a column with a static value. One way to do this is using the inherent pandas `.fillna(0)` function: there is no ambiguity in imputation here–the static value with which to substitute the null data point in the column is the argument being passed to the function (the value in the brackets).

However, if the number of null values in a column is significant and it's not immediately obvious what the appropriate central value is that can be used to replace each null value, then we can either delete the rows having null values or delete the column altogether from the modeling perspective, as it may not add any significant value. This can be done by using the `.dropna()` function on the DataFrame. The parameters that can be passed to the function are:

- **axis**: This defines whether to drop rows or columns, which is determined by assigning the parameter a value of 0 or 1 respectively.
- **how**: A value of `all` or `any` can be assigned to this parameter to indicate whether the row/column should contain all null values to drop the column, or whether to drop the column if there is at least one null value.
- **thresh**: This defines the minimum number of null values the row/column should have in order to be dropped.

Additionally, if an appropriate replacement for a null value for a categorical feature cannot be determined, a possible alternative to deleting the column is to create a new category in the feature that can represent the null values.

> **Note**
>
> If it is immediately obvious how a null value for a column can be replaced from an intuitive understanding or domain knowledge, then we can replace the value on the spot. In many cases, however, such inferences become more obvious at later stages in the exploration process. In these cases, we can substitute null values as and when we find an appropriate way to do so.

Exercise 13: Imputation Using pandas

Let's look at missing values and replace them with zeros in time-based (continuous) features having at least one null value (month, day, hour, minute, and second). We do this because for cases where we do not have recorded values, it would be safe to assume that the events take place at the beginning of the time duration.

1. Create a list containing the names of the columns whose values we want to impute:

   ```
   time_features = ['month', 'day', 'hour', 'minute', 'second']
   ```

2. Impute the null values using `.fillna()`. We will replace the missing values in these columns with `0` using the inherent pandas `.fillna()` function and pass `0` as an argument to the function:

   ```
   data[time_features] = data[time_features].fillna(0)
   ```

3. Use the `.info()` function to view null value counts for the imputed columns:

   ```
   data[time_features].info()
   ```

The output will be as follows:

```
<class 'pandas.core.frame.DataFrame'>
RangeIndex: 6072 entries, 0 to 6071
Data columns (total 5 columns):
month     6072 non-null float64
day       6072 non-null float64
hour      6072 non-null float64
minute    6072 non-null float64
second    6072 non-null float64
dtypes: float64(5)
memory usage: 237.3 KB
```

Figure 2.10: Null value counts

As we can see now, all values for our features in the DataFrame are now non-null.

Exercise 14: Imputation Using scikit-learn

Let's replace the null values in the description-related categorical features using scikit-learn's **SimpleImputer** class. In *Exercise 12: Visualizing Missing Values*, we saw that almost all of these features comprised more than 50% of null values in the data. Replacing these null values with a central value might bias any model we try to build using the features, deeming them irrelevant. Let's instead replace the null values with a separate category, having value **NA**:

1. Create a list containing the names of the columns whose values we want to impute:

    ```
    description_features = [
        'injuries_description', 'damage_description',
        'total_injuries_description', 'total_damage_description'
    ]
    ```

2. Create an object of the **SimpleImputer** class. Here, we first create an **imp** object of the **SimpleImputer** class and initialize it with parameters that represent how we want to impute the data. The parameters we will pass to initialize the object are:

    missing_values: This is the placeholder for the missing values, that is, all occurrences of the values in the **missing_values** parameter will be imputed.

    strategy: This is the imputation strategy, which can be one of **mean**, **median**, **most_frequent** (that is, the mode), or **constant**. While the first three can only be used with numeric data and will replace missing values using the specified central value along each column, the last one will replace missing values with a constant as per the **fill_value** parameter.

fill_value: This specifies the value with which to replace all occurrences of **missing_values**. If left to the default, the imputed value will be **0** when imputing numerical data and the **missing_value** string for strings or object data types:

```
imp = SimpleImputer(missing_values=np.nan, strategy='constant', fill_value='NA')
```

3. Perform the imputation. We will use **imp.fit_transform()** to actually perform the imputation. It takes the DataFrame with null values as input and returns the imputed DataFrame:

   ```
   data[description_features] = imp.fit_transform(data[description_features])
   ```

4. Use the **.info()** function to view null value counts for the imputed columns:

   ```
   data[description_features].info()
   ```

   The output will be as follows:

   ```
   <class 'pandas.core.frame.DataFrame'>
   RangeIndex: 6072 entries, 0 to 6071
   Data columns (total 4 columns):
   injuries_description        6072 non-null object
   damage_description          6072 non-null object
   total_injuries_description  6072 non-null object
   total_damage_description    6072 non-null object
   dtypes: object(4)
   memory usage: 189.8+ KB
   ```

   Figure 2.11: The null value counts

Exercise 15: Imputation Using Inferred Values

Let's replace the null values in the continuous **damage_millions_dollars** feature with information from the categorical **damage_description** feature. Although we may not know the exact dollar amount that was incurred, the categorical feature gives us information on the range of the amount that was incurred due to damage from the earthquake:

1. Find how many rows have null **damage_millions_dollars** values, and how many of those have non-null **damage_description** values:

   ```
   print(data[pd.isnull(data.damage_millions_dollars)].shape[0])
   print(data[pd.isnull(data.damage_millions_dollars) & (data.damage_description != 'NA')].shape[0])
   ```

The output will be as follows:

```
5594
3849
```

Figure 2.12: Count of rows with null values

As we can see, 3,849 of 5,594 null values can be easily substituted with the help of another variable.

2. Find the mean **damage_millions_dollars** value for each category. Since each of the categories in **damage_description** represent a range of values, we find the mean **damage_millions_dollars** value for each category from the non-null values already available. These provide a reasonable estimate for the most likely value for that category:

```
category_means = data[['damage_description', 'damage_millions_dollars']].groupby('damage_description').mean()
category_means
```

The output will be as follows:

damage_description	damage_millions_dollars
1	0.417211
2	3.078840
3	13.818806
4	3574.998799
NA	NaN

Figure 2.13: The mean damage_millions_dollars value for each category

3. Store the mean values as a dictionary. In this step, we will convert the DataFrame containing the mean values to a dictionary (a Python **dict** object) so that accessing them is convenient.

Additionally, since the value for the newly created **NA** category (the imputed value in the previous exercise) was **NaN** and the value for the **0** category was absent (no rows had **damage_description** equal to **0** in the dataset), we explicitly added these values in the dictionary as well:

```
replacement_values = category_means.damage_millions_dollars.to_dict()

replacement_values['NA'] = -1
replacement_values['0'] = 0
replacement_values
```

The output will be as follows:

```
{'1': 0.4172105263157895,
 '2': 3.0788402777777772,
 '3': 13.818805970149256,
 '4': 3574.9987991266385,
 'NA': -1,
 '0': 0}
```

Figure 2.14: The dictionary of mean values

4. Create a series of replacement values. For each value in the **damage_description** column, we map the categorical value onto the mean value using the **map** function. The **.map()** function is used to map the keys in the column to the corresponding values for each element from the **replacement_values** dictionary:

   ```
   imputed_values = data.damage_description.map(replacement_values)
   ```

5. Replace null values in the column. We do this by using **np.where** as a ternary operator: the first argument is the mask, the second is the series from which to take the value if the mask is positive, and the third is the series from which to take the value if the mask is negative.

   This ensures that the array returned by **np.where** only replaces the null values in **damage_millions_dollars** with values from the **imputed_values** series:

   ```
   data['damage_millions_dollars'] = np.where(condition=data.damage_millions_
   dollars.isnull(),
                       x=imputed_values,
                       y=data.damage_millions_dollars)
   ```

6. Use the `.info()` function to view null value counts for the imputed columns:

    ```
    data[['damage_millions_dollars']].info()
    ```

    The output will be as follows:

    ```
    <class 'pandas.core.frame.DataFrame'>
    RangeIndex: 6072 entries, 0 to 6071
    Data columns (total 1 columns):
    damage_millions_dollars    6072 non-null float64
    dtypes: float64(1)
    memory usage: 47.5 KB
    ```

    Figure 2.15: The null value counts

    We can see that, after replacement, there are no null values in the **damage_millions_dollars** column.

Activity 2: Summary Statistics and Missing Values

In this activity, we'll revise some of the summary statistics and missing value exploration we have looked at thus far in this chapter. We will be using a new dataset, taken from Kaggle's *House Prices: Advanced Regression Techniques* competition (available at https://www.kaggle.com/c/house-prices-advanced-regression-techniques/data or on GitHub at https://github.com/TrainingByPackt/Applied-Supervised-Learning-with-Python). While the Earthquakes dataset used in the exercises is aimed at solving a classification problem (when the target variable has only discrete values), the dataset we will use in the activities will be aimed at solving a regression problem (when the target variable takes on a range of continuous values). We'll use pandas functions to generate summary statistics and visualize missing values using a nullity matrix and nullity correlation heatmap.

The steps to be performed are as follows:

1. Read the data.

2. Use pandas' `.info()` and `.describe()` methods to view the summary statistics of the dataset.

3. Find the total count and total percentage of missing values in each column of the DataFrame and display them for columns having at least one null value, in descending order of missing percentages.

4. Plot the nullity matrix and nullity correlation heatmap.

5. Delete the columns having more than 80% of values missing.
6. Replace null values in the **FireplaceQu** column with **NA** values.

> **Note**
>
> The solution for this activity can be found on page 307.

Distribution of Values

In this section, we'll look at how individual variables behave—what kind of values they take, what the distribution across those values is, and how those distributions can be represented visually.

Target Variable

The target variable can either have values that are continuous (in the case of a regression problem) or discrete (as in the case of a classification problem). The problem statement we're looking at in this chapter involves predicting whether or not an earthquake caused a tsunami, that is, the **flag_tsunami** variable, which takes on two discrete values only—making it a classification problem.

One way of visualizing how many earthquakes resulted in tsunamis and how many didn't is a bar chart, where each bar represents a single discrete value of the variable, and the height of the bars is equal to the count of the data points having the corresponding discrete value. This gives us a good comparison of the absolute counts of each category.

Exercise 16: Plotting a Bar Chart

Let's look at how many of the earthquakes in our dataset resulted in a tsunami. We will do this by using the **value_counts()** method over the column and directly using the **.plot(kind='bar')** function on the returned pandas series. Follow these steps:

1. Use **plt.figure()** to initiate the plotting:

   ```
   plt.figure(figsize=(8,6))
   ```

2. Next, type in our primary plotting command:

   ```
   data.flag_tsunami.value_counts().plot(kind='bar')
   ```

3. Set the display parameters and display the plot:

   ```
   plt.ylabel('Number of data points')
   plt.xlabel('flag_tsunami')
   plt.show()
   ```

   The output will be as follows:

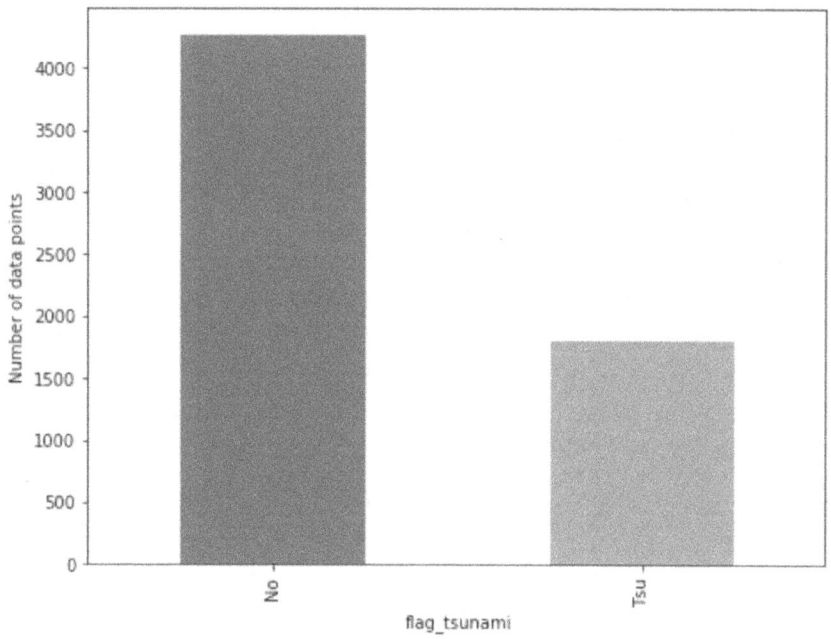

Figure 2.16: Bar chart showing how many earthquakes resulted in a tsunami

From this bar plot, we can see that most of the earthquakes did not result in tsunamis, and that less than one-third of the earthquakes did. This shows us that the dataset is slightly imbalanced.

Let's look more closely at what these Matplotlib commands do:

- `plt.figure(figsize=(8,6))`: This command defines how big our plot should be, by providing width and height values. This is always the first command before any plotting command is written.

- `plt.xlabel()` and `plt.ylabel()`: These commands take a string as input, and allow us to specify what the labels for the X and Y axes on the plot should be.

- `plt.show()`: This is the final command written when plotting that displays the plot inline within the Jupyter notebook.

Categorical Data

Categorical variables are ones that take discrete values representing different categories or levels of observation that can either be string objects, or integer values. For example, our target variable, `flag_tsunami`, is a categorical variable having two categories: `Tsu` and `No`.

Categorical variables can be of two types:

- **Nominal variables**: Variables in which the categories are labeled without any order of precedence are called nominal variables. An example of a nominal variable from our dataset would be `location_name`. The values that this variable takes cannot be said to be ordered, that is, one location is not *greater* than the other. Similarly, more examples of such a variable would be color, types of footwear, ethnicity type, and so on.

- **Ordinal variables**: Variables that have some order associated with them are called ordinal variables. An example from our dataset would be `damage_description`, since each value represents an increasing value of damage incurred. Another example could be day of the week, which would have values from Monday to Sunday, which have some order associated with them and we know that Thursday comes after Wednesday but before Friday.

  Although ordinal variables can be represented by object data types, they are often represented as numerical data types as well, often making it difficult to differentiate between them and continuous variables.

One of the major challenges faced when dealing with categorical variables in a dataset is high cardinality, that is, a large number of categories or distinct values with each value appearing a relatively small number of times. For example, `location_name` has a large number of unique values, with each value occurring a small fraction of times in the dataset.

Additionally, non-numerical categorical variables will always require some form of preprocessing to be converted into a numerical format so that they can be ingested for training by a machine learning model. It can be a challenge to encode categorical variables numerically without losing out on contextual information that despite being easy for humans to interpret (due to domain knowledge or otherwise just plain common sense), would be hard for a computer to automatically understand. For example, a geographical feature such as country or location name by itself would give no indication of the geographical proximity of different values, but that might just be an important feature—what if earthquakes that occur at locations in South-East Asia trigger more tsunamis than those that occur in Europe? There would be no way of capturing that information by merely numerically encoding the feature.

Exercise 17: Datatypes for Categorical Variables

Let's find which variables in our Earthquake dataset are categorical and which are continuous. As we now know, categorical variables can also have numerical values, so having a numeric data type doesn't guarantee that a variable is continuous:

1. Find all the columns that are numerical and object types. We use the `.select_dtypes()` method on the DataFrame to create a subset DataFrame having numeric (`np.number`) and categorical (`np.object`) columns, and then print the column names for each. For numeric columns, use this:

   ```
   numeric_variables = data.select_dtypes(include=[np.number])
   numeric_variables.columns
   ```

   The output will be as follows:

   ```
   Index(['id', 'year', 'month', 'day', 'hour', 'minute', 'second', 'focal_depth',
          'eq_primary', 'eq_mag_mw', 'eq_mag_ms', 'eq_mag_mb', 'intensity',
          'latitude', 'longitude', 'injuries', 'damage_millions_dollars',
          'total_injuries', 'total_damage_millions_dollars'],
         dtype='object')
   ```

   Figure 2.17: All columns that are numerical

   For categorical columns, use this:

   ```
   object_variables = data.select_dtypes(include=[np.object])
   Object_variables.columns
   ```

   The output will be as follows:

   ```
   Index(['flag_tsunami', 'country', 'state', 'location_name', 'region_code',
          'injuries_description', 'damage_description',
          'total_injuries_description', 'total_damage_description'],
         dtype='object')
   ```

   Figure 2.18: All columns that are object types

   Here, it is evident that the columns of object type are categorical variables. To differentiate between the categorical and continuous variables from the numeric columns, let's see how many unique values there are for each of these features.

2. Find the number of unique values for numeric features. We use the **select_dtypes** method on the DataFrame to find the number of unique values in each column and sort the resulting series in ascending order. For numeric columns, use this:

   ```
   numeric_variables.nunique().sort_values()
   ```

   The output will be as follows:

   ```
   intensity                        11
   month                            13
   hour                             24
   day                              32
   eq_mag_mb                        47
   eq_mag_mw                        54
   eq_mag_ms                        55
   minute                           60
   eq_primary                       64
   focal_depth                     197
   total_damage_millions_dollars   233
   damage_millions_dollars         248
   injuries                        338
   total_injuries                  344
   second                          576
   year                            946
   latitude                       2885
   longitude                      3654
   id                             6072
   dtype: int64
   ```

   Figure 2.19: Number of unique values for numeric features

   For categorical columns, use this:

   ```
   object_variables.nunique().sort_values()
   ```

   The output will be as follows:

   ```
   flag_tsunami                       2
   injuries_description               5
   damage_description                 5
   total_injuries_description         5
   total_damage_description           5
   region_code                       18
   state                             29
   country                          155
   location_name                   3821
   dtype: int64
   ```

   Figure 2.20: Number of unique values for categorical columns

For the numeric variables, we can see that the top nine have significantly fewer unique values than the remaining rows, and it's likely that these are categorical variables. However, we must keep in mind that it is possible that some of them might just be continuous variables with a low range of rounded-up values. Also, **month** and **day** would not be considered categorical variables here.

Exercise 18: Calculating Category Value Counts

For columns with categorical values, it would be useful to see what the unique values (categories) of the feature are, along with what the frequencies of these categories are, that is, how much does each distinct value occur in the dataset. Let's find the number of occurrences of each **0** to **4** label and **NaN** values for the **injuries_description** categorical variable:

1. Use the **value_counts()** function on the **injuries_description** column to find the frequency of each category. Using **value_counts** gives us the frequencies of each value in decreasing order in the form of a pandas series:

   ```
   counts = data.injuries_description.value_counts(dropna=False)
   counts
   ```

   The output should be as follows:

   ```
   NA      4723
   1        666
   3        347
   2        193
   4        143
   Name: injuries_description, dtype: int64
   ```

   Figure 2.21: Frequency of each category

2. Sort the values in increasing order of the ordinal variable. If we want the frequencies in the order of the values themselves, we can reset the index to give us a DataFrame and sort values by the index (that is, the ordinal variable):

    ```
    counts.reset_index().sort_values(by='index')
    ```

	index	injuries_description
1	1	666
3	2	193
2	3	347
4	4	143
0	NA	4723

Figure 2.22: Sorted values

Exercise 19: Plotting a Pie Chart

Since our target variable in our sample data is categorical, the example in *Exercise 16: Plotting a Bar Chart* showed us one way of visualizing how the categorical values are distributed (using a bar chart). Another plot that can make it easy to see how each category functions as a fraction of the overall dataset is a pie chart. Let's plot a pie chart to visualize the distribution of the discrete values of the **damage_description** variable:

1. Format the data into the form that needs to be plotted. Here, we run **value_counts()** over the column and sort the series by index:

    ```
    counts = data.damage_description.value_counts()
    counts = counts.sort_index()
    ```

2. Plot the pie chart. The **plt.pie()** category plots the pie chart using the count data. We will use the same three steps for plotting as described in *Exercise 16: Plotting a Bar Chart*:

    ```
    plt.figure(figsize=(10,10))
    plt.pie(counts, labels=counts.index)
    plt.title('Pie chart showing counts for\ndamage_description categories')
    plt.show()
    ```

The output will be:

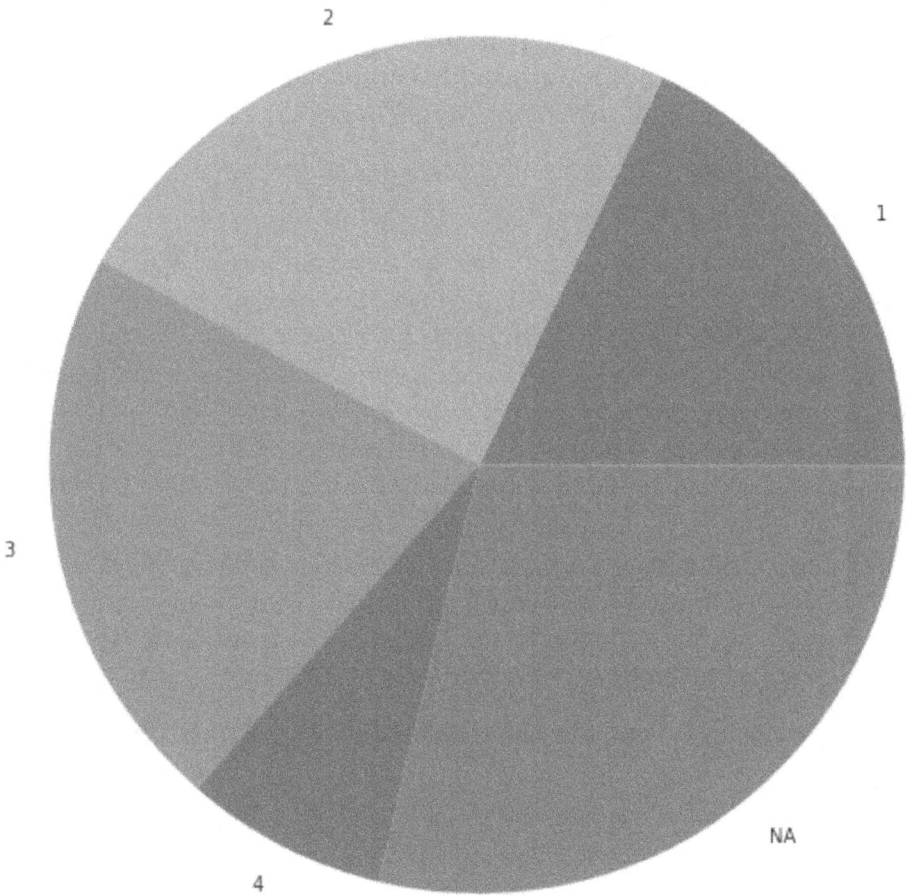

Figure 2.23: Pie chart showing counts for damage_description categories

Continuous Data

Continuous variables can take any number of values and are usually integer (for example, number of deaths) or float data types (for example, the height of a mountain). It's useful to get an idea of the basic statistics of the values in the feature: the minimum, maximum, and percentile values we see from the output of the `describe()` function gives us a fair estimate of this.

However, for continuous variables, it is also very useful to see how the values are distributed in the range they operate in. Since we cannot simply find the counts of individual values, instead we order the values in ascending order, group them into evenly-sized intervals, and find the counts for each interval. This gives us the underlying frequency distribution, and plotting this gives us a histogram, which allows us to examine the shape, central values, and amount of variability in the data.

Histograms give us an easy view of the data that we're looking at. They tell us about the behavior of the values at a glance in terms of the underlying distribution (for example, a normal or exponential distribution), the presence of outliers, skewness, and more.

> **Note**
>
> It is easy to get confused between a bar chart and a histogram. The major difference is that a histogram is used to plot continuous data that has been binned to visualize the frequency distribution, while bar charts can be used for a variety of other use cases, including to represent categorical variables as we have done. Additionally, it is not just the height of the bar that indicates the frequency of that bin, but also the width of the bin itself, which is not the case in a bar chart.

One of the most common frequency distributions is a Gaussian (or normal) distribution. This is a symmetric distribution that has a bell-shaped curve, which indicates that the values near the middle of the range have the highest occurrences in the dataset with a symmetrically decreasing frequency of occurrences as we move away from the middle.

It is a probability distribution and the area under the curve equals one.

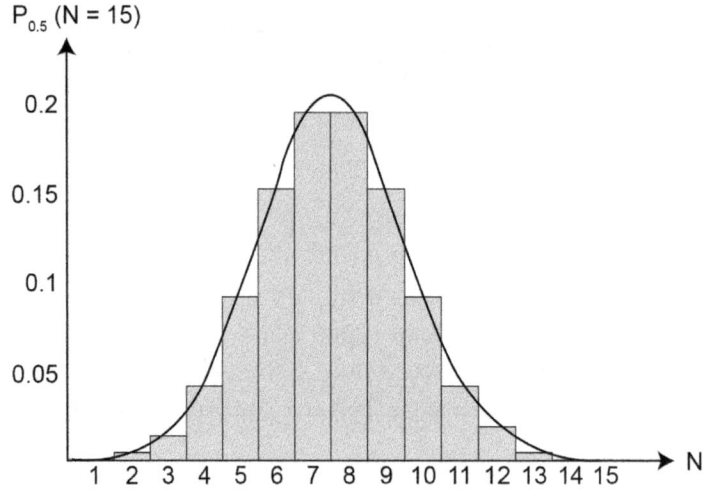

Figure 2.24: Normal distribution

Skewness

A distribution is said to be skewed if it is not symmetric in nature, and skewness measures the asymmetry of a variable about its mean. The value can be positive or negative (or undefined). In the former case, the tail is on the right-hand side of the distribution, while the latter indicates that the tail is on the left-hand side.

However, it must be noted that a thick and short tail would have the same effect on the value of skewness as a long, thin tail.

Kurtosis

Kurtosis is a measure of the *tailedness* of the distribution of a variable and is used to measure the presence of outliers in one tail versus the other. A high value of kurtosis indicates a fatter tail and the presence of outliers. In a similar way to the concept of skewness, kurtosis also describes the shape of the distribution.

Exercise 20: Plotting a Histogram

Let's plot the histogram for the **eq_primary** feature using the Seaborn library:

1. Use **plt.figure()** to initiate the plotting:

    ```
    plt.figure(figsize=(10,7))
    ```

2. **sns.distplot()** is the primary command that we will use to plot the histogram. The first parameter is the one-dimensional data over which to plot the histogram, the bins parameter defines the number and size of the bins. Use this as follows:

    ```
    sns.distplot(data.eq_primary.dropna(), bins=np.linspace(0,10,21))
    ```

3. Display the plot using **plt.show()**:

   ```
   plt.show()
   ```

   The output will be as follows:

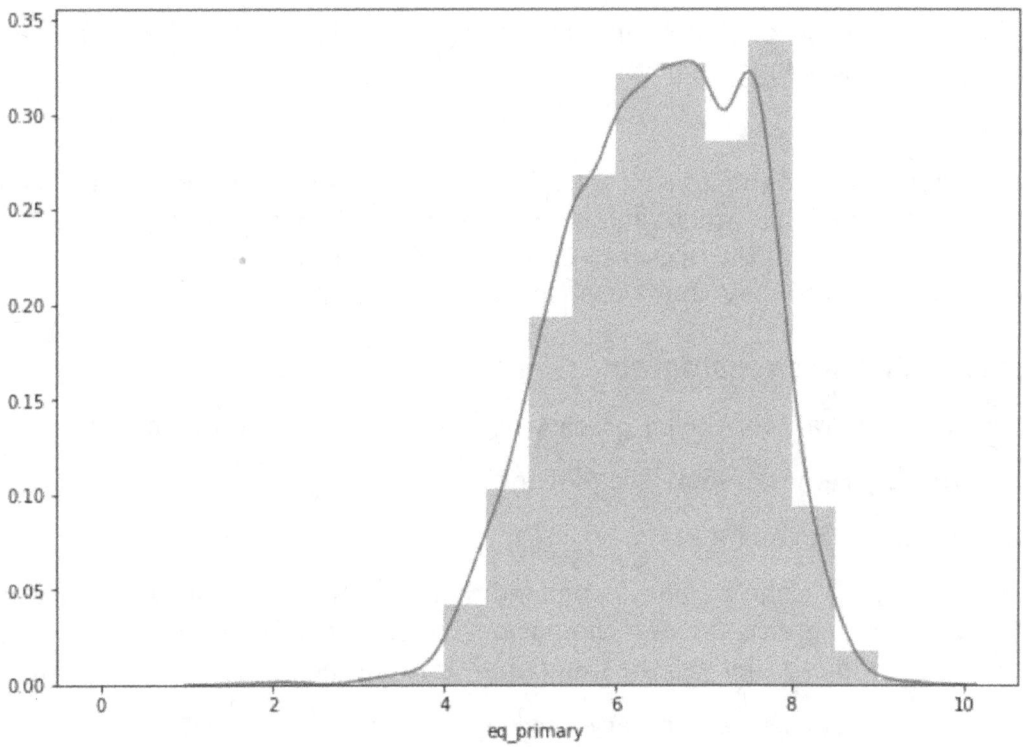

Figure 2.25: Histogram for the eq_primary feature

The plot gives us a normed (or normalized) histogram, which means that the area under the bars of the histogram equals unity. Additionally, the line over the histogram is the **kernel density estimate**, which gives us an idea of what the probability distribution for the variable would look like.

From the plot, we can see that the values of **eq_primary** lie mostly between 5 and 8, which means that most earthquakes had a magnitude with a moderate to high value, with barely any earthquakes having a low or very high magnitude.

Exercise 21: Skew and Kurtosis

Let's calculate the skew and kurtosis values for all the features in the dataset using the core pandas functions available to us:

1. Use the `.skew()` DataFrame method to calculate the skew for all features and then sort the values in ascending order:

   ```
   data.skew().sort_values()
   ```

   The output will be:

   ```
   year                            -3.859655
   latitude                        -1.038393
   region_code                     -0.539048
   longitude                       -0.457442
   intensity                       -0.442065
   eq_primary                      -0.295823
   eq_mag_ms                       -0.243581
   eq_mag_mb                       -0.058037
   month                           -0.012936
   day                              0.036121
   eq_mag_mw                        0.154842
   id                               0.300563
   hour                             0.570365
   minute                           0.618738
   second                           1.096737
   focal_depth                      5.866408
   total_damage_millions_dollars   13.227907
   total_injuries                  22.191856
   injuries                        24.428284
   damage_millions_dollars         47.532464
   dtype: float64
   ```

   Figure 2.26: Skew values for all the features in the dataset

2. Use the `.kurt()` DataFrame method to calculate the kurtosis for all features:

    data.kurt()

The output will be:

```
id                               -0.866617
year                             19.532730
month                            -1.202962
day                              -1.228782
hour                             -1.132145
minute                           -1.050225
second                           -0.272400
focal_depth                      40.911649
eq_primary                       -0.327067
eq_mag_mw                        -0.593857
eq_mag_ms                        -0.486214
eq_mag_mb                         0.432798
intensity                         0.072622
latitude                          0.384692
longitude                        -0.777352
region_code                      -1.324200
injuries                        672.946635
damage_millions_dollars        2725.970362
total_injuries                  569.624067
total_damage_millions_dollars   202.895621
dtype: float64
```

Figure 2.27: Kurtosis values for all the features in the dataset

Here, we can see that the kurtosis values for some variables deviate significantly from 0. This means that these columns have a long tail. But the values that are at the tail end of these variables (which indicate the number of people dead, injured, and the monetary value of damage), in our case, may be outliers that we may need to pay special attention to. Larger values might, in fact, indicate an additional force that added to the devastation caused by an earthquake, that is, a tsunami.

Activity 3: Visually Representing the Distribution of Values

In this activity, we will revise what we learned in the previous section about different types of data. We will use the same dataset we used in *Activity 2: Summary Statistics and Missing Values*, that is, *House Prices: Advanced Regression Techniques* (available at https://www.kaggle.com/c/house-prices-advanced-regression-techniques/data or on GitHub at https://github.com/TrainingByPackt/Applied-Supervised-Learning-with-Python). We'll use different types of plots to visually represent the distribution of values for this dataset.

The steps to be performed are as follows:

1. Plot a histogram using Matplotlib for the target variable, `SalePrice`.
2. Find the number of unique values within each column having an object type.
3. Create a DataFrame representing the number of occurrences for each categorical value in the `HouseStyle` column.
4. Plot a pie chart representing these counts.
5. Find the number of unique values within each column having a number type.
6. Plot a histogram using Seaborn for the `LotArea` variable.
7. Calculate the skew and kurtosis values for the values in each column.

> **Note**
>
> The solution for this activity can be found on page 312.

Relationships within the Data

There are two reasons why it is important to find relationships between variables in the data:

- Finding which features are potentially important can be deemed essential, since finding ones that have a strong relationship with the target variable will aid in the feature selection process.

- Finding relationships between different features themselves can be useful, since variables in the dataset are usually never completely independent of every other variable and this can affect our modeling in a number of ways.

Now, there are a number of ways we can visualize these relationships, and this really depends on the types of variable we are trying to find the relationship between, and how many we are considering as part of the equation or comparison.

Relationship between Two Continuous Variables

To find a relationship between two continuous variables is basically to see how one varies as the value of the other is increased. The most common way to visualize this would be using a scatter plot, in which we take each variable along a single axis (the X and Y axes in a two-dimensional plane when we have two variables) and plot each data point using a marker in the X-Y plane. This visualization gives us a good idea of whether any kind of relationship exists between the two variables at all.

If we want to quantize the relationship between the two variables, however, the most common method is to find the correlation between them. If the target variable is continuous and it has a high degree of correlation with another variable, this is an indication that the feature would be an important part of the model.

Pearson's Coefficient of Correlation

Pearson's Coefficient of Correlation is a correlation coefficient that is commonly used to show the linear relationship between a pair of variables. The formula returns a value between −1 and +1, where:

- +1 indicates a strong positive relationship
- −1 indicates a strong negative relationship
- 0 indicates no relationship at all

It's also useful to find correlations between pairs of features themselves. Although the presence of highly correlated features wouldn't worsen the model, they wouldn't necessarily make any model better, either. For the sake of simplicity, it is always better to keep only one from a set of highly correlated features.

> **Note**
>
> When fitting a linear model, having features that are highly correlated to each other can result in an unpredictable and widely varying model. This is because the coefficients of each feature in a linear model can be interpreted as the unit change in the target variable, keeping all other features constant. When a set of features are not independent (that is, are correlated), however, we cannot determine the effect of the independent changes to the target variable due to each feature, resulting in widely varying coefficients.

To find the pairwise correlation for every numeric feature in a DataFrame with every other feature, we can use the `.corr()` function on the DataFrame.

Exercise 22: Plotting a Scatter Plot

Let's plot a scatter plot between the primary earthquake magnitude on the X axis and the corresponding number of injuries on the Y axis:

1. Filter out null values. Since we know that there are null values in both columns, let's first filter the data to include only the non-null rows:

   ```
   data_to_plot = data[~pd.isnull(data.injuries) & ~pd.isnull(data.eq_primary)]
   ```

2. Create and display the scatter plot. We will use Matplotlib's `plt.scatter(x=..., y=...)` as the primary command for plotting the data. The **x** and **y** parameters state which feature is to be considered along which axis. They take a single-dimensional data structure such as a list, a tuple, or a pandas series. We can also send the **scatter** function more parameters that define, say, the icon to use to plot an individual data point. For example, to use a red cross as the icon, we would need to send the following parameters: `marker='x', c='r'`:

   ```
   plt.figure(figsize=(12,9))

   plt.scatter(x=data_to_plot.eq_primary, y=data_to_plot.injuries)
   ```

```
plt.xlabel('Primary earthquake magnitude')
plt.ylabel('No. of injuries')
plt.show()
```

The output will be as follows:

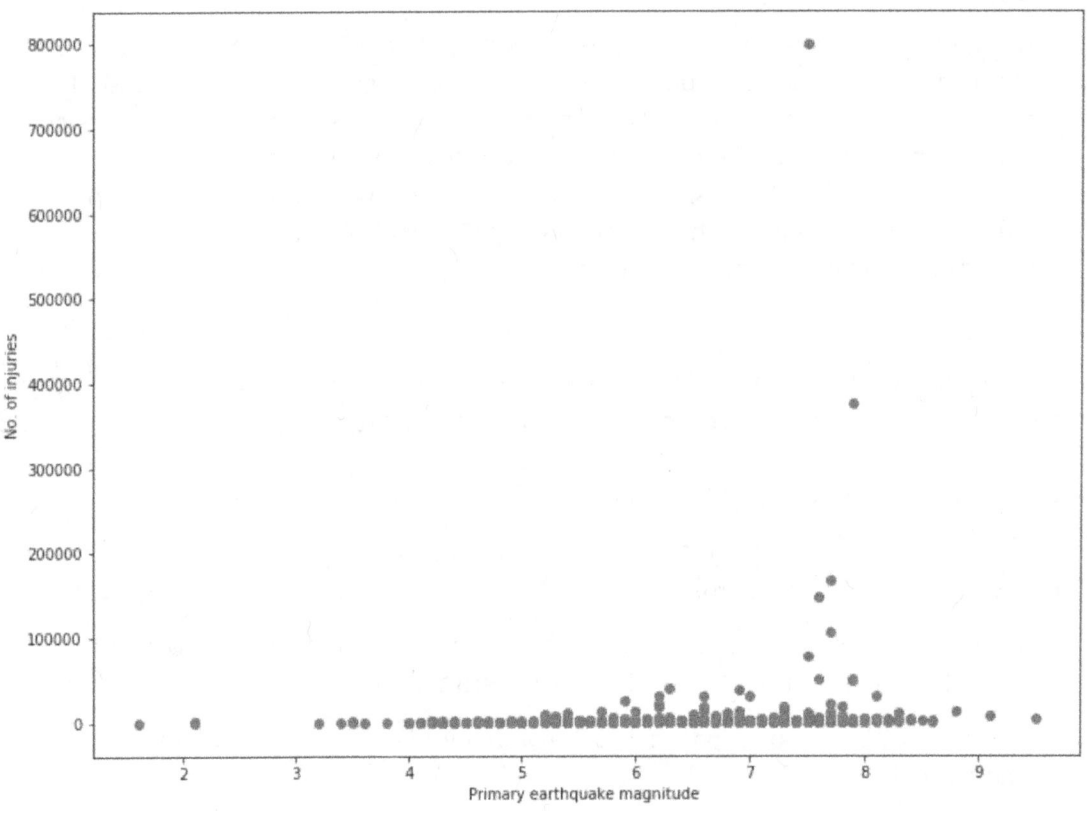

Figure 2.28: Scatter plot

From the plot, we can infer that although there doesn't seem to be a trend between the number of people who were injured and the earthquake magnitude, there are an increasing number of earthquakes with large injury counts as the magnitude increases. However, for the majority of earthquakes, there does not seem to be a relationship.

Exercise 23: Correlation Heatmap

Let's plot a correlation heatmap between all the numeric variables in our dataset using Seaborn's `sns.heatmap()` function on the inter-feature correlation values in the dataset.

Relationships within the Data | 91

The optional parameters passed to the **sns.heatmap()** function are **square** and **cmap**, which indicate that the plot should be such that each pixel is square and specify which color scheme to use, respectively:

1. Plot a basic heatmap with all the features:

   ```
   plt.figure(figsize = (12,10))
   sns.heatmap(data.corr(), square=True, cmap="YlGnBu")
   plt.show()
   ```

   The output will be:

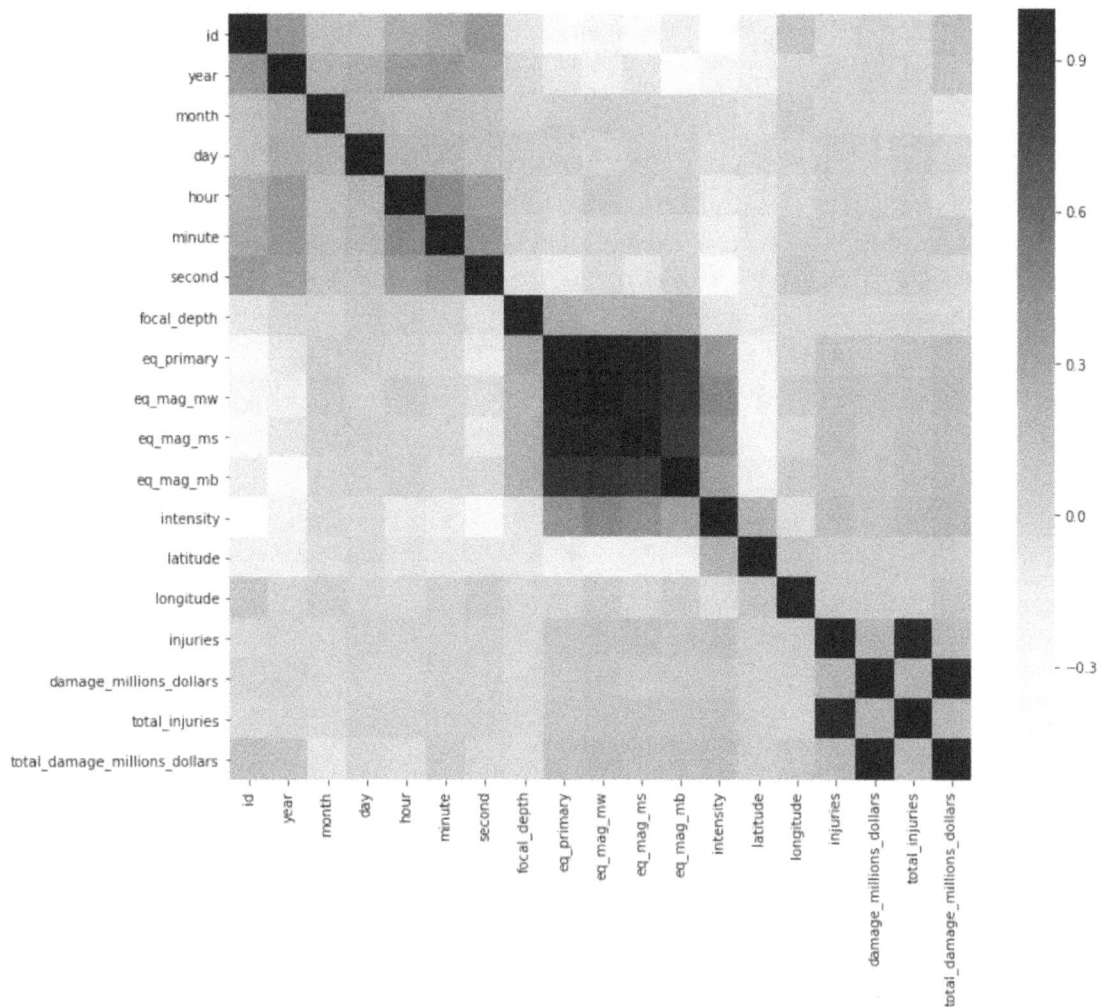

Figure 2.29: Correlation heatmap

We can see from the color bar on the right of the plot that the minimum value, around **-0.2**, is the lightest shade, which is a misrepresentation of the correlation values, which vary from -1 to 1.

2. Plot a subset of features in a more customized heatmap. We will specify the upper and lower limits using the **vmin** and **vmax** parameters, and plot the heatmap again with annotations specifying the pairwise correlation values on a subset of features. We will also change the color scheme to one that can be better interpreted–while the neutral white will represent no correlation, increasingly darker shades of blue and red will represent higher positive and negative correlation values respectively:

```
feature_subset = [
    'focal_depth', 'eq_primary', 'eq_mag_mw', 'eq_mag_ms', 'eq_mag_mb', 'intensity',
    'latitude', 'longitude', 'injuries', 'damage_millions_dollars',
    'total_injuries', 'total_damage_millions_dollars']

plt.figure(figsize = (12,10))
sns.heatmap(data[feature_subset].corr(), square=True, annot=True,
cmap="RdBu", vmin=-1, vmax=1)
plt.show()
```

The output will be as follows:

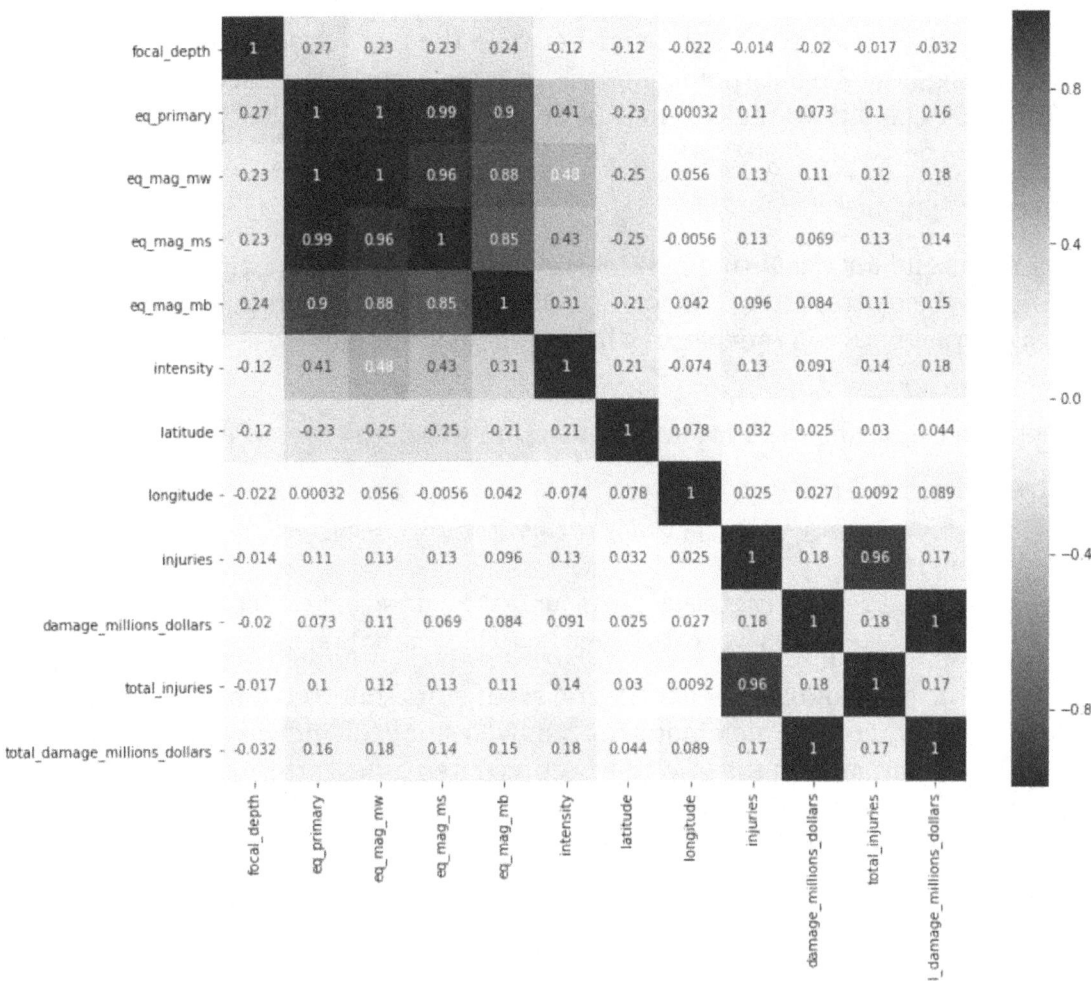

Figure 2.30: Customized correlation heatmap

Now, while we can calculate the value of correlation, this only gives us an indication of a linear relationship. To better judge whether there's a possible dependency, we could plot a scatter plot between pairs of features, which is mostly useful when the relationship between the two variables is not known and visualizing how the data points are scattered or distributed could give us an idea of whether (and how) the two may be related.

Exercise 24: Pairplot

A pairplot is useful for visualizing multiple relationships between pairs of features at once, and can be plotted using Seaborn's `.pairplot()` function. In this exercise, we will look at a pairplot between the features having the highest pair-wise correlation in the dataset:

1. Define a list having the subset of features on which to create the pairplot:

   ```
   feature_subset = [
       'focal_depth', 'eq_primary', 'eq_mag_mw', 'eq_mag_ms', 'eq_mag_mb',
   'intensity',
       'latitude', 'longitude', 'injuries', 'damage_millions_dollars',
       'total_injuries', 'total_damage_millions_dollars']
   ```

2. Create the pairplot using Seaborn. The arguments sent to the plotting function are: **kind='scatter'**, which indicates that we want each individual plot between the pair of variables in the grid to be represented as a scatter plot, and **diag_kind='kde'**, which indicates that we want the plots along the diagonal (where both the features in the pair are the same) to be a kernel density estimate.

   It should also be noted here that the plots symmetrically across the diagonal from each other will essentially be the same, just with the axes reversed:

   ```
   plt.figure(figsize = (12,10))
   sns.heatmap(data[feature_subset].corr(), square=True, annot=True,
   cmap="RdBu", vmin=-1, vmax=1)
   plt.show()
   ```

The output will be as follows:

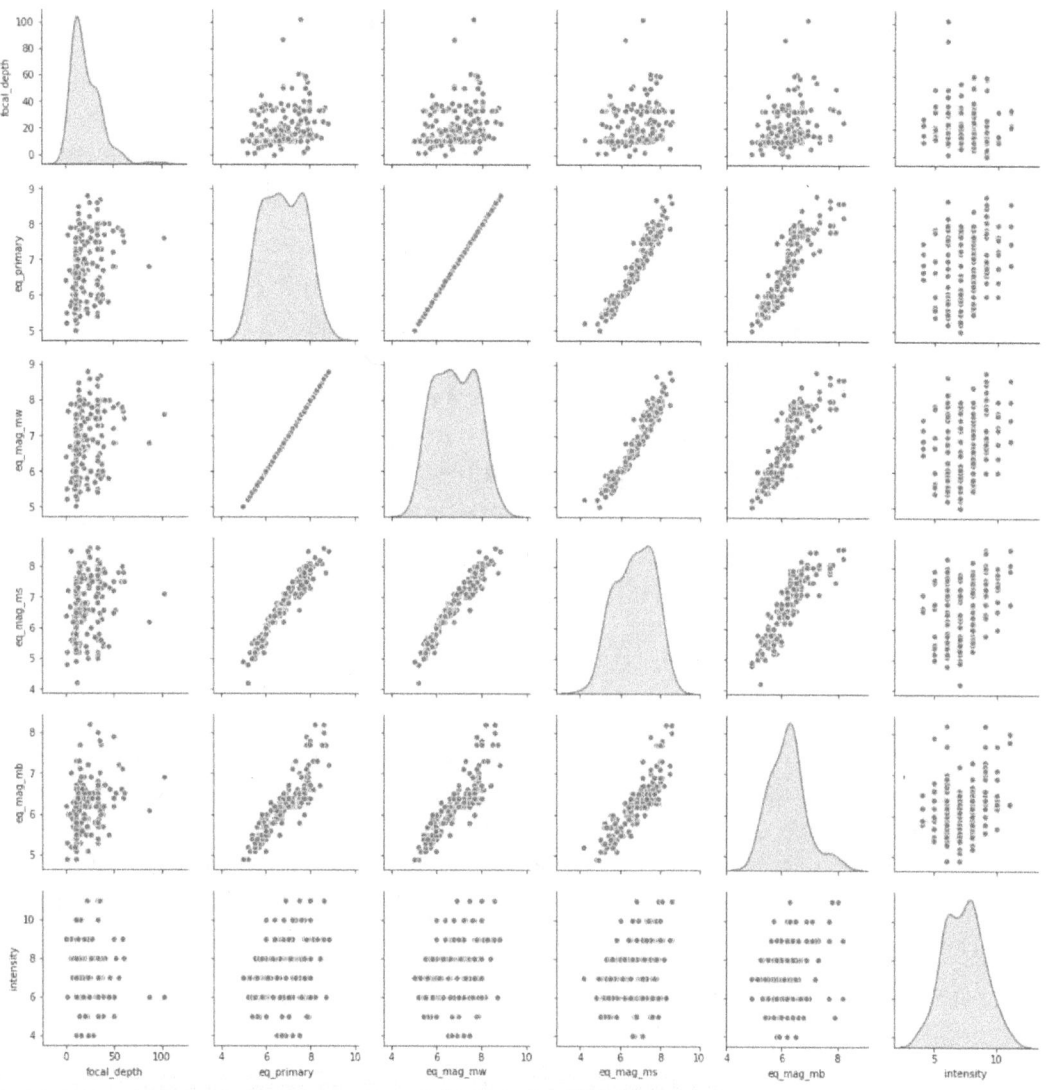

Figure 2.31: Pairplot between the features having the highest pair-wise correlation

Relationship between a Continuous and a Categorical Variable

A common way to see the relationship between two variables when one is categorical and the other is continuous can be using a bar plot or a box plot.

- A bar plot helps compare the value of a variable for a discrete set of parameters and is one of the most common types of plots. Each bar represents a categorical value and the height of the bar usually represents an aggregated value of the continuous variable over that category (such as average, sum, or count of the values of the continuous variable in that category).

- A box plot is a rectangle drawn to represent the distribution of the continuous variable for each discrete value of the categorical variable. It not only allows us to visualize outliers efficiently but also allows us to compare the distribution of the continuous variable across categories of the categorical variable. The lower and upper edges of the rectangle represent the first and third quartiles respectively, the line down through the middle represents the median value, and the points (or fliers) above and below the rectangle represent outlier values.

Exercise 25: Bar Chart

Let's visualize the total number of tsunamis created by earthquakes of each intensity level using a bar chart:

1. Preprocess the **flag_tsunami** variable. Before we can use the **flag_tsunami** variable, we need to preprocess it to convert the **No** values to zeros and the **Tsu** values to ones. This will give us the binary target variable. To do this, we set the values in the column using the **.loc** operator, with **:** indicating that values need to be set for all rows, and the second parameter specifying the name of the column for which values are to be set:

    ```
    data.loc[:,'flag_tsunami'] = data.flag_tsunami.apply(lambda t: int(str(t) == 'Tsu'))
    ```

2. Remove all rows having null **intensity** values from the data we want to plot:

    ```
    subset = data[~pd.isnull(data.intensity)][['intensity','flag_tsunami']]
    ```

3. Find the total number of tsunamis for each **intensity** level and display the DataFrame. To get the data in a format using which a bar plot can be visualized, we will need to group the rows by each intensity level, and then sum over the **flag_tsunami** values to get the total number of tsunamis for each intensity level:

   ```
   data_to_plot = subset.groupby('intensity').sum()
   data_to_plot
   ```

   The output will be as follows:

intensity	flag_tsunami
2.0	0
3.0	8
4.0	19
5.0	38
6.0	63
7.0	91
8.0	119
9.0	132
10.0	130
11.0	58
12.0	4

   Figure 2.32: Total number of tsunamis for each intensity level

4. Plot the bar chart, using Matplotlib's **plt.bar(x=..., height=...)** method, which takes two arguments, one specifying the x values at which bars need to be drawn, and the second specifying the height of each bar. Both of these are one-dimensional data structures that must have the same length:

   ```
   plt.figure(figsize=(12,9))
   plt.bar(x=data_to_plot.index, height=data_to_plot.flag_tsunami)
   plt.xlabel('Earthquake intensity')
   plt.ylabel('No. of tsunamis')
   plt.show()
   ```

The output will be as follows:

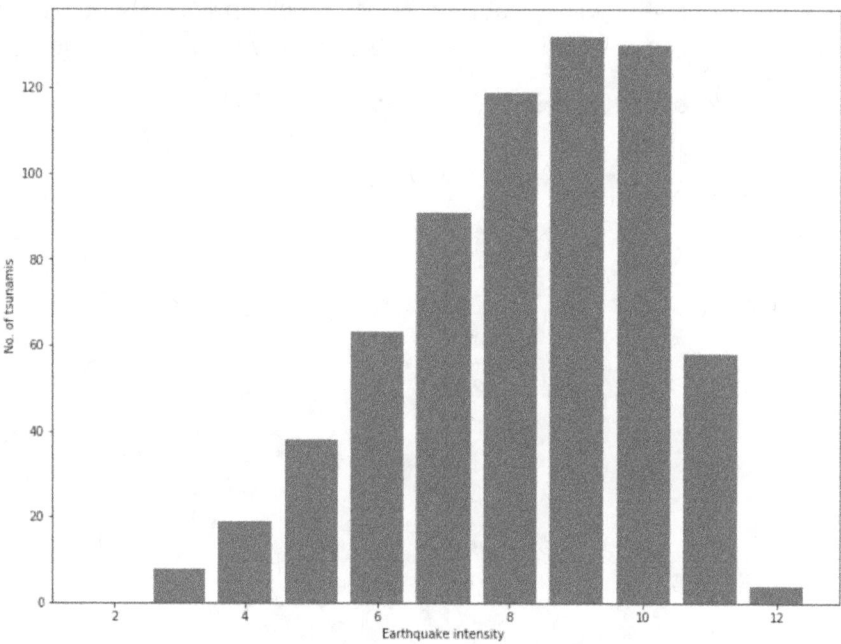

Figure 2.33: Bar chart

From this plot, we can see that as the earthquake intensity increases, the number of tsunamis caused also increases, but beyond an intensity of 9, the number of tsunamis seems to suddenly drop.

Think about why this could be happening. Perhaps it's just that there are fewer earthquakes with an intensity that high, and hence fewer tsunamis. Or it could be an entirely independent factor; maybe high-intensity earthquakes have historically occurred on land and couldn't trigger a tsunami. Explore the data to find out.

Exercise 26: Box Plot

In this exercise, we'll plot a box plot that represents the variation in **eq_primary** over the countries with at least 100 earthquakes:

1. Find countries with over 100 earthquakes. We will find the value counts for all the countries in the dataset. Then, we'll create a series comprising only those countries having a count greater than 100:

   ```
   country_counts = data.country.value_counts()
   top_countries = country_counts[country_counts > 100]
   top_countries
   ```

The output will be as follows:

```
CHINA          590
JAPAN          403
INDONESIA      379
IRAN           377
ITALY          325
TURKEY         321
USA            260
GREECE         260
PHILIPPINES    210
MEXICO         198
CHILE          193
PERU           180
RUSSIA         149
Name: country, dtype: int64
```

Figure 2.34: Countries with over 100 earthquakes

2. Subset the DataFrame to filter in only those rows having countries in the preceding set. To filter the rows, we use the `.isin()` method on the pandas series to select those rows containing a value in the array-like object passed as a parameter:

   ```
   subset = data[data.country.isin(top_countries.index)]
   ```

3. Create and display the box plot. The primary command for plotting the data is **sns.boxplot(x=..., y=..., data=..., order=)**. The **x** and **y** parameters are the names of the columns in the DataFrame to be plotted on each axis—the former is assumed to be the categorical variable and the latter the continuous. The **data** parameter takes the DataFrame from which to take the data and **order** takes a list of category names that indicates the order in which to display the categories on the X axis:

   ```
   plt.figure(figsize=(15, 15))
   sns.boxplot(x='country', y="eq_primary", data=subset, order=top_countries.index)
   plt.show()
   ```

The output will be as follows:

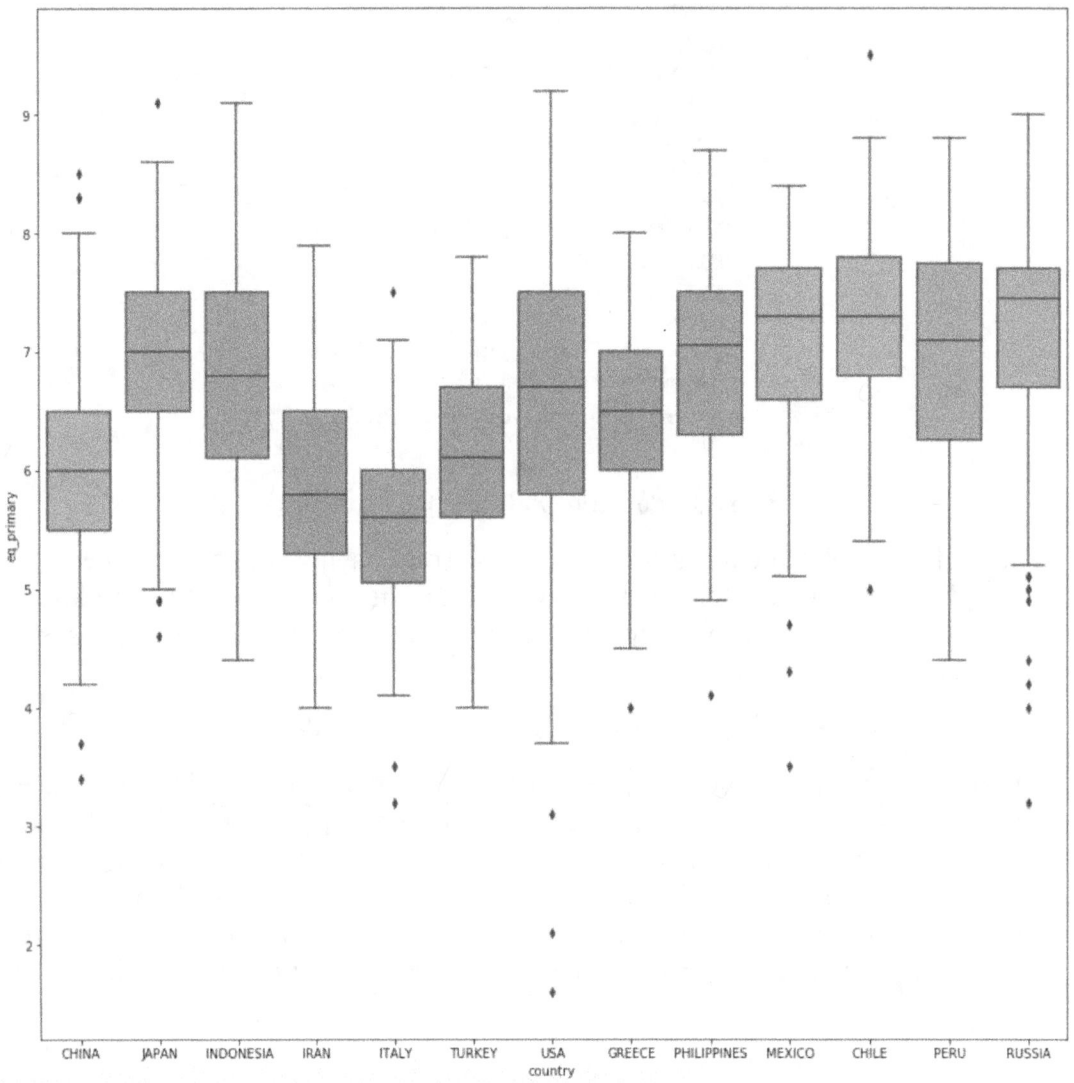

Figure 2.35: Box plot

Relationship between Two Categorical Variables

When we are looking at only a pair of categorical variables to find a relationship between them, the most intuitive way to do this is to divide the data on the basis of the first category, and then subdivide it further on the basis of the second categorical variable and look at the resultant counts to find the distribution of data points. While this might seem confusing, a popular way to visualize this is using stacked bar charts. As in a regular bar chart, each bar would represent a categorical value. But each bar would again be subdivided into color-coded categories that would provide an indication of what fraction of the data points in the primary category fall into each subcategory (that is, the second category). The variable with a larger number of categories is usually considered the primary category.

Exercise 27: Stacked Bar Chart

In this exercise, we'll plot a stacked bar chart that represents the number of tsunamis that occurred for for each intensity level:

1. Find the number of data points that fall into each grouped value of **intensity** and **flag_tsunami**:

   ```
   grouped_data = data.groupby(['intensity', 'flag_tsunami']).size()
   grouped_data
   ```

   The output will be as follows:

   ```
   intensity  flag_tsunami
   2.0        0                 5
   3.0        0                10
              1                 8
   4.0        0                37
              1                19
   5.0        0                74
              1                38
   6.0        0               151
              1                63
   7.0        0               342
              1                91
   8.0        0               470
              1               119
   9.0        0               356
              1               132
   10.0       0               494
              1               130
   11.0       0                79
              1                58
   12.0       0                68
              1                 4
   dtype: int64
   ```

   Figure 2.36: Data points falling into each grouped value of intensity and flag_tsunami

2. Use the `.unstack()` method on the resultant DataFrame to get the level 1 index (`flag_tsunami`) as a column:

   ```
   data_to_plot = grouped_data.unstack()
   data_to_plot
   ```

   The output will be as follows:

flag_tsunami	0	1
intensity		
2.0	5.0	NaN
3.0	10.0	8.0
4.0	37.0	19.0
5.0	74.0	38.0
6.0	151.0	63.0
7.0	342.0	91.0
8.0	470.0	119.0
9.0	356.0	132.0
10.0	494.0	130.0
11.0	79.0	58.0
12.0	68.0	4.0

   Figure 2.37: The level 1 index

3. Create the stacked bar chart. We first use the `sns.set()` function to indicate that we want to use Seaborn as our visualization library. Then, we can easily use the native `.plot()` function in pandas to plot a stacked bar chart by passing the `kind='bar'` and `stacked=True` arguments:

   ```
   sns.set()
   data_to_plot.plot(kind='bar', stacked=True, figsize=(12,8))
   plt.show()
   ```

The output will be as follows:

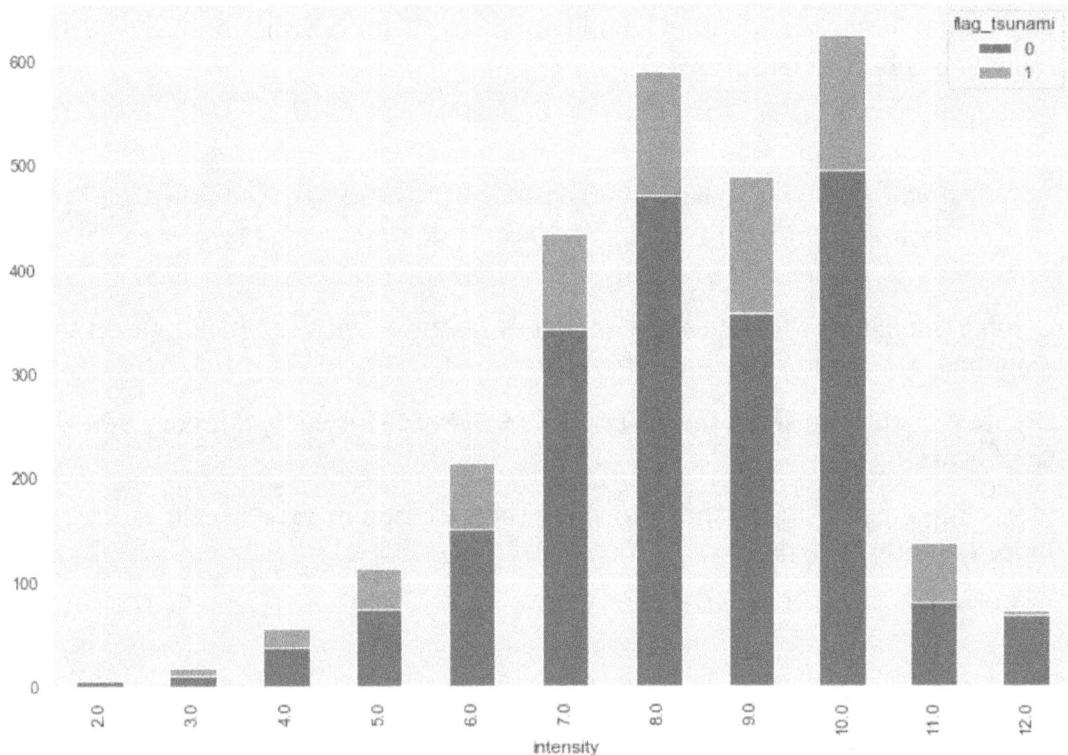

Figure 2.38: A stacked bar chart

The plot now lets us visualize and interpret the fraction of earthquakes that caused tsunamis at each intensity level. In *Exercise 25: Bar Chart*, we saw the number of tsunamis drop for earthquakes having intensity greater than 9. From this plot, we can now confirm that this was primarily because the number of earthquakes themselves dropped beyond level 10; the fraction of tsunamis even increased for level 11.

Activity 4: Relationships Within the Data

In this activity, we will revise what we learned in the previous section about relationships between data. We will use the same dataset we used in *Activity 2: Summary Statistics and Missing Values*, that is, *House Prices: Advanced Regression Techniques* (available at https://www.kaggle.com/c/house-prices-advanced-regression-techniques/data or on GitHub at https://github.com/TrainingByPackt/Applied-Supervised-Learning-with-Python). We'll use different plots to highlight relationships between values in this dataset.

The steps to be performed are as follows:

1. Plot the correlation heatmap for the dataset.

2. Plot a more compact heatmap having annotations for correlation values using the following subset of features:

   ```
   feature_subset = [
       'GarageArea',
   'GarageCars','GarageCond','GarageFinish','GarageQual','GarageType',
       'GarageYrBlt','GrLivArea','LotArea','MasVnrArea','SalePrice'
   ]
   ```

3. Display the pairplot for the same subset of features, with the KDE plot on the diagonals and scatter plot elsewhere.

4. Create a boxplot to show the variation in **SalePrice** for each category of **GarageCars**.

5. Plot a line graph using Seaborn to show the variation in **SalePrice** for older and more recently built flats.

> **Note**
>
> The solution for this activity can be found on page 319.

Summary

In this chapter, we started by talking about why data exploration is an important part of the modeling process and how it can help in not only preprocessing the dataset for the modeling process, but also help us engineer informative features and improve model accuracy. This chapter focused on not only gaining a basic overview of the dataset and its features, but also gaining insights by creating visualizations that combine several features.

We looked at how to find the summary statistics of a dataset using core functionality from pandas. We looked at how to find missing values and talked about why they're important, while learning how to use the Missingno library to analyze them and the pandas and scikit-learn libraries to impute the missing values.

Then, we looked at how to study the univariate distributions of variables in the dataset and visualize them for both categorical and continuous variables using bar charts, pie charts, and histograms. Lastly, we learned how to explore relationships between variables, and about how they can be represented using scatter plots, heatmaps, box plots, and stacked bar charts, to name a few.

In the following chapters, we will start exploring supervised machine learning algorithms. Now that we have an idea of how to explore a dataset that we have, we can proceed to the modeling phase. The next chapter will introduce regression: a class of algorithms that are primarily used to build models for continuous target variables.

3
Regression Analysis

Learning Objectives

By the end of this chapter, you will be able to:

- Describe regression models and explain the difference between regression and classification problems
- Explain the concept of gradient descent, how it is used in linear regression problems, and how it can be applied to other model architectures
- Use linear regression to construct a linear model for data in an *x-y* plane
- Evaluate the performance of linear models and use the evaluation to choose the best model
- Use feature engineering to create dummy variables for constructing more complicated linear models
- Construct time series regression models using autoregression

This chapter covers regression problems and analysis, introducing us to linear regression as well as multiple linear regression, gradient descent, and autoregression.

Introduction

In the first two chapters, we were introduced to the concept of supervised machine learning in Python and the essential techniques required for loading, cleaning, exploring, and visualizing raw data sources. We discussed the criticality of the correlations between the specified inputs and desired output for the given problem, as well as how the initial data preparation process can sometimes take a lot of the time spent on the entire project.

In this chapter, we will delve into the model building process and will construct our first supervised machine learning solution using linear regression. So, let's get started.

Regression and Classification Problems

We discussed two distinct methods, supervised learning and unsupervised learning, in *Chapter 1, Python Machine Learning Toolkit*. Supervised learning problems aim to map input information to a known output value or label, but there are two further subcategories to consider. Both supervised and unsupervised learning problems can be further divided into regression or classification problems. Regression problems, which are the subject of this chapter, aim to predict or model continuous values, for example, predicting the temperature tomorrow in degrees Celsius or determining the location of a face within an image. In contrast, classification problems, rather than returning a continuous value, predict membership of one of a specified number of classes or categories. The example supervised learning problem in *Chapter 1, Python Machine Learning Toolkit*, where we wanted to determine or predict whether a wig was from the 1960s or 1980s, is a good example of a supervised classification problem. There, we attempted to predict whether a wig was from one of two distinct groups or classes; class 1 being the 1960s and class 2 being the 1980s. Other classification problems include predicting whether a passenger of the Titanic survived or perished or the classic MNIST problem (http://yann.lecun.com/exdb/mnist/). MNIST is a database of 70,000 labeled images of handwritten digits 0 through 9. The task in classifying examples from MNIST is to take one of the 70,000 input images and predict or classify which digit 0-9 is written in the image; so, the model must predict the membership of the image in one of 10 different classes.

Data, Models, Training, and Evaluation

Before we begin our deep dive into regression problems, we will first look at the four major stages involved in creating any machine learning model, supervised regression or otherwise. These stages are as follows:

1. Data preparation
2. Model architecture specification

3. The design and execution of the training process
4. The evaluation of the trained model

It is advised that you ensure you are completely confident in your understanding of this pipeline and of what is described within this section, as each of these stages is critical in achieving high or even reasonable system performance. We will consider each of these stages in the context of the wig classification problem from *Chapter 1, Python Machine Learning Toolkit*.

Data Preparation

The first stage of the pipeline, data preparation, was the focus of a significant component of *Chapter 1, Python Machine Learning Toolkit*, and thus will not be the subject of further analysis in this section. It is important, however, that the criticality of the data specification, collection, and cleaning/tidying process is well understood. We cannot expect to produce a high-performing system if the input data is sub-optimal. One common phrase that you should always remember with regard to data quality is *junk in, junk out*. If you put junk data in, you are going to get a junk result out. In our wig example, we are looking for a sample size at least in the order of hundreds, ideally thousands, that have been correctly labeled as either from the 1960s or 1980s. We do not want samples that have been incorrectly labeled or aren't even from either era.

Model Architecture

The second stage, model architecture specification, will be described in more detail in this chapter. This stage defines the type of model that is to be used, as well as the types and values of the parameters that comprise the model itself. The model is essentially a mathematical equation that is used to define the relationship between the input data and the desired result. As with any equation, the model is composed of variables and constants combined by a set of processes, for example, addition, subtraction, or convolution. The nature and values of the model parameters will vary depending upon the type of model selected and the level of complexity at which the model is able to describe the relationship being observed. Simpler models will contain fewer parameters with greater constraints on their values, while more complex models have a greater number of possibly varying parameters. In this chapter, we will be employing a linear model, which is one of the simpler models available, compared with some others, such as convolutional neural network models, which may have more than one million parameters that need to be optimized for a good result. This simplicity should not be mistaken for a lack of power, or a lack of ability to describe relationships within data, but simply that fewer parameters are available for tuning (that is, changing the values to optimize performance).

Model Training

The third stage of the system pipeline is the design and execution of the training process, that is, the mechanism by which the values for the parameters of the model are determined. In a supervised learning problem, we can think about the training process as being analogous to being a student within a classroom. In a typical classroom environment, the teacher already has the answers to a given problem and is attempting to show the students how to solve the problem given some set of inputs. In such a scenario, the student is the model, and the parameters are all within the student's brain and are the means by which the student correctly answers the problem.

The training process is the method the teacher uses to train the student to correctly answer the problem; this method can be tweaked and changed in response to the student's ability to learn and understand the content. Once a model architecture has been defined (that is, the student in the class), it is the training process that is used to provide the guidance and constraints required to approach an optimal solution. Just as some students perform better in different learning environments, so do models. Thus, there is an additional set of parameters known as **hyperparameters**, which, while not being used within the model itself to make predictions given some set of input data, are defined, used, and tuned in an attempt to optimize the performance of the model against a specified cost (or error) function (for example, root mean squared error). We will also discuss hyperparameters in more detail in this chapter, but for the time being, it is simplest to think about hyperparameters as the environment in which the actual parameters of the model are determined.

Model Evaluation

The final stage of the pipeline is the evaluation of the model, which yields the final performance metric. This is the mechanism through which we know whether the model is worth publishing, better than a previous version, or has been effectively translated across programming languages or development environments. We will cover some of these metrics in more detail in *Chapter 6, Model Evaluation*, and as such this will not be discussed in detail at this stage. Just keep in mind that whichever validation technique is selected, it needs to be capable of consistently reporting and independently measuring the performance of the model against the dataset. Again, using our wig dataset as the example, the evaluation stage would look at how many correct predictions the model achieved, given wig images and the known eras as the labels.

Linear Regression

We will start our investigation into regression problems with the selection of a linear model. Linear models, while being a great first choice due to their intuitive nature, are also very powerful in their predictive power, assuming datasets contain some degree of linear or polynomial relationship between the input features and values. The intuitive nature of linear models often arises from the ability to view data as plotted on a graph and observe a trending pattern in the data with, say, the output (the y axis value for the data) trending positively or negatively with the input (x axis value). While often not presented as such, the fundamental components of linear regression models are also often learned during high school mathematics classes. You may recall that the equation of a straight line, or linear model, is defined as follows:

$$y = mx + b$$

Figure 3.1: Equation of a straight line

Here, x is the input value and y is the corresponding output or predicted value. The parameters of the model are the gradient or slope of the line (change in y values divided by change in x) defined by m as well as the y-intercept value b, which indicates where the line crosses the y axis. With such a model, we can provide values for the m and b parameters to construct a linear model. For example, $y = 2x + 1$, has a slope of 2, indicating the changes in y values are at a rate of twice that of x; the line crosses the y intercept at 1:

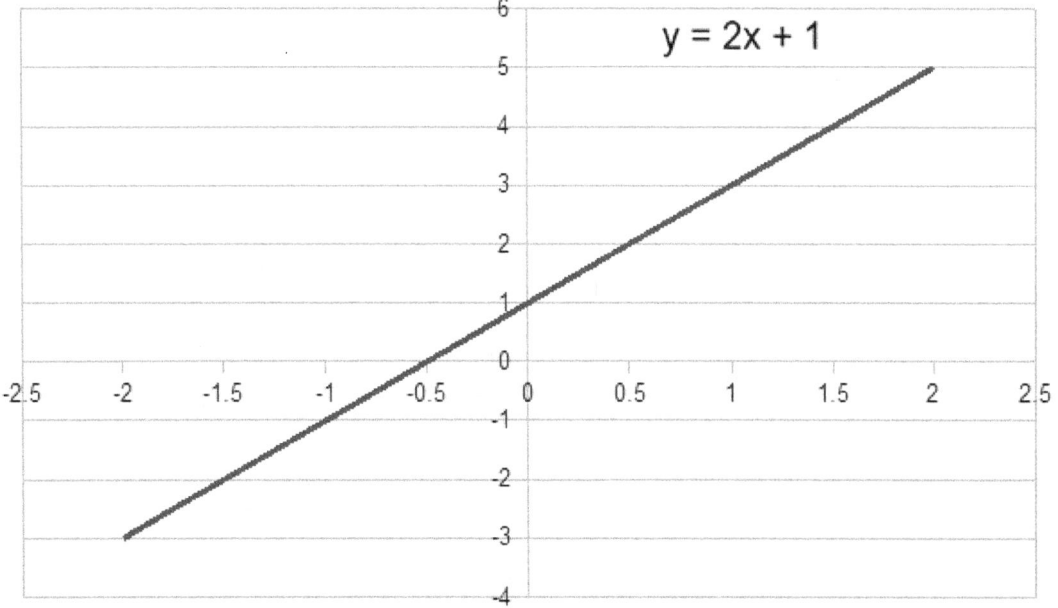

Figure 3.2: Parameters of a straight line

So, we have an understanding of the parameters that are required to define a straight line, but this isn't really doing anything particularly interesting. We just dictated the parameters of the model to construct a line. What we want to do is take a dataset and construct a model that best describes a dataset. As mentioned before, this dataset needs to have something that approximates a linear relationship between the input features and output values. For this purpose, we have created a synthetic dataset of recorded air temperatures from the years 1841 to 2010, which is available in the accompanying code bundle of this book or on GitHub at https://github.com/TrainingByPackt/Supervised-Learning-with-Python. This dataset is composed of values designed to demonstrate the subject matter of this chapter and should not be mistaken for data collected from a scientific study.

Exercise 28: Plotting Data with a Moving Average

As we discussed in *Chapter 1, Python Machine Learning Toolkit*, a thorough understanding of the dataset being used is critical if a high-performing model is to be built. So, with this in mind, let's use this exercise to load, plot, and interrogate the data source:

1. Import the **numpy**, **pandas**, and **matplotlib** packages with alternative handles:

    ```
    Import numpy as np
    import pandas as pd
    import matplotlib.pyplot as plt
    ```

2. Use the pandas **read_csv** function to load the CSV file containing the **synth_temp.csv** dataset, and then display the first five lines of data:

    ```
    df = pd.read_csv('synth_temp.csv')
    df.head()
    ```

    The output will be as follows:

	AverageTemperature	Year
0	12.980258	1841
1	13.689697	1842
2	12.485703	1843
3	14.202069	1844
4	12.831530	1845

    Figure 3.3: The first five rows

3. Since we are only interested in the data from 1901 to 2010, remove all rows prior to 1901:

   ```
   df = df.loc[df.Year > 1901]
   df.head()
   ```

   The output will be:

	AverageTemperature	Year
366	16.973653	1902
367	17.181773	1903
368	17.436933	1904
369	17.688948	1905
370	17.811166	1906

   Figure 3.4: The first five rows after removing all rows prior to 1901

4. The original dataset contains multiple temperature measurements per year, with more measurements for the later years (12 for 2010) and less for the earlier years (6 for 1841); however, we are interested in a list of yearly average temperatures. Group the data by year and use the **agg** method of the DataFrame to create the yearly averages:

   ```
   df_group_year = df.groupby('Year').agg(np.mean)
   df_group_year.head()
   ```

   The output will be:

Year	AverageTemperature
1902	17.438122
1903	17.375456
1904	17.558674
1905	17.740646
1906	17.501770

   Figure 3.5: Yearly average data

5. Given that the data is quite noisy, a moving average filter would provide a useful indicator of the overall trend. A moving average filter simply computes the average over the last N values and assigns this average to the (N+1)th sample. Compute the values for a moving average signal for the temperature measurements using a window of 10 years:

```
window = 10
rolling = df_group_year.AverageTemperature.rolling(window).mean()
rolling.head(n=20)
```

We will get the following output:

```
Year
1902           NaN
1903           NaN
1904           NaN
1905           NaN
1906           NaN
1907           NaN
1908           NaN
1909           NaN
1910           NaN
1911     17.501145
1912     17.502700
1913     17.500737
1914     17.487112
1915     17.466333
1916     17.460069
1917     17.475434
1918     17.463959
1919     17.472423
1920     17.474037
1921     17.480317
Name: AverageTemperature, dtype: float64
```

Figure 3.6: Values for a moving average signal

Notice that the first 9 samples are **NaN**, which is because of the size of the moving average filter window. The window size is 10, thus 9 (10-1) samples are required to generate the first average, and thus the first 9 samples are **NaN**.

6. Finally, plot the measurements by year along with the moving average signal:

```
fig = plt.figure(figsize=(10, 7))
ax = fig.add_axes([1, 1, 1, 1]);

# Temp measurements
ax.scatter(df_group_year.index, df_group_year.AverageTemperature,
label='Raw Data', c='k');
```

```
ax.plot(df_group_year.index, rolling, c='k', linestyle='--',
label=f'{window} year moving average');

ax.set_title('Mean Air Temperature Measurements')
ax.set_xlabel('Year')
ax.set_ylabel('Temperature (degC)')
ax.set_xticks(range(df_group_year.index.min(), df_group_year.index.max(),
10))
ax.legend();
```

The output will be as follows:

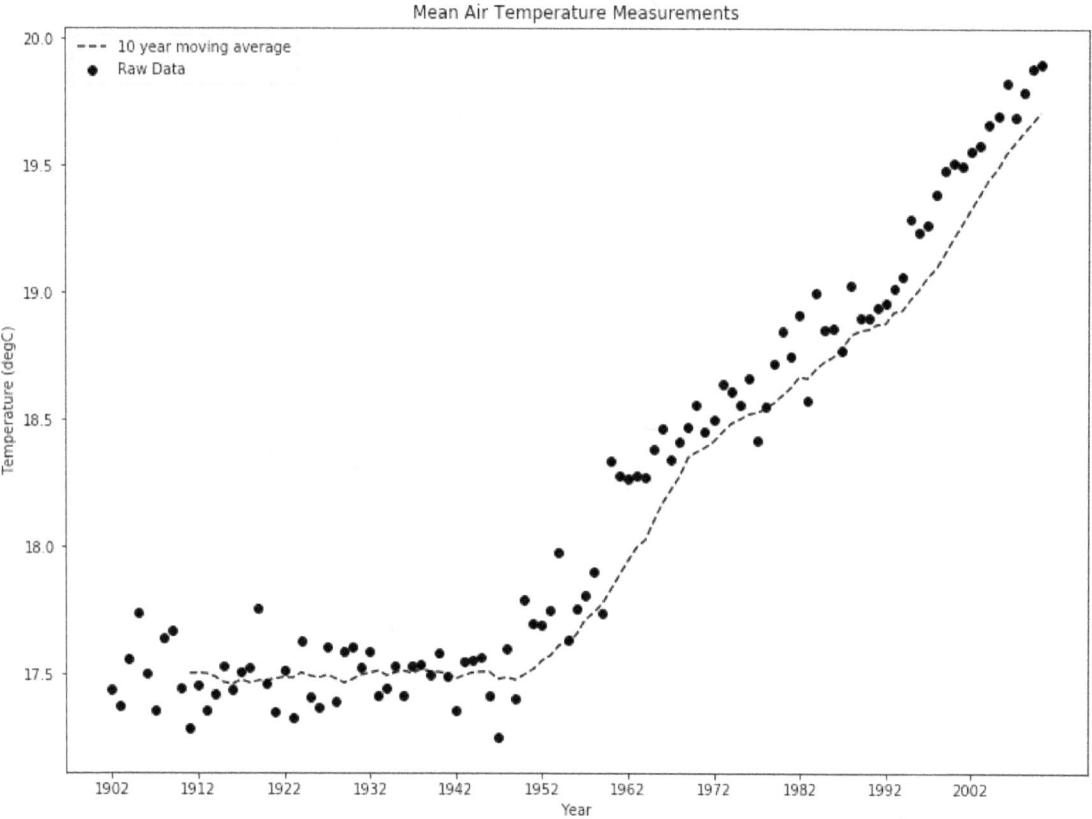

Figure 3.7: Mean annual air temperature

Figure 3.7 is the expected output of this exercise and is a plot of the mean land temperature measurements for each year with a 10-year moving average trending. By simply looking at this plot, we can immediately make a couple of interesting observations. The first observation that we can make is that the temperature remained relatively consistent from the year 1901 to about 1960, after which there is an increasing trend until the data ends in 2010. Secondly, there is a reasonable amount of scatter or noise in the measurements.

Activity 5: Plotting Data with a Moving Average

For this activity, we have acquired a dataset of weather information from Austin, Texas (`austin_weather.csv`), available in the accompanying source code, and will be looking at the changes in average daily temperature. We will plot a moving average filter for this dataset.

Before we begin, we will need to import a few libraries, which can be done as follows:

```
import numpy as np
import pandas as pd
import matplotlib.pyplot as plt
```

The steps to be performed are as follows:

1. Load the dataset into a pandas DataFrame from the CSV file.
2. We only need the `Date` and `TempAvgF` columns; remove all others from the dataset.
3. Initially, we will only be interested in the first year's data, so we need to extract that information only. Create a column in the DataFrame for the year value and extract the year value as an integer from the strings in the `Date` column and assign these values to the `Year` column.

   Note that temperatures are recorded daily.

4. Repeat this process to extract the month values and store the values as integers in a `Month` column.
5. Copy the first year's worth of data to a DataFrame.
6. Compute a 20-day moving average filter.

7. Plot the raw data and moving average signal, with the x axis being the day number in the year.

> **Note**
>
> The solution for this activity can be found on page 325.

Least Squares Method

The field of machine learning and artificial intelligence evolved essentially as a specialized branch of statistics, and as such it is important to reflect on these origins from time to time to have a thorough understanding of how models are able to be used as predictive tools. It is also interesting to see the points where machine learning grew out of statistics and compare the more modern methods available today. Linear regression models are a great example of this as they can be used to demonstrate more classical solving techniques such as the least squares method, as well as more modern methods, such as gradient descent, which we will also cover in this chapter. Linear models also have the additional advantage of containing mathematical concepts commonly learned in high school, such as the equation of a straight line, providing a useful platform for describing the methods used to fit data.

The traditional method of solving linear models, which is executed by toolkits such as scikit-learn, SciPy, Minitab, and Excel, is the **least squares method**, and this is the first method we will cover. Referring to our standard equation for a straight line (*Figure 3.1*), m is the slope or gradient of the line and c is the y axis offset. These values can be directly calculated in the least squares method by first determining the average x and y values, which will be denoted as $\bar{x}$ and $\bar{y}$ respectively. With the mean values calculated, we can then calculate the gradient, m, by multiplying the differences in x values from the mean with the differences in y values from the mean and dividing by the squared differences in x from the mean. The offset can then be calculated by solving for b using the newly calculated m and $\bar{x}$ and $\bar{y}$. This is represented mathematically as follows:

$$m = \frac{\sum_{i=1}^{N}(x_i - \bar{x})(y_i - \bar{y})}{\sum_{i=1}^{N}(x_i - \bar{x})^2}$$

$$b = \bar{y} - m\bar{x}$$

Figure 3.8: Least squares method

118 | Regression Analysis

We can consider this in more practical terms, recalling that the gradient is simply the change in the vertical (or y) values divided by the horizontal (or x) values. In the context of mean annual air temperature over time, we can see that we are taking the sum of the differences in the individual temperature values from the mean value multiplied by the individual differences in the time values from the mean. By dividing the result by the sum of the squared differences in time from the mean, the trending gradient is completed, providing part of the temperature over time model.

Now, we don't need to worry about computing these values by hand, though it wouldn't be that hard to do. But specialized libraries such as SciPy and scikit-learn can be used do to the work for us as well as worrying about some of the details such as computational efficiency. For the purposes of this section, we will use scikit-learn as our library of choice as it provides a great introduction to the scikit-learn interface.

One implementation detail to note is that the scikit-learn linear regression model is actually a wrapper around the SciPy ordinary least squares function and provides some additional convenience methods:

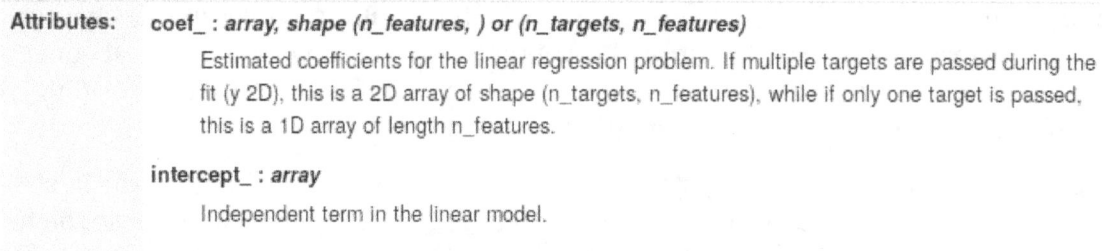

Figure 3.9: scikit-learn's implementation of linear regression

The scikit-learn Model API

The scikit-learn API uses a reasonably simple code pattern irrespective of the type of model being constructed. Put simply, the model must first be defined with all appropriate hyperparameters that are relevant to the training or fitting process. In defining the model, a model object is returned, which is then used during the second stage of model construction, which is training or fitting. Calling the `fit` method on the model object with the appropriate training data will then train the model with the defined hyperparameters. We will now use this pattern to construct our first linear regression model.

Exercise 29: Fitting a Linear Model Using the Least Squares Method

In this exercise, we will construct our first linear regression model using the least squares method.

1. We will use the scikit-learn **LinearRegression** model for this exercise, so import the class from the **linear_regression** module of scikit-learn:

   ```
   from sklearn.linear_model import LinearRegression
   ```

2. Construct a linear regression model using the default values; that is, compute a value for the y intercept and do not normalize the input data:

   ```
   model = LinearRegression()
   model
   ```

   ```
   In [8]: model = LinearRegression()
           model
   Out[8]: LinearRegression(copy_X=True, fit_intercept=True, n_jobs=None,
                   normalize=False)
   ```

   Figure 3.10: Linear regression model

3. Now we are ready to fit or train the model to the data. We will provide the year values as the input and the mean yearly temperature as the output. Note that the `fit` method of scikit-learn models expects 2D arrays to be provided as the **X** and **Y** value. As such, the year or index values need to be reshaped to suit the method. Get the values of the index as a NumPy array using the `.values` method and reshape the values to **((-1, 1))** which is an N x 1 array. The value -1 in a NumPy shape definition represents that its value is inferred from the current shape of the array and the target shape:

   ```
   model.fit(df_group_year.index.values.reshape((-1, 1)), gf_group_year.AverageTemperature)
   ```

The output will be as follows:

```
In [9]:  # Note the year values need to be provided as an N x 1 array
         model.fit(df_group_year.index.values.reshape((-1, 1)), df_group_year.AverageTemperature)
Out[9]:  LinearRegression(copy_X=True, fit_intercept=True, n_jobs=None,
                  normalize=False)
```

Figure 3.11: Output of the fit method

4. Get the parameters for the model by printing the values for **model.coef_** (which is the value for *m*) and **model.intercept_** (which is the value for the *y* intercept):

    ```python
    print(f'm = {model.coef_[0]}')
    print(f'c = {model.intercept_}')

    print('\nModel Definition')
    print(f'y = {model.coef_[0]:0.4}x + {model.intercept_:0.4f}')
    ```

    The output will be:

    ```
    m = 0.023146460838006862
    c = -27.080386660799967

    Model Definition
    y = 0.02315x + -27.0804
    ```

Figure 3.12: Output of model co-efficient and model intercept

5. Now that we have our generated model, we can predict some values to construct our trendline. So, let's use the first, last, and average year value as the input to predict the local temperature. Construct a NumPy array with these values and call the array **trend_x**. Once you are done, pass the values for **trend_x** to the **predict** method of the model to get the predicted values:

    ```python
    trend_x = np.array([
        df_group_year.index.values.min(),
        df_group_year.index.values.mean(),
        df_group_year.index.values.max()
    ])

    trend_y = model.predict(trend_x.reshape((-1, 1)))
    trend_y
    ```

The output will be as follows:

```
In [11]:  trend_x = np.array([
              df_group_year.index.values.min(),
              df_group_year.index.values.mean(),
              df_group_year.index.values.max()
          ])

          trend_y = model.predict(trend_x.reshape((-1, 1)))
          trend_y
Out[11]:  array([16.94418185, 18.19409074, 19.44399962])
```

Figure 3.13: Array showing min, mean, and max

6. Now plot the trendline produced by the model, with the model parameters over the previous plot with the raw data:

```
fig = plt.figure(figsize=(10, 7))
ax = fig.add_axes([1, 1, 1, 1]);

# Temp measurements
ax.scatter(df_group_year.index, df_group_year.AverageTemperature,
label='Raw Data', c='k');
ax.plot(df_group_year.index, rolling, c='k', linestyle='--',
label=f'{window} year moving average');
ax.plot(trend_x, trend_y, c='k', label='Model: Predicted trendline')

ax.set_title('Mean Air Temperature Measurements')
ax.set_xlabel('Year')
ax.set_ylabel('Temperature (degC)')
ax.set_xticks(range(df_group_year.index.min(), df_group_year.index.max(),
10))
ax.legend();
```

The output will be as follows:

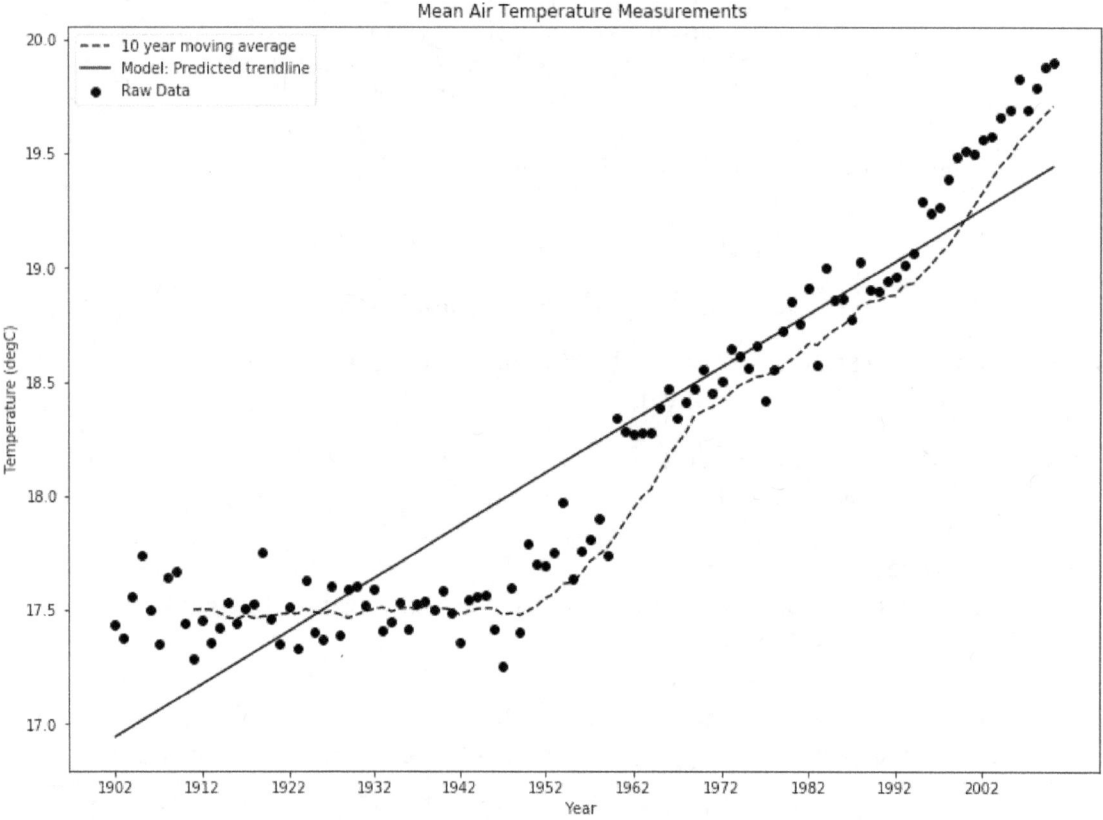

Figure 3.14: Linear regression – a first simple linear model

Now that we have the model, we need to evaluate its performance to see how well it fits the data and to compare against other models we may like to generate. We will cover this topic in much more detail in *Chapter 6, Model Evaluation*, where we'll look at validation and cross validation, but for the moment we will compute the **R-squared** value for the model against the dataset. R-squared, which is commonly reported in statistical-based modeling, is a ratio of the sum of squares between the predicted and actual values and the actual value from its own mean. A perfect fit will have an r² of 1, and the score decreases to 0 as the performance degrades.

$$r^2 = \frac{\sum(y_{pred} - y_{true})^2}{\sum(y_{true} - \overline{y_{true}})^2}$$

Figure 3.15: R-squared score

We can compute the R² value using the **score** method:

```
# Note the year values need to be provided as an N x 1 array
r2 = model.score(df_group_year.index.values.reshape((-1, 1)), df_group_year.AverageTemperature)
print(f'r2 score = {r2:0.4f}')
```

We'll get an output like this:

```
In [13]: # Note the year values need to be provided as an N x 1 array
         r2 = model.score(df_group_year.index.values.reshape((-1, 1)), df_group_year.AverageTemperature)
         print(f'r2 score = {r2:0.4f}')
         r2 score = 0.8618
```

Figure 3.16: R-squared score for the model against the dataset

So, looking at the trendline in *Figure 3.14*, we can see that the linear model is OK. It definitely performs better in the linear region of the moving average post 1960, but could use some improvement for the data earlier than 1970. Is there something we can do to manage this? It seems something that two separate linear models could perform better than one. The data prior to 1960 could form one model and the post-1960 data another? We could do that and just split the data and create two separate models, evaluate them separately, and put them together in a piece-wise fashion. But we could also include similar features in our existing model through the use of dummy variables.

> **Note**
>
> Before continuing, it is important to note that when reporting the performance of machine learning models, the data used to train the model is *not* to be used to evaluate the model, as it will give an optimistic view of the model's performance. We will cover the concept of validation, which includes evaluating and reporting model performance, in *Chapter 6, Model Evaluation*. For the purpose of this chapter, however, we will use the training data to check the model's performance; just remember that once you have completed *Chapter 6, Model Evaluation*, you will know better.

Activity 6: Linear Regression Using the Least Squares Method

For this activity, we will use the Austin, Texas weather dataset that we used in the previous activity. We will plot a linear regression model using the least squares method for the dataset.

Before we begin, we will need to import a few libraries and load data from a previous activity, which can be done as follows:

```
import numpy as np
import pandas as pd
import matplotlib.pyplot as plt
from sklearn.linear_model import LinearRegression
```

```
# Loading the data from activity 5
df = pd.read_csv('activity2_measurements.csv')
df_first_year = df[:365]
rolling = pd.read_csv('activity2_rolling.csv')
window = 20
```

The steps to be performed are as follows:

1. Visualize the measurements.
2. Visualize the rolling average values.
3. Create a linear regression model using the default parameters, that is, calculate a y intercept for the model and do not normalize the data.
4. Now fit the model, where the input data is the day number for the year (1 to 365) and the output is the average temperature. To make later calculations easier, insert a column (**DayOfYear**) that corresponds with the day of the year for that measurement.
5. Fit the model with the **DayOfYear** values as the input and **df_first_year.TempAvgF** as the output.
6. Print the parameters of the model.
7. Let's check the trendline provided by the model. Plot this simply using the first, middle, and last values (days in years) in the linear equation.
8. Plot the values with the trendline.

9. Evaluate the performance of the model.

10. Let's check how well the model fits the data. Calculate the r^2 score to find out.

> **Note**
>
> The solution for this activity can be found on page 329.

Linear Regression with Dummy Variables

Dummy variables are categorical variables that we can introduce into a model, using information provided within the existing dataset. The design and selection of these variables is considered a component of feature engineering, and depending upon the choice of variables, the results may vary. We made the observation earlier that the moving average begins to continually increase from approximately 1960 and that the initial plateau ends at approximately 1945. We will introduce two dummy variables, **Gt_1960** and **Gt_1945**; these variables will indicate whether the time period for the measurements is greater than the year 1960 and greater than the year 1945. Dummy variables are typically assigned the values 0 or 1 to indicate the lack of or presence of the assigned category for each row. In our example, given the magnitude of the **Year** values, we will need to increase the positive value of the dummy variables as, with a value of 1, they will have little to no effect given that the values for **Year** are in the thousands. Throughout the following exercise, we will demonstrate that regression models can be composed of both discrete and continuous values and that, depending on an appropriate choice of dummy variables, performance can be improved.

Exercise 30: Introducing Dummy Variables

In this exercise, we will introduce two dummy variables into our linear regression model:

1. For convenience, assign the index values of the **df_group_year** DataFrame to the **Year** column:

   ```
   df_group_year['Year'] = df_group_year.index
   ```

2. Create a dummy variable with a column labeled **Gt_1960**, where the value is **0** if the year is less than 1960 and **10** if greater:

   ```
   df_group_year['Gt_1960'] = [0 if year < 1960 else 10 for year in df_group_year.Year] # Dummy Variable - greater than 1960
   df_group_year.head(n=2)
   ```

The output will be as follows:

	AverageTemperature	Year	Gt_1960
Year			
1902	17.438122	1902	0
1903	17.375456	1903	0

Figure 3.17: Added column Gt_1960

3. Create a dummy variable with a column labeled **Gt_1945**, where the value is **0** if the year is less than 1945 and **10** if greater:

   ```
   df_group_year['Gt_1945'] = [0 if year < 1945 else 10 for year in df_group_
   year.Year]# Dummy Variable - greater than 1945
   df_group_year.head(n=2)
   ```

The output will be:

	AverageTemperature	Year	Gt_1960	Gt_1945
Year				
1902	17.438122	1902	0	0
1903	17.375456	1903	0	0

Figure 3.18: Added column Gt_1945

4. Call the **tail()** method to look at the last two rows of the **df_group_year** DataFrame to confirm that the post 1960 and 1945 labels have been correctly assigned:

   ```
   df_group_year.tail(n=2)
   ```

The output will be:

	AverageTemperature	Year	Gt_1960	Gt_1945
Year				
2009	19.884571	2009	10	10
2010	19.903760	2010	10	10

Figure 3.19: Last two values

5. Fit the linear model with the additional dummy variables by passing the **Year**, **Gt_1960**, and **Gt_1945** columns as inputs to the model, with **AverageTemperature** again as the output:

   ```
   # Note the year values need to be provided as an N x 1 array
   model.fit(df_group_year[['Year', 'Gt_1960', 'Gt_1945']], df_group_year.
   AverageTemperature)
   ```

   The output will be:

   ```
   In [18]: # Note the year values need to be provided as an N x 1 array
            model.fit(df_group_year[['Year', 'Gt_1960', 'Gt_1945']], df_group_year.AverageTemperature)
   Out[18]: LinearRegression(copy_X=True, fit_intercept=True, n_jobs=None,
                    normalize=False)
   ```

   Figure 3.20: Linear model fitted on data

6. Check the R-squared score for the new model against the training data to see whether we made an improvement:

   ```
   # Note the year values need to be provided as an N x 1 array
   r2 = model.score(df_group_year[['Year', 'Gt_1960', 'Gt_1945']], df_group_
   year.AverageTemperature)
   print(f'r2 score = {r2:0.4f}')
   ```

   The output will be as follows:

   ```
   In [19]: # Note the year values need to be provided as an N x 1 array
            r2 = model.score(df_group_year[['Year', 'Gt_1960', 'Gt_1945']], df_group_year.AverageTemperature)
            print(f'r2 score = {r2:0.4f}')
            r2 score = 0.9128
   ```

   Figure 3.21: R-squared score for the model

7. We have made an improvement! This is a reasonable step in accuracy given that the first model's performance was 0.8618. We will plot another trendline, but we will need more values than before to accommodate the additional complexity of the dummy variables. Use **linspace** to create 20 linearly spaced values between 1902 and 2013:

   ```
   # Use linspace to get a range of values, in 20 year increments
   x = np.linspace(df_group_year['Year'].min(), df_group_year['Year'].max(),
   20)
   x
   ```

We'll get this output:

```
array([1902.        , 1907.68421053, 1913.36842105, 1919.05263158,
       1924.73684211, 1930.42105263, 1936.10526316, 1941.78947368,
       1947.47368421, 1953.15789474, 1958.84210526, 1964.52631579,
       1970.21052632, 1975.89473684, 1981.57894737, 1987.26315789,
       1992.94736842, 1998.63157895, 2004.31578947, 2010.        ])
```

Figure 3.22: Array of 20 years created using linspace

8. Create an array of zeros in the shape 20 x 3 and fill the first column of values with x, the second column with the dummy variable value for greater than 1960, and the third column with the dummy variable value for greater than 1945:

```
trend_x = np.zeros((20, 3))
trend_x[:,0] = x # Assign to the first column
trend_x[:,1] = [10 if _x > 1960 else 0 for _x in x] # Assign to the second column
trend_x[:,2] = [10 if _x > 1945 else 0 for _x in x] # Assign to the third column
trend_x
```

The output will be:

```
array([[1902.        ,  0.        ,  0.        ],
       [1907.68421053,  0.        ,  0.        ],
       [1913.36842105,  0.        ,  0.        ],
       [1919.05263158,  0.        ,  0.        ],
       [1924.73684211,  0.        ,  0.        ],
       [1930.42105263,  0.        ,  0.        ],
       [1936.10526316,  0.        ,  0.        ],
       [1941.78947368,  0.        ,  0.        ],
       [1947.47368421,  0.        , 10.        ],
       [1953.15789474,  0.        , 10.        ],
```

Figure 3.23: Finding trend_x

9. Now get the *y* values for the trendline by making predictions for **trend_x**:

   ```
   trend_y = model.predict(trend_x)
   trend_y
   ```

   The output will be as follows:

   ```
   array([17.06063456, 17.17806179, 17.29548901, 17.41291624, 17.53034347,
          17.6477707 , 17.76519793, 17.88262516, 17.57196656, 17.68939379,
          17.80682102, 18.51649321, 18.63392043, 18.75134766, 18.86877489,
          18.98620212, 19.10362935, 19.22105658, 19.33848381, 19.45591104])
   ```

   Figure 3.24: Finding trend_y

10. Plot the trendline:

    ```
    fig = plt.figure(figsize=(10, 7))
    ax = fig.add_axes([1, 1, 1, 1]);

    # Temp measurements
    ax.scatter(df_group_year.index, df_group_year.AverageTemperature,
    label='Raw Data', c='k');
    ax.plot(df_group_year.index, rolling, c='k', linestyle='--',
    label=f'{window} year moving average');
    ax.plot(trend_x[:,0], trend_y, c='k', label='Model: Predicted trendline')

    ax.set_title('Mean Air Temperature Measurements')
    ax.set_xlabel('Year')
    ax.set_ylabel('Temperature (degC)')
    ax.set_xticks(range(df_group_year.index.min(), df_group_year.index.max(),
    10))
    ax.legend();
    ```

The output will be as follows:

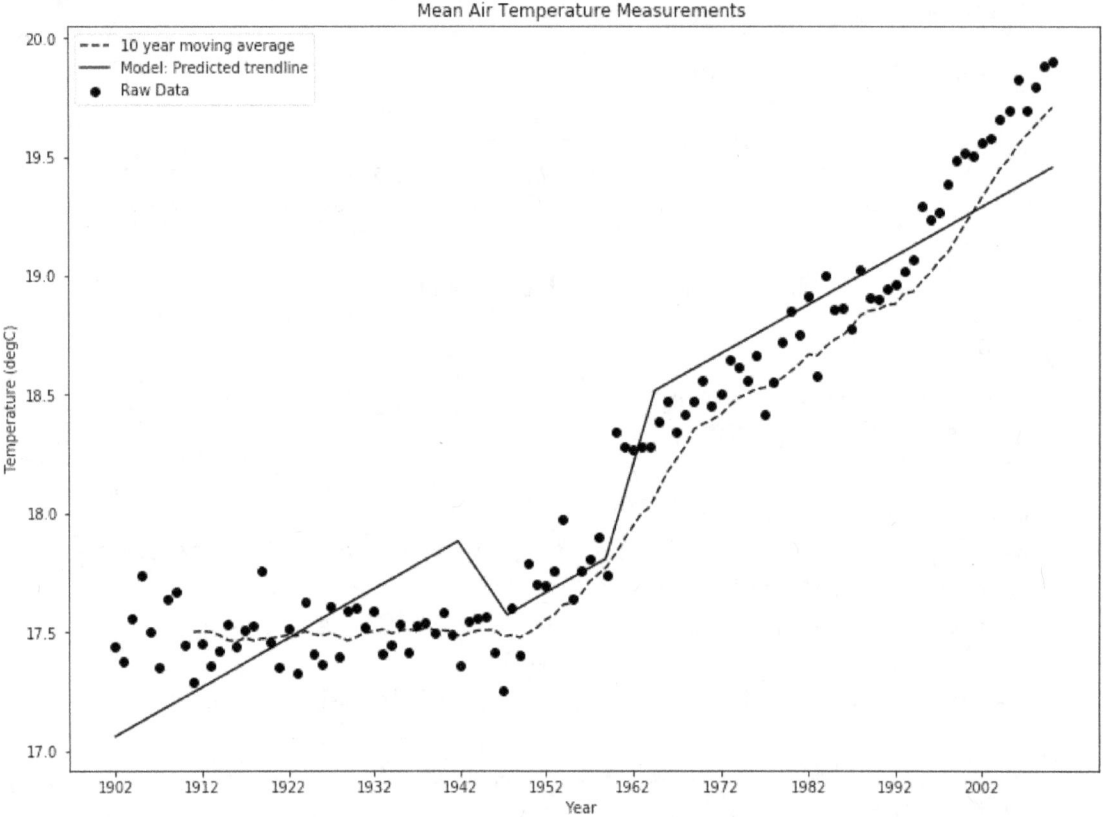

Figure 3.25: Predictions using dummy variables

Incorporating dummy variables made quite an improvement to the model, but looking at the trendline, it doesn't seem like a reasonable path for natural phenomena such as temperature to take and could be suffering from overfitting. We will cover overfitting in more detail in *Chapter 5, Ensemble Modeling*; however, let's use linear regression to fit a model with a smoother prediction curve, such as a parabola.

Activity 7: Dummy Variables

For this activity, we will use the Austin, Texas weather dataset that we used in the previous activity. In this activity, we will use dummy variables to enhance our linear regression model for this dataset.

Linear Regression | 131

Before we begin, we will need to import a few libraries and load data from a previous activity, which can be done as follows:

```
import numpy as np
import pandas as pd
import matplotlib.pyplot as plt
from sklearn.linear_model import LinearRegression

# Loading the data from activity 5
df = pd.read_csv('activity2_measurements.csv')
df_first_year = pd.read_csv('activity_first_year.csv')
rolling = pd.read_csv('activity2_rolling.csv')
window = 20

# Trendline values
trend_x = np.array([
    1,
    182.5,
    365
])
```

The steps to be performed are as follows:

1. Plot the raw data (**df**) and moving average (**rolling**).
2. Looking at the result of the previous step, there seems to be an inflection point around day 250. Create a dummy variable to introduce this feature into the linear model.
3. Check the first and last samples to confirm that the dummy variable is correct.
4. Use a least squares linear regression model and fit the model to the **DayOfYear** values and the dummy variable to predict **TempAvgF**.
5. Compute the R^2 score.
6. Using the **DayOfYear** values, create a set of predictions using the model to construct a trendline.

7. Plot the trendline against the data and moving average.

> **Note**
>
> The solution for this activity can be found on page 334.

Parabolic Model with Linear Regression

Linear regression models are not simply constrained to straight-line linear models. We can fit some more complicated models using the exact same techniques. We have mentioned that there seems to be some parabolic characteristics to the data, so let's try fitting a parabolic model. As a reminder, the equation for a parabola is:

$$y = ax^2 + mx + c$$

Figure 3.26: Equation for a parabola

The addition of this squared term transforms the model from a straight line to one that has a parabolic (or arc like) trajectory.

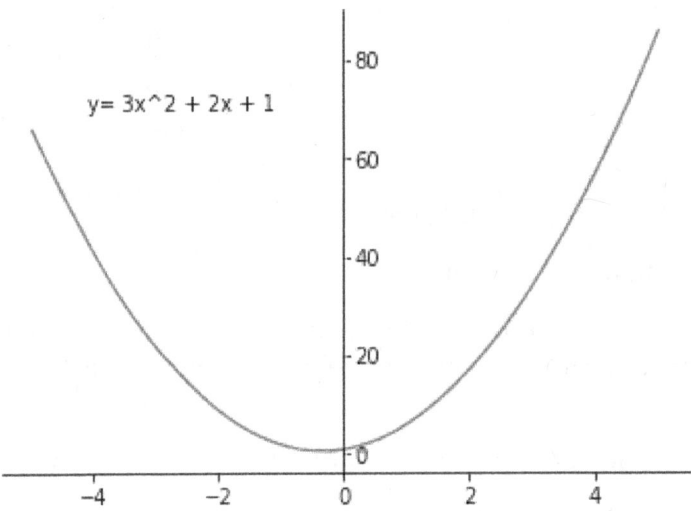

Figure 3.27: Parabolic curve

Exercise 31: Parabolic Models with Linear Regression

In order to fit a parabolic model using linear regression, we just need to manipulate our inputs a little. In this exercise, we'll see how to do it:

1. The first thing we need to do is provide a squared term for year values. For convenience, create a copy of the index and store it in a **Year** column. Now square the **Year** column to provide parabolic features and assign the result to the **Year2** column:

   ```
   df_group_year['Year'] = df_group_year.index
   df_group_year['Year2'] = df_group_year.index ** 2
   df_group_year.head()
   ```

   We'll get this:

Year	AverageTemperature	Year	Gt_1960	Gt_1945	Year2
1902	17.438122	1902	0	0	3617604
1903	17.375456	1903	0	0	3621409
1904	17.558674	1904	0	0	3625216
1905	17.740646	1905	0	0	3629025
1906	17.501770	1906	0	0	3632836

   Figure 3.28: First five rows

2. Fit the data to the model. This time, we will need to provide two sets of values as the inputs to the model, **Year** and **Year2**, which is equivalent to passing x and x^2 to the parabolic equation. As we are providing two columns of data, we do not need to reshape the input data as it will be provided as an N x 2 array by default. The target y value remains the same:

   ```
   # Note the year values need to be provided as an N x 1 array
   model.fit(df_group_year[['Year2', 'Year']], df_group_year.AverageTemperature)
   ```

The output will be as follows:

```
In [26]:  # Note the year values need to be provided as an N x 1 array
          model.fit(df_group_year[['Year2', 'Year']], df_group_year.AverageTemperature)
Out[26]:  LinearRegression(copy_X=True, fit_intercept=True, n_jobs=None,
                   normalize=False)
```

Figure 3.29: Model fitted

3. Print the parameters of the model by looking at the coefficients and the intercept; there will now be two coefficients to print:

    ```
    print(f'a = {model.coef_[0]}')
    print(f'm = {model.coef_[1]}')
    print(f'c = {model.intercept_}')

    print('\nModel Definition')
    print(f'y = {model.coef_[0]:0.4}x^2 + {model.coef_[1]:0.4}x + {model.intercept_:0.4f}')
    ```

The output will be:

```
a = 0.0002814670724607414
m = -1.0779527266284135
c = 1049.5159662796232

Model Definition
y = 0.0002815x^2 + -1.078x + 1049.5160
```

Figure 3.30: Model coefficients and intercept

4. Evaluate the performance of the model using the **score** method. Has the performance improved?

    ```
    # Note the year values need to be provided as an N x 1 array
    r2 = model.score(df_group_year[['Year2', 'Year']], df_group_year.AverageTemperature)
    print(f'r2 score = {r2:0.4f}')
    ```

We'll get the following output:

```
In [28]:  # Note the year values need to be provided as an N x 1 array
          r2 = model.score(df_group_year[['Year2', 'Year']], df_group_year.AverageTemperature)
          print(f'r2 score = {r2:0.4f}')

          r2 score = 0.9627
```

Figure 3.31: R-squared score

5. Yes, the model has improved slightly on the dummy variable method, but let's look at the trendline to see whether it is a more reasonable fit. Plot the trendline as we did before. Again, to effectively plot the parabolic arc of the trendline, we will need more predicted values. Use **linspace** to create 20 linearly spaced values between 1902 and 2013:

   ```
   # Use linspace to get a range of values, in 20 yr increments
   x = np.linspace(df_group_year['Year'].min(), df_group_year['Year'].max(), 20)
   x
   ```

   We'll get this:

   ```
   array([1902.       , 1907.68421053, 1913.36842105, 1919.05263158,
          1924.73684211, 1930.42105263, 1936.10526316, 1941.78947368,
          1947.47368421, 1953.15789474, 1958.84210526, 1964.52631579,
          1970.21052632, 1975.89473684, 1981.57894737, 1987.26315789,
          1992.94736842, 1998.63157895, 2004.31578947, 2010.        ])
   ```

   Figure 3.32: Finding 20 increments using linspace

6. Now the model we trained takes two columns of year data as an input: the first column containing squared yearly values and the second just the year value itself. To provide the data to the model, create a NumPy array (**trend_x**) of zeros with 20 rows and 2 columns. Square the values for **x** and assign to the first column of **trend_x**, and simply assign **x** to the second column of **trend_x**:

   ```
   trend_x = np.zeros((20, 2))
   trend_x[:,0] = x ** 2 # Assign to the first column
   trend_x[:,1] = x # Assign to the second column
   trend_x
   ```

The output will be:

```
array([[3.61760400e+06, 1.90200000e+03],
       [3.63925905e+06, 1.90768421e+03],
       [3.66097871e+06, 1.91336842e+03],
       [3.68276300e+06, 1.91905263e+03],
       [3.70461191e+06, 1.92473684e+03],
       [3.72652544e+06, 1.93042105e+03],
       [3.74850359e+06, 1.93610526e+03],
       [3.77054636e+06, 1.94178947e+03],
       [3.79265375e+06, 1.94747368e+03],
       [3.81482576e+06, 1.95315789e+03],
       [3.83706239e+06, 1.95884211e+03],
       [3.85936365e+06, 1.96452632e+03],
       [3.88172952e+06, 1.97021053e+03],
       [3.90416001e+06, 1.97589474e+03],
       [3.92665512e+06, 1.98157895e+03],
       [3.94921486e+06, 1.98726316e+03],
       [3.97183921e+06, 1.99294737e+03],
       [3.99452819e+06, 1.99863158e+03],
       [4.01728178e+06, 2.00431579e+03],
       [4.04010000e+06, 2.01000000e+03]])
```

Figure 3.33: Trends for the x variable

7. Now get the y values for the trendline by making predictions for **trend_x**:

    ```
    trend_y = model.predict(trend_x)
    trend_y
    ```

    We'll get this:

```
array([17.48628743, 17.45415991, 17.44022092, 17.44447048, 17.46690858,
       17.50753523, 17.56635041, 17.64335414, 17.73854641, 17.85192723,
       17.98349658, 18.13325448, 18.30120092, 18.48733591, 18.69165943,
       18.9141715 , 19.15487211, 19.41376127, 19.69083897, 19.98610521])
```

Figure 3.34: Trends for the y variable

8. Plot the trendline as per the straight-line model. Remember that the x axis values for **trend_y** are the years; that is, the second column of **trend_x**, and not the years squared:

    ```
    fig = plt.figure(figsize=(10, 7))
    ax = fig.add_axes([1, 1, 1, 1]);
    
    # Temp measurements
    ax.scatter(df_group_year.index, df_group_year.AverageTemperature,
    label='Raw Data', c='k');
    ```

```
ax.plot(df_group_year.index, rolling, c='k', linestyle='--',
label=f'{window} year moving average');
ax.plot(trend_x[:,1], trend_y, c='k', label='Model: Predicted trendline')

ax.set_title('Mean Air Temperature Measurements')
ax.set_xlabel('Year')
ax.set_ylabel('Temperature (degC)')
ax.set_xticks(range(df_group_year.index.min(), df_group_year.index.max(),
10))
ax.legend();
```

The output will be as follows:

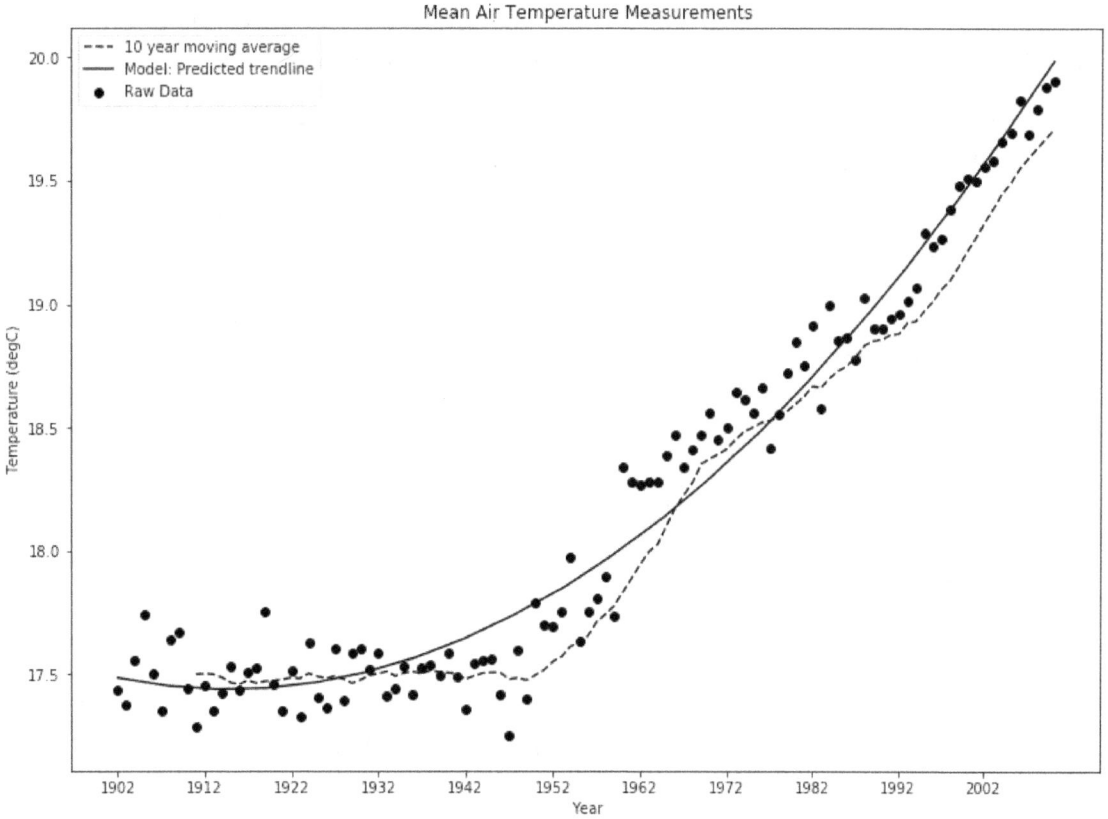

Figure 3.35: Linear regression with a parabolic model

Referring to *Figure 3.35*, we can see the performance benefit in using the parabolic model, with the trendline almost following the 10-year moving average. This is a reasonably good fit given the amount of noise in the yearly average raw data. In such a case, it should not be expected that the model will fit the data perfectly. If our model was to perfectly fit the observed examples, there would be a very strong case for overfitting the data, leading to poor predictive power with unseen examples.

Activity 8: Other Model Types with Linear Regression

We have tried a standard linear model as well as a dummy variable. In this activity, we will experiment with a few different functions to try and get a better fit for the data. For each different function, try to make sure you print the function parameters, R^2 value, and plot the trendline against the original and moving average data.

Try a few different functions, experiment with the data, and see how good your predictions can get. In this activity, we will use the sine function.

Before we begin, we will need to import a few libraries and load data from a previous activity, which can be done as follows:

```
import numpy as np
import pandas as pd
import matplotlib.pyplot as plt
from sklearn.linear_model import LinearRegression



# Loading the data from activity 5
df = pd.read_csv('activity2_measurements.csv')
df_first_year = pd.read_csv('activity_first_year.csv')
rolling = pd.read_csv('activity2_rolling.csv')
window = 20

# Trendline values
trend_x = np.array([
    1,
    182.5,
    365
])
```

The steps to be performed are as follows:

1. Use a sine curve function as the basis of the model.
2. Print the parameters of the model.
3. Compute the r2 value to measure the performance.
4. Construct the trendline values.
5. Plot the trendline with the raw data and the moving average.

> **Note**
> The solution for this activity can be found on page 338.

Generic Model Training

The least squares method of constructing a linear regression model is a useful and accurate method of training, assuming that the dimensionality of the dataset is low and that the system memory is sufficiently large to be able to manage the dataset and, in the case of the scikit-learn implementation, the matrix division operation. In recent times, large datasets have become more readily available, with universities, governments, and even some companies releasing large datasets for free online; as such, it may be relatively easy to exceed system memory when using the least squares method of regression modeling. In this situation, we will need to employ a different method of training the algorithm, such as gradient descent, which is not *as* susceptible to high dimensionality, allows large datasets to be trained, and avoids the use of memory intensive matrix operations. Before we look at gradient descent in a little more detail, we will revisit the process of training a model in a more general form, as most training methods, including gradient descent, adhere to this generic process (*Figure* 3.36). The training process involves the repeated exposure of the model and its parameters to a set of example training data and passing the predicted values issued by the model to a specified cost or error function.

The cost function is used to determine how close the model is to its target values and a measure of progress throughout the training process. The final piece of the process is the definition of the training hyperparameters, which, as discussed at the start of this chapter, are the means by which the process of updating the model is regulated:

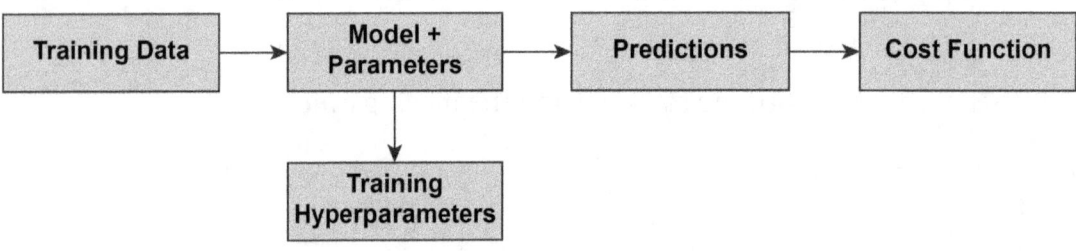

Figure 3.36: Generic training process

Gradient Descent

The process of gradient descent can be summarized as a means of updating the parameters of the model proportionally and in response to an error within the system, as defined by the cost function. There are a number of cost functions that can be selected, depending on the type of model being fitted or the problem being solved. We will select the simple but effective mean squared error cost function, but first we will rewrite our model equation in notation consistent with that generally used within machine learning literature. Using the equation of a straight line as our model:

$$y = mx + b$$

Figure 3.37: Equation of a straight line

It can be rewritten as:

$$h(x) = \Theta_1 x_1 + \Theta_0$$

$$h(x) = \sum_{i=0}^{1} \Theta_i x_i$$

Figure 3.38: Shortened linear model

Where $h(x)$ is the prediction made by the model and, by convention, $x_0 - 1$ is used to represent the intercept term. With the new model notation, we can define the mean squared error function as follows:

$$J(\Theta) = \frac{1}{N}\sum_{i=1}^{N}\left(h(x^{(i)}) - y_t^{(i)}\right)^2$$

Figure 3.39: Mean squared error

Where y_t is the corresponding ground truth value and N is the number of training samples.

With these two functions defined, we can now look at the gradient descent algorithm in greater detail:

1. Gradient descent starts by taking an initial, random guess at the values for all θ.
2. A prediction for each of the samples in the training set is made using the random values for θ.
3. The error for those parameters $J(\theta)$ is then computed.
4. The values for θ are then modified, making a small adjustment proportional to the error, in an attempt to minimize the error. More formally, the update process takes the current value for θ_j and subtracts the component of $J(\theta)$ attributed to θ_j times the small adjustment γ, otherwise known as the learning rate.

Without delving too deeply into the mathematical details, the equation to update the parameters or weights (θ_j) can be written as follows:

$$\theta_j := \theta_j - \gamma \frac{\delta}{\delta \theta_j} J(\Theta)$$

$$\theta_j := \theta_j + \gamma \sum_{i=1}^{N} \left(y^{(i)} - h_\Theta(x^{(i)})\right) x_j^{(i)}$$

Figure 3.40: Gradient descent update step

Let's discuss this equation:

- The := operator denotes variable reassignment or update as a computer programming concept.
- This training process will continue until convergence; that is, until the changes to the weights are so small that there is essentially no change to the parameters, or until we intervene and stop the process, as is the case in cross-validation.

- The value assigned to the learning rate is critical for the training process as it defines how large the changes to the weights are and subsequently how big the steps to take down the error curve are. If the value is too small, the training process may take far too long or may get stuck in areas of local minima of the error curve and not find an optimal global value. Alternatively, if the steps are too large, the training process can become unstable, as they pass over the local and global minima.

This process is visualized in the following graph:

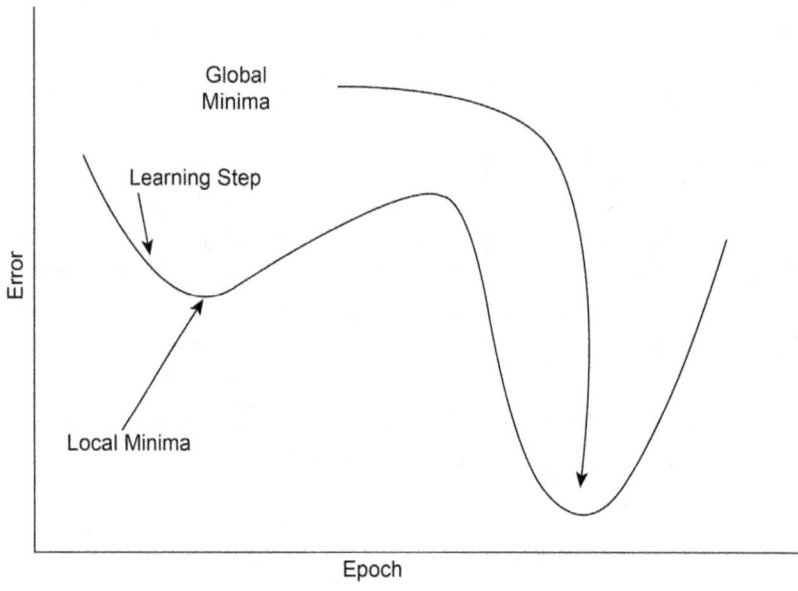

Figure 3.41: Gradient descent process

> **Note**
>
> As a general hint for setting the learning rate, start larger, say around 0.1, and if a solution cannot be found, that is, the error is a **NaN** (not a number), reduce by a factor of 10. Keep going until the training is continuing and the error is continually reducing. Once you are happy with the model and are almost done, reduce the learning rate by a small amount and let the training run for longer.

While this process may sound complicated, it isn't anywhere near as scary as it looks. Gradient descent can be summarized by making a one-time only guess at the values for the weights, calculating the error in the guess, making small adjustments to the weights, and continually repeating the process until the error converges at a minimum value. To reinforce our understanding, let's look at a more concrete example. We will use gradient descent to train the original linear regression model we constructed in *Exercise 29: Fitting a Linear Model Using the Least Squares Method*, replacing the least squares method with gradient descent.

Exercise 32: Linear Regression with Gradient Descent

Before we can start the gradient descent process, we need to spend a little bit of time setting up the model. In our Jupyter notebook, perform these steps:

1. Write a function to define our linear model. This is where the advantage of using the shortened form of the linear model (*Figure 3.38*) comes in handy. We can use linear algebra multiplication between the weights (theta) and the input values, x, which is the equivalent of $h(x) = \sum_{i=0}^{1} \theta_i x_i$:

   ```
   def h_x(weights, x):
       return np.dot(weights, x).flatten()
   ```

2. In order to use this linear algebra multiplication technique, we must modify the input data by inserting a row of ones to represent the bias term. Create an array of ones with a shape of two columns (one for the gradient term of the weights and one for the bias term). Insert the normalized **Year** values into the first row of the newly created array.

   To use the input data in a gradient descent process, we must also normalize all of the values to be between 0 and 1. This is a critical aspect of the process, as if one variable has values in the order of, say 1,000, and the second in the order of 10, then the first variable will be 100 times more influential in the training process and could lead to the inability to train the model. By ensuring that all variables are scaled between 0 and 1, they will have equal influence during training. Scale the input by dividing the values for **Year** by the maximum value:

   ```
   x = np.ones((2, len(df_group_year)))
   x[0,:] = df_group_year.Year
   x[1,:] = 1
   x /= x.max()
   x[:,:5]
   ```

You'll get this output:

```
Out[35]: array([[9.46268657e-01, 9.46766169e-01, 9.47263682e-01, 9.47761194e-01,
         9.48258706e-01],
        [4.97512438e-04, 4.97512438e-04, 4.97512438e-04, 4.97512438e-04,
         4.97512438e-04]])
```

Figure 3.42: Modified data

3. As we have learned, we need to take an initial guess at the values for the weights. We need to define two weight values, one for the gradient and one for the y intercept. To ensure that the same first random number is initialized each time, seed the NumPy random number generator. Seeding the random number generator ensures that each time the script is run, the same set of random numbers are produced. This ensures the consistency of the same model in multiple runs and provides the opportunity to check the performance of the model against possible changes:

```
np.random.seed(255) # Ensure the same starting random values
```

4. Initialize the weights with a normally distributed random number with a mean of 0 and standard deviation of 0.1. We want the initialized weights to be random, but still close to zero to give them a chance to find a good solution. In order to execute the matrix multiplication operation in **h_x**, reshape the random numbers to one row and two columns (one for the gradient and one for the y intercept):

```
Theta = np.random.randn(2).reshape((1, 2)) * 0.1
Theta
```

We'll get the following output:

```
In [37]: Theta = np.random.randn(2).reshape((1, 2)) * 0.1
         Theta
Out[37]: array([[-0.15134119, -0.01970609]])
```

Figure 3.43: Theta value

5. Define the ground truth values as the average yearly temperatures:

```
y_true = df_group_year.AverageTemperature.values
```

6. Define the cost function (mean squared error) as a Python function:

```
def J_theta(pred, true):
    return np.mean((pred - true) ** 2) # mean squared error
```

7. Define the learning rate as discussed earlier. This is a very important parameter and it must be set appropriately. As mentioned earlier, set it too small and the model may take a very long time to find a minimum; set it too large and it may not reach it at all. Define the learning rate as **1e-6**:

   ```
   gamma = 1e-6
   ```

8. Define a function that implements a step of gradient descent (*Figure 3.40*). The function will take the predicted and true values as well as the values for *x* and *gamma*, and return the value to be added to the weights (theta):

   ```
   def update(pred, true, x, gamma):
       return gamma * np.sum((true - pred) * x, axis=1)
   ```

9. Define the maximum number of epochs (or iterations) we want the training process to run for. Each epoch predicts the values of *y* (the normalized annual mean land temperature) given *x* and updates the weights in accordance with the error in the predictions:

   ```
   max_epochs = 100000
   ```

10. Make an initial prediction and calculate the error or cost in that prediction using the defined **h_x** and **J_theta** functions:

    ```
    y_pred = h_x(Theta, x)
    print(f'Initial cost J(Theta) = {J_theta(y_pred, y_true): 0.3f}')
    ```

    The output will be as follows:

    ```
    y_pred = h_x(Theta, x)
    print(f'Initial cost J(Theta) = {J_theta(y_pred, y_true): 0.3f}')
    Initial cost J(Theta) =  337.025
    ```

    Figure 3.44: Initial cost of J theta

11. Complete the first update step by hand. Use the newly predicted values to call the **update** function, make another call to **h_x** to get the predicted values, and get the new error:

    ```
    Theta += update(y_pred, y_true, x, gamma)

    y_pred = h_x(Theta, x)
    print(f'Initial cost J(Theta) = {J_theta(y_pred, y_true): 0.3f}')
    ```

We'll get the following output:

```
Theta += update(y_pred, y_true, x, gamma)

y_pred = h_x(Theta, x)
print(f'Initial cost J(Theta) = {J_theta(y_pred, y_true): 0.3f}')

Initial cost J(Theta) =   336.955
```

Figure 3.45: Updated cost of J theta

12. Notice the small reduction in the error; as such, many epochs of training will be required. Put the **predict** and **update** function calls in a **for** loop for **max_epochs** and print the corresponding error at each tenth epoch:

```
error_hist = []
epoch_hist = []
for epoch in range(max_epochs):
    Theta += update(y_pred, y_true, x, gamma)
    y_pred = h_x(Theta, x)
    
    if (epoch % 10) == 0:
        _err = J_theta(y_pred, y_true)
        error_hist.append(_err)
        epoch_hist.append(epoch)
        print(f'epoch:{epoch:4d} J(Theta) = {_err: 9.3f}')
```

The output will be as follows:

```
epoch:99810 J(Theta) =      0.275
epoch:99820 J(Theta) =      0.275
epoch:99830 J(Theta) =      0.275
epoch:99840 J(Theta) =      0.275
epoch:99850 J(Theta) =      0.275
epoch:99860 J(Theta) =      0.275
epoch:99870 J(Theta) =      0.275
epoch:99880 J(Theta) =      0.275
epoch:99890 J(Theta) =      0.275
epoch:99900 J(Theta) =      0.275
epoch:99910 J(Theta) =      0.275
epoch:99920 J(Theta) =      0.275
epoch:99930 J(Theta) =      0.275
epoch:99940 J(Theta) =      0.275
epoch:99950 J(Theta) =      0.275
epoch:99960 J(Theta) =      0.275
epoch:99970 J(Theta) =      0.275
epoch:99980 J(Theta) =      0.275
epoch:99990 J(Theta) =      0.275
```

Figure 3.46: Ten epochs

13. Visualize the training history by plotting **epoch_hist** versus **error_hist**:

    ```
    plt.figure(figsize=(10, 7))
    plt.plot(epoch_hist, error_hist);
    plt.title('Training History');
    plt.xlabel('epoch');
    plt.ylabel('Error');
    ```

    The output will be:

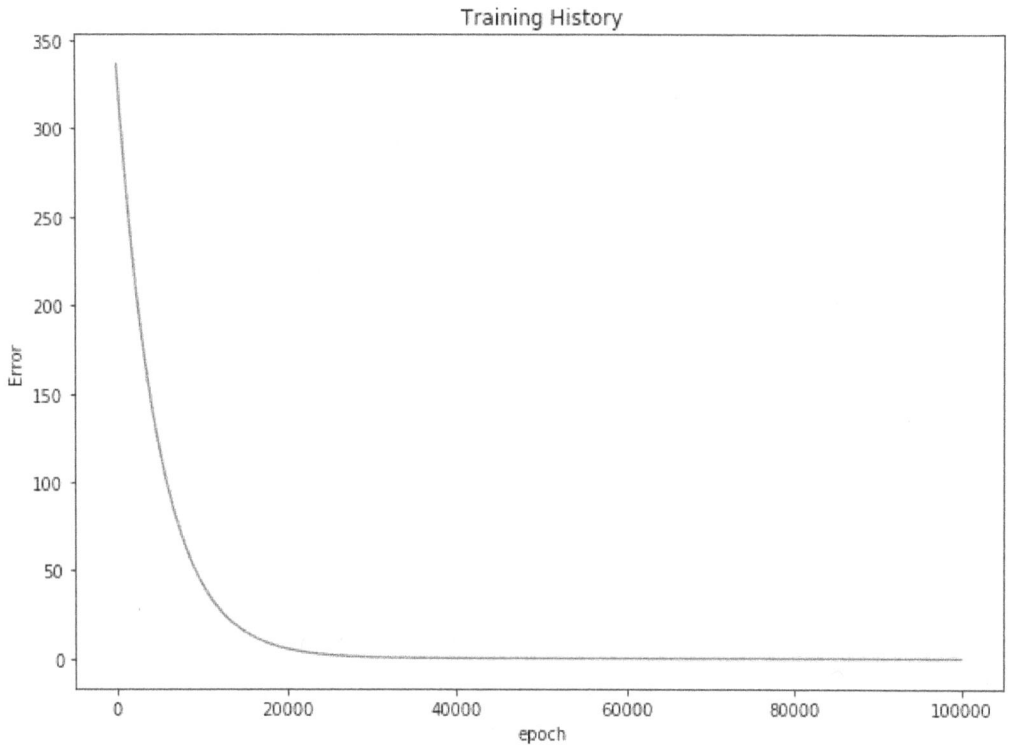

Figure 3.47: Training history curve: a very important tool

Notice that the error reaches an asymptote at 30,000 epochs, and thus **max_epochs** could be reduced.

14. Use the **r2_score** function from **sklearn.metrics** to compute the R-squared score for the model trained using gradient descent:

    ```
    from sklearn.metrics import r2_score
    r2_score(y_true, y_pred)
    ```

    We'll get the following output:

    ```
    In [47]: from sklearn.metrics import r2_score
             r2_score(y_true, y_pred)
    Out[47]: 0.5535787754767713
    ```

    Figure 3.48: R-squared score

15. To plot the trendline for the new model, again create 20 linearly spaced year values between 1901 and 2013:

    ```
    # Use linspace to get a range of values, in 20 yr increments
    x = np.linspace(df_group_year['Year'].min(), df_group_year['Year'].max(), 20)
    x
    ```

    The output will be as follows:

    ```
    array([1902.       , 1907.68421053, 1913.36842105, 1919.05263158,
           1924.73684211, 1930.42105263, 1936.10526316, 1941.78947368,
           1947.47368421, 1953.15789474, 1958.84210526, 1964.52631579,
           1970.21052632, 1975.89473684, 1981.57894737, 1987.26315789,
           1992.94736842, 1998.63157895, 2004.31578947, 2010.       ])
    ```

    Figure 3.49: Values using linspace

16. In order to use this data with our model, we must first normalize the maximum value to scale between 0 and 1 and insert a row of ones. Execute this step in a similar way to when the data was prepared for training in *Step 2*.

    ```
    trend_x = np.ones((2, len(x)))
    trend_x[0,:] = x
    trend_x[1,:] = 1
    trend_x /= trend_x.max()
    trend_x
    ```

The output will be as follows:

```
array([[9.46268657e-01, 9.49096622e-01, 9.51924588e-01, 9.54752553e-01,
        9.57580518e-01, 9.60408484e-01, 9.63236449e-01, 9.66064415e-01,
        9.68892380e-01, 9.71720346e-01, 9.74548311e-01, 9.77376277e-01,
        9.80204242e-01, 9.83032207e-01, 9.85860173e-01, 9.88688138e-01,
        9.91516104e-01, 9.94344069e-01, 9.97172035e-01, 1.00000000e+00],
       [4.97512438e-04, 4.97512438e-04, 4.97512438e-04, 4.97512438e-04,
        4.97512438e-04, 4.97512438e-04, 4.97512438e-04, 4.97512438e-04,
        4.97512438e-04, 4.97512438e-04, 4.97512438e-04, 4.97512438e-04,
        4.97512438e-04, 4.97512438e-04, 4.97512438e-04, 4.97512438e-04,
        4.97512438e-04, 4.97512438e-04, 4.97512438e-04, 4.97512438e-04]])
```

Figure 3.50: Trends in x

17. Call the **h_x** model function with the weights saved from the training process to get predicted *y* values for the trendline:

    ```
    trend_y = h_x(Theta, trend_x)
    trend_y
    ```

```
array([17.69802689, 17.75091824, 17.80380958, 17.85670093, 17.90959228,
       17.96248362, 18.01537497, 18.06826631, 18.12115766, 18.174049  ,
       18.22694035, 18.2798317 , 18.33272304, 18.38561439, 18.43850573,
       18.49139708, 18.54428842, 18.59717977, 18.65007111, 18.70296246])
```

Figure 3.51: Trends in y

18. Plot the trendline with the data:

    ```
    fig = plt.figure(figsize=(10, 7))
    ax = fig.add_axes([1, 1, 1, 1]);

    # Temp measurements
    ax.scatter(df_group_year.index, df_group_year.AverageTemperature,
    label='Raw Data', c='k');
    ax.plot(df_group_year.index, rolling, c='k', linestyle='--',
    label=f'{window} year moving average');
    ax.plot(x, trend_y, c='k', label='Model: Predicted trendline')


    ax.set_title('Mean Air Temperature Measurements')
    ax.set_xlabel('Year')
    ax.set_ylabel('Temperature (degC)')
    ax.set_xticks(range(df_group_year.index.min(), df_group_year.index.max(),
    10))
    ax.legend();
    ```

The output will be as follows:

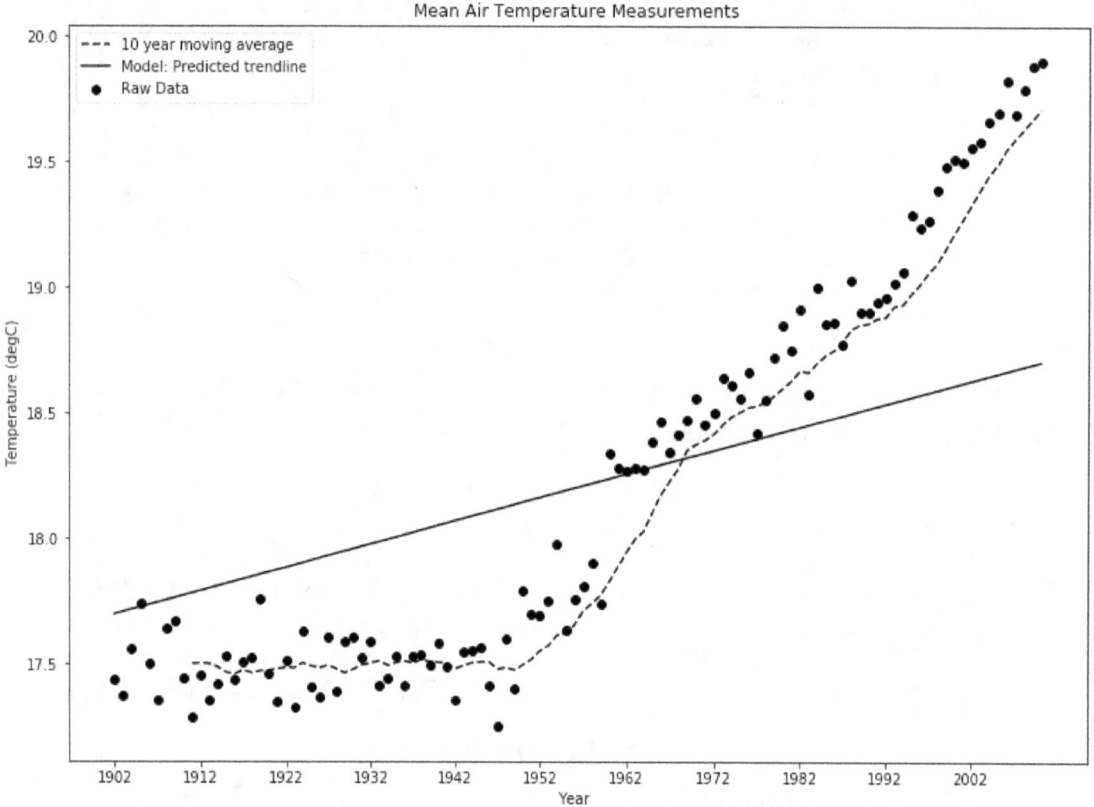

Figure 3.52: Mean air temperature measurements using gradient descent

Congratulations! You have just trained your first model with gradient descent. This is an important step as this simple tool can be used to construct more complicated models such as logistic regression and neural network models. We must first, however, note one important observation: the r-squared value produced by the gradient descent model is not as high as the least squares model.

In the first step of gradient descent, we guess some plausible values for the weights, and then make small adjustments to the weights in an attempt to reduce the error and stop training only when the error stops reducing. Gradient descent finds its power in two specific applications:

- Solving more complicated models for which a mathematically optimal solution has yet to be or cannot be found

- Providing a means of training with datasets or parameters that are so large that physical hardware restrictions, such as available memory, prevent the use of other methods such as least squares

So, if the dataset is not excessively large and can be solved optimally, we should definitely use the more precise method. That being said, there are many more options available to modify the gradient descent process, including different types of gradient descent algorithms and more advanced uses of learning rate and the way the data is supplied during training. These modifications fall outside the scope of this book, as an entire book could be written on the gradient descent process and methods for improving performance.

Exercise 33: Optimizing Gradient Descent

In the previous exercise, we implemented gradient descent directly; however, we would not typically use this implementation. The scikit-learn method of gradient descent contains a number of optimizations and can be used in only a few lines of code:

1. Import the **SGDRegressor** class and construct a model using the same parameters as used in the previous exercise:

    ```
    from sklearn.linear_model import SGDRegressor
    model = SGDRegressor(
        max_iter=100000,
        learning_rate='constant',
        eta0=1e-6,
        random_state=255,
        tol=1e-6,
        penalty='none',
    )
    ```

2. Use the year values, divided by the maximum year value, as an input and fit with the **AverageTemperature** values as the ground truth:

    ```
    x = df_group_year.Year / df_group_year.Year.max()
    y_true = df_group_year.AverageTemperature.values.ravel()
    model.fit(x.values.reshape((-1, 1)), y_true)
    ```

3. Predict the values using the trained model and determine the r-squared value:

    ```
    y_pred = model.predict(x.values.reshape((-1, 1)))
    r2_score(y_true, y_pred)
    ```

4. Plot the trendline as determined by the model in addition to the raw data and the moving average:

    ```
    fig = plt.figure(figsize=(10, 7))
    ax = fig.add_axes([1, 1, 1, 1]);
    
    # Temp measurements
    ```

```
ax.scatter(df_group_year.index, df_group_year.AverageTemperature,
label='Raw Data', c='k');
ax.plot(df_group_year.index, rolling, c='k', linestyle='--',
label=f'{window} year moving average');
ax.plot(x, trend_y, c='k', label='Model: Predicted trendline')


ax.set_title('Mean Air Temperature Measurements')
ax.set_xlabel('Year')
ax.set_ylabel('Temperature (degC)')
ax.set_xticks(range(df_group_year.index.min(), df_group_year.index.max(),
10))
ax.legend();
```

The output will be as follows:

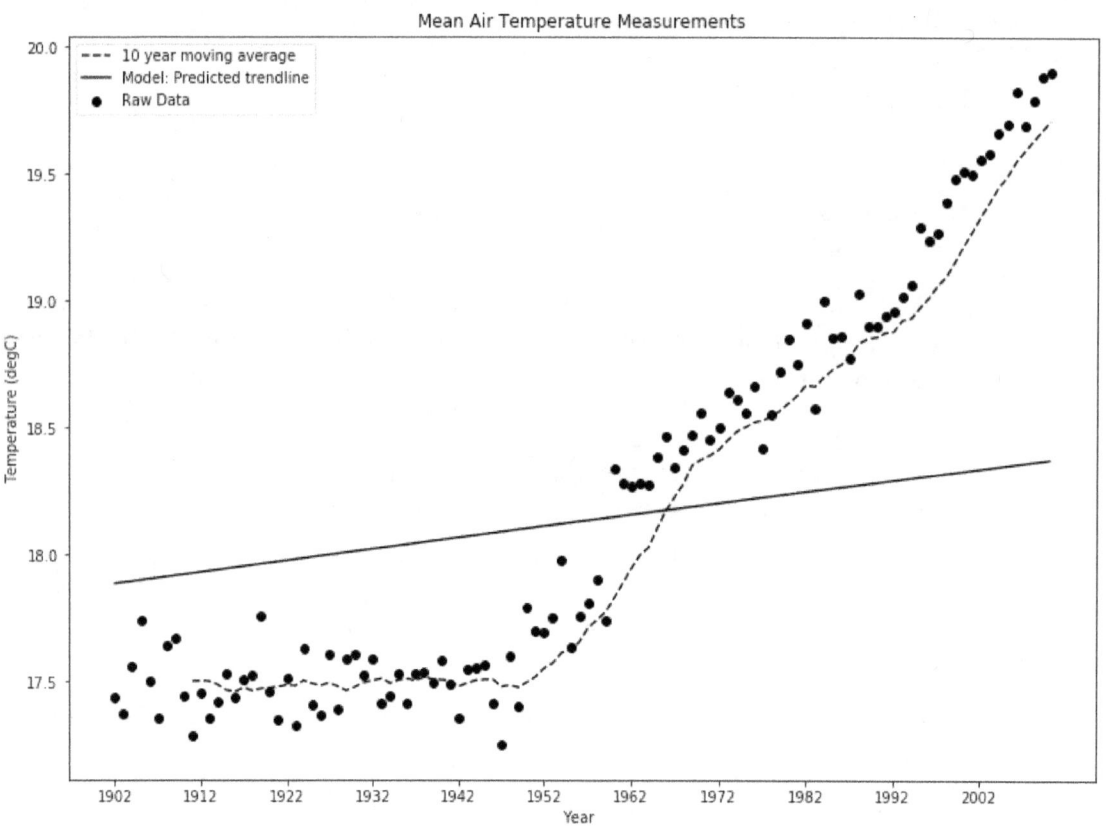

Figure 3.53: Optimized gradient descent predicted trendline

Compare this graph to the one constructed using the manual implementation of gradient descent. Notice the similarities: this provides us with confidence that both implementations of gradient descent are correct.

Activity 9: Gradient Descent

In this activity, we will implement the same model as *Activity 6, Linear Regression Using the Least Squares Method*; however, we will use the gradient descent process.

Before we begin, we will need to import a few libraries and load data from a previous activity, which can be done as follows:

```
import numpy as np
import pandas as pd
import matplotlib.pyplot as plt
from sklearn.linear_model import SGDRegressor


# Loading the data from activity 5
df = pd.read_csv('activity2_measurements.csv')
df_first_year = pd.read_csv('activity_first_year.csv')
rolling = pd.read_csv('activity2_rolling.csv')
window = 20

# Trendline values
trend_x = np.array([
    1,
    182.5,
    365
])
```

The steps to be performed are as follows:

1. Create a generic gradient descent model and normalize the day of year values to be between 0 and 1.
2. Fit the model.
3. Print the details of the model.
4. Prepare the *x* (`trend_x`) trendline values by dividing by the maximum. Predict `y_trend_values` using the gradient descent model.
5. Plot the data and the moving average with the trendline.

> **Note**
> The solution for this activity can be found on page 341.

Multiple Linear Regression

We have already covered regular linear regression, as well as linear regression with polynomial terms, and considered training them with both the least squares method and gradient descent. This section of the chapter will consider an additional type of linear regression: multiple linear regression, where more than one type of variable (or feature) is used to construct the model. To examine multiple linear regression, we will use a modified version of the Boston Housing Dataset, available from https://archive.ics.uci.edu/ml/index.php. The modified dataset can be found in the accompanying source code or on GitHub at https://github.com/TrainingByPackt/Supervised-Learning-with-Python and has been reformatted for simplified use. This dataset contains a list of different attributes for property in the Boston area, including the crime rate per capita by town, the percentage of the population with a lower socio-economic status, as well as the average number of rooms per dwelling, and the median value of owner-occupied homes in the area.

Exercise 34: Multiple Linear Regression

We will use the Boston Housing Dataset to construct a multiple linear model that predicts the median value of owner-occupied homes given the percentage of the population with a lower socio-economic status and the average number of rooms per dwelling:

1. Import the required dependencies:

   ```
   import numpy as np
   import pandas as pd
   import matplotlib.pyplot as plt
   from sklearn.linear_model import LinearRegression
   ```

2. Read in the housing database:

   ```
   df = pd.read_csv('housing_data.csv')
   df.head()
   ```

   The **head()** function will return the following output:

	CRIM	ZN	INDUS	CHAS	NOX	RM	AGE	DIS	RAD	TAX	PTRATIO	LSTAT	MEDV
0	0.00632	18.0	2.31	0	0.538	6.575	65.2	4.0900	1	296.0	15.3	4.98	24.0
1	0.02731	0.0	7.07	0	0.469	6.421	78.9	4.9671	2	242.0	17.8	9.14	21.6
2	0.02729	0.0	7.07	0	0.469	7.185	61.1	4.9671	2	242.0	17.8	4.03	34.7
3	0.03237	0.0	2.18	0	0.458	6.998	45.8	6.0622	3	222.0	18.7	2.94	33.4
4	0.06905	0.0	2.18	0	0.458	7.147	54.2	6.0622	3	222.0	18.7	5.33	36.2

   Figure 3.54: First five rows

3. Plot both columns: average number of rooms (**RM**) and the percentage of the population of a lower socio-economic status (**PTRATIO**):

   ```
   fig = plt.figure(figsize=(10, 7))
   fig.suptitle('Parameters vs Median Value')
   ax1 = fig.add_subplot(121)
   ax1.scatter(df.LSTAT, df.MEDV, marker='*', c='k');
   ax1.set_xlabel('% lower status of the population')
   ax1.set_ylabel('Median Value in $1000s')
   ax2 = fig.add_subplot(122, sharey=ax1)
   ax2.scatter(df.RM, df.MEDV, marker='*', c='k');
   ax2.get_yaxis().set_visible(False)
   ax2.set_xlabel('average number of rooms per dwelling');
   ```

The output will be as follows:

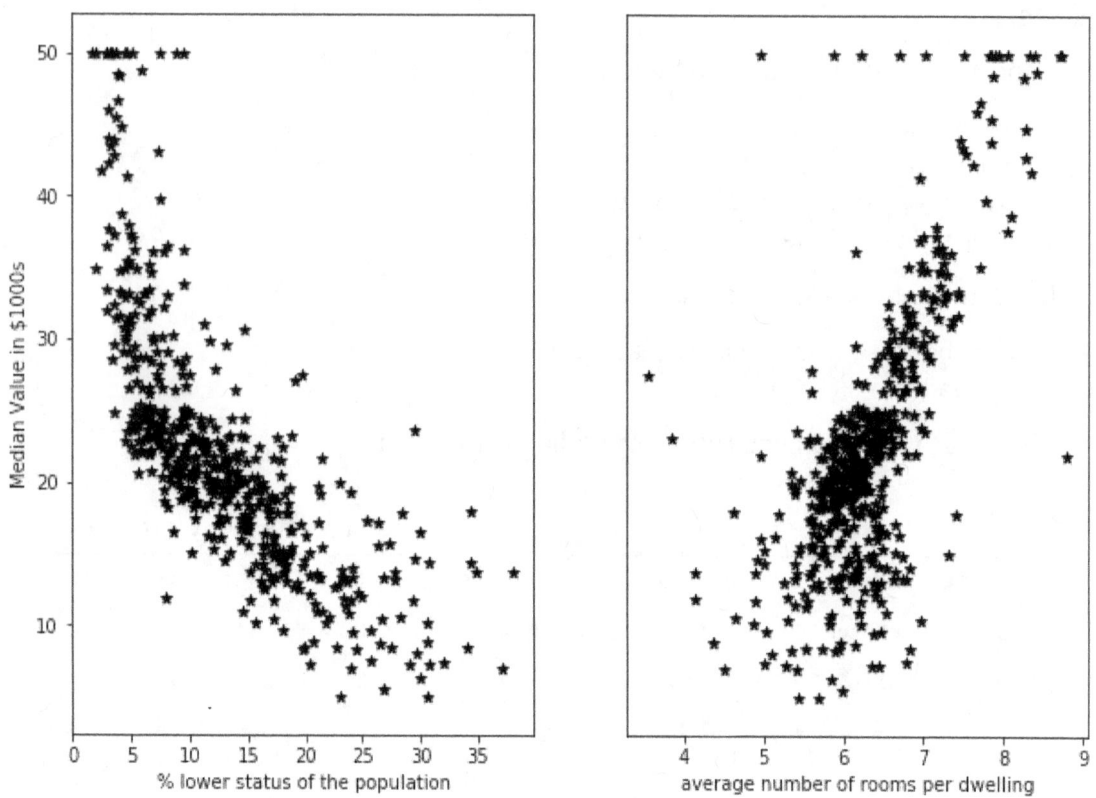

Figure 3.55: Parameters versus the median value

4. Construct a linear regression model for the percentage of lower socio-economic status (**LSTAT**) versus the median property value (**MEDV**), and compute the performance of the model in terms of the R-squared value:

```
model = LinearRegression()
model.fit(df.LSTAT.values.reshape((-1, 1)), df.MEDV.values.reshape((-1, 1)))
model.score(df.LSTAT.values.reshape((-1, 1)), df.MEDV.values.reshape((-1, 1)))
```

We'll get the following output:

```
Out[4]: 0.5441462975864797
```

Figure 3.56: Model score using LSTAT

5. Compute the prediction performance of the linear model trained using the average number of rooms to predict the property value:

   ```
   model.fit(df.RM.values.reshape((-1, 1)), df.MEDV.values.reshape((-1, 1)))
   model.score(df.RM.values.reshape((-1, 1)), df.MEDV.values.reshape((-1, 1)))
   ```

   The output will be as follows:

   ```
   Out[5]: 0.4835254559913343
   ```

   Figure 3.57: Model score using RM

6. Create a multiple linear regression model using both the **LSTAT** and **RM** values as input to predict the median property value:

   ```
   model.fit(df[['LSTAT', 'RM']], df.MEDV.values.reshape((-1, 1)))
   model.score(df[['LSTAT', 'RM']], df.MEDV.values.reshape((-1, 1)))
   ```

   The output will be:

   ```
   Out[6]: 0.6385616062603403
   ```

   Figure 3.58: Model score using LSTAT and RM

Autoregression Models

Autoregression models are part of a more classical statistical modeling technique that is used on time series data (that is, any dataset that changes with time) and extends upon the linear regression techniques covered in this chapter. Autoregression models are commonly used in the economics and finance industry as they are particularly powerful in time series datasets with a sizeable number of measurements. To reflect this, we will change our dataset to the S&P daily closing prices from 1986 to 2018, which is available in the accompanying source code.

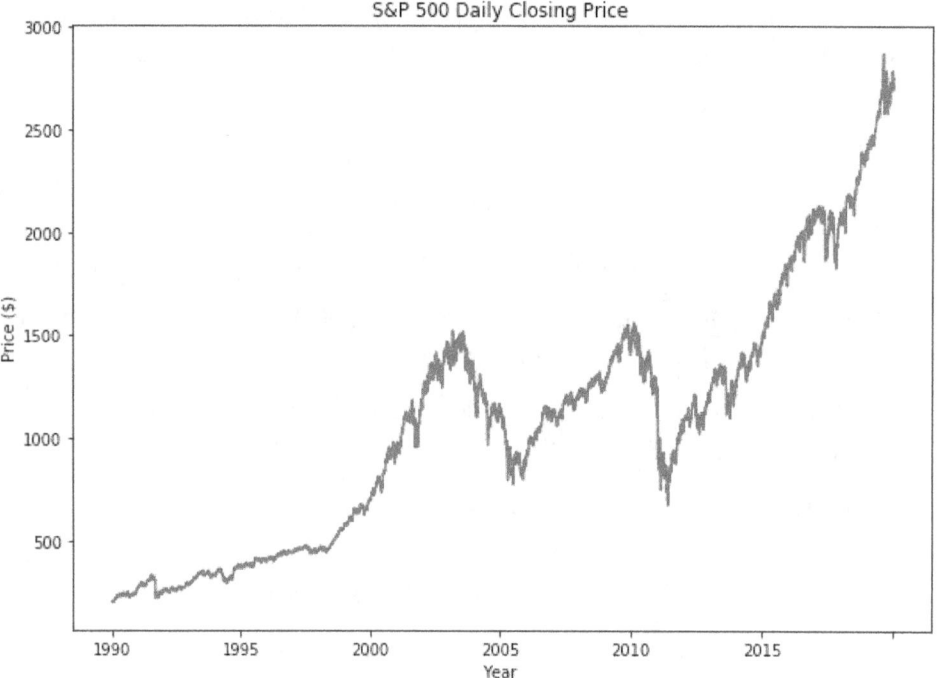

Figure 3.59: S&P 500 Daily Closing Price

The main principle behind autoregression models is that, given enough previous observations, a reasonable prediction for the future can be made; that is, we are essentially constructing a model using the dataset as a regression against itself, hence **autoregression**. This relationship can be modeled mathematically as a linear equation:

$$y_t = \theta_0 + \theta_1 y_{t-1} + \epsilon_t$$

Figure 3.60: First-order autoregression model

Where y_t is the predicted value for time, t, θ_0 is the first weight of the model, θ_1 is the second weight with $y_t - 1$ as the previous value in the dataset, and ϵ_t is an error term.

The equation in *Figure 3.60* represents a model using only the previous value in the dataset to make a prediction. This is a first-order autoregression model and can be extended to include more previous samples.

The equation in *Figure 3.61* provides an example of a second-order model, including the previous two values.

Similarly, a kth order autoregression model contains values with corresponding parameters between $y_{t-1} \ldots y_{t-(k-1)}$, adding more context about the previous observations about the model. Again, referring to the equation in *Figure 3.61* and the kth order autoregression, the recursive properties of the autoregression model can also be observed. Each prediction uses the previous value(s) in its summation, and thus, if we take the previously predicted values, they themselves use the predictions of the previous value, hence the recursion.

$$y_t = \theta_0 + \theta_1 y_{t-1} + \theta_2 y_{t-2} + \epsilon_t$$
$$y_t = \theta_0 + \theta_1 y_{t-1} + \theta_2 y_{t-2} + \cdots + \theta_{t-(k-1)} y_{t-(k-1)} + \epsilon_t$$

Figure 3.61: Second and k^{th} order autoregression model

Exercise 35: Creating an Autoregression Model

We will use the S&P 500 model to create an autoregression model:

1. Load the S&P 500 dataset, extract the year represented as two digits in the column date, and create a new column, **Year**, with the year represented in the four-digit format (for example, 02-Jan-86 will become 1986 and 31-Dec-04 will become 2004):

    ```
    df = pd.read_csv('spx.csv')
    yr = []
    for x in df.date:
        x = int(x[-2:])
        if x < 10:
            x = f'200{x}'
        elif x < 20:
            x = f'20{x}'
        else:
            x = f'19{x}'
        yr.append(x)
    df['Year'] = yr
    df.head()
    ```

We'll get the following output:

```
In [56]: df = pd.read_csv('spx.csv')
         yr = []
         for x in df.date:
             x = int(x[-2:])
             if x < 10:
                 x = f'200{x}'
             elif x < 20:
                 x = f'20{x}'
             else:
                 x = f'19{x}'
             yr.append(x)
         df['Year'] = yr
         df.head()
```

Out[56]:

	date	close	Year
0	02-Jan-86	209.59	1986
1	03-Jan-86	210.88	1986
2	06-Jan-86	210.65	1986
3	07-Jan-86	213.80	1986
4	08-Jan-86	207.97	1986

Figure 3.62: First five rows

2. Plot the raw dataset with years along the *x* axis in multiples of five:

```
plt.figure(figsize=(10, 7))
plt.plot(df.close.values);
yrs = [yr for yr in df.Year.unique() if (int(yr[-2:]) % 5 == 0)]
plt.xticks(np.arange(0, len(df), len(df) // len(yrs)), yrs);
plt.title('S&P 500 Daily Closing Price');
plt.xlabel('Year');
plt.ylabel('Price ($)');
```

The output will be as follows:

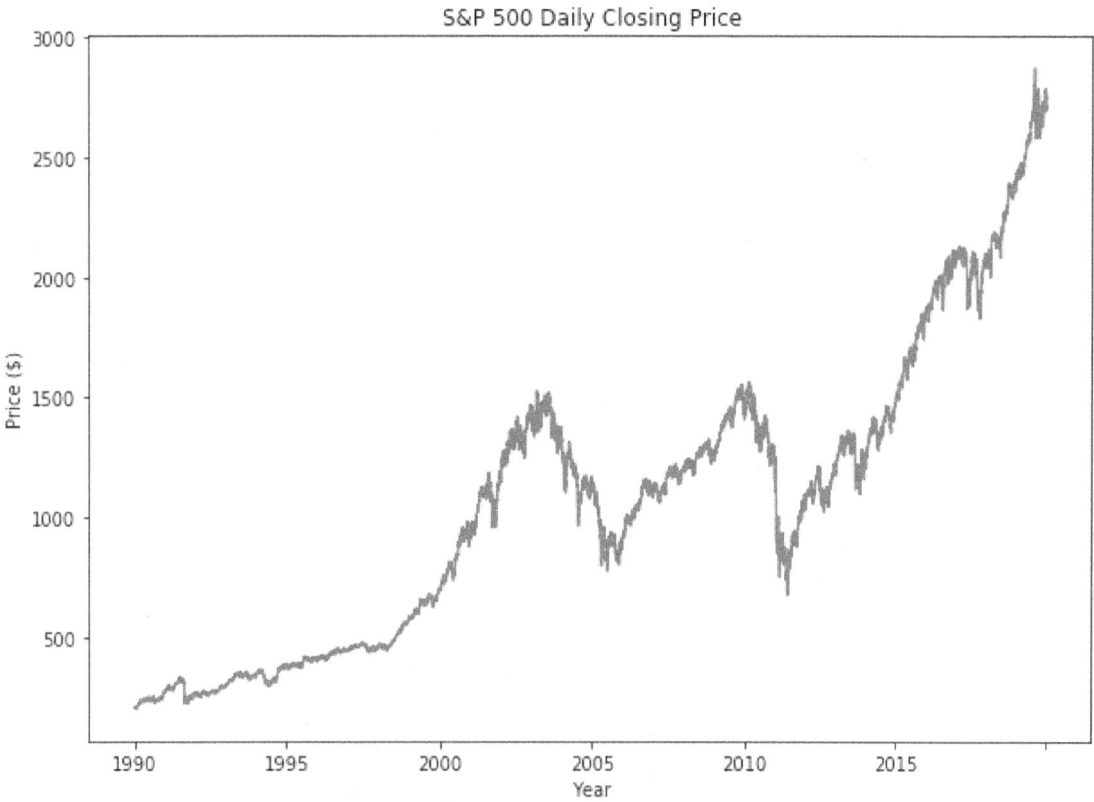

Figure 3.63: Plot of closing price through the years

3. Before we can construct an autoregression model, we must first check to see whether the model is able to be used as a regression against itself. To do that, we can once again use the pandas library to check for correlations between the dataset and a copy of the dataset that is shifted by a defined number of samples, known as **lag**. For a more concrete understanding of this regression, print out the first 10 values of the closing prices. Then, using the pandas **shift** method, introduce a sample lag of **3** into the first 10 values of the closing price and look at the result:

```
df.close[:10].values
df.close[:10].shift(3).values
```

We'll get this output:

```
In [69]:  df.close[:10].values
Out[69]:  array([209.59, 210.88, 210.65, 213.8 , 207.97, 206.11, 205.96, 206.72,
                 206.64, 208.26])

In [70]:  df.close[:10].shift(3).values
Out[70]:  array([   nan,    nan,    nan, 209.59, 210.88, 210.65, 213.8 , 207.97,
                 206.11, 205.96])
```

Figure 3.64: Values with a lag of three

Notice the introduction of three NaN values into the array and that the last three values have dropped off the array. This is the effect of shifting, essentially sliding the dataset forward in time by the period defined by the lag.

4. Shift the dataset by a lag of 100 and plot the result:

```
plt.figure(figsize=(15, 7))
plt.plot(df.close.values, label='Original Dataset', c='k', linestyle='-');
plt.plot(df.close.shift(100), c='k', linestyle=':', label='Lag 100');
yrs = [yr for yr in df.Year.unique() if (int(yr[-2:]) % 5 == 0)]
plt.xticks(np.arange(0, len(df), len(df) // len(yrs)), yrs);
plt.title('S&P 500 Daily Closing Price');
plt.xlabel('Year');
plt.ylabel('Price ($)');
plt.legend();
```

The output will be as follows:

Figure 3.65: Plot of closing price over the year

5. Now that we have an understanding of the time shift, we will confirm that the data can be correlated against itself. To do this, use the pandas **autocorrelation_plot** method to check for randomness within the data:

```
plt.figure(figsize=(10, 7))
pd.plotting.autocorrelation_plot(df.close);
```

The output will be as follows:

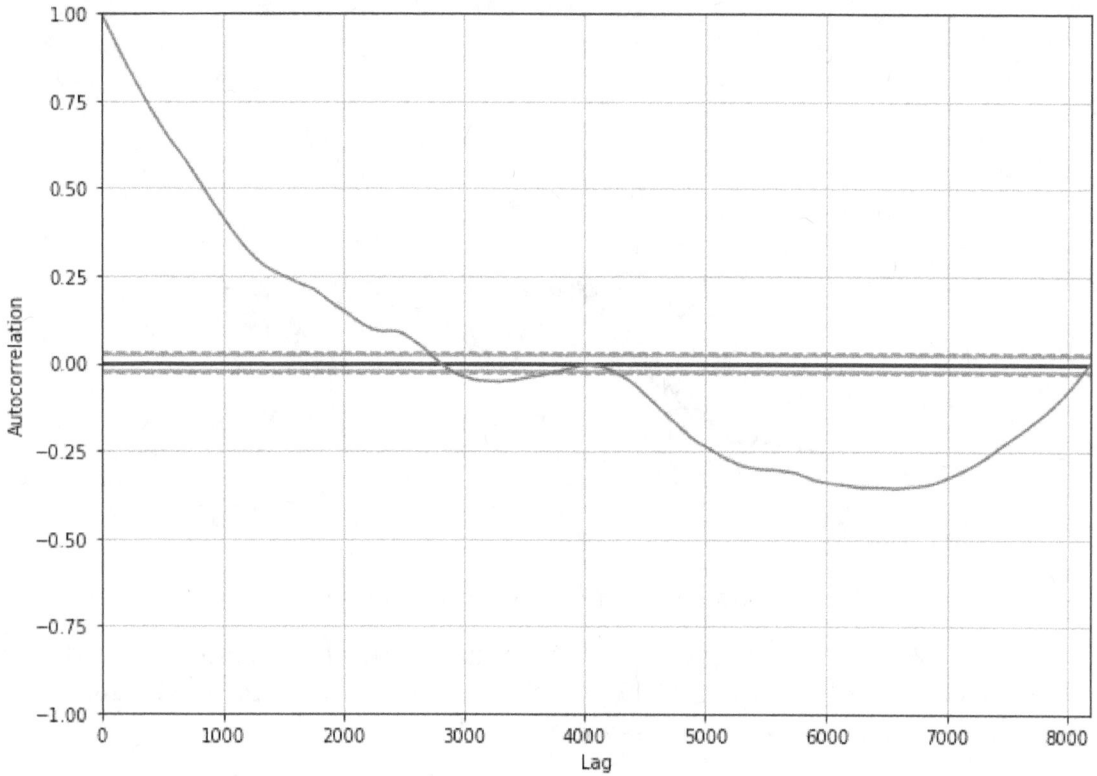

Figure 3.66: Relation of autocorrelation versus the lag

All of the information required to determine whether autoregression is possible is defined within this plot. We can see on the x axis, the values for **Lag** range from 0 to 8,000 samples, and the values for **Autocorrelation** vary from approximately -0.4 to 1. There are five other additional lines of interest; however, at this scale on the y axis, it is difficult to see them.

6. Set the y axis limits to be between -0.1 and 0.1:

```
plt.figure(figsize=(10, 7))
ax = pd.plotting.autocorrelation_plot(df.close);
ax.set_ylim([-0.1, 0.1]);
```

The output will be as follows:

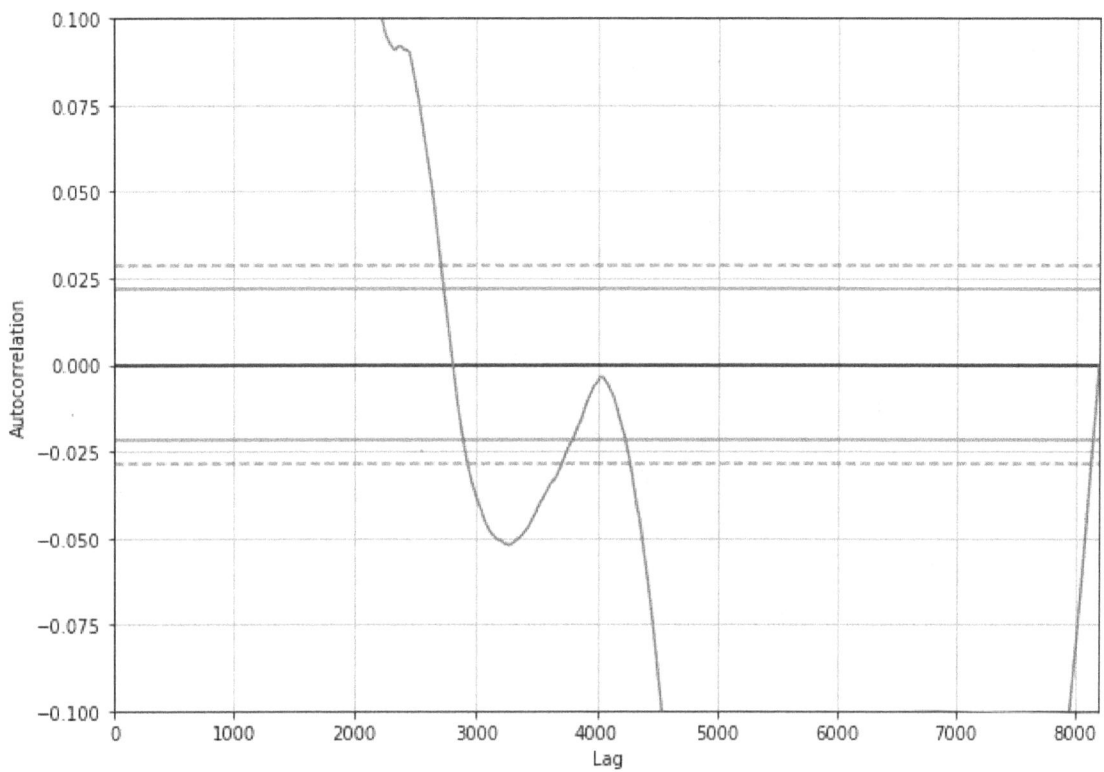

Figure 3.67: Plot of autocorrelation versus lag

We can see in the enhanced view that there are two gray dashed lines, which represent the 99% confidence band that the series is non-random. The solid gray line represents the 95% confidence band. Once the autocorrelation plot approaches zero within these bands, the time series with the specified lag becomes sufficiently random that autoregression models would not be appropriate.

7. To further solidify our understanding, create a plot of the closing prices versus the closing prices with a lag of 100 samples. According to our autocorrelation plot, there is a high correlation between these sets. What does that look like?

```
plt.figure(figsize=(10,7))
ax = pd.plotting.lag_plot(df.close, lag=100);
```

The output will be:

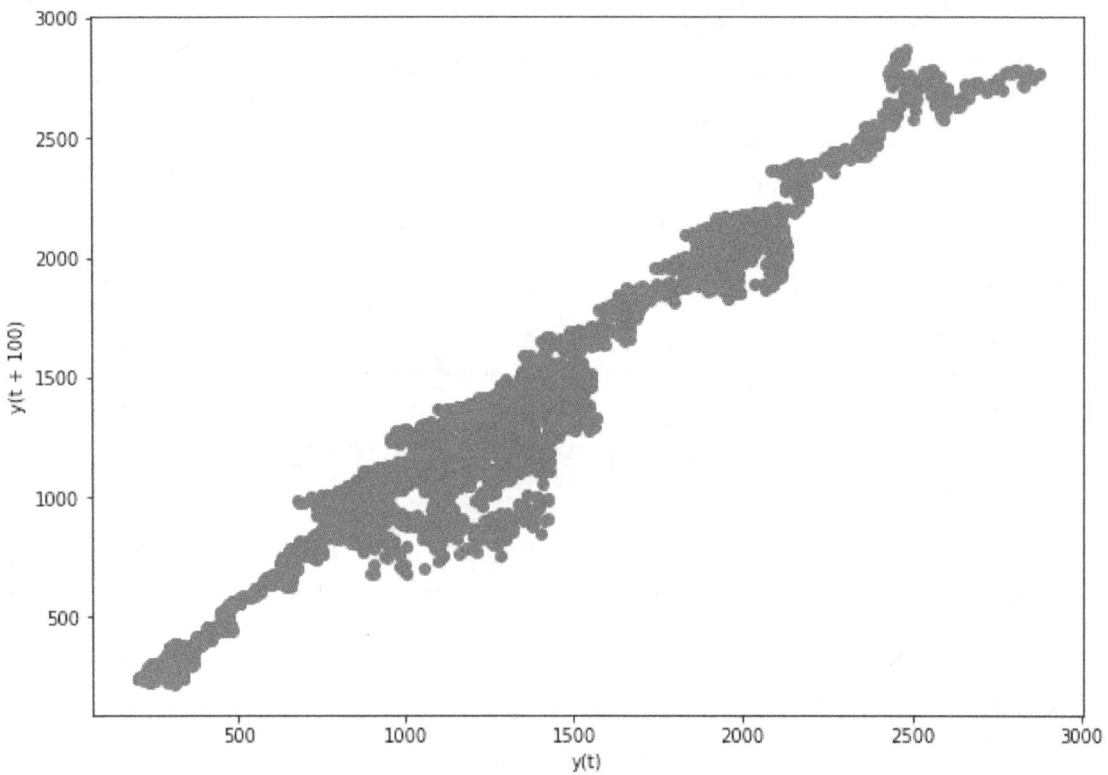

Figure 3.68: Autocorrelation plot

8. Create a plot of closing prices versus closing prices with a lag of 4,000 samples. Again, looking at the autocorrelation plot at a lag of 4,000, the autocorrelation value is approximately 0, indicating that there is no real correlation between the two and it is mostly random:

```
plt.figure(figsize=(10,7))
ax = pd.plotting.lag_plot(df.close, lag=4000);
```

The output will be:

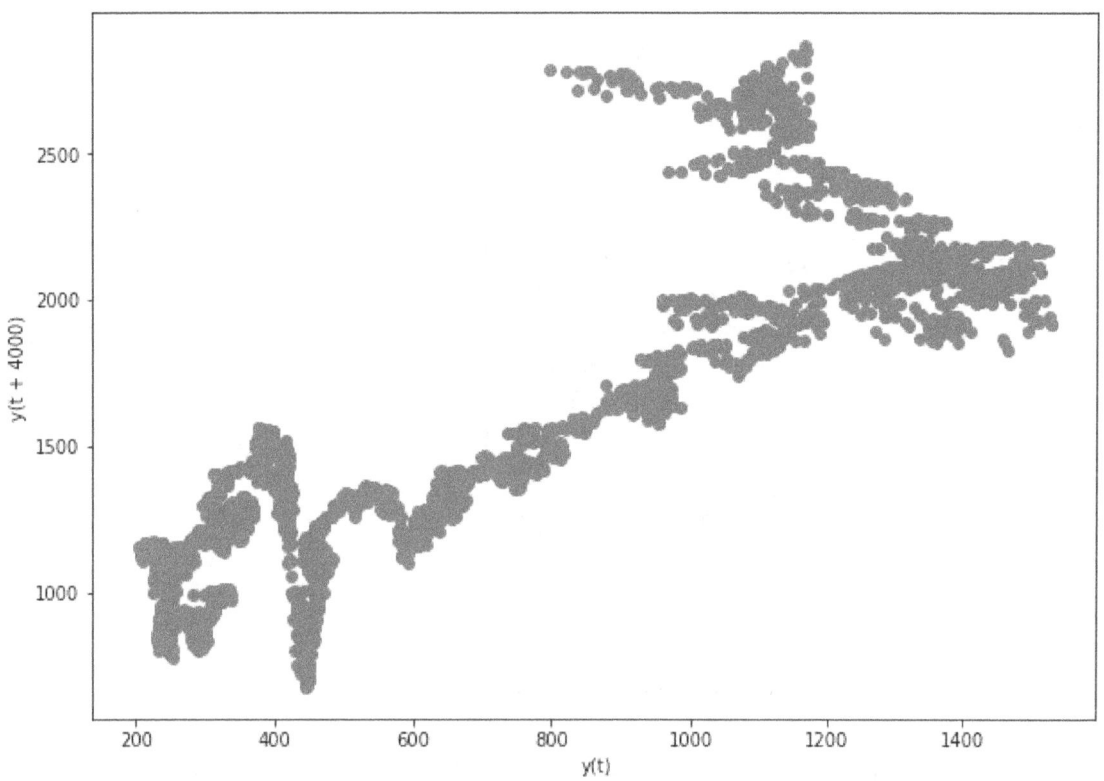

Figure 3.69: Plot of closing prices versus closing prices with a lag of 4,000 samples

9. Now we are ready to create our model. To do this, however, we will need another Python package, the **statsmodel** package (http://www.statsmodels.org), which is similar to scikit-learn but is dedicated to creating models and executing tests using the more classical statistical techniques. Install the **statsmodel** package. You can do this either using **conda install** or **pip**. For the Anaconda installation, the **conda install** method is preferred:

    ```
    #!pip install statsmodels
    !conda install -c conda-forge statsmodels
    ```

10. Import the autoregression class (**AR**) from **statsmodel** and construct the model using the closing price data:

    ```
    from statsmodels.tsa.ar_model import AR
    model = AR(df.close)
    ```

11. Fit the model using the `fit` method and print out the lag that was selected for use and the coefficients of the model:

    ```
    model_fit = model.fit()
    print('Lag: %s' % model_fit.k_ar)
    print('Coefficients: %s' % model_fit.params)
    ```

    The output will be:

    ```
    Lag: 36
    Coefficients: const      0.114237
    L1.close     0.944153
    L2.close     0.008452
    L3.close     0.046900
    L4.close    -0.014887
    L5.close    -0.024734
    L6.close     0.025849
    L7.close    -0.004821
    L8.close     0.009209
    L9.close    -0.010451
    L10.close    0.033449
    L11.close   -0.029657
    ```

    Figure 3.70: Lag coefficients

    Note that there are 36 coefficients for each of the weights and one constant; only an extract is shown for simplicity. All coefficients can be found in the **Ex7-AutoRegressors.ipynb** Jupyter notebook in the accompanying source code.

12. Use the model to create a set of predictions starting at sample 36 (the lag) and finishing at 500 samples after the dataset has ended:

    ```
    predictions = model_fit.predict(start=36, end=len(df) + 500)
    predictions[:10].values
    ```

    We'll get the following output:

    ```
    array([224.22071026, 224.18191256, 224.47901622, 224.15407352,
           226.46426347, 226.72721775, 225.6576946 , 224.52871226,
           224.56431615, 225.15588295])
    ```

    Figure 3.71: Prediction values

13. Plot the predictions' values over the top of the original dataset:

    ```
    plt.figure(figsize=(10, 7))
    plt.plot(predictions, c='g', linestyle=':', label='Predictions');
    plt.plot(df.close.values, label='Original Dataset');
    yrs = [yr for yr in df.Year.unique() if (int(yr[-2:]) % 5 == 0)]
    plt.xticks(np.arange(0, len(df), len(df) // len(yrs)), yrs);
    plt.title('S&P 500 Daily Closing Price');
    plt.xlabel('Year');
    plt.ylabel('Price ($)');
    plt.legend();
    ```

    This will give the following output:

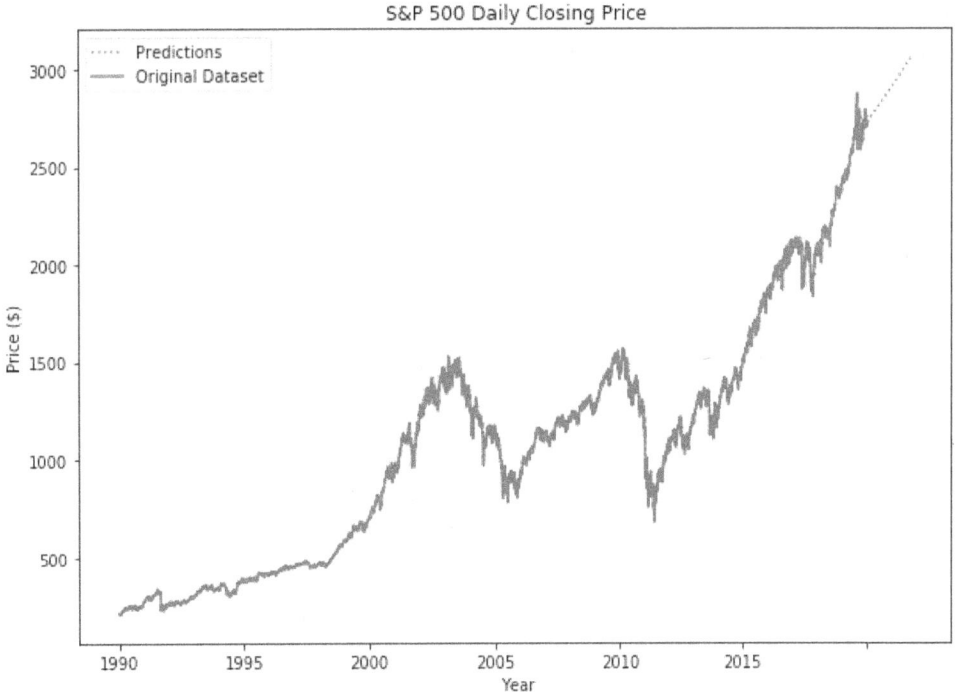

Figure 3.72: Plot of price through the year

Note that the predictions do an excellent job of following the dataset, and that after the dataset has ended, the predictions are relatively linear. Given that the model is constructed from the previous samples, it makes sense that it becomes less certain once the dataset has finished, particularly as there are no repetitive patterns in the data.

14. The fit seems really close – what does the difference between the predictions and original dataset look like? Enhance the model to observe the differences:

    ```
    plt.figure(figsize=(10, 7))
    plt.plot(predictions, c='g', linestyle=':', label='Predictions');
    plt.plot(df.close.values, label='Original Dataset');
    yrs = [yr for yr in df.Year.unique() if (int(yr[-2:]) % 5 == 0)]
    plt.xticks(np.arange(0, len(df), len(df) // len(yrs)), yrs);
    plt.title('S&P 500 Daily Closing Price');
    plt.xlabel('Year');
    plt.ylabel('Price ($)');
    plt.xlim([2000, 2500])
    plt.ylim([420, 500])
    plt.legend();
    ```

    This provides the following plot:

Figure 3.73: Predictions on the original dataset values

From this exercise using an autoregressor, we can see that there is significant predictive power in using these models when there is missing data from the set or when we are attempting to predict between measurement intervals. The autoregressor model shown for the S&P 500 dataset was able to effectively provide predictions within the range of observed samples. However, outside of this range, when predicting future values for which no measurements have been taken, the predictive power may be somewhat limited.

Activity 10: Autoregressors

In this activity, we will now use autoregressors to model the Austin weather dataset and predict future values:

Before we begin, we will need to import a few libraries and load data from a previous activity, which can be done as follows:

```
import numpy as np
import pandas as pd
import matplotlib.pyplot as plt
from statsmodels.tsa.ar_model import AR

# Loading the data from activity 5
df = pd.read_csv('activity2_measurements.csv')
```

The steps to be performed are as follows:

1. Plot the complete set of average temperature values (**df.TempAvgF**) with years on the *x* axis.

2. Create a 20-day lag and plot the lagged data on the original dataset.

3. Construct an autocorrelation plot to see whether the average temperature can be used with an autoregressor.

4. Choose an acceptable lag and an unacceptable lag and construct lag plots using these values.

5. Create an autoregressor model, note the selected lag, calculate the r^2 value, and plot the autoregressor model with the original plot. The model is to project past the available data by 1,000 samples.

6. Fit the model to the data.
7. Create a set of predictions for 1,000 days after the last sample.
8. Plot the predictions, as well as the original dataset.
9. Enhance the view to look for differences by showing the 100th to 200th sample.

> **Note**
> The solution for this activity can be found on page 344.

Summary

In this chapter, we took our first big leap into constructing machine learning models and making predictions with labeled datasets. We began our analysis by looking at a variety of different ways to construct linear models, starting with the precise least squares method, which is very good when modeling small amounts of data that can be processed using the available computer memory. The performance of our vanilla linear model was improved using dummy variables, which we created from categorical variables, adding additional features and context to the model. We then used linear regression analysis with a parabolic model to further improve performance, fitting a more natural curve to the dataset. We also implemented the gradient descent algorithm, which we noticed, while not as precise as the least squares method was for our limited dataset, was most powerful when the dataset cannot be processed on the resources available on the system.

Finally, we investigated the use of autoregression models, which predict future values based on the experience of previous data in the set. Using autoregressors, we were able to accurately model the closing price of the S&P 500 over the years 1986 – 2018.

Now that we have experience with supervised regression problems, we will turn our attention to classification problems in the next chapter.

Classification

Learning Objectives

By the end of this chapter, you will be able to:

- Implement logistic regression and explain how it can be used to classify data into specific groups or classes
- Use the K-nearest neighbors clustering algorithm for classification
- Use decision trees for data classification, including the ID3 algorithm
- Describe the concept of entropy within data
- Explain how decision trees such as ID3 aim to reduce entropy
- Use decision trees for data classification

This chapter introduces classification problems, classification using linear and logistic regression, K-nearest neighbors classification, and decision trees.

Introduction

In the previous chapter, we began our supervised machine learning journey using regression techniques, predicting the continuous variable output given a set of input data. We will now turn to the other sub-type of machine learning problems that we previously described: classification problems. Recall that classification tasks aim to predict, given a set of input data, which one of a specified number of groups of classes data belongs to.

In this chapter, we will extend the concepts learned in *Chapter 3, Regression Analysis*, and will apply them to a dataset labeled with classes, rather than continuous values, as output.

Linear Regression as a Classifier

We covered linear regression in the context of predicting continuous variable output in the previous chapter, but it can also be used to predict the class that a set of data is a member of. Linear regression classifiers are not as powerful as other types of classifiers that we will cover in this chapter, but they are particularly useful in understanding the process of classification. Let's say we had a fictional dataset containing two separate groups, Xs and Os, as shown in *Figure 4.1*. We could construct a linear classifier by first using linear regression to fit the equation of a straight line to the dataset. For any value that lies above the line, the X class would be predicted, and for any value beneath the line, the O class would be predicted. Any dataset that can be separated by a straight line is known as linearly separable, which forms an important subset of data types in machine learning problems. While this may not be particularly helpful in the context of a linear regression-based classifier, it often is in the case of other classifiers, such as **support vector machines** (**SVM**), decision trees, and linear neural network-based classifiers.

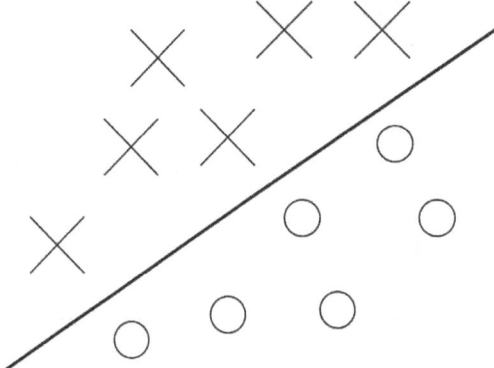

Figure 4.1: Linear regression as a classifier

Exercise 36: Linear Regression as a Classifier

This exercise contains a contrived example of using linear regression as a classifier. In this exercise, we will use a completely fictional dataset, and test how linear regression fares as a classifier. The dataset is composed of manually selected x and y values for a scatterplot that are approximately divided into two groups. The dataset has been specifically designed for this exercise, to demonstrate how linear regression can be used as a classifier, and this is available in the accompanying code files for this book, as well as on GitHub, at https://github.com/TrainingByPackt/Supervised-Learning-with-Python.

1. Load the `linear_classifier.csv` dataset into a pandas DataFrame:

   ```
   df = pd.read_csv('linear_classifier.csv')
   df.head()
   ```

   The output will be as follows:

	x	y	labels
0	1	13	x
1	8	18	o
2	9	25	x
3	5	25	x
4	4	17	x

   Figure 4.2: First five rows

   Looking through the dataset, each row contains a set of x, y coordinates, as well as the label corresponding to which class the data belongs to, either a cross (**x**) or a circle (**o**).

2. Produce a scatterplot of the data with the marker for each point as the corresponding class label:

   ```
   plt.figure(figsize=(10, 7))
   for label, label_class in df.groupby('labels'):
       plt.scatter(label_class.values[:,0], label_class.values[:,1],
                   label=f'Class {label}', marker=label, c='k')
   plt.legend()
   plt.title("Linear Classifier");
   ```

We'll get the following scatterplot:

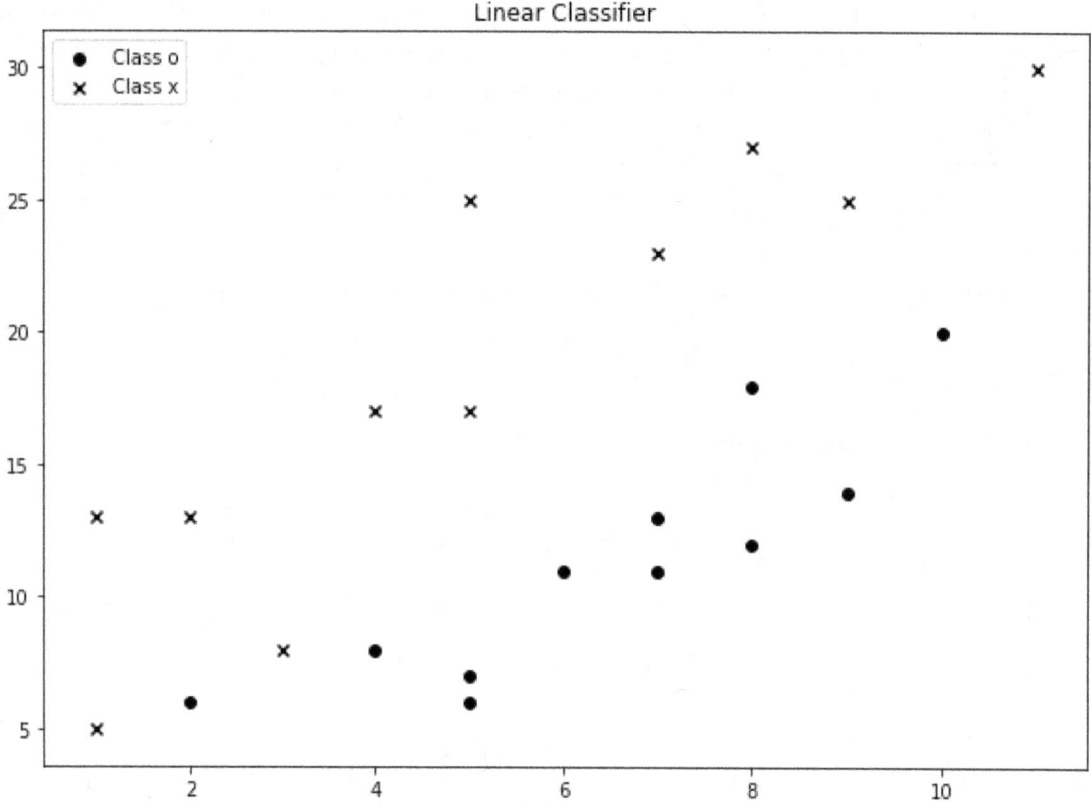

Figure 4.3 Scatterplot of a linear classifier

3. Using the scikit-learn `LinearRegression` API from the previous chapter, fit a linear model to the x, y coordinates of the dataset and print out the linear equation:

```
# Fit a linear regression model
model = LinearRegression()
model.fit(df.x.values.reshape((-1, 1)), df.y.values.reshape((-1, 1)))

# Print out the parameters
print(f'y = {model.coef_[0][0]}x + {model.intercept_[0]}')
```

The output will be:

y = 1.6363401395709483x + 5.50840010338589

Figure 4.4: Output of model fitting

4. Plot the fitted trendline over the dataset:

```
# Plot the trendline
trend = model.predict(np.linspace(0, 10).reshape((-1, 1)))

plt.figure(figsize=(10, 7))
for label, label_class in df.groupby('labels'):
    plt.scatter(label_class.values[:,0], label_class.values[:,1],
                label=f'Class {label}', marker=label, c='k')
plt.plot(np.linspace(0, 10), trend, c='k', label='Trendline')
plt.legend()
plt.title("Linear Classifier");
```

The output will be as follows:

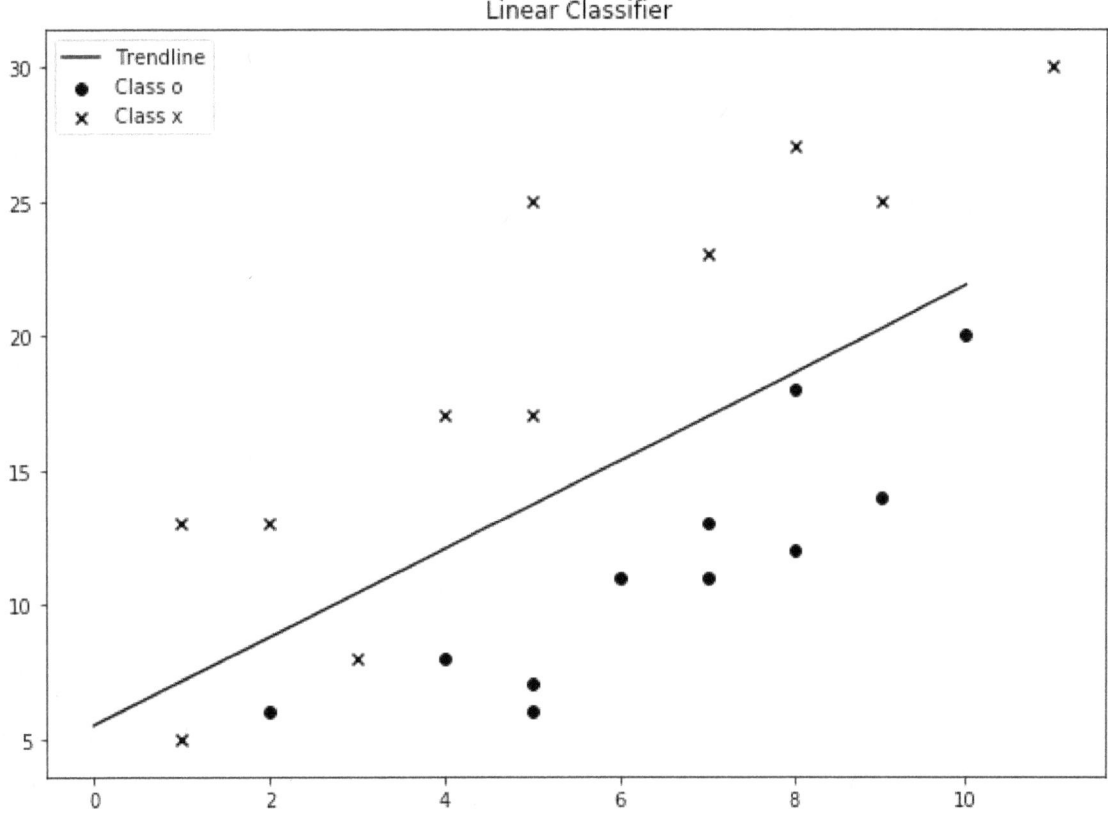

Figure 4.5: Scatterplot with trendline

5. With the fitted trendline, the classifier can then be applied. For each row in the dataset, determine whether the x, y point lies above or below the linear model (or trendline). If the point lies below the trendline, the model predicts the **o** class, if above the line, the **x** class is predicted. Include these values as a column of predicted labels:

```
# Make predictions
y_pred = model.predict(df.x.values.reshape((-1, 1)))
pred_labels = []

for _y, _y_pred in zip(df.y, y_pred):
    if _y < _y_pred:
        pred_labels.append('o')
    else:
        pred_labels.append('x')
df['Pred Labels'] = pred_labels
df.head()
```

The output will be as follows:

	x	y	labels	Pred Labels
0	1	13	x	x
1	8	18	o	o
2	9	25	x	x
3	5	25	x	x
4	4	17	x	x

Figure 4.6: First five rows

6. Plot the points with the corresponding ground truth labels. For those points where the labels were correctly predicted, plot the corresponding class. For those incorrect predictions, plot a diamond:

```
plt.figure(figsize=(10, 7))
for idx, label_class in df.iterrows():
    if label_class.labels != label_class['Pred Labels']:
        label = 'D'
        s=70
    else:
```

```
            label = label_class.labels
            s=50
    plt.scatter(label_class.values[0], label_class.values[1],
                label=f'Class {label}', marker=label, c='k', s=s)

plt.plot(np.linspace(0, 10), trend, c='k', label='Trendline')
plt.title("Linear Classifier");

incorrect_class = mlines.Line2D([], [], color='k', marker='D',
                    markersize=10, label='Incorrect Classification');
plt.legend(handles=[incorrect_class]);
```

The output will be as follows:

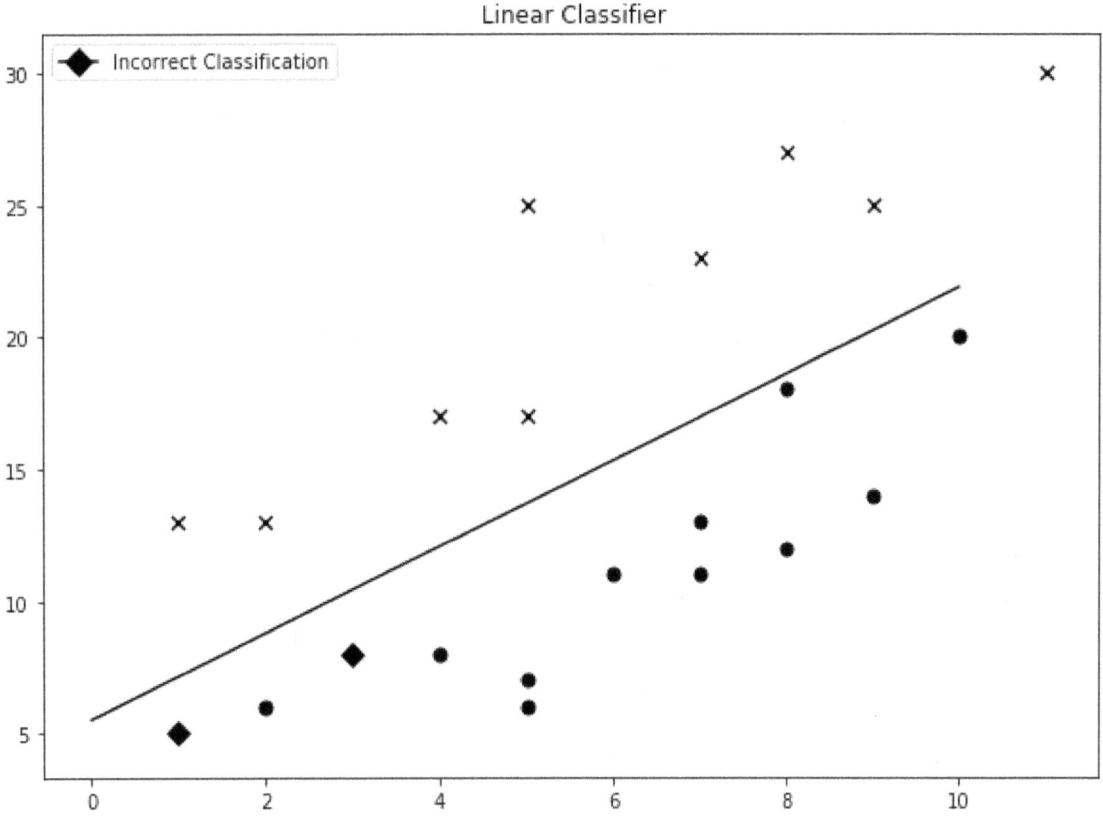

Figure 4.7: Scatterplot showing incorrect predictions

We can see that, in this plot, the linear classifier made two incorrect predictions in this completely fictional dataset, one at $x = 1$, another at $x = 3$.

But what if our dataset is not linearly separable and we cannot classify the data using a straight line model, which is very frequently the case. In this scenario, we turn to other classification methods, many of which use different models, but the process logically flows from our simplified linear classifier model.

Logistic Regression

The **logistic** or **logit** model is one such non-linear model that has been effectively used for classification tasks in a number of different domains. In this section, we will use it to classify images of hand-written digits. In understanding the logistic model, we also take an important step in understanding the operation of a particularly powerful machine learning model, **artificial neural networks**. So, what exactly is the logistic model? Like the linear model, which is composed of a linear or straight-line function, the logistic model is composed of the standard logistic function, which, in mathematical terms, looks something like this:

$$p(x) = \frac{1}{1 + e^{-(\beta_0 + \beta_1 x)}}$$

Figure 4.8: Logistic function

In practical terms, when trained, this function returns the probability of the input information belonging to a particular class or group.

Say we would like to predict whether a single entry of data belongs to one of two groups. As in the previous example, in linear regression, this would equate to y being either zero or one, and x can take a value between $-\infty$ and $+\infty$:

$$y = \beta_0 + \beta_1 x; 0 \leq y \leq 1, -\infty < x < \infty$$

Figure 4.9: Equation for y

A range of zero to one and $-\infty$ to $+\infty$ are significantly different; to improve this, we will calculate the odds ratio, which will then vary from greater than zero to less than $+\infty$, which is a step in the right direction:

$$p = \frac{Y}{(1-Y)} = \beta_0 + \beta_1 x; 0 < 0 < \infty, -\infty < x < \infty$$

Figure 4.10: Odds ratio

We can use the mathematical relationships of the natural log to reduce this even further. As the odds ratio approaches zero, $ln(O)$ss approaches $-\infty$; similarly, as the odds ratio approaches one, $ln(O)$ approaches $+\infty$. This is exactly what we want; that is, for the two classification options to be as far apart as possible:

$$ln(p) = ln\left(\frac{Y}{(1-Y)}\right) = \beta_0 + \beta_1 x; -\infty < ln(p) < +\infty, -\infty < x < +\infty$$

Figure 4.11: Natural log of classified points

With a little bit of equation re-arranging we get the logistic function:

$$y = \beta_0 + \beta_{1x}; 0 \leq y \leq 1, -\infty < x < \infty$$

Figure 4.12: Logistic function

Notice the exponents of e, that is, $(\beta_0 + \beta_1 x)$, and that this relationship is a linear function with two training parameters or *weights*, β_0 and $-\infty$, as well as the input feature, x. If we were to plot the logistic function over the range (-6, 6), we would get the following result:

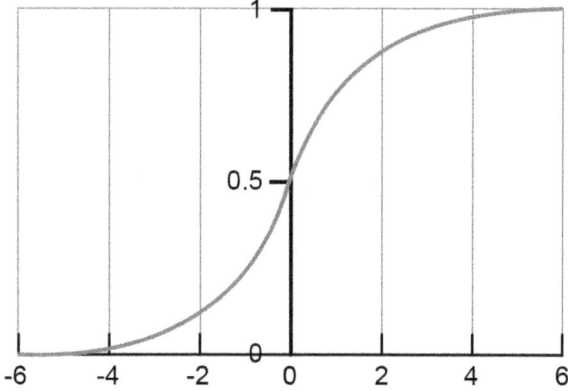

Figure 4.13: Logistic function curve

Examining *Figure 4.13*, we can see some features that are important for a classification task. The first thing to note is that, if we look at the probability values on the y axis at the extremes of the function, the values are almost at zero when $x = -6$ and at one when $x = 6$. While it looks like the values are in fact zero and one, this is not exactly the case. The logistic function approaches zero and one at these extremes and will only equal zero and one when x is at a positive or negative infinity. In practical terms, what this means is that the logistic function will never return a probability of one or greater or less than or equal to zero, which is perfect for a classification task. We can never have a probability of greater than one, as, by definition, a probability of one is a certainty of an event occurring. Likewise, we cannot have a probability of less than zero, as, by definition, a probability of zero is a certainty of the event not occurring. The fact that the logistic function approaches but never equals one or zero means that there is always some uncertainty in the outcome or the classification.

The final feature to notice about the logistic function is that at $x = 0$, the probability is 0.5, which, if we were to get this result, would indicate that the model is equally uncertain about the outcome of the corresponding class; that is, it really has no idea. Typically, this is the default position at the start of training, and, as the model is exposed to training data, it becomes more confident in its decisions.

> **Note**
>
> It is very important to correctly understand and interpret the probability information provided by classification models such as linear regression. Consider this probability score as the chance of the input information belonging to a particular class given the variability in the information provided by the training data. One common mistake is to use this probability score as an objective measure of whether the model can be trusted about its prediction; unfortunately, this isn't necessarily the case. *A model can provide a probability of 99.99% that some data belongs to a particular class and still be 99.99% wrong.*

What we do use the probability value for is selecting the predicted class by the classifier. Say we had a model that was to predict whether some set of data belonged to class A or class B. If the logistic model returned a probability of 0.7 for class A, then we would return class A as the predicted class for the model. If the probability was only 0.2, the predicted class for the model would be class B.

Exercise 37: Logistic Regression as a Classifier – Two-Class Classifier

For this exercise, we will be using a sample of the famous MNIST dataset (available at http://yann.lecun.com/exdb/mnist/ or on GitHub at https://github.com/TrainingByPackt/Supervised-Learning-with-Python), which is a sequence of images of handwritten postcode digits, zero through nine, with corresponding labels. The MNIST dataset is comprised of 60,000 training samples and 10,000 test samples, where each sample is a grayscale image with a size of 28 x 28 pixels. In this exercise, we will use logistic regression to build a classifier. The first classifier we will build is a two-class classifier, where we will determine whether the image is a handwritten zero or a one:

1. For this exercise, we will need to import a few dependencies. Execute the following import statements:

    ```python
    import struct
    import numpy as np
    import gzip
    import urllib.request
    import matplotlib.pyplot as plt
    from array import array
    from sklearn.linear_model import LogisticRegression
    ```

2. We will also need to download the MNIST datasets. You will only need to do this once, so after this step, feel free to comment out or remove these cells. Download the image data, as follows:

    ```python
    request = urllib.request.urlopen('http://yann.lecun.com/exdb/mnist/train-images-idx3-ubyte.gz')

    with open('train-images-idx3-ubyte.gz', 'wb') as f:
        f.write(request.read())

    request = urllib.request.urlopen('http://yann.lecun.com/exdb/mnist/t10k-images-idx3-ubyte.gz')

    with open('t10k-images-idx3-ubyte.gz', 'wb') as f:
        f.write(request.read())
    ```

3. Download the corresponding labels for the data:

   ```
   request = urllib.request.urlopen('http://yann.lecun.com/exdb/mnist/train-labels-idx1-ubyte.gz')

   with open('train-labels-idx1-ubyte.gz', 'wb') as f:
       f.write(request.read())

   request = urllib.request.urlopen('http://yann.lecun.com/exdb/mnist/t10k-labels-idx1-ubyte.gz')

   with open('t10k-labels-idx1-ubyte.gz', 'wb') as f:
       f.write(request.read())
   ```

4. Once all the files have been successfully downloaded, check out the files in the local directory using the following command for Windows:

   ```
   !dir *.gz
   ```

   The output will be as follows:

   ```
   In [24]:  1  !ls *.gz # or !dir *.gz for windows
             t10k-images-idx3-ubyte.gz    train-images-idx3-ubyte.gz
             t10k-labels-idx1-ubyte.gz    train-labels-idx1-ubyte.gz
   ```

   Figure 4.14: Files in directory

   > **Note**
   >
   > For Linux and macOS, check out the files in the local directory using the `!ls *.gz` command.

5. Load the downloaded data. Don't worry too much about the exact details of reading the data, as these are specific to the MNIST dataset:

   ```
   with gzip.open('train-images-idx3-ubyte.gz', 'rb') as f:
       magic, size, rows, cols = struct.unpack(">IIII", f.read(16))
       img = np.array(array("B", f.read())).reshape((size, rows, cols))

   with gzip.open('train-labels-idx1-ubyte.gz', 'rb') as f:
       magic, size = struct.unpack(">II", f.read(8))
       labels = np.array(array("B", f.read()))

   with gzip.open('t10k-images-idx3-ubyte.gz', 'rb') as f:
   ```

```
        magic, size, rows, cols = struct.unpack(">IIII", f.read(16))

        img_test = np.array(array("B", f.read())).reshape((size, rows, cols))

    with gzip.open('t10k-labels-idx1-ubyte.gz', 'rb') as f:
        magic, size = struct.unpack(">II", f.read(8))
        labels_test = np.array(array("B", f.read()))
```

6. As always, having a thorough understanding of the data is key, so create an image plot of the first 10 images in the training sample. Notice the grayscale images and that the corresponding labels are the digits zero through nine:

```
for i in range(10):
    plt.subplot(2, 5, i + 1)
    plt.imshow(img[i], cmap='gray');
    plt.title(f'{labels[i]}');
    plt.axis('off')
```

The output will be as follows:

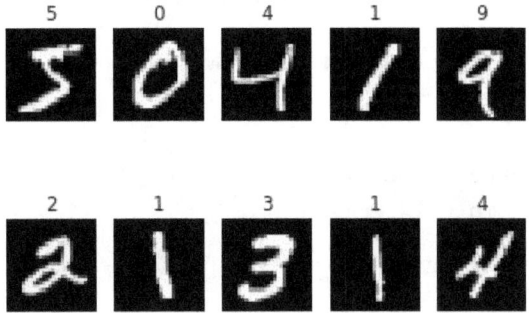

Figure 4.15: Training images

7. As the initial classifier is aiming to classify either images of zeros or images of ones, we must first select these samples from the dataset:

```
samples_0_1 = np.where((labels == 0) | (labels == 1))[0]
images_0_1 = img[samples_0_1]
labels_0_1 = labels[samples_0_1]

samples_0_1_test = np.where((labels_test == 0) | (labels_test == 1))
images_0_1_test = img_test[samples_0_1_test].reshape((-1, rows * cols))
labels_0_1_test = labels_test[samples_0_1_test]
```

8. Visualize one sample from the zero selection and another from the handwritten one digits to ensure we have correctly allocated the data.

   Here's the code for zero:

   ```
   sample_0 = np.where((labels == 0))[0][0]
   plt.imshow(img[sample_0], cmap='gray');
   ```

   The output will be as follows:

   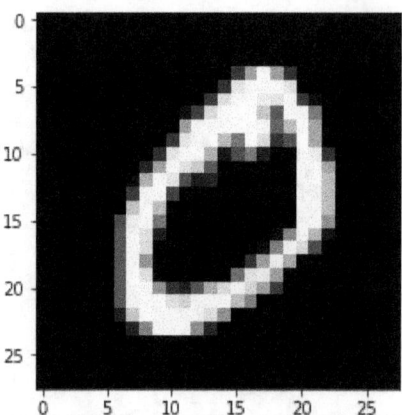

   Figure 4.16: First handwritten image

   Here's the code for one:

   ```
   sample_1 = np.where((labels == 1))[0][0]
   plt.imshow(img[sample_1], cmap='gray');
   ```

   The output will be as follows:

   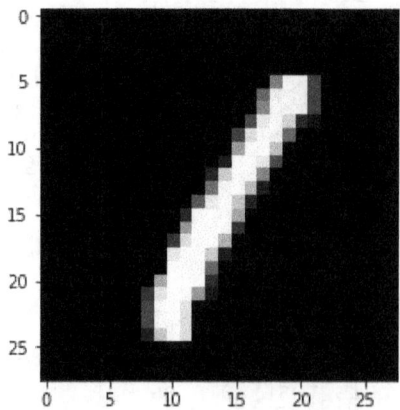

   Figure 4.17: Second handwritten image

9. We are almost at the stage where we can start building the model, however, as each sample is an image and has data in a matrix format, we must first re-arrange each of the images. The model needs the images to be provided in vector form, that is, all the information for each image is stored in one row. Do that as follows:

    ```
    images_0_1 = images_0_1.reshape((-1, rows * cols))
    images_0_1.shape
    ```

10. Now we can build and fit the logistic regression model with the selected images and labels:

    ```
    model = LogisticRegression(solver='liblinear')
    model.fit(X=images_0_1, y=labels_0_1)
    ```

    The output will be:

    ```
    Out[12]: LogisticRegression(C=1.0, class_weight=None, dual=False, fit_intercept=True,
                       intercept_scaling=1, max_iter=100, multi_class='warn',
                       n_jobs=None, penalty='l2', random_state=None, solver='liblinear',
                       tol=0.0001, verbose=0, warm_start=False)
    ```

    Figure 4.18: Logistic Regression Model

    Note how the scikit-learn API calls for logistic regression are consistent with that of linear regression. There is an additional argument, **solver**, which specifies the type of optimization process to be used. We have provided this argument here with the default value to suppress a future warning in this version of scikit-learn that requires **solver** to be specified. The specifics of the **solver** argument are out of scope for this chapter and has only been included to suppress the warning message.

11. Check the performance of this model against the corresponding training data:

    ```
    model.score(X=images_0_1, y=labels_0_1)
    ```

    We'll get the following output:

    ```
    In [13]:   1  model.score(X=images_0_1, y=labels_0_1)
    Out[13]:  1.0
    ```

    Figure 4.19: Model score

    In this example, the model was able to predict the training labels with 100% accuracy.

12. Display the first two predicted labels for the training data using the model:

    ```
    model.predict(images_0_1)[:2]
    ```

The output will be:

```
In [18]:  1  model.predict(images_0_1)[:2]
Out[18]: array([0, 1], dtype=uint8)
```

Figure 4.20: The first two labels the model predicted

13. How is the logistic regression model making the classification decisions? Look at some of the probabilities produced by the model for the training set:

    ```
    model.predict_proba(images_0_1)[:2]
    ```

    The output will be as follows:

    ```
    In [21]:  1  model.predict_proba(images_0_1)[:2]
    Out[21]: array([[9.99999999e-01, 9.89532236e-10],
                    [4.56461513e-09, 9.99999995e-01]])
    ```

    Figure 4.21: Array of probabilities

    We can see that, for each prediction made, there are two probability values. The first corresponding to the probability of the class being zero, the second the probability of the class being one, both of which add up to one. We can see that, in the first example, the prediction probability is 0.9999999 for class zero and thus the prediction is class zero. Similarly, the inverse is true for the second example.

14. Compute the performance of the model against the test set to check its performance against data that it has not seen:

    ```
    model.score(X=images_0_1_test, y=labels_0_1_test)
    ```

    The output will be:

    ```
    In [15]:  1  model.score(X=images_0_1_test, y=labels_0_1_test)
    Out[15]: 0.9995271867612293
    ```

    Figure 4.22: Model score

> **Note**
>
> Refer to *Chapter 6, Model Evaluation*, for better methods of objectively measuring the model performance.

We can see here that logistic regression is a powerful classifier that is able to distinguish between hand-written samples of zero and one.

Exercise 38: Logistic Regression – Multiclass Classifier

In the previous exercise, we examined using logistic regression to classify between one of two groups. Logistic regression, however, can also be used to classify a set of input information to k different groups and it is this multiclass classifier we will be investigating in this exercise. The process for loading the MNIST training and test data is identical to the previous exercise:

1. Load the training/test images and the corresponding labels:

    ```
    with gzip.open('train-images-idx3-ubyte.gz', 'rb') as f:
        magic, size, rows, cols = struct.unpack(">IIII", f.read(16))
        img = np.array(array("B", f.read())).reshape((size, rows, cols))

    with gzip.open('train-labels-idx1-ubyte.gz', 'rb') as f:
        magic, size = struct.unpack(">II", f.read(8))
        labels = np.array(array("B", f.read()))

    with gzip.open('t10k-images-idx3-ubyte.gz', 'rb') as f:
        magic, size, rows, cols = struct.unpack(">IIII", f.read(16))
        img_test = np.array(array("B", f.read())).reshape((size, rows, cols))

    with gzip.open('t10k-labels-idx1-ubyte.gz', 'rb') as f:
        magic, size = struct.unpack(">II", f.read(8))
        labels_test = np.array(array("B", f.read()))
    ```

2. Given that the training data is so large, we will select a subset of the overall data to reduce the training time as well as the system resources required for the training process:

    ```
    np.random.seed(0) # Give consistent random numbers
    selection = np.random.choice(len(img), 5000)
    selected_images = img[selection]
    selected_labels = labels[selection]
    ```

    Note that, in this example, we are using data from all 10 classes, not just classes zero and one, so we are making this example a multiclass classification problem.

3. Again, reshape the input data in vector form for later use:

   ```
   selected_images = selected_images.reshape((-1, rows * cols))
   selected_images.shape
   ```

   The output will be as follows:

   ```
   In [8]:  1  selected_images = selected_images.reshape((-1, rows * cols))
            2  selected_images.shape

   Out[8]: (5000, 784)
   ```

   Figure 4.23: Reshaping the data

4. The next cell is intentionally commented out. Leave this code commented out for the moment:

   ```
   # selected_images = selected_images / 255.0
   # img_test = img_test / 255.0
   ```

5. Construct the logistic model. There are a few extra arguments, as follows: the **lbfgs** value for **solver** is geared up for multiclass problems, with additional **max_iter** iterations required for converging on a solution. The **multi_class** argument is set to **multinomial** to calculate the loss over the entire probability distribution:

   ```
   model = LogisticRegression(solver='lbfgs', multi_class='multinomial', max_iter=500, tol=0.1)
   model.fit(X=selected_images, y=selected_labels)
   ```

   The output will be as follows:

   ```
   Out[7]: LogisticRegression(C=1.0, class_weight=None, dual=False, fit_intercept=True,
                      intercept_scaling=1, max_iter=500, multi_class='multinomial',
                      n_jobs=None, penalty='l2', random_state=None, solver='lbfgs',
                      tol=0.1, verbose=0, warm_start=False)
   ```

   Figure 4.24: Logistic regression model

   > **Note**
   >
   > Refer to the documentation at https://scikit-learn.org/stable/modules/generated/sklearn.linear_model.LogisticRegression.html for more information on the arguments.

6. Determine the accuracy score against the training set:

   ```
   model.score(X=selected_images, y=selected_labels)
   ```

   The output will be:

   ```
   In [10]:   1  model.score(X=selected_images, y=selected_labels)
   Out[10]: 1.0
   ```

   Figure 4.25: Model score

7. Determine the first two predictions for the training set and plot the images with the corresponding predictions:

   ```
   model.predict(selected_images)[:2]
   ```

   ```
   Out[9]: array([4, 1], dtype=uint8)
   ```

   Figure 4.26: Model score predicted values

8. Show the images for the first two samples of the training set to see whether we are correct:

   ```
   plt.subplot(1, 2, 1)
   plt.imshow(selected_images[0].reshape((28, 28)), cmap='gray');
   plt.axis('off');
   plt.subplot(1, 2, 2)
   plt.imshow(selected_images[1].reshape((28, 28)), cmap='gray');
   plt.axis('off');
   ```

   The output will be as follows:

   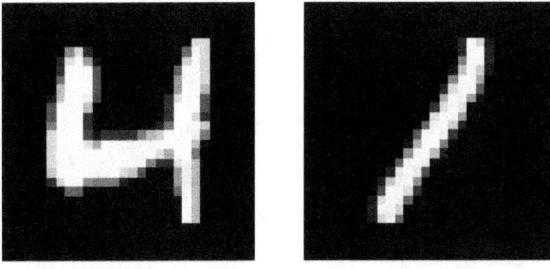

   Figure 4.27: Images plotted using prediction

9. Again, print out the probability scores provided by the model for the first sample of the training set. Confirm that there are 10 different values for each of the 10 classes in the set:

```
model.predict_proba(selected_images)[0]
```

The output will be as follows:

```
Out[11]: array([2.96442210e-43, 1.48526160e-86, 6.42369611e-35, 4.47099135e-69,
                1.00000000e+00, 4.86942544e-54, 4.59375153e-37, 2.07618567e-50,
                5.98339087e-32, 1.31118343e-38])
```

Figure 4.28: Array of predicted values

Notice that, in the probability array of the first sample, the fifth (index four) sample is the highest probability, thus indicating a prediction of four.

10. Compute the accuracy of the model against the test set. This will provide a reasonable estimate of the model's *in the wild* performance, as it has never seen the data in the test set. It is expected that the accuracy rate of the test set will be slightly lower than the training set, given that the model has not been exposed to this data:

```
model.score(X=img_test.reshape((-1, rows * cols)), y=labels_test)
```

The output will be as follows:

```
Out[12]: 0.878
```

Figure 4.29: Model score

When checked against the test set, the model produced accuracy of 87.8%. When applying a test set, a performance drop is expected, as this is the very first time the model has seen these samples; while, during training, the training set was repeatedly shown to the model.

11. Find the cell with the commented-out code, as shown in *step four*. Uncomment the code in this cell:

```
selected_images = selected_images / 255.0
img_test = img_test / 255.0
```

This cell simply scales all the image values to between zero and one. Grayscale images are comprised of pixels with values between and including 0 – 255, where 0 is black and 255 is white.

12. Click **Restart & Run-All** to rerun the entire notebook.
13. Find the training set error:

    ```
    model.score(X=selected_images, y=selected_labels)
    ```

    We'll get the following score:

    ```
    Out[8]: 0.986
    ```

    Figure 4.30: Training set model score

14. Find the test set error:

    ```
    model.score(X=img_test.reshape((-1, rows * cols)), y=labels_test)
    ```

    We'll get the following score:

    ```
    Out[12]: 0.9002
    ```

    Figure 4.31: Test set model score

What effect did normalizing the images have on the overall performance of the system? The training error is worse! We went from 100% accuracy in the training set to 98.6%. Yes, there was a reduction in the performance of the training set, but an increase in the test set from 87.8% accuracy to 90.02%. The test set performance is of more interest, as the model has not seen this data before, and so it is a better representation of the performance than we could expect once the model is in the field. So, why do we get a better result? Again, review *Figure* 4.13, and notice the shape of the curve as it approaches and . The curve saturates or flattens at almost zero and almost one. So, if we use an image (or x values) of between 0 and 255, the class probability defined by the logistic function is well within this flat region of the curve. Predictions within this region are highly unlikely to change very much, as they will need to have very large changes in x values for any meaningful change in y. Scaling the images to be between zero and one initially puts the predictions closer to $p(x) = 0.5$, and so, changes in x can have a bigger impact on the value for y. This allows for more sensitive predictions and results in getting a couple of predictions in the training set wrong, but more in the test set right. It is recommended, for your logistic regression models, that you scale the input values to be between either zero and one or negative-one and one prior to training and testing.

The following function will scale values of a NumPy array between negative-one and one with a mean of approximately zero:

```
def scale_input(x):
    mean_x = x.mean()
    x = x - mean_x
    max_x = x / no.max(abs(x))
    return x
```

Activity 11: Linear Regression Classifier – Two-Class Classifier

In this activity, we will build a two-class linear regression-based classifier using the MNIST dataset to classify between two digits: zero and one.

The steps to be performed are as follows:

1. Import the required dependencies:

   ```
   import struct
   import numpy as np
   import gzip
   import urllib.request
   import matplotlib.pyplot as plt
   from array import array
   from sklearn.linear_model import LinearRegression
   ```

2. Load the MNIST data into memory.

3. Visualize a sample of the data.

4. Construct a linear classifier model to classify the digits zero and one. The model we are going to create is to determine whether the samples are either the digits zero or one. To do this, we first need to select only those samples.

5. Visualize the selected information with images of one sample of zero and one sample of one.

6. In order to provide the image information to the model, we must first flatten the data out so that each image is 1 x 784 pixels in shape.

7. Let's construct the model; use the **LinearRegression** API and call the **fit** function.

8. Determine the R^2 score against the training set.

9. Determine the label predictions for each of the training samples, using a threshold of 0.5. Values greater than 0.5 classify as one; values less than or equal to 0.5 classify as zero.

10. Compute the classification accuracy of the predicted training values versus the ground truth.

11. Compare the performance against the test set.

> **Note**
>
> The solution for this activity can be found on page 352.

Activity 12: Iris Classification Using Logistic Regression

In this activity, we will be using the well-known Iris Species dataset (available at https://en.wikipedia.org/wiki/Iris_flower_data_set or on GitHub at https://github.com/TrainingByPackt/Supervised-Learning-with-Python) created in 1936 by botanist, Ronald Fisher. The dataset contains sepal and petal length and width measurements for three different iris flower species: iris setosa, iris versicolor, and iris virginica. In this activity, we will use the measurements provided in the dataset to classify the different flower species.

The steps to be performed are as follows:

1. Import the required packages. For this activity, we will require the pandas package for loading the data, the Matplotlib package for plotting, and scikit-learn for creating the logistic regression model. Import all the required packages and relevant modules for these tasks:

    ```
    import pandas as pd
    import matplotlib.pyplot as plt
    from sklearn.linear_model import LogisticRegression
    ```

2. Load the iris dataset using pandas and examine the first five rows.

3. The next step is feature engineering. We need to select the most appropriate features that will provide the most powerful classification model. Plot a number of different features versus the allocated species classifications, for example, sepal length versus petal length and species. Visually inspect the plots and look for any patterns that could indicate separation between each of the species.

4. Select the features by writing the column names in the following list:

    ```
    selected_features = [
        '', # List features here
    ]
    ```

198 | Classification

5. Before we can construct the model, we must first convert the **species** values into labels that can be used within the model. Replace the **Iris-setosa** species string with the value **0**, the **Iris-versicolor** species string with the value **1**, and the **Iris-virginica** species string with the value **2**.

6. Create the model using the **selected_features** and the assigned **species** labels.

7. Compute the accuracy of the model against the training set.

8. Construct another model using your second choice **selected_features** and compare the performance.

9. Construct another model using all available information and compare the performance.

> **Note**
> The solution for this activity can be found on page 357.

Classification Using K-Nearest Neighbors

Now that we are comfortable with creating multiclass classifiers using logistic regression and are getting reasonable performance with these models, we will turn our attention to another type of classifier: the **K-nearest neighbors** (**K-NN**) clustering method of classification. This is a handy method, as it can be used in both supervised classification problems as well as in unsupervised problems.

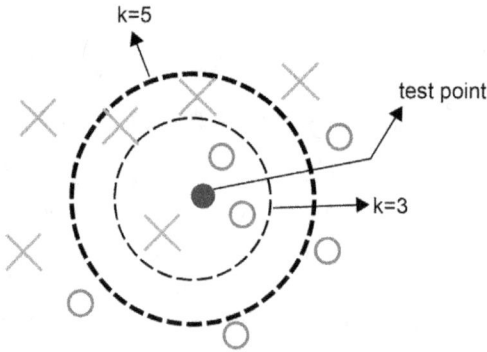

Figure 4.32: Visual representation of K-NN

The solid circle approximately in the center is the test point requiring classification, while the inner circle shows the classification process where K=3 and the outer circle where K=5.

K-NN is one of the simplest "learning" algorithms available for data classification. The use of learning in quotation marks is explicit, as K-NN doesn't really learn from the data and encode these learnings in parameters or weights like other methods, such as logistic regression. K-NN uses instance-based or lazy learning in that it simply stores or memorizes all the training samples and the corresponding classes. It derives its name, K-nearest neighbors, from the fact that, when a test sample is provided to the algorithm for class prediction, it uses a majority vote of the K-nearest points to determine the corresponding class. If we look at *Figure 4.35*, the solid circle is the test point to be classified. If we use K=3, the nearest three points lie within the inner dotted circle, and, in this case, the classification would be a hollow circle. If, however we were to take K=5, the nearest five points lie within the outer dotted circle and the classification would be a cross (three crosses to two hollow circles).

This figure highlights a few characteristics of K-NN classification that should be considered:

- The selection of K is quite important. In this simple example, switching K from three to five flipped the class prediction due to the proximity of both classes. As the final classification is taken by a majority vote, it is often useful to use odd numbers of K to ensure that there is a winner in the voting process. If an even value of K is selected, and a tie in the vote occurs, then there are a number of different methods available for breaking the tie, including:

    Reducing K by one until the tie is broken

    Selecting the class on the basis of the smallest Euclidean distance to the nearest point

    Applying a weighting function to bias the test point toward those neighbors which are closer

- K-NN models have the ability to form extremely complex non-linear boundaries, which can be advantageous in classifying images or datasets with interesting boundaries. Considering that, in *Figure 4.35*, the test point changes from a hollow circle classification to a cross with an increase in K, we can see here that a complex boundary could be formed.

- K-NN models can be highly sensitive to local features in the data, given that the classification process is only really dependent on the nearby points.

- As K-NN models memorize all the training information to make predictions, they can struggle with generalizing to new, unseen data.

There is another variant of K-NN, which, rather than specifying the number of nearest neighbors, specifies the size of the radius around the test point at which to look. This method, known as the **radius neighbors classification**, will not be considered in this chapter, but in understanding K-NN, you will also develop an understanding of radius neighbors classification and how to use the model through scikit-learn.

> **Note**
>
> Our explanation of K-NN classification and the next exercise examines modeling data with two features or two dimensions as it enables simple visualization and a greater understanding of the K-NN modeling process. K-NN classification, like linear and logistic regression, is not limited to use in only two dimensions; it can be applied in N dimensional datasets as well. This will be examined in further detail in *Activity 13: K-NN Multiclass Classifier*, wherein we'll classify MNIST using K-NN. Remember, just because there are too many dimensions to plot, it doesn't mean it cannot be classified with N dimensions.

Exercise 39: K-NN Classification

To allow visualization of the K-NN process, we will turn our attention in this exercise to a different dataset, the well-known Iris dataset. This dataset is provided as part of the accompanying code files for this book:

1. For this exercise, we need to import pandas, Matplotlib, and the **KNeighborsClassifier** of scikit-learn. We will use the shorthand notation **KNN** for quick access:

    ```
    import pandas as pd
    import matplotlib.pyplot as plt
    from sklearn.neighbors import KNeighborsClassifier as KNN
    ```

2. Load the Iris dataset and examine the first five rows:

    ```
    df = pd.read_csv('iris-data.csv')
    df.head()
    ```

The output will be:

	Sepal Length	Sepal Width	Petal Length	Petal Width	Species
0	5.1	3.5	1.4	0.2	Iris-setosa
1	4.9	3.0	1.4	0.2	Iris-setosa
2	4.7	3.2	1.3	0.2	Iris-setosa
3	4.6	3.1	1.5	0.2	Iris-setosa
4	5.0	3.6	1.4	0.2	Iris-setosa

Figure 4.33: First five rows

3. At this stage, we need to choose the most appropriate features from the dataset for use with the classifier. We could simply select all four (sepal and petal, length and width), however, as this exercise is designed to allow visualization of the K-NN process, we will only select sepal length and petal width. Construct a scatterplot for sepal length versus petal width for each of the classes in the dataset with the corresponding species:

```
markers = {
    'Iris-setosa': {'marker': 'x', 'facecolor': 'k', 'edgecolor': 'k'},
    'Iris-versicolor': {'marker': '*', 'facecolor': 'none', 'edgecolor': 'k'},
    'Iris-virginica': {'marker': 'o', 'facecolor': 'none', 'edgecolor': 'k'},
}
plt.figure(figsize=(10, 7))
for name, group in df.groupby('Species'):
    plt.scatter(group['Sepal Length'], group['Petal Width'],
                label=name,
                marker=markers[name]['marker'],
                facecolors=markers[name]['facecolor'],
                edgecolor=markers[name]['edgecolor'])

plt.title('Species Classification Sepal Length vs Petal Width');
plt.xlabel('Sepal Length (mm)');
plt.ylabel('Petal Width (mm)');
plt.legend();
```

The output will be as follows:

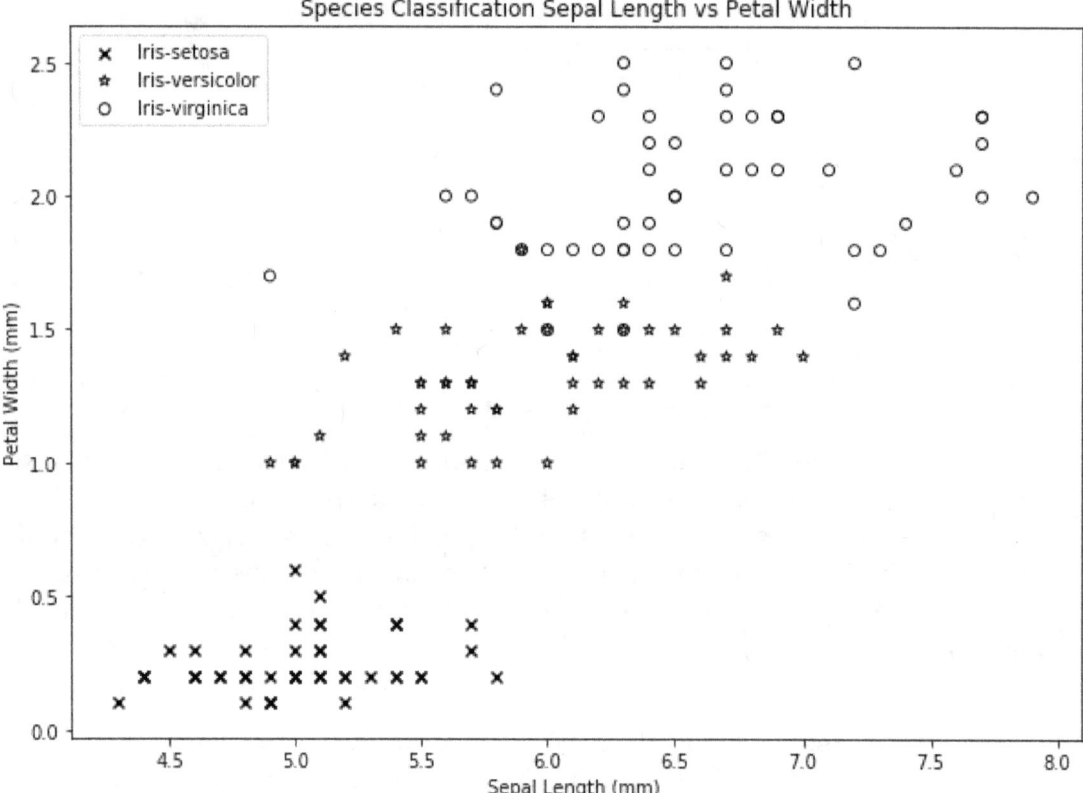

Figure 4.34: Scatterplot of iris data

4. Looking at this graph, we can see that the species are reasonably well separated by the petal width, with the greatest similarity between the Iris versicolor and the Iris virginica species. There are a couple of Iris virginica species points that lie within the Iris versicolor cluster. As a test point for later use, select one of these points at the boundary—sample 134:

```
df_test = df.iloc[134]
df = df.drop([134]) # Remove the sample
df_test
```

The output will be:

```
Sepal Length          6.1
Sepal Width           2.6
Petal Length          5.6
Petal Width           1.4
Species        Iris-virginica
Name: 134, dtype: object
```

Figure 4.35: Boundary sample

5. Plot the data again, highlighting the location of the test sample/point:

   ```
   plt.figure(figsize=(10, 7))
   for name, group in df.groupby('Species'):
       plt.scatter(group['Sepal Length'], group['Petal Width'],
                   label=name,
                   marker=markers[name]['marker'],
                   facecolors=markers[name]['facecolor'],
                   edgecolor=markers[name]['edgecolor'])

   plt.scatter(df_test['Sepal Length'], df_test['Petal Width'], label='Test Sample', c='k', marker='D')
   plt.title('Species Classification Sepal Length vs Petal Width');
   plt.xlabel('Sepal Length (mm)');
   plt.ylabel('Petal Width (mm)');
   plt.legend();
   ```

The output will be as follows:

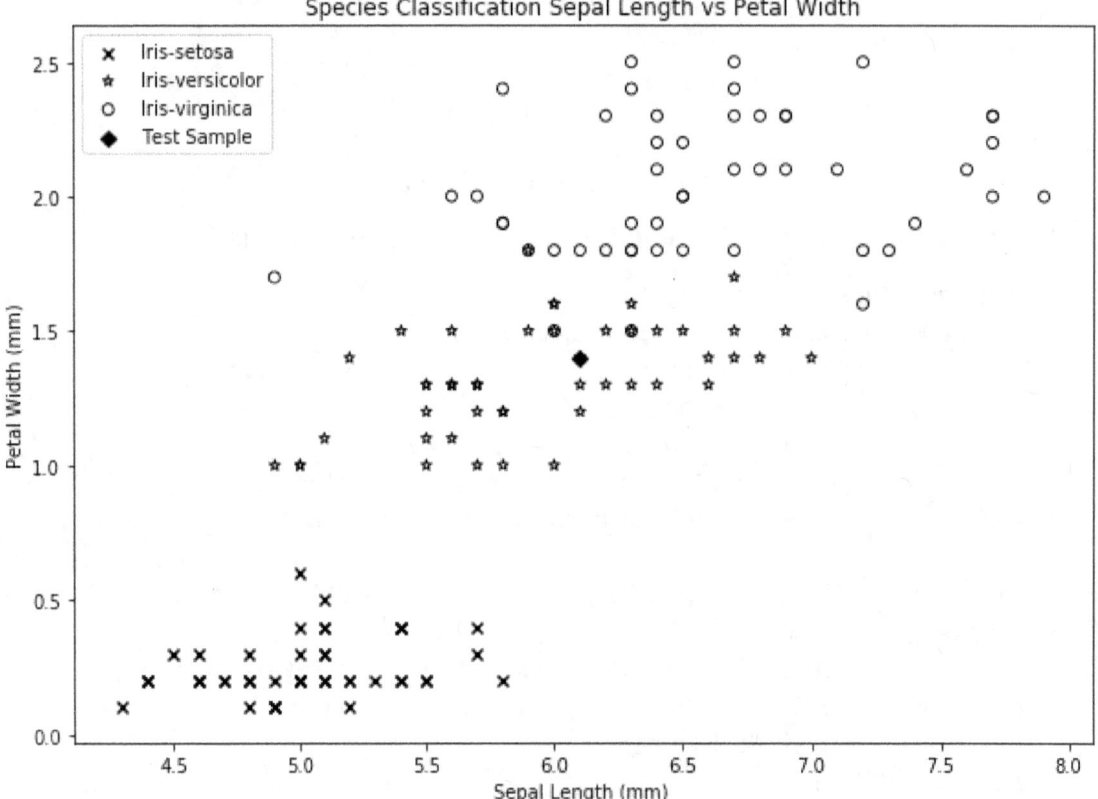

Figure 4.36: Scatterplot with the test sample

6. Construct a K-NN classifier model with K = 3 and fit it to the training data:

```
model = KNN(n_neighbors=3)
model.fit(X=df[['Petal Width', 'Sepal Length']], y=df.Species)
```

The output will be:

```
KNeighborsClassifier(algorithm='auto', leaf_size=30, metric='minkowski',
        metric_params=None, n_jobs=None, n_neighbors=3, p=2,
        weights='uniform')
```

Figure 4.37: K Neighbor classifier

7. Check the performance of the model against the training set:

    ```
    model.score(X=df[['Petal Width', 'Sepal Length']], y=df.Species)
    ```

    The output will show the performance score:

    ```
    In [6]:   1  model.score(X=df[['Petal Width', 'Sepal Length']], y=df.Species)
    Out[6]: 0.9731543624161074
    ```

    Figure 4.38: Model score

    As the accuracy is over 97% on the test set, the next step will be to check the test sample.

8. Predict the species of the test sample:

    ```
    model.predict(df_test[['Petal Width', 'Sepal Length']].values.reshape((-1, 2)))[0]
    ```

    The output will be as follows:

    ```
    In [7]:   1  model.predict(df_test[['Petal Width', 'Sepal Length']].values.reshape((-1, 2)))[0]
    Out[7]: 'Iris-versicolor'
    ```

    Figure 4.39: Predicted test sample

9. Verify it with the actual species of the sample:

    ```
    df.iloc[134].Species
    ```

    The output will be:

    ```
    In [8]:   1  df.iloc[134].Species
    Out[8]: 'Iris-virginica'
    ```

    Figure 4.40: Species of the sample

This prediction is clearly incorrect but is not surprising given the location of the test point on the boundary. What would be helpful would be to know where the boundary for the model is drawn. We will draw this boundary in the next exercise.

Exercise 40: Visualizing K-NN Boundaries

To visualize the decision boundaries produced by the K-NN classifier, we need to sweep over the prediction space, that is, the minimum and maximum values for petal width and sepal length, and determine the classifications made by the model at those points. Once we have this sweep, we can then plot the classification decisions made by the model.

1. Import all the relevant packages. We will also need NumPy for this exercise:

    ```
    import numpy as np
    import pandas as pd
    import matplotlib.pyplot as plt
    from matplotlib.colors import ListedColormap
    from sklearn.neighbors import KNeighborsClassifier as KNN
    ```

2. Load the Iris dataset into a pandas DataFrame:

    ```
    df = pd.read_csv('iris-data.csv')
    df.head()
    ```

    The output will be:

	Sepal Length	Sepal Width	Petal Length	Petal Width	Species
0	5.1	3.5	1.4	0.2	Iris-setosa
1	4.9	3.0	1.4	0.2	Iris-setosa
2	4.7	3.2	1.3	0.2	Iris-setosa
3	4.6	3.1	1.5	0.2	Iris-setosa
4	5.0	3.6	1.4	0.2	Iris-setosa

    Figure 4.41: First five rows

3. While we could use the species strings to create the model in the previous exercise, in plotting the decision boundaries, it would be more useful to map the species to separate integer values. To do this, create a list of the labels for later reference and iterate through this list, replacing the existing label with the corresponding index in the list:

```
labelled_species = [
    'Iris-setosa',
    'Iris-versicolor',
    'Iris-virginica',
]

for idx, label in enumerate(labelled_species):
    df.Species = df.Species.replace(label, idx)
df.head()
```

The output will be as follows:

	Sepal Length	Sepal Width	Petal Length	Petal Width	Species
0	5.1	3.5	1.4	0.2	0
1	4.9	3.0	1.4	0.2	0
2	4.7	3.2	1.3	0.2	0
3	4.6	3.1	1.5	0.2	0
4	5.0	3.6	1.4	0.2	0

Figure 4.42: First five rows

Notice the use of the **enumerate** function in the **for** loop definition. When iterating through the **for** loop, the **enumerate** function provides the index of the value in the list as well as the value itself through each iteration. We assign the index of the value to the **idx** variable and the value to **label**. Using **enumerate** in this way provides an easy way to replace the species strings with a unique integer label.

4. Construct a K-NN classification model, again using three nearest neighbors and fit to the sepal length and petal width with the newly labeled species data:

   ```
   model = KNN(n_neighbors=3)
   model.fit(X=df[['Sepal Length', 'Petal Width']], y=df.Species)
   ```

   The output will be as follows:

   ```
   KNeighborsClassifier(algorithm='auto', leaf_size=30, metric='minkowski',
             metric_params=None, n_jobs=None, n_neighbors=3, p=2,
             weights='uniform')
   ```

   Figure 4.43: K Neighbors classifier

5. To visualize our decision boundaries, we need to create a mesh or range of predictions across the information space, that is, all values of sepal length and petal width. Starting with 1mm less than the minimum for both the petal width and sepal length, and finishing at 1mm more than the maximum for petal width and sepal length, use the **arange** function of NumPy to create a range of values between these limits in increments of 0.1 (spacing):

   ```
   spacing = 0.1 # 0.1mm
   petal_range = np.arange(df['Petal Width'].min() - 1, df['Petal Width'].max() + 1, spacing)
   sepal_range = np.arange(df['Sepal Length'].min() - 1, df['Sepal Length'].max() + 1, spacing)
   ```

6. Use the NumPy **meshgrid** function to combine the two ranges into a grid:

   ```
   xx, yy = np.meshgrid(sepal_range, petal_range) # Create the mesh
   ```

   Check out **xx**:

   ```
   xx
   ```

   The output will be:

   ```
   array([[3.3, 3.4, 3.5, ..., 8.6, 8.7, 8.8],
          [3.3, 3.4, 3.5, ..., 8.6, 8.7, 8.8],
          [3.3, 3.4, 3.5, ..., 8.6, 8.7, 8.8],
          ...,
          [3.3, 3.4, 3.5, ..., 8.6, 8.7, 8.8],
          [3.3, 3.4, 3.5, ..., 8.6, 8.7, 8.8],
          [3.3, 3.4, 3.5, ..., 8.6, 8.7, 8.8]])
   ```

   Figure 4.44: Array of meshgrid xx values

Check out **yy**:

> yy

The output will be:

```
array([[-0.9, -0.9, -0.9, ..., -0.9, -0.9, -0.9],
       [-0.8, -0.8, -0.8, ..., -0.8, -0.8, -0.8],
       [-0.7, -0.7, -0.7, ..., -0.7, -0.7, -0.7],
       ...,
       [ 3.2,  3.2,  3.2, ...,  3.2,  3.2,  3.2],
       [ 3.3,  3.3,  3.3, ...,  3.3,  3.3,  3.3],
       [ 3.4,  3.4,  3.4, ...,  3.4,  3.4,  3.4]])
```

Figure 4.45: Array of meshgrid yy values

7. Concatenate the mesh into a single NumPy array using **np.c_**:

   ```
   pred_x = np.c_[xx.ravel(), yy.ravel()] # Concatenate the results
   pred_x
   ```

   We'll get the following output:

```
array([[ 3.3, -0.9],
       [ 3.4, -0.9],
       [ 3.5, -0.9],
       ...,
       [ 8.6,  3.4],
       [ 8.7,  3.4],
       [ 8.8,  3.4]])
```

Figure 4.46: Array of predicted values

While this function call looks a little mysterious, it simply concatenates the two separate arrays together (refer to https://docs.scipy.org/doc/numpy/reference/generated/numpy.c_.html) and is shorthand for concatenate.

8. Produce the class predictions for the mesh:

   ```
   pred_y = model.predict(pred_x).reshape(xx.shape)
   pred_y
   ```

   We'll get the following output:

   ```
   array([[0, 0, 0, ..., 1, 1, 2],
          [0, 0, 0, ..., 1, 1, 2],
          [0, 0, 0, ..., 1, 2, 2],
          ...,
          [2, 2, 2, ..., 2, 2, 2],
          [2, 2, 2, ..., 2, 2, 2],
          [2, 2, 2, ..., 2, 2, 2]])
   ```

   Figure 4.47: Array of predicted y values

9. To consistently visualize the boundaries, we will need two sets of consistent colors; a lighter set of colors for the decision boundaries and a darker set of colors for the points of the training set themselves. Create two **ListedColormaps**:

   ```
   # Create color maps
   cmap_light = ListedColormap(['#F6A56F', '#6FF6A5', '#A56FF6'])
   cmap_bold = ListedColormap(['#E6640E', '#0EE664', '#640EE6'])
   ```

10. To highlight the decision boundaries, first plot the training data according to the iris species, using the **cmap_bold** color scheme and different markers for each of the different species:

    ```
    markers = {
        'Iris-setosa': {'marker': 'x', 'facecolor': 'k', 'edgecolor': 'k'},
        'Iris-versicolor': {'marker': '*', 'facecolor': 'none', 'edgecolor': 'k'},
        'Iris-virginica': {'marker': 'o', 'facecolor': 'none', 'edgecolor': 'k'},
    }
    plt.figure(figsize=(10, 7))
    for name, group in df.groupby('Species'):
        species = labelled_species[name]
        plt.scatter(group['Sepal Length'], group['Petal Width'],
                    c=cmap_bold.colors[name],
                    label=labelled_species[name],
                    marker=markers[species]['marker']
                    )
    ```

```
plt.title('Species Classification Sepal Length vs Petal Width');
plt.xlabel('Sepal Length (mm)');
plt.ylabel('Petal Width (mm)');
plt.legend();
```

The output will be as follows:

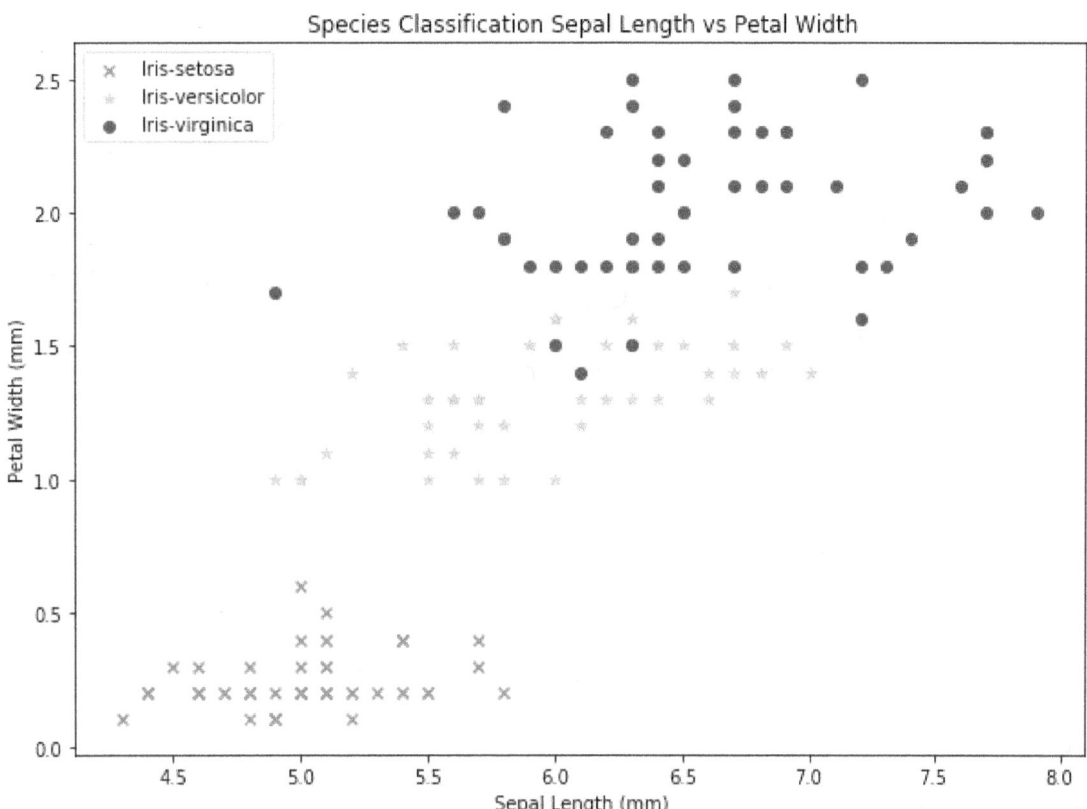

Figure 4.48: Scatterplot with highlighted decision boundaries

11. Using the prediction mesh made previously, plot the decision boundaries in addition to the training data:

    ```
    plt.figure(figsize=(10, 7))
    plt.pcolormesh(xx, yy, pred_y, cmap=cmap_light);
    plt.scatter(df['Sepal Length'], df['Petal Width'], c=df.Species,
    cmap=cmap_bold, edgecolor='k', s=20);
    plt.title('Species Decision Boundaries Sepal Length vs Petal Width');
    plt.xlabel('Sepal Length (mm)');
    plt.ylabel('Petal Width (mm)');
    ```

    The output will be as follows:

    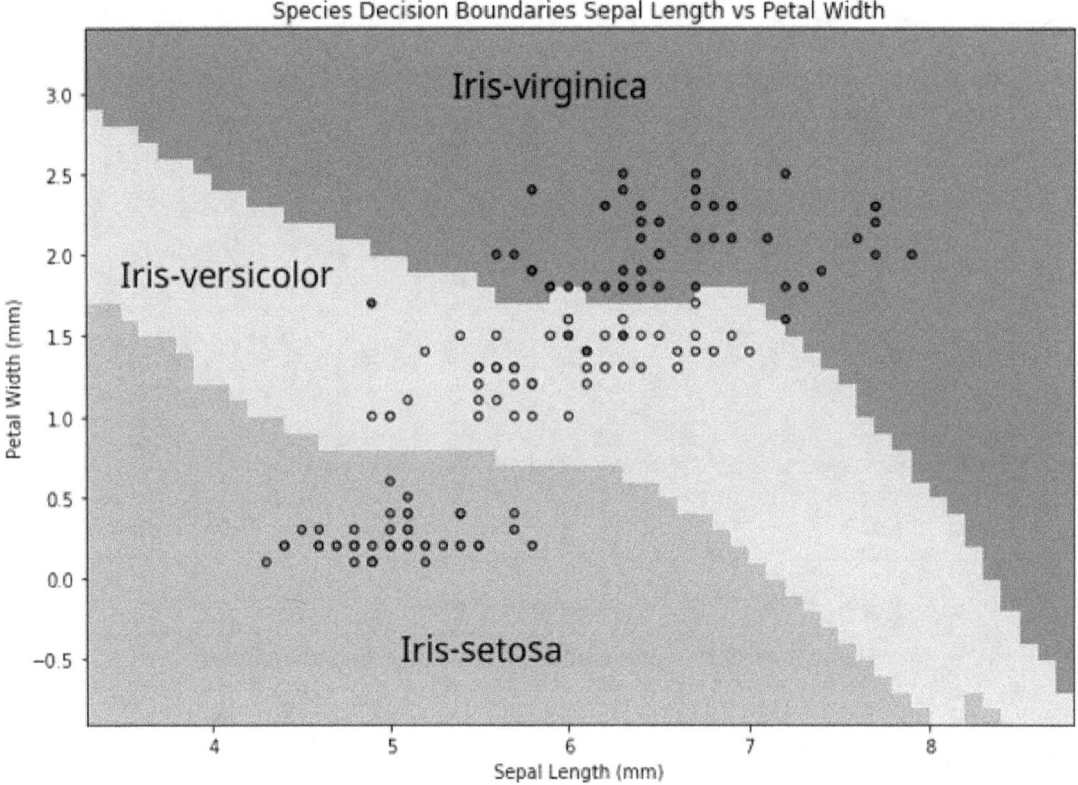

    Figure 4.49: The decision boundaries

    > **Note**
    >
    > *Figure 4.49* has been modified for grayscale print and has additional labels, indicating the prediction boundaries of the classes.

Activity 13: K-NN Multiclass Classifier

In this activity, we will use the K-NN model to classify the MNIST dataset into 10 different digit-based classes.

The steps to be performed are as follows:

1. Import the following packages:

    ```
    import struct
    import numpy as np
    import gzip
    import urllib.request
    import matplotlib.pyplot as plt
    from array import array
    from sklearn.neighbors import KNeighborsClassifier as KNN
    ```

2. Load the MNIST data into memory. First the training images, then the training labels, then the test images, and finally, the test labels.

3. Visualize a sample of the data.

4. Construct a K-NN classifier, with three nearest neighbors to classify the MNIST dataset. Again, to save processing power, randomly sample 5,000 images for use in training.

5. In order to provide the image information to the model, we must first flatten the data out so that each image is 1 x 784 pixels in shape.

6. Build the three-neighbor KNN model and fit the data to the model. Note that, in this activity, we are providing 784 features or dimensions to the model, not simply 2.

7. Determine the score against the training set.

8. Display the first two predictions for the model against the training data.

9. Compare the performance against the test set.

> **Note**
>
> The solution for this activity can be found on page 360.

Classification Using Decision Trees

The final classification method that we will be examining in this chapter is **decision trees**, which have found particular use in applications such as natural language processing. There are a number of different machine learning algorithms that fall within the overall umbrella of decision trees, such as ID3, CART, and the powerful random forest classifiers (covered in *Chapter 5, Ensemble Modeling*). In this chapter, we will investigate the use of the ID3 method in classifying categorical data, and we will use the scikit-learn CART implementation as another means of classifying the Iris dataset. So, what exactly are decision trees?

As the name suggests, decision trees are a learning algorithm that apply a sequential series of decisions based on input information to make the final classification. Recalling your childhood biology class, you may have used a process similar to decision trees in the classification of different types of animals via dichotomous keys. Just like the example dichotomous key shown in *Figure 4.50*, decision trees aim to classify information following the result of a number of decision or question steps:

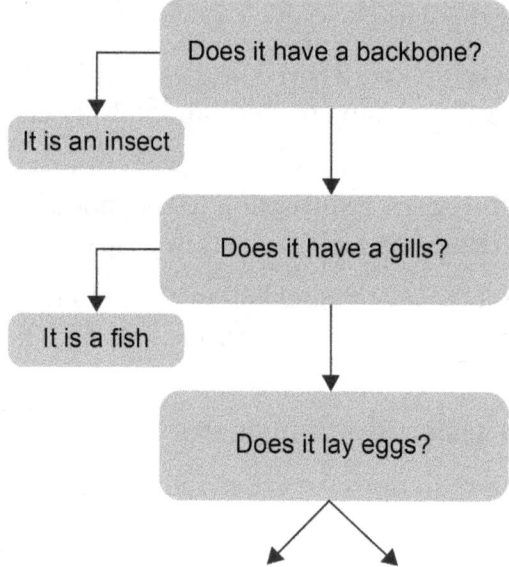

Figure 4.50: Animal classification using dichotomous key

Depending upon the decision tree algorithm being used, the implementation of the decision steps may vary slightly, but we will be considering the implementation of the ID3 algorithm specifically. The **Iterative Dichotomiser 3** (**ID3**) algorithm aims to classify the data on the basis of each decision providing the largest information gain. To further understand this design, we also need to understand two additional concepts: entropy and information gain.

> **Note**
>
> The ID3 algorithm was first proposed by the Australian researcher Ross Quinlan in 1985 (https://doi.org/10.1007/BF00116251).

- **Entropy**: In the context of information theory, entropy is the average rate at which information is provided by a random source of data. Mathematically speaking, this entropy is defined as:

$$H(s) = - \sum_i P_i \log P_i$$

Figure 4.51: Entropy equation

In this scenario, when the random source of data produces a low probability value, the event carries more information, as it is unexpected compared to when a high-probability event occurs.

- **Information gain**: Somewhat related to entropy is the amount of information gained about a random variable by observing another random variable. Given a dataset, S, and an attribute to observe, a, the information gain is defined mathematically as:

$$IG(S, a) = H(S) - H(S|a) = H(S) - \sum_{t \in T} p(t) H(t)$$

Figure 4.52: Information gain equation

The information gain of dataset S, for attribute a, is equal to the entropy of S minus the entropy of S conditional on attribute a, or the entropy of dataset S minus the proportion of elements in t to the elements in S, times the entropy of t, where t is one of the categories in attribute a.

216 | Classification

If at first you find the mathematics here a little daunting, don't worry, for it is far simpler than it seems. To clarify the ID3 process, we will walk through the process using the same dataset as was provided by Quinlan in the original paper.

Exercise 41: ID3 Classification

In the original paper, Quinlan provided a small dataset of 10 weather observation samples labeled with either **P** to indicate that the weather was suitable for, say, a Saturday morning game of cricket, or baseball for our North American friends. If the weather was not suitable for a game, label **N** was provided. The example dataset described in the paper will be created in the exercise.

1. In a Jupyter notebook, create a pandas DataFrame of the following training set:

   ```
   df = pd.DataFrame()
   df['Outlook'] = [
       'sunny', 'sunny', 'overcast', 'rain', 'rain', 'rain',
       'overcast', 'sunny', 'sunny', 'rain', 'sunny',
       'overcast', 'overcast', 'rain'
   ]
   df['Temperature'] = [
       'hot', 'hot', 'hot', 'mild', 'cool', 'cool', 'cool',
       'mild', 'cool', 'mild', 'mild', 'mild', 'hot', 'mild',
   ]
   df['Humidity'] = [
       'high', 'high', 'high', 'high', 'normal', 'normal', 'normal',
       'high', 'normal', 'normal', 'normal', 'high', 'normal', 'high'
   ]
   df['Windy'] = [
       'Weak', 'Strong', 'Weak', 'Weak', 'Weak', 'Strong', 'Strong', 'Weak',
   'Weak', 'Weak',
       'Strong', 'Strong', 'Weak', 'Strong'
   ]
   df['Decision'] = [
       'N', 'N', 'P', 'P', 'P', 'N', 'P', 'N', 'P', 'P',
       'P', 'P', 'P', 'N'
   ]
   df
   ```

The output will be as follows:

	Outlook	Temperature	Humidity	Windy	Decision
0	sunny	hot	high	Weak	N
1	sunny	hot	high	Strong	N
2	overcast	hot	high	Weak	P
3	rain	mild	high	Weak	P
4	rain	cool	normal	Weak	P
5	rain	cool	normal	Strong	N
6	overcast	cool	normal	Strong	P
7	sunny	mild	high	Weak	N
8	sunny	cool	normal	Weak	P
9	rain	mild	normal	Weak	P
10	sunny	mild	normal	Strong	P
11	overcast	mild	high	Strong	P
12	overcast	hot	normal	Weak	P
13	rain	mild	high	Strong	N

Figure 4.53: Pandas DataFrame

2. In the original paper, the ID3 algorithm starts by taking a small sample of the training set at random and fitting the tree to this window. This can be a useful method for large datasets, but given that ours is quite small, we will simply start with the entire training set. The first step is to calculate the entropy for the **Decision** column, where there are two possible values, or classes, **P** and **N**:

```
# Probability of P
p_p = len(df.loc[df.Decision == 'P']) / len(df)

# Probability of N
p_n = len(df.loc[df.Decision == 'N']) / len(df)

entropy_decision = -p_n * np.log2(p_n) - p_p * np.log2(p_p)
print(f'H(S) = {entropy_decision:0.4f}')
```

We'll get the following output:

$$H(S) = 0.9403$$

Figure 4.54: Entropy decision

3. We will need to repeat this calculation, so wrap it into a function:

```
def f_entropy_decision(data):
    p_p = len(data.loc[data.Decision == 'P']) / len(data)
    p_n = len(data.loc[data.Decision == 'N']) / len(data)
    return -p_n * np.log2(p_n) - p_p * np.log2(p_p)
```

4. The next step is to calculate which attribute provides the highest information gain out of **Outlook**, **Temperature**, **Humidity**, and **Windy**. Starting with the **Outlook** parameter, determine the probability of each decision given sunny, overcast, and rainy conditions. We need to evaluate the following equation:

$$IG(S, a) = H(S) - H(S|a) = H(S) - \sum_{t \in T} p(t) H(t)$$

Figure 4.55: Information gain

Construct this equation in Python using the pandas **groupby** method:

```
IG_decision_Outlook = entropy_decision # H(S)

# Create a string to print out the overall equation
overall_eqn = 'Gain(Decision, Outlook) = Entropy(Decision)'

# Iterate through the values for outlook and compute the probabilities
# and entropy values
for name, Outlook in df.groupby('Outlook'):
    num_p = len(Outlook.loc[Outlook.Decision == 'P'])
    num_n = len(Outlook.loc[Outlook.Decision != 'P'])
    num_Outlook = len(Outlook)
    print(f'p(Decision=P|Outlook={name}) = {num_p}/{num_Outlook}')
    print(f'p(Decision=N|Outlook={name}) = {num_n}/{num_Outlook}')
    print(f'p(Decision|Outlook={name}) = {num_Outlook}/{len(df)}')
    print(f'Entropy(Decision|Outlook={name}) = '\
        f'-{num_p}/{num_Outlook}.log2({num_p}/{num_Outlook}) - '\
        f'{num_n}/{num_Outlook}.log2({num_n}/{num_Outlook})')
```

```
            entropy_decision_outlook = 0

        # Cannot compute log of 0 so add checks
        if num_p != 0:
            entropy_decision_outlook -= (num_p / num_Outlook) \
                * np.log2(num_p / num_Outlook)

        # Cannot compute log of 0 so add checks
        if num_n != 0:
            entropy_decision_outlook -= (num_n / num_Outlook) \
                * np.log2(num_n / num_Outlook)

        IG_decision_Outlook -= (num_Outlook / len(df)) * entropy_decision_
    outlook
        print()
        overall_eqn += f' - p(Decision|Outlook={name}).'
        overall_eqn += f'Entropy(Decision|Outlook={name})'
    print(overall_eqn)
    print(f'Gain(Decision, Outlook) = {IG_decision_Outlook:0.4f}')
```

The output will be as follows:

```
p(Decision=P|Outlook=overcast) = 4/4
p(Decision=N|Outlook=overcast) = 0/4
p(Decision|Outlook=overcast) = 4/14
Entropy(Decision|Outlook=overcast) = -4/4.log2(4/4) - 0/4.log2(0/4)

p(Decision=P|Outlook=rain) = 3/5
p(Decision=N|Outlook=rain) = 2/5
p(Decision|Outlook=rain) = 5/14
Entropy(Decision|Outlook=rain) = -3/5.log2(3/5) - 2/5.log2(2/5)

p(Decision=P|Outlook=sunny) = 2/5
p(Decision=N|Outlook=sunny) = 3/5
p(Decision|Outlook=sunny) = 5/14
Entropy(Decision|Outlook=sunny) = -2/5.log2(2/5) - 3/5.log2(3/5)

Gain(Decision, Outlook) = Entropy(Decision) - p(Decision|Outlook=overcast).Entropy(Decision|Outlook=overcast) - p(Decisi
on|Outlook=rain).Entropy(Decision|Outlook=rain) - p(Decision|Outlook=sunny).Entropy(Decision|Outlook=sunny)
Gain(Decision, Outlook) = 0.2467
```

Figure 4.56: Probabilities entropies and gains

The final gain equation for **Outlook** can be re-written as:

$$G(Decision, Outlook) = H(Decision)$$
$$- p(Decision|Outlook = overcast)H(Decision|Outlook = overcast)$$
$$- p(Decision|Outlook = sunny)H(Decision|Outlook = sunny)$$
$$- p(Decision|Outlook = rain)H(Decision|Outlook = rain)$$

Figure 4.57: Equation of information gain

5. We need to repeat this process quite a few times, so wrap it in a function for ease of use later:

```
def IG(data, column, ent_decision=entropy_decision):
    IG_decision = ent_decision
    for name, temp in data.groupby(column):
        p_p = len(temp.loc[temp.Decision == 'P']) / len(temp)
        p_n = len(temp.loc[temp.Decision != 'P']) / len(temp)

        entropy_decision = 0

        if p_p != 0:
            entropy_decision -= (p_p) * np.log2(p_p)

        if p_n != 0:
            entropy_decision -= (p_n) * np.log2(p_n)

        IG_decision -= (len(temp) / len(df)) * entropy_decision
    return IG_decision
```

6. Repeat this process for each of the other columns to compute the corresponding information gain:

```
for col in df.columns[:-1]:
    print(f'Gain(Decision, {col}) = {IG(df, col):0.4f}')
```

We'll get the following output:

```
Gain(Decision, Outlook) = 0.2467
Gain(Decision, Temperature) = 0.0292
Gain(Decision, Humidity) = 0.1518
Gain(Decision, Windy) = 0.0481
```

Figure 4.58: Gains

7. This information provides the first decision of the tree. We want to split on the maximum information gain, thus we split on **Outlook**. Look at the data splitting on **Outlook**:

```
for name, temp in df.groupby('Outlook'):
    print('-' * 15)
    print(name)
    print('-' * 15)
    print(temp)
    print('-' * 15)
```

The output will be as follows:

```
---------------
overcast
---------------
    Outlook  Temperature  Humidity  Windy   Decision
2   overcast        hot      high   Weak       P
6   overcast       cool    normal   Strong     P
11  overcast       mild      high   Strong     P
12  overcast        hot    normal   Weak       P
---------------
---------------
rain
---------------
    Outlook  Temperature  Humidity  Windy   Decision
3   rain           mild      high   Weak       P
4   rain           cool    normal   Weak       P
5   rain           cool    normal   Strong     N
9   rain           mild    normal   Weak       P
13  rain           mild      high   Strong     N
---------------
---------------
sunny
---------------
    Outlook  Temperature  Humidity  Windy   Decision
0   sunny           hot      high   Weak       N
1   sunny           hot      high   Strong     N
7   sunny          mild      high   Weak       N
8   sunny          cool    normal   Weak       P
10  sunny          mild    normal   Strong     P
---------------
```

Figure 4.59: Information gain

Notice that all the overcast records have a decision of **P**. This provides our first terminating leaf of the decision tree. If it is overcast, we are going to play, while if it is rainy or sunny, there is a chance we will not play. The decision tree so far can be represented as in the following figure:

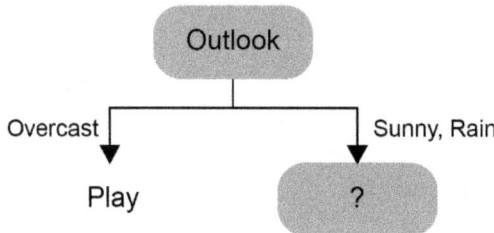

Figure 4.60: Decision tree

> **Note**
>
> This figure was created manually for reference and is not contained in or obtained from the accompanying source code.

8. We now repeat this process, splitting by information gain until all the data is allocated and all branches of the tree terminate. First, remove the overcast samples, as they no longer provide any additional information:

   ```
   df_next = df.loc[df.Outlook != 'overcast']
   df_next
   ```

We'll get the following output:

	Outlook	Temperature	Humidity	Windy	Decision
0	sunny	hot	high	Weak	N
1	sunny	hot	high	Strong	N
3	rain	mild	high	Weak	P
4	rain	cool	normal	Weak	P
5	rain	cool	normal	Strong	N
7	sunny	mild	high	Weak	N
8	sunny	cool	normal	Weak	P
9	rain	mild	normal	Weak	P
10	sunny	mild	normal	Strong	P
13	rain	mild	high	Strong	N

Figure 4.61: Data after removing the overcast samples

9. Now, we will turn our attention to the sunny samples and will rerun the gain calculations to determine the best way to split the sunny information:

   ```
   df_sunny = df_next.loc[df_next.Outlook == 'sunny']
   ```

10. Recompute the entropy for the sunny samples:

    ```
    entropy_decision = f_entropy_decision(df_sunny)
    entropy_decision
    ```

    The output will be:

    ```
    In [32]:  1  entropy_decision = f_entropy_decision(df_sunny)
              2  entropy_decision
    Out[32]:  0.9709505944546686
    ```

    Figure 4.62: Entropy decision

11. Run the gain calculations for the sunny samples:

    ```
    for col in df_sunny.columns[1:-1]:
        print(f'Gain(Decision, {col}) = {IG(df_sunny, col, entropy_decision):0.4f}')
    ```

    The output will be as follows:

    ```
    Gain(Decision, Temperature) = 0.8281
    Gain(Decision, Humidity) = 0.9710
    Gain(Decision, Windy) = 0.6313
    ```

    Figure 4.63: Gains

12. Again, we select the largest gain, which is **Humidity**. Group the data by **Humidity**:

    ```
    for name, temp in df_sunny.groupby('Humidity'):
        print('-' * 15)
        print(name)
        print('-' * 15)
        print(temp)
        print('-' * 15)
    ```

    The output will be:

    ```
    ---------------
    high
    ---------------
       Outlook Temperature Humidity  Windy Decision
    0    sunny         hot     high   Weak        N
    1    sunny         hot     high Strong        N
    7    sunny        mild     high   Weak        N
    ---------------
    ---------------
    normal
    ---------------
       Outlook Temperature Humidity  Windy Decision
    8    sunny        cool   normal   Weak        P
    10   sunny        mild   normal Strong        P
    ---------------
    ```

    Figure 4.64: After grouping data according to humidity

We can see here that we have two terminating leaves in that when the **Humidity** is high there is a decision not to play, and, vice versa, when the **Humidity** is normal, there is the decision to play. So, updating our representation of the decision tree, we have:

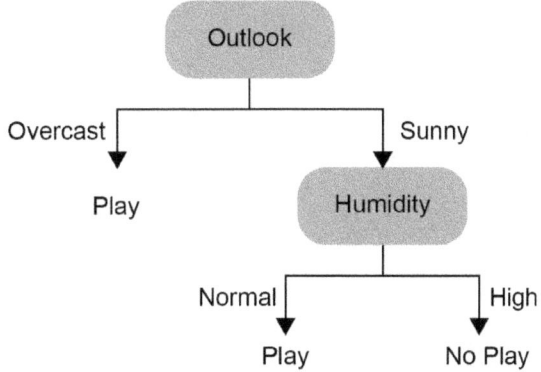

Figure 4.65: Decision tree with two values

13. So, the last set of data that requires classification is the rainy outlook data. Extract only the **rain** data and rerun the entropy calculation:

    ```
    df_rain = df_next.loc[df_next.Outlook == 'rain']
    entropy_decision = f_entropy_decision(df_rain)
    entropy_decision
    ```

    The output will be:

    Out[14]: 0.9709505944546686

    Figure 4.66: Entropy decision

14. Repeat the gain calculation with the **rain** subset:

    ```
    for col in df_rain.columns[1:-1]:
        print(f'Gain(Decision, {col}) = {IG(df_rain, col, entropy_decision):0.4f}')
    ```

    The output will be:

    ```
    Gain(Decision, Temperature) = 0.6313
    Gain(Decision, Humidity) = 0.6313
    Gain(Decision, Windy) = 0.9710
    ```

    Figure 4.67: Gains

15. Again, splitting on the attribute with the largest gain value requires splitting on the **Windy** values. So, group the remaining information by **Windy**:

   ```
   for name, temp in df_rain.groupby('Windy'):
       print('-' * 15)
       print(name)
       print('-' * 15)
       print(temp)
       print('-' * 15)
   ```

   The output will be:

   ```
   ---------------
   Strong
   ---------------
       Outlook Temperature Humidity  Windy Decision
   5      rain        cool   normal Strong        N
   13     rain        mild     high Strong        N
   ---------------
   ---------------
   Weak
   ---------------
       Outlook Temperature Humidity Windy Decision
   3      rain        mild     high  Weak        P
   4      rain        cool   normal  Weak        P
   9      rain        mild   normal  Weak        P
   ---------------
   ```

   Figure 4.68: Data grouped according to Windy

Finally, we have all the terminating leaves required to complete the tree, as splitting on **Windy** provides two sets, all of which indicate either play (**P**) or no-play (**N**) values. Our complete decision tree is as follows:

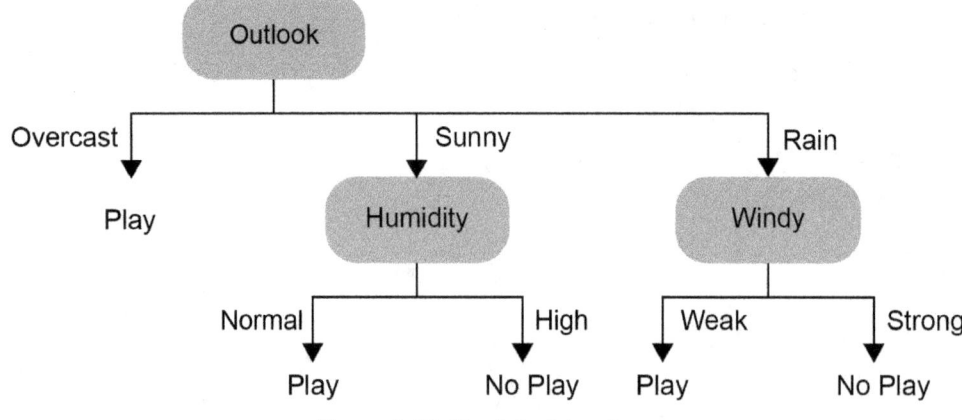

Figure 4.69: Final decision tree

We can see here that decision trees, very much like K-NN models, consume the entire training set to construct the model. So, how do we make predictions with unseen information? Simply follow the tree. Look at the decision being made at each node and apply the data from the unseen sample. The prediction will then end up being the label specified at the terminating leaf. Let's say we had a weather forecast for the upcoming Saturday and we wanted to predict whether we were going to play or not. The weather forecast is as follows:

Attribute	Value
Outlook	Rain
Temperature	Mild
Humidity	Normal
Windy	Strong

Figure 4.70: Weather forecast for upcoming Saturday

The decision tree for this would be as follows (the dashed circles indicate selected leaves in the tree):

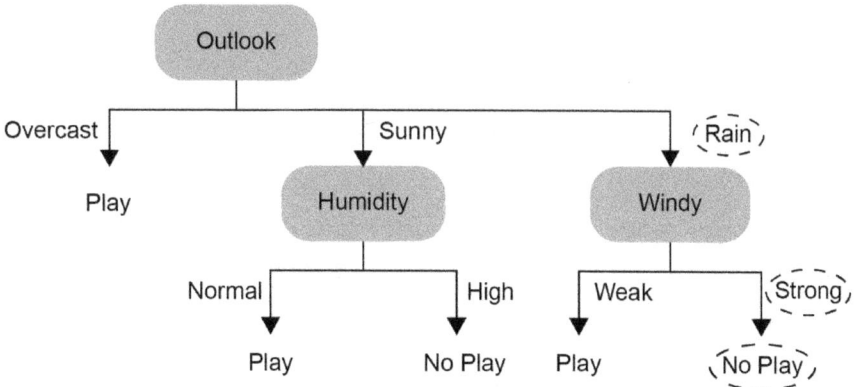

Figure 4.71: Making a new prediction using a decision tree

Now, hopefully, you have a reasonable understanding of the underlying concept of decision trees and the process of making sequential decisions. We have covered one of the first decision tree methodologies in this exercise, but there are certainly more available, and many of the more modern methods, such as random forests, do not suffer as much from overfitting (see *Chapter 5, Ensemble Modeling*, for more information) as ID3. With the principles of decision trees in our toolkit, we will now look at applying a more complicated model using the functionality provided in scikit-learn.

The scikit-learn decision tree methods implement the **CART (Classification and Regression Tree)** method, which provides the ability to use decision trees in both classification and regression problems. CART differs from ID3 in that the decisions are made by comparing the values of features against a calculated value, for example, for the Iris dataset, *is the petal width less than x mm?*

Exercise 42: Iris Classification Using a CART Decision Tree

In this exercise, we will classify the Iris data using scikit-learn's decision tree classifier, which can be used in both classification and regression problems:

1. Import the required packages:

   ```
   import numpy as np
   import pandas as pd
   import matplotlib.pyplot as plt
   from sklearn.tree import DecisionTreeClassifier
   ```

2. Load the Iris dataset:

   ```
   df = pd.read_csv('iris-data.csv')
   df.head()
   ```

   The output will be as follows:

	Sepal Length	Sepal Width	Petal Length	Petal Width	Species
0	5.1	3.5	1.4	0.2	Iris-setosa
1	4.9	3.0	1.4	0.2	Iris-setosa
2	4.7	3.2	1.3	0.2	Iris-setosa
3	4.6	3.1	1.5	0.2	Iris-setosa
4	5.0	3.6	1.4	0.2	Iris-setosa

   Figure 4.72: First five rows

3. Take a random sample of 10 rows to use for testing. Decision trees can overfit the training data, so this will provide an independent measure of the accuracy of the tree:

   ```
   np.random.seed(10)
   samples = np.random.randint(0, len(df), 10)
   df_test = df.iloc[samples]
   df = df.drop(samples)
   ```

4. Fit the model to the training data and check the corresponding accuracy:

   ```
   model = DecisionTreeClassifier()
   model = model.fit(df[['Sepal Length', 'Sepal Width', 'Petal Length', 'Petal Width']], df.Species)
   model.score(df[['Sepal Length', 'Sepal Width', 'Petal Length', 'Petal Width']], df.Species)
   ```

   The output will be as follows:

   ```
   In [4]:  1  model = DecisionTreeClassifier()
            2  model = model.fit(df[['Sepal Length', 'Sepal Width', 'Petal Length', 'Petal Width']], df.Species)
            3  model.score(df[['Sepal Length', 'Sepal Width', 'Petal Length', 'Petal Width']], df.Species)

   Out[4]: 1.0
   ```

   Figure 4.73: Output of the model score

   Our model achieves 100% accuracy on the training set.

5. Check the performance against the test set:

   ```
   model.score(df_test[['Sepal Length', 'Sepal Width', 'Petal Length', 'Petal Width']], df_test.Species)
   ```

   The output will be as follows:

   ```
   In [5]:  1  model.score(df_test[['Sepal Length', 'Sepal Width', 'Petal Length', 'Petal Width']], df_test.Species)

   Out[5]: 1.0
   ```

   Figure 4.74: Output of the model score using df_test

6. One of the great things about decision trees is that we can visually represent the model and see exactly what is going on. Install the required dependency:

   ```
   !conda install python-graphviz
   ```

7. Import the graphing package:

   ```
   import graphviz
   from sklearn.tree import export_graphviz
   ```

8. Plot the model:

   ```
   dot_data = export_graphviz(model, out_file=None)
   graph = graphviz.Source(dot_data)
   graph
   ```

   We'll get the following output:

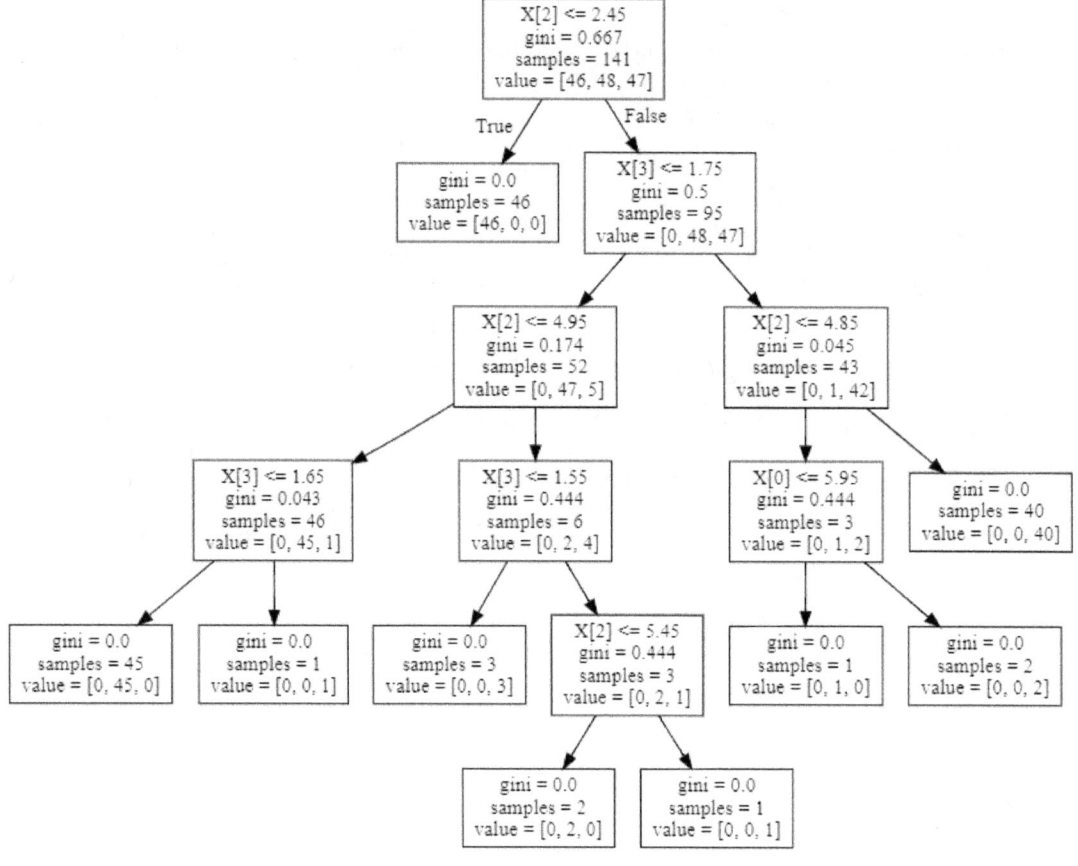

Figure 4.75: Decisions of the CART decision tree

This figure illustrates the decisions of the CART decision tree in the scikit-learn model. The first line of the node is the decision that is made at each step. The first node X[2] <= 2.45 indicates that the training data is split on column two (petal length) on the basis of being less than or equal to 2.45. Those samples with a petal length of less than 2.45 (of which there are 46) are all of the iris setosa class, and, as such, all of a `gini` (a metric similar to information gain) of zero. If the petal length is greater than 2.45, the next decision is whether the petal width (column three) is less than or equal to 1.75mm. This decision/branching process continues until the tree has been exhausted and all terminating leaves have been constructed.

Summary

We covered a number of powerful and extremely useful classification models in this chapter, starting with the use of linear regression as a classifier, then we observed a significant performance increase through the use of the logistic regression classifier. We then moved on to **memorizing** models, such as K-NN, which, while simple to fit, was able to form complex non-linear boundaries in the classification process, even with images as input information into the model. We then finished our introduction to classification problems, looking at decision trees and the ID3 algorithm. We saw how decision trees, like K-NN models, memorize the training data using rules and decision gates to make predictions with quite a high degree of accuracy.

In the next chapter, we will be extending what we have learned in this chapter. It will cover ensemble techniques, including boosting and the very effective random forest method.

5

Ensemble Modeling

Learning Objectives

By the end of the chapter, you will be able to:

- Explain the concepts of bias and variance and how they lead to underfitting and overfitting
- Explain the concepts behind bootstrapping
- Implement a bagging classifier using decision trees
- Implement adaptive boosting and gradient boosting models
- Implement a stacked ensemble using a number of classifiers

This chapter covers bias and variance, and underfitting and overfitting, and then introduces ensemble modeling.

Introduction

In the previous chapters, we discussed the two types of supervised learning problems: regression and classification. We looked at a number of algorithms for each type and delved into how those algorithms worked.

But there are times when these algorithms, no matter how complex they are, just don't seem to perform well on the data that we have. There could be a variety of causes and reasons – perhaps the data is not good enough, perhaps there really is no trend where we are trying to find one, or perhaps the model itself is too complex.

Wait. What? How can a model being *too complex* be a problem? Oh, but it can! If a model is too complex and there isn't enough data, the model could fit so well to the data that it learns even the noise and outliers, which is never what we want.

Oftentimes, where a single complex algorithm can give us a result that is way off, aggregating the results from a group of models can give us a result that's closer to the actual truth. This is because there is a high likelihood that the errors from all the individual models would cancel out when we take them all into account when making a prediction.

This approach to grouping multiple algorithms to give an aggregated prediction is what **ensemble modeling** is based on. The ultimate goal of an ensemble method is to combine several underperforming **base estimators** (that is, individual algorithms) in such a way that the overall performance of the system improves and the **ensemble** of algorithms results in a model that is more robust and can generalize well compared to an individual algorithm.

In this chapter, we'll discuss how building an ensemble model can help us build a robust system that makes accurate predictions without increasing variance. We will start by talking about some reasons a model may not perform well, and then move on to discussing the concepts of bias and variance, as well as overfitting and underfitting. We will introduce ensemble modeling as a solution for these performance issues and discuss different ensemble methods that could be used to overcome different types of problems when it comes to underperforming models.

The chapter will discuss three types of ensemble methods. Namely, bagging, boosting, and stacking. Each of these will be discussed right from the basic theory to discussions on which use cases each type deals with well and which use cases each type might not be a good fit for. This chapter will also walk you through a number of exercises to implement the models using the scikit-learn library in Python.

Exercise 43: Importing Modules and Preparing the Dataset

In this exercise, we'll import all the modules we will need for this chapter and get our dataset in shape for the exercises to come:

1. Import all the modules required to manipulate the data and evaluate the model:

   ```
   import pandas as pd
   import numpy as np

   %matplotlib inline
   import matplotlib.pyplot as plt

   from sklearn.model_selection import train_test_split
   from sklearn.metrics import accuracy_score
   from sklearn.model_selection import KFold
   ```

2. The dataset that we will use in this chapter is the Titanic dataset, which was introduced in the previous chapters as well. Read the dataset and print the first five rows:

   ```
   data = pd.read_csv('titanic.csv')
   data.head()
   ```

   The output is as follows:

	PassengerId	Survived	Pclass	Name	Sex	Age	SibSp	Parch	Ticket	Fare	Cabin	Embarked
0	1	0	3	Braund, Mr. Owen Harris	male	22.0	1	0	A/5 21171	7.2500	NaN	S
1	2	1	1	Cumings, Mrs. John Bradley (Florence Briggs Th...	female	38.0	1	0	PC 17599	71.2833	C85	C
2	3	1	3	Heikkinen, Miss. Laina	female	26.0	0	0	STON/O2. 3101282	7.9250	NaN	S
3	4	1	1	Futrelle, Mrs. Jacques Heath (Lily May Peel)	female	35.0	1	0	113803	53.1000	C123	S
4	5	0	3	Allen, Mr. William Henry	male	35.0	0	0	373450	8.0500	NaN	S

   Figure 5.1: The first five rows

3. In order to make the dataset ready for use, we will add a **preprocess** function, which will preprocess the dataset to get it into a format that is ingestible by the scikit-learn library.

   This chapter assumes that the dataset has already been preprocessed and is ready for use, but we will add a **preprocess** function, which will preprocess the dataset to get it into a format that is ingestible by the **Scikit-learn** library.

   First, we create a **fix_age** function to preprocess the **age** function and get an integer value. If the age is null, the function returns a value of -1 to differentiate it from available values, and if the value is a fraction less than 1, multiply the age value by 100. We then apply this function to the **age** column.

   Then, we convert the **Sex** column into a binary variable with 1 for female and 0 for male values, and subsequently create dummy binary columns for the **Embarked** column using pandas' **get_dummies** function. Following this, we combine the DataFrame containing the dummy columns with the remaining numerical columns to create the final DataFrame, which is returned by the function:

   ```
   def preprocess(data):
       def fix_age(age):
           if np.isnan(age):
               return -1
           elif age < 1:
               return age*100
           else:
               return age

       data.loc[:, 'Age'] = data.Age.apply(fix_age)
       data.loc[:, 'Sex'] = data.Sex.apply(lambda s: int(s == 'female'))

       embarked = pd.get_dummies(data.Embarked, prefix='Emb')
   [['Emb_C','Emb_Q','Emb_S']]
       cols = ['Pclass','Sex','Age','SibSp','Parch','Fare']

       return pd.concat([data[cols], embarked], axis=1).values
   ```

4. Split the dataset into training and validation sets.

   We split the dataset into two parts – one on which we will train the models during the exercises (**train**), and another on which we will make predictions to evaluate the performance of each of those models (**val**). We will use the function we wrote in the previous step to preprocess the training and validation datasets separately.

Here, the `Survived` binary variable is the target variable that determines whether or not the individual in each row survived the sinking of the Titanic, so we create `y_train` and `y_val` as the dependent variable columns from both the splits:

```
train, val = train_test_split(data, test_size=0.2, random_state=11)

x_train = preprocess(train)
y_train = train['Survived'].values

x_val = preprocess(val)
y_val = val['Survived'].values
```

Let's begin.

Overfitting and Underfitting

Let's say we fit a supervised learning algorithm to our data and subsequently use the model to perform a prediction on a hold-out validation set. The performance of this model will be considered to be good based on how well it generalizes, that is, the predictions it makes for data points in an independent validation dataset.

Sometimes we find that the model is not able to make accurate predictions and gives poor performance on the validation data. This poor performance can be the result of a model that is too simple to model the data appropriately, or a model that is too complex to generalize to the validation dataset. In the former case, the model has a **high bias** and results in **underfitting**, while in the latter case, the model has a **high variance** and results in **overfitting**.

Bias

The bias in the prediction of a machine learning model represents the difference between the predicted values and the true values. A model is said to have a high bias if the average predicted values are far off from the true values and is conversely said to have a low bias if the average predicted values are close to the true values.

A high bias indicates that the model cannot capture the complexity in the data and is unable to identify the relevant relationships between the inputs and outputs.

Variance

The variance in prediction of a machine learning model represents how scattered the predicted values are compared to the true values. A model is said to have high variance if the predictions are scattered and unstable and is conversely said to have low variance if the predictions are consistent and not very scattered.

A high variance indicates the model's inability to generalize and make accurate predictions on data points previously unseen by the model:

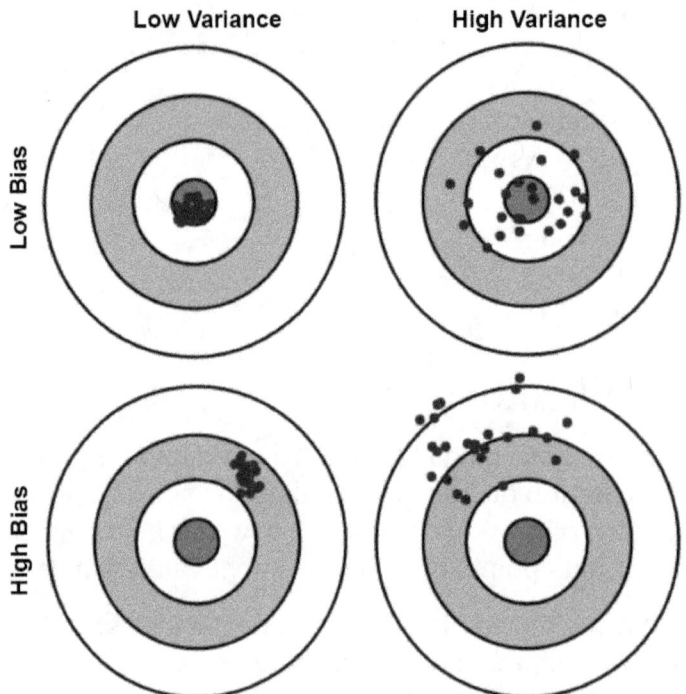

Figure 5.2: Visual representation of data points having high and low bias and variance

Underfitting

Let's say that we fit a simple model on the training dataset, one with a low model complexity, such as a simple linear model. We have fit a function that's able to represent the relationship between the X and Y data points in the training data to some extent, but we see that the training error is still high.

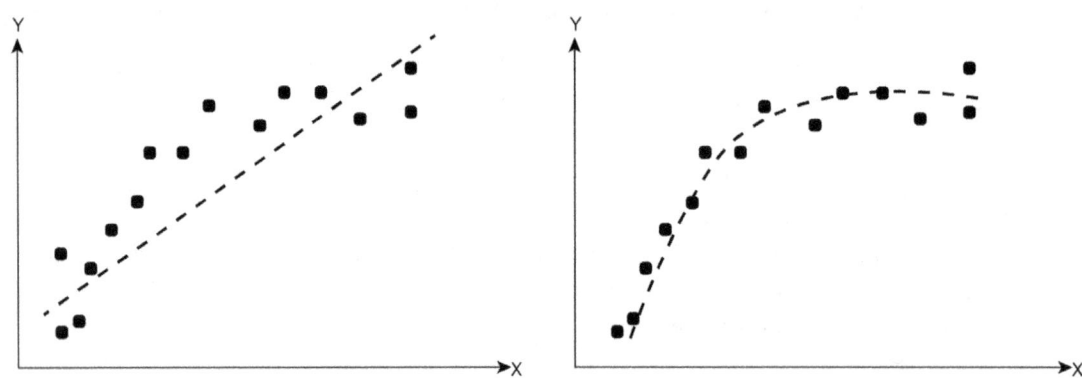

Figure 5.3: Underfitting versus an ideal fit in regression

For example, look at the two regression plots shown in *Figure 5.3*; while the first plot shows a model that fits a straight line to the data, the second plot shows a model that attempts to fit a relatively more complex polynomial to the data, one that seems to represent the mapping between X and Y quite well.

We can say that the first model demonstrates underfitting, since it shows the characteristics of a high bias and low variance; that is, while it is unable to capture the complexity in the mapping between the inputs and outputs, it is consistent in its predictions. This model will have a high prediction error on both the training data and validation data.

Overfitting

Let's say that we trained a highly complex model that is able to make predictions on the training dataset almost perfectly. We have managed to fit a function to represent the relationship between the X and Y data points in the training data such that prediction error on the training data is extremely low:

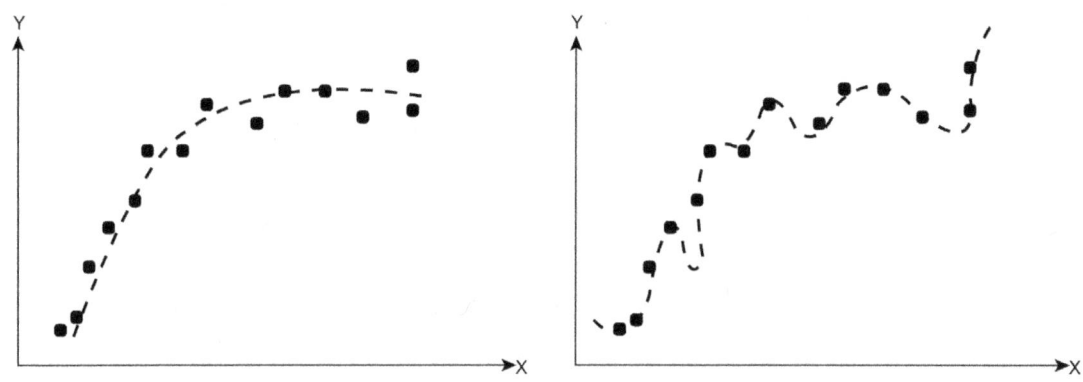

Figure 5.4: An ideal fit versus overfitting in regression

Looking at the two plots in *Figure 5.4*, we can see that the second plot shows a model that attempts to fit a highly complex function to the data points, compared to the plot on the left, which represents the ideal fit for the given data.

It is evident that, when we try to use the first model to predict the Y values for X data points that did not appear in the training set, we will see that the predictions are way off from the corresponding true values. This is a case of overfitting: the phenomenon where the model fits the data *too well* so that it is unable to generalize to new data points, since the model learns even the random noise and outliers in the training data.

This model shows the characteristics of high variance and low bias: while the average predicted values would be close to the true values, they would be quite scattered compared to the true values.

Overcoming the Problem of Underfitting and Overfitting

From the previous sections, we can see that, as we move from an overly simplistic to an overly complex model, we go from having an underfitting model with high bias and low variance to an overfitting model with a low bias and high variance. The goal of any supervised machine learning algorithm is to achieve low bias and low variance and find that sweet spot between underfitting and overfitting. This will help the algorithm generalize well from the training data to validation data points as well, resulting in good prediction performance on data the model has never seen.

The best way to improve performance when the model underfits the data is to increase the model complexity so as to identify the relevant relationships in the data. This can be done by adding new features, or by creating an ensemble of high-bias models. However, in this case, adding more data to train on would not help, as the constraining factor is model complexity and more data will not help to reduce the model's bias.

Overfitting is, however, more difficult to tackle. Here are some common techniques used to overcome the problem posed by overfitting:

- **To get more data**: A highly complex model can easily overfit to a small dataset but not be able to as easily on a larger dataset.
- **Dimensionality Reduction**: Reducing the number of features can help make the model less complex.
- **Regularization**: A new term is added to the cost function to adjust the coefficients (especially the high-degree coefficients in linear regression) toward a low value.
- **Ensemble modeling**: Aggregating the predictions of several overfitting models can effectively eliminate high variance in prediction and perform better than individual models that overfit to the training data.

We will talk in more detail about the nuances and considerations involved in the first three in *Chapter 6, Model Evaluation*; this chapter will focus on different ensemble modeling techniques. Some of the common types of ensembles are:

- **Bagging**: A shorter term for **bootstrap aggregation**, this technique is also used to decrease the model's variance and avoid overfitting. It involves taking a subset of features and data points at a time, training a model on each subset, and subsequently aggregating the results from all the models into a final prediction.
- **Boosting**: This technique is used to reduce bias rather than to reduce variance, and involves incrementally training new models that focus on the misclassified data points in the previous model.

- **Stacking**: The aim of this technique is to increase the predictive power of the classifier, as it involves training multiple models and then using a combiner algorithm to make the final prediction by using the predictions from all these models additional inputs.

Let's start with bagging, and then move on to boosting and stacking.

Bagging

The term bagging is derived from a technique called bootstrap aggregation. In order to implement a successful predictive model, it's important to know in what situation we could benefit from using bootstrapping methods to build ensemble models. In this section, we'll talk about a way to use bootstrap methods to create an ensemble model that minimizes variance and look at how we can build an ensemble of decision trees, that is, the Random Forest algorithm. But what is bootstrapping and how does it help us build robust ensemble models?

Bootstrapping

The bootstrap method refers to random sampling with replacement, that is, drawing multiple samples (each known as a resample) from the dataset consisting of randomly chosen data points, where there can be an overlap in the data points contained in each resample and each data point has an equal probability of being selected from the overall dataset:

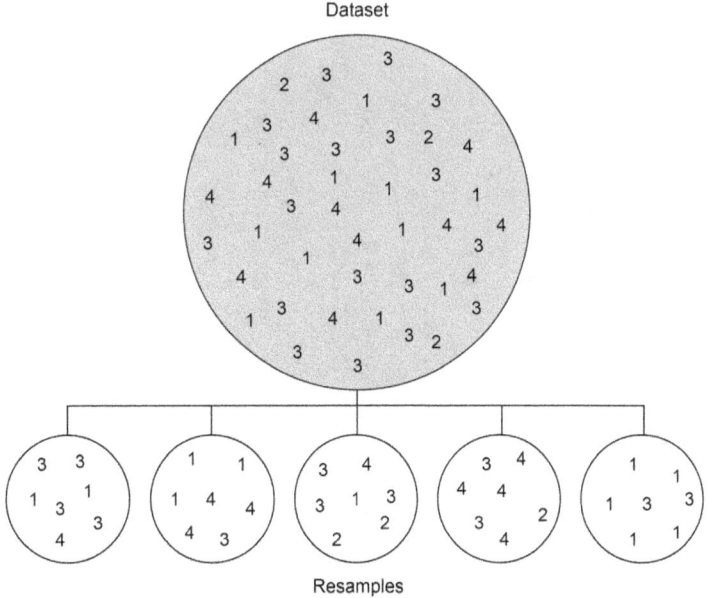

Figure 5.5: Randomly choosing data points

242 | Ensemble Modeling

From the previous diagram, we can see that each of the five bootstrapped samples taken from the primary dataset is different and has different characteristics. As such, training models on each of these resamples would result in different predictions.

The following are the advantages of bootstrapping:

- Each resample can contain different characteristics from that of the entire dataset, allowing us a different perspective of how the data behaves.
- Algorithms that utilize bootstrapping can be more robust and handle unseen data better, especially on smaller datasets that have a tendency to cause overfitting.
- The bootstrap method can test the stability of a prediction by testing models using datasets with different variations and characteristics, resulting in a model that is more robust.

Bootstrap Aggregation

Now that we are aware of what bootstrapping is, what exactly does a bagging ensemble do? It is essentially an ensemble model that generates multiple versions of a predictor on each resample and uses these to get an aggregated predictor. The aggregation step gives us a *meta prediction*, which involves taking an average over the models when predicting a continuous numerical value for regression problems, and also involves taking a vote when predicting a class for classification problems.

The following diagram gives us a visual representation of how a bagging estimator is built from the bootstrap sampling shown in *Figure 5.5*:

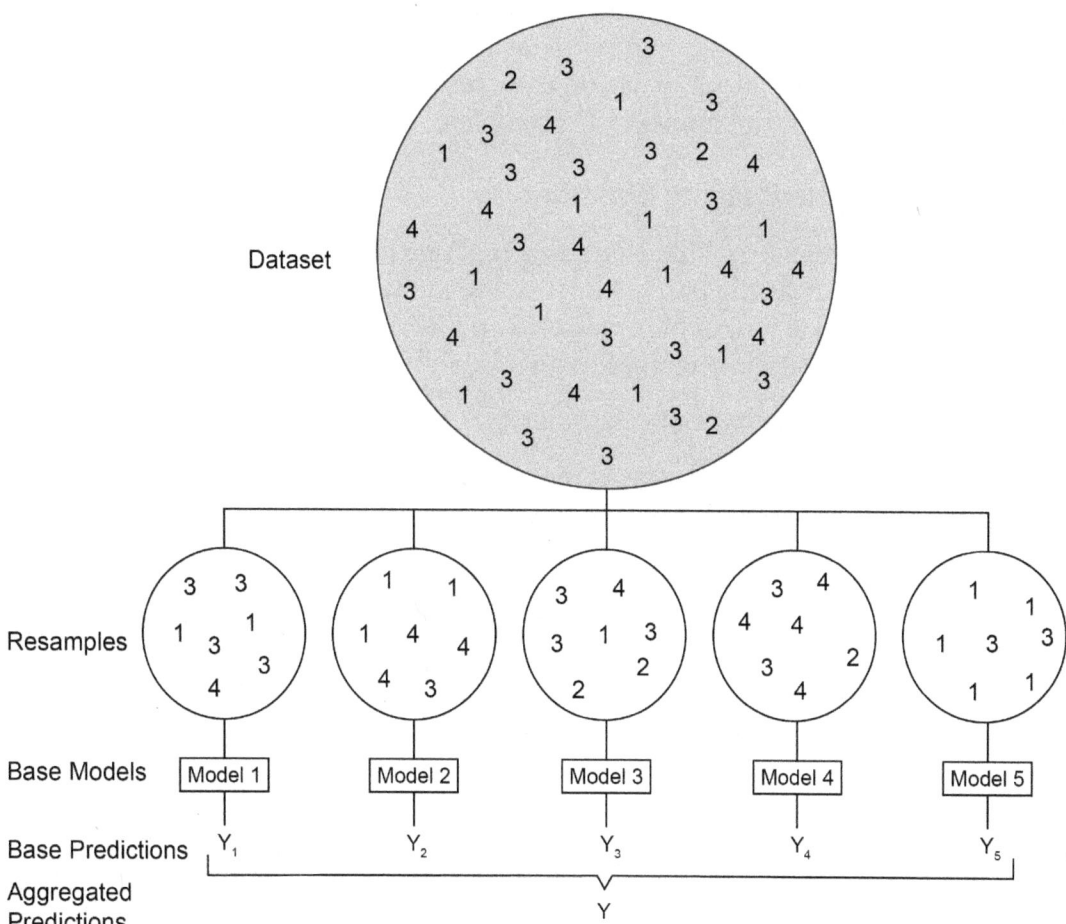

Figure 5.6: Bagging estimator built from bootstrap sampling

Since each model is essentially independent of the others, all the base models can be trained in parallel, considerably speeding up the training process and allowing us to take advantage of the computational power we have on our hands today.

Bagging essentially helps reduce the variance of the entire ensemble by introducing randomization into its construction procedure and is usually used with a base predictor that has a tendency to overfit the training data. The primary point of consideration here would be the stability (or lack thereof) of the training dataset: Bagging can improve accuracy in cases where a slight perturbation in the data could result in a significant change in the trained model.

scikit-learn uses `BaggingClassifier` and `BaggingRegressor` to implement generic bagging ensembles for classification and regression tasks respectively. The primary inputs to these are the base estimators to use on each resample, along with the number of estimators to use (that is, the number of resamples).

Exercise 44: Using the Bagging Classifier

In this exercise, we will use scikit-learn's `BaggingClassifier` as our ensemble with `DecisionTreeClassifier` as the base estimator. We know that decision trees are prone to overfitting, and so will have a high variance and low bias, both being important characteristics for the base estimators to be used in bagging ensembles:

1. Import the base and ensemble classifiers:

   ```
   from sklearn.tree import DecisionTreeClassifier
   from sklearn.ensemble import BaggingClassifier
   ```

2. Specify the hyperparameters and initialize the model.

   Here, we will first specify the hyperparameters of the base estimator, for which we are using the decision tree classifier with the entropy or information gain as the splitting criterion. We will not specify any limits on the depth of the tree or size/number of leaves to each tree to grow fully. Following this, we will define the hyperparameters for the bagging classifier and pass the base estimator object to the classifier as a hyperparameter.

   We will take 50 base estimators for our example, which will run in parallel and utilize all the processes available in the machine (which is done by specifying `n_jobs=-1`). Additionally, we will specify `max_samples` as 0.5, indicating that the number of datapoints in the bootstrap should be half that in the total dataset. We will also set a random state (to any arbitrary value, which will stay constant throughout) to maintain the reproducibility of the results:

   ```
   dt_params = {
       'criterion': 'entropy',
       'random_state': 11
   }
   dt = DecisionTreeClassifier(**dt_params)

   bc_params = {
       'base_estimator': dt,
       'n_estimators': 50,
       'max_samples': 0.5,
       'random_state': 11,
   ```

```
        'n_jobs': -1
}
bc = BaggingClassifier(**bc_params)
```

3. Fit the bagging classifier model to the training data and calculate the prediction accuracy.

   Let's fit the bagging classifier and find the meta predictions for both the training and validation set. Following this, let's find the prediction accuracy on the training and validation datasets:

   ```
   bc.fit(x_train, y_train)
   bc_preds_train = bc.predict(x_train)
   bc_preds_val = bc.predict(x_val)

   print('Bagging Classifier:\n> Accuracy on training data = {:.4f}\n> Accuracy on validation data = {:.4f}'.format(
       accuracy_score(y_true=y_train, y_pred=bc_preds_train),
       accuracy_score(y_true=y_val, y_pred=bc_preds_val)
   ))
   ```

   The output is as follows:

   ```
   Bagging Classifier:
   > Accuracy on training data = 0.9284
   > Accuracy on validation data = 0.8603
   ```

   Figure 5.7: Prediction accuracy of the bagging classifier

4. Fit the decision tree model to the training data to compare prediction accuracy.

   Let's also fit the decision tree (from the object we initialized in *step two*) so that we will be able to compare the prediction accuracies of the ensemble with that of the base predictor:

   ```
   dt.fit(x_train, y_train)
   dt_preds_train = dt.predict(x_train)
   dt_preds_val = dt.predict(x_val)

   print('Decision Tree:\n> Accuracy on training data = {:.4f}\n> Accuracy on validation data = {:.4f}'.format(
       accuracy_score(y_true=y_train, y_pred=dt_preds_train),
       accuracy_score(y_true=y_val, y_pred=dt_preds_val)
   ))
   ```

The output is as follows:

```
Decision Tree:
> Accuracy on training data = 0.9831
> Accuracy on validation data = 0.7598
```

Figure 5.8: Prediction accuracy of the decision tree

Here, we can see that, although the decision tree has a much higher training accuracy than the bagging classifier, its accuracy on the validation dataset is lower, a clear signal that the decision tree is overfitting to the training data. The bagging ensemble, on the other hand, reduces the overall variance and results in a much more accurate prediction.

Random Forest

An issue that is commonly faced with decision trees is that the split on each node is performed using a **greedy** algorithm that minimizes the entropy of the leaf nodes. Keeping this in mind, the base estimator decision trees in a bagging classifier can still be similar in terms of the features they split on, and so can have predictions that are quite similar. However, bagging is only useful in reducing the variance in predictions if the predictions from the base models are not correlated.

The Random Forest algorithm attempts to overcome this problem by not only bootstrapping the data points in the overall training dataset, but also bootstrapping the features available for each tree to split on. This ensures that when the greedy algorithm is searching for the *best* feature to split on, the overall *best* feature may not always be available in the bootstrapped features for the base estimator and so would not be chosen – resulting in base trees that have different structures. This simple tweak lets the best estimators be trained in such a way that the predictions from each tree in the forest have a lower probability of being correlated to the predictions from other trees.

Each base estimator in the Random Forest has a random sample of data points as well as a random sample of features. And since the ensemble is made up of decision trees, the algorithm is called a Random Forest.

Exercise 45: Building the Ensemble Model Using Random Forest

The two primary parameters that Random Forest takes is the fraction of features and the fraction of data points to bootstrap to train each base decision tree on.

In this exercise, we will use scikit-learn's `RandomForestClassifier` to build the ensemble model:

1. Import the ensemble classifier:

   ```
   from sklearn.ensemble import RandomForestClassifier
   ```

2. Specify the hyperparameters and initialize the model.

   Here, we will use entropy as the splitting criterion for the decision trees in a forest comprising 100 trees. As before, we will not specify any limits on the depth of the trees or size/number of leaves. Unlike the bagging classifier, which took `max_samples` as an input during initialization, the Random Forest algorithm takes in only `max_features`, indicating the number (or fraction) of features in the bootstrap sample. We will specify the value for this as 0.5, so that only three out of six features are considered for each tree:

   ```
   rf_params = {
       'n_estimators': 100,
       'criterion': 'entropy',
       'max_features': 0.5,
       'min_samples_leaf': 10,
       'random_state': 11,
       'n_jobs': -1
   }
   rf = RandomForestClassifier(**rf_params)
   ```

3. Fit the Random Forest classifier model to the training data and calculate the prediction accuracy.

   Let's fit the Random Forest model and find the meta predictions for both the training and validation set. Following this, let's find the prediction accuracy on the training and validation datasets:

   ```
   rf.fit(x_train, y_train)
   rf_preds_train = rf.predict(x_train)
   rf_preds_val = rf.predict(x_val)
   ```

```
print('Random Forest:\n> Accuracy on training data = {:.4f}\n> Accuracy on 
validation data = {:.4f}'.format(
    accuracy_score(y_true=y_train, y_pred=rf_preds_train),
    accuracy_score(y_true=y_val, y_pred=rf_preds_val)
))
```

The output is as follows:

```
Random Forest:
> Accuracy on training data = 0.8230
> Accuracy on validation data = 0.8603
```

Figure 5.9: Accuracy on training and validation using Random Forest

If we compare the prediction accuracies of Random Forest on our dataset to that of the bagging classifier, we can see that the accuracy on the validation set is pretty much the same, although the latter has higher accuracy on the training dataset.

Boosting

The second ensemble technique we'll be looking at is **boosting**, which involves incrementally training new models that focus on the misclassified data points in the previous model and utilizes weighted averages to turn weak models (underfitting models having high bias) into stronger models. Unlike bagging, where each base estimator could be trained independently of the others, the training of each base estimator in a boosted algorithm depends on the previous one.

Although boosting also uses the concept of bootstrapping, it's done differently from bagging, since each sample of data is weighted, implying that some bootstrapped samples can be used for training more often than other samples. When training each model, the algorithm keeps track of which features are most useful and which data samples have the most prediction error; these are given higher weightage and are considered to require more iterations to properly train the model.

When predicting the output, the boosting ensemble takes a weighted average of the predictions from each base estimator, giving a higher weight to the ones that had lower errors during the training stage. This means that, for the data points that are misclassified by the model in an iteration, the weights for those data points are increased so that the next model is more likely to classify it correctly.

As was the case with bagging, the results from all the boosting base estimators are aggregated to produce a meta prediction. However, unlike bagging, the accuracy of a boosted ensemble increases significantly with the number of base estimators in the boosted ensemble:

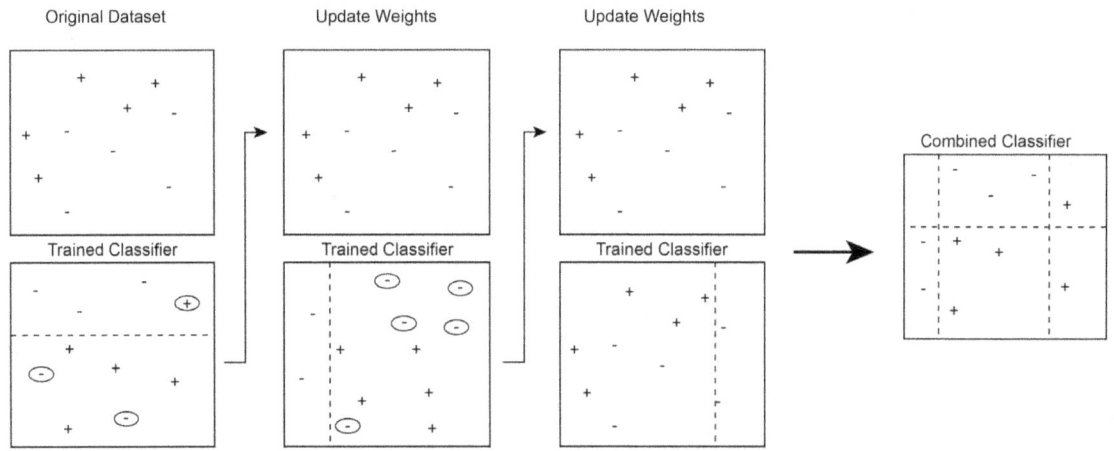

Figure 5.10: A boosted ensemble

In the diagram, we can see that, after each iteration, the misclassified points have increased weights (represented by larger icons) so that the next base estimator that is trained is able to focus on those points. The final predictor has aggregated the decision boundaries from each of its base estimators.

Adaptive Boosting

Let's talk about a boosting technique called **adaptive boosting**, which is best used to boost the performance of decision stumps for binary classification problems. Decision stumps are essentially decision trees with a maximum depth of one (only one split is made on a single feature), and, as such, are weak learners. The primary principle that adaptive boosting works on is the same: to improve the areas where the base estimator fails to turn an ensemble of weak learners to a strong learner.

To start with, the first base estimator takes a bootstrap of data points from the main training set and fits a decision stump to classify the sampled points, after which the trained decision tree stump is fit to the complete training data. For the samples that are misclassified, the weights are increased so that there is a higher probability of these data points being selected in the bootstrap for the next base estimator. A decision stump is again trained on the new bootstrap to classify the data points in the sample. Subsequently, the mini ensemble comprising the two base estimators is used to classify the data points in the entire training set. The misclassified data points from the second round are given a higher weight to improve their probability of selection, and so on until the ensemble reaches the limit on the number of base estimators it should contain.

One drawback of adaptive boosting is that the algorithm is easily influenced by noisy data points and outliers since it tries to fit every point perfectly. As such, it is prone to overfitting if the number of estimators is very high.

Exercise 46: Adaptive Boosting

In this exercise, we'll use scikit-learn's implementation of adaptive boosting for classification, `AdaBoostClassifier`:

1. Import the classifier:

   ```
   from sklearn.ensemble import AdaBoostClassifier
   ```

2. Specify the hyperparameters and initialize the model.

   Here, we will first specify the hyperparameters of the base estimator, for which we are using the decision tree classifier with a maximum depth of one, that is, a decision stump. Following this, we will define the hyperparameters for the AdaBoost classifier and pass the base estimator object to the classifier as a hyperparameter:

   ```
   dt_params = {
       'max_depth': 1,
       'random_state': 11
   }
   dt = DecisionTreeClassifier(**dt_params)

   ab_params = {
       'n_estimators': 100,
       'base_estimator': dt,
       'random_state': 11
   }
   ab = AdaBoostClassifier(**ab_params)
   ```

3. Fit the model to the training data.

   Let's fit the AdaBoost model and find the meta predictions for both the training and validation set. Following this, let's find the prediction accuracy on the training and validation datasets:

   ```
   ab.fit(x_train, y_train)
   ab_preds_train = ab.predict(x_train)
   ab_preds_val = ab.predict(x_val)

   print('Adaptive Boosting:\n> Accuracy on training data = {:.4f}\n> Accuracy on validation data = {:.4f}'.format(
       accuracy_score(y_true=y_train, y_pred=ab_preds_train),
       accuracy_score(y_true=y_val, y_pred=ab_preds_val)
   ))
   ```

The output is as follows:

```
Adaptive Boosting:
> Accuracy on training data = 0.8244
> Accuracy on validation data = 0.8547
```

Figure 5.11: Accuracy of training and validation data using adaptive boosting

4. Calculate the prediction accuracy of the model on the training and validation data for a varying number of base estimators.

   Earlier, we claimed that the accuracy tends to increase with an increasing number of base estimators, but also that the model has a tendency to overfit if too many base estimators are used. Let's calculate the prediction accuracies so that we can find the point where the model begins to overfit the training data:

```
ab_params = {
    'base_estimator': dt,
    'random_state': 11
}

n_estimator_values = list(range(10, 210, 10))
train_accuracies, val_accuracies = [], []

for n_estimators in n_estimator_values:
    ab = AdaBoostClassifier(n_estimators=n_estimators, **ab_params)
    ab.fit(x_train, y_train)
    ab_preds_train = ab.predict(x_train)
    ab_preds_val = ab.predict(x_val)

    train_accuracies.append(accuracy_score(y_true=y_train, y_pred=ab_preds_train))
    val_accuracies.append(accuracy_score(y_true=y_val, y_pred=ab_preds_val))
```

5. Plot a line graph to visualize the trend of the prediction accuracies on both the training and validation datasets:

```
plt.figure(figsize=(10,7))
plt.plot(n_estimator_values, train_accuracies, label='Train')
plt.plot(n_estimator_values, val_accuracies, label='Validation')

plt.ylabel('Accuracy score')
plt.xlabel('n_estimators')

plt.legend()
plt.show()
```

The output is as follows:

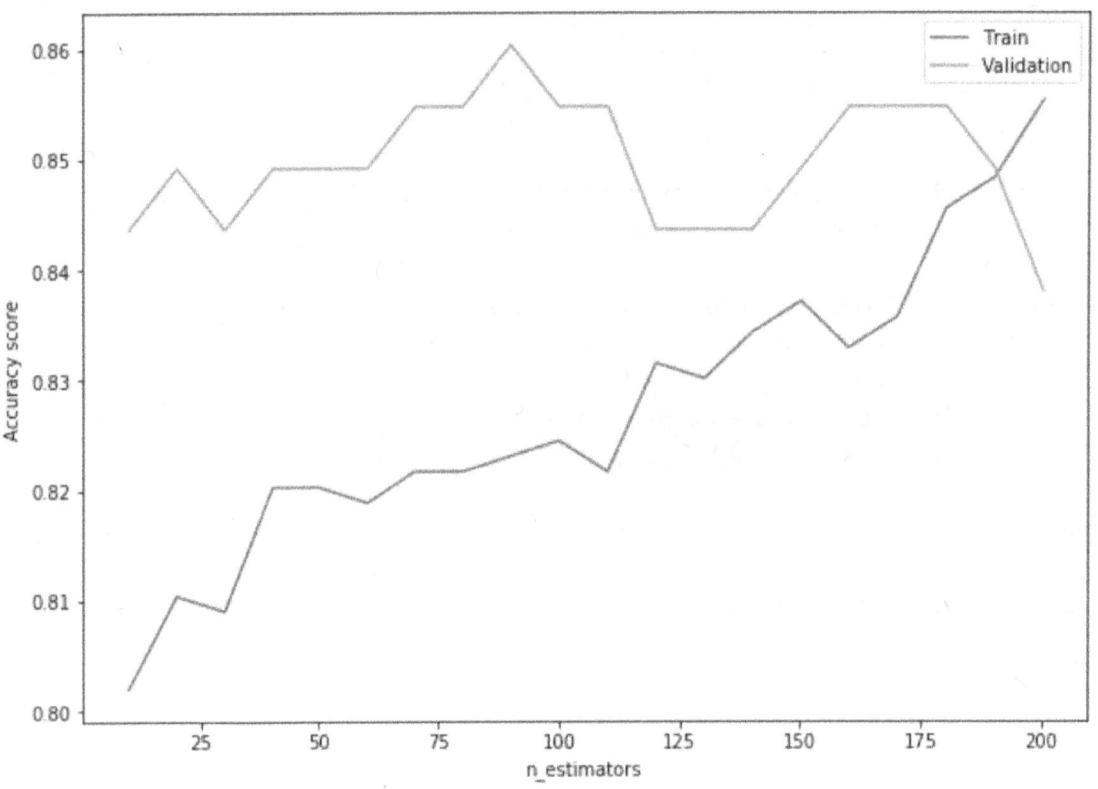

Figure 5.12: The trend of the prediction accuracies

As was mentioned earlier, we can see that the training accuracy almost consistently increases as the number of decision tree stumps increases from 10 to 200. However, the validation accuracy fluctuates between 0.84 and 0.86 and begins to drop as the number of decision stumps goes higher. This happens because the AdaBoost algorithm is trying fit the noisy data points and outliers as well.

Gradient Boosting

Gradient boosting is an extension to the boosting method that visualizes boosting as an optimization problem. A loss function is defined that is representative of the error residuals (the difference between the predicted and true values), and the gradient descent algorithm is used to optimize the loss function.

In the first step, a base estimator (which would be a weak learner) is added and trained on the entire training dataset. The loss associated with the prediction is calculated, and, in order to reduce the error residuals, the loss function is updated to add more base estimators for the data points where the existing estimators are performing poorly. Subsequently, the algorithm iteratively adds new base estimators and computes the loss to allow the optimization algorithm to update the model and minimize the residuals themselves.

In the case of adaptive boosting, decision stumps were used as the weak learners for the base estimators. However, for gradient boosting methods, larger trees can be used, but the weak learners should still be constrained by providing a limit to the maximum number of layers, nodes, splits, or leaf nodes. This ensures that the base estimators are still weak learners, but they can be constructed in a greedy manner.

From *Chapter 3, Regression Analysis*, we know that the gradient descent algorithm can be used to minimize a set of parameters, such as the coefficients in a regression equation. When building an ensemble, however, we have decision trees instead of parameters that need to be optimized. After calculating the loss at each step, the gradient descent algorithm then has to modify the parameters of the new tree that's to be added to the ensemble in such a way that reduces the loss. This approach is more commonly known as **functional gradient descent**.

Ensemble Modeling

Exercise 47: GradientBoostingClassifier

The two primary parameters that Random Forest takes is the fraction of features and the fraction of data points to bootstrap to train each base decision tree on.

In this exercise, we will use scikit-learn's **GradientBoostingClassifier** to build the boosting ensemble model:

1. Import the ensemble classifier:

   ```
   from sklearn.ensemble import GradientBoostingClassifier
   ```

2. Specify the hyperparameters and initialize the model.

   Here, we will use 100 decision trees as the base estimator, with each tree having a maximum depth of three and a minimum of five samples in each of its leaves. Although we are not using decision stumps, as in the previous example, the tree is still small and would be considered a weak learner:

   ```
   gbc_params = {
       'n_estimators': 100,
       'max_depth': 3,
       'min_samples_leaf': 5,
       'random_state': 11
   }
   gbc = GradientBoostingClassifier(**gbc_params)
   ```

3. Fit the gradient boosting model to the training data and calculate the prediction accuracy.

   Let's fit the ensemble model and find the meta predictions for both the training and validation set. Following this, we will find the prediction accuracy on the training and validation datasets:

   ```
   gbc.fit(x_train, y_train)
   gbc_preds_train = gbc.predict(x_train)
   gbc_preds_val = gbc.predict(x_val)

   print('Gradient Boosting Classifier:\n> Accuracy on training data = {:.4f}\
   n> Accuracy on validation data = {:.4f}'.format(
       accuracy_score(y_true=y_train, y_pred=gbc_preds_train),
       accuracy_score(y_true=y_val, y_pred=gbc_preds_val)
   ))
   ```

The output is as follows:

```
Gradient Boosting Classifier:
> Accuracy on training data = 0.8947
> Accuracy on validation data = 0.8771
```

Figure 5.13: Prediction accuracy on the training and validation datasets

We can see that the gradient boosting ensemble has greater accuracy on both the training and validation datasets compared to those for the adaptive boosting ensemble.

Stacking

Stacking, or stacked generalization (also called meta ensembling), is a model ensembling technique that involves combining information from multiple predictive models and using them as features to generate a new model. The stacked model will most likely outperform each of the individual models due the smoothing effect it adds, as well as due to its ability to "choose" the base model that performs best in certain scenarios. Keeping this in mind, stacking is usually most effective when each of the base models is significantly different from each other.

Stacking uses the predictions of the base models as additional features when training the final model – these are known as **meta features**. The stacked model essentially acts as a classifier that determines where each model is performing well and where it is performing poorly.

However, you cannot simply train the base models on the full training data, generate predictions on the full validation dataset, and then output these for second-level training. This runs the risk of your base model predictions already having "seen" the test set and therefore overfitting when feeding these predictions.

It is important to note that the value of the meta features for each row cannot be predicted using a model that contained that row in the training data, as we then run the risk of overfitting since the base predictions would have already "seen" the target variable for that row. The common practice is to divide the training data into k subsets so that, when finding the meta features for each of those subsets, we only train the model on the remaining data. Doing this also avoids the problem of overfitting the data the model has already "seen":

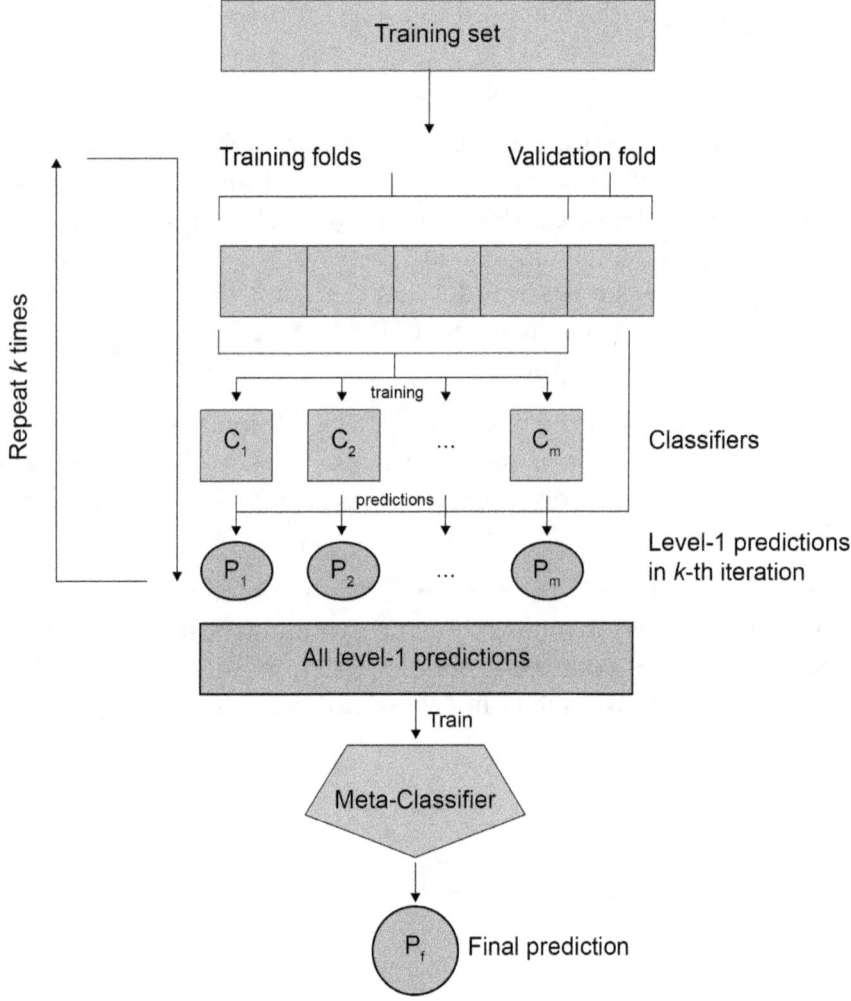

Figure 5.14: A stacking ensemble

The preceding diagram shows how this is done: we divide the training data into k folds and find the predictions from the base models on each fold by training the model on the remaining $k-1$ folds. So, once we have the meta predictions for each of the folds, we can use those meta predictions along with the original features to train the stacked model.

Exercise 48: Building a Stacked Model

In this exercise, we will use a support vector machine (scikit-learn's **LinearSVC**) and k-nearest neighbors (scikit-learn's **KNeighborsClassifier**) as the base predictors, and the stacked model will be a logistic regression classifier.

1. Import the base models and the model used for stacking:

    ```
    # Base models
    from sklearn.neighbors import KNeighborsClassifier
    from sklearn.svm import LinearSVC
    # Stacking model
    from sklearn.linear_model import LogisticRegression
    ```

2. Create a new training set with additional columns for predictions from base predictors.

    We need to create two new columns for predicted values from each model to be used as features for the ensemble model in both the test and train set. Since NumPy arrays are immutable, we will create a new array that will have the same number of rows as the training dataset, and two columns more than those in the training dataset. Once the dataset is created, let's print it to see what it looks like:

    ```
    x_train_with_metapreds = np.zeros((x_train.shape[0], x_train.shape[1]+2))
    x_train_with_metapreds[:, :-2] = x_train
    x_train_with_metapreds[:, -2:] = -1
    print(x_train_with_metapreds)
    ```

    The output is as follows:

    ```
    [[ 3.   0.  16.  ...   1.  -1.  -1.]
     [ 1.   0.  47.  ...   1.  -1.  -1.]
     [ 3.   0.  32.  ...   1.  -1.  -1.]
     ...
     [ 3.   0.  20.  ...   1.  -1.  -1.]
     [ 3.   0.  22.  ...   1.  -1.  -1.]
     [ 3.   0.  25.  ...   0.  -1.  -1.]]
    ```

    Figure 5.15: The new columns for the predicted values

    As we can see, there are two extra columns filled with -1 values at the end of each row.

3. Train base models using the k-fold strategy.

   Let's take *k*=5. For each of the five folds, train on the other four folds and predict on the fifth fold. These predictions should then be added into the placeholder columns for base predictions in the new NumPy array.

   First, we initialize the **KFold** object with the value of **k** and a random state to maintain reproducibility. The **kf.split()** function takes the dataset to split as an input and returns an iterator, each element in the iterator corresponding to the list of indices in the training and validation folds respectively. These index values in each loop over the iterator can be used to subdivide the training data for training and prediction for each row.

   Once the data is adequately divided, we train the two base predictors on four-fifths of the data and predict the values on the remaining one-fifth of the rows. These predictions are then inserted into the two placeholder columns we initialized with **-1** in *step 2*:

   ```
   kf = KFold(n_splits=5, random_state=11)

   for train_indices, val_indices in kf.split(x_train):
       kfold_x_train, kfold_x_val = x_train[train_indices], x_train[val_indices]
       kfold_y_train, kfold_y_val = y_train[train_indices], y_train[val_indices]

       svm = LinearSVC(random_state=11, max_iter=1000)
       svm.fit(kfold_x_train, kfold_y_train)
       svm_pred = svm.predict(kfold_x_val)

       knn = KNeighborsClassifier(n_neighbors=4)
       knn.fit(kfold_x_train, kfold_y_train)
       knn_pred = knn.predict(kfold_x_val)

       x_train_with_metapreds[val_indices, -2] = svm_pred
       x_train_with_metapreds[val_indices, -1] = knn_pred
   ```

4. Create a new validation set with additional columns for predictions from base predictors.

   As we did in *step 2*, we will add two placeholder columns for the base model predictions in the validation dataset as well:

   ```
   x_val_with_metapreds = np.zeros((x_val.shape[0], x_val.shape[1]+2))
   x_val_with_metapreds[:, :-2] = x_val
   x_val_with_metapreds[:, -2:] = -1
   print(x_val_with_metapreds)
   ```

   The output is as follows:

   ```
   [[ 3.  1. -1. ...  1. -1. -1.]
    [ 3.  0. 27. ...  1. -1. -1.]
    [ 3.  0. -1. ...  0. -1. -1.]
    ...
    [ 3.  0. 22. ...  1. -1. -1.]
    [ 1.  0. -1. ...  1. -1. -1.]
    [ 1.  0. 25. ...  0. -1. -1.]]
   ```

   Figure 5.16: Additional columns for predictions from base predictors

5. Fit base models on the complete training set to get meta features for the validation set.

   Next, we will train the two base predictors on the complete training dataset to get the meta prediction values for the validation dataset. This is similar to what we did for each fold in *step 3*:

   ```
   svm = LinearSVC(random_state=11, max_iter=1000)
   svm.fit(x_train, y_train)

   knn = KNeighborsClassifier(n_neighbors=4)
   knn.fit(x_train, y_train)

   svm_pred = svm.predict(x_val)
   knn_pred = knn.predict(x_val)

   x_val_with_metapreds[:, -2] = svm_pred
   x_val_with_metapreds[:, -1] = knn_pred
   ```

6. Train the stacked model and use the final predictions to calculate accuracy.

    The last step is to train the logistic regression model on all the columns of the training dataset plus the meta predictions from the base estimators. We use the model to find the prediction accuracies for both the training and validation datasets:

    ```
    lr = LogisticRegression(random_state=11)
    lr.fit(x_train_with_metapreds, y_train)
    lr_preds_train = lr.predict(x_train_with_metapreds)
    lr_preds_val = lr.predict(x_val_with_metapreds)
    print('Stacked Classifier:\n> Accuracy on training data = {:.4f}\n> Accuracy on validation data = {:.4f}'.format(
        accuracy_score(y_true=y_train, y_pred=lr_preds_train),
        accuracy_score(y_true=y_val, y_pred=lr_preds_val)
    ))
    ```

    The output is as follows:

    ```
    Stacked Classifier:
    > Accuracy on training data = 0.7865
    > Accuracy on validation data = 0.8883
    ```

    Figure 5.17: Accuracy using a stacked classifier

7. Compare the accuracy with that of base models.

    To get a sense of the performance boost from stacking, we calculate the accuracies of the base predictors on the training and validation datasets and compare it to that of the stacked model:

    ```
    print('SVM:\n> Accuracy on training data = {:.4f}\n> Accuracy on validation data = {:.4f}'.format(
        accuracy_score(y_true=y_train, y_pred=svm.predict(x_train)),
        accuracy_score(y_true=y_val, y_pred=svm_pred)
    ))
    print('kNN:\n> Accuracy on training data = {:.4f}\n> Accuracy on validation data = {:.4f}'.format(
        accuracy_score(y_true=y_train, y_pred=knn.predict(x_train)),
        accuracy_score(y_true=y_val, y_pred=knn_pred)
    ))
    ```

The output is as follows:

```
SVM:
> Accuracy on training data = 0.6924
> Accuracy on validation data = 0.7654
kNN:
> Accuracy on training data = 0.7921
> Accuracy on validation data = 0.6704
```

Figure 5.18: Accuracy of training and validation data using SVM and K-NN

As we can see, not only does the stacked model give us a validation accuracy that is significantly higher than either of the base predictors, but it also has the highest accuracy, of nearly 89%, of all the ensemble models discussed in this chapter.

Activity 14: Stacking with Standalone and Ensemble Algorithms

In this activity, we'll use the *Kaggle House Prices: Advanced Regression Techniques* database (available at https://www.kaggle.com/c/house-prices-advanced-regression-techniques/data or on GitHub at https://github.com/TrainingByPackt/Applied-Supervised-Learning-with-Python), that we did EDA on in *Chapter 2, Exploratory Data Analysis and Visualization*. This dataset is aimed toward solving a regression problem (that is, the target variable takes on a range of continuous values). In this activity, we will use decision trees, K-nearest neighbors, Random Forest, and gradient boosting algorithms to train individual regressors on the data. Then, we will build a stacked linear regression model that uses all these algorithms and compare the performance of each. We will use the **mean absolute error** (**MAE**) as the evaluation metric for this activity.

The steps to be performed are as follows:

1. Import the relevant libraries.
2. Read the data.
3. Preprocess the dataset to remove null values and one-hot encode categorical variables to prepare the data for modeling.
4. Divide the dataset into train and validation DataFrames.
5. Initialize dictionaries in which to store the train and validation MAE values.

6. Train a decision tree model with the following hyperparameters and save the scores:

    ```
    dt_params = {
        'criterion': 'mae',
        'min_samples_leaf': 10,
        'random_state': 11
    }
    ```

7. Train a k-nearest neighbors model with the following hyperparameters and save the scores:

    ```
    knn_params = {
        'n_neighbors': 5
    }
    ```

8. Train a Random Forest model with the following hyperparameters and save the scores:

    ```
    rf_params = {
        'n_estimators': 50,
        'criterion': 'mae',
        'max_features': 'sqrt',
        'min_samples_leaf': 10,
        'random_state': 11,
        'n_jobs': -1
    }
    ```

9. Train a gradient boosting model with the following hyperparameters and save the scores:

    ```
    gbr_params = {
        'n_estimators': 50,
        'criterion': 'mae',
        'max_features': 'sqrt',
        'min_samples_leaf': 10,
        'random_state': 11
    }
    ```

10. Prepare the training and validation datasets, with the four meta estimators having the same hyperparameters that were used in the previous steps.

11. Train a linear regression model as the stacked model.

12. Visualize the train and validation errors for each individual model and the stacked model.

> **Note**
>
> The solution for this activity can be found on page 364.

Summary

In this chapter, we started off with a discussion on overfitting and underfitting and how these can affect the performance of a model on unseen data. The chapter looked at ensemble modeling as a solution for these and went on to discuss different ensemble methods that could be used, and how they could decrease the overall bias or variance encountered when making predictions.

We first discussed bagging algorithms and introduced the concept of bootstrapping. Then, we looked at Random Forest as a classic example of a Bagged ensemble and solved exercises that involved building a bagging classifier and Random Forest classifier on the previously seen Titanic dataset.

We then moved on to discussing boosting algorithms, how they successfully reduce bias in the system, and gained an understanding of how to implement adaptive boosting and gradient boosting. The last ensemble method we discussed was stacking, which, as we saw from the exercise, gave us the best accuracy score of all the ensemble methods we implemented.

Although building an ensemble model is a great way to decrease bias and variance, and they generally outperform any single model by itself, they themselves come with their own problems and use cases. While bagging is great when trying to avoid overfitting, boosting can reduce both bias and variance, though it may still have a tendency to overfit. Stacking, on the other hand, is a good choice for when one model performs well on a portion of the data while another model performs better on another portion of the data.

In the next chapter, we will explore more ways to overcome the problems of overfitting and underfitting in detail by looking at validation techniques, that is, ways to judge our model's performance, and how to use different metrics as indicators to build the best possible model for our use case.

Model Evaluation

Learning Objectives

By the end of this chapter, you will be able to:

- Explain the importance of evaluating models
- Evaluate regression and classification models using a number of metrics
- Choose the right metric for evaluating and tuning a model
- Explain the importance of hold-out datasets and types of sampling
- Perform hyperparameter tuning to find the best model
- Calculate feature importance and explain why they are important

This chapter introduces us to how we can improve a model's performance by using hyperparameters and model evaluation metrics.

Introduction

In the previous three chapters, we discussed the two types of supervised learning problems, regression and classification, followed by ensemble models, which were built from a combination of base models. We built several models and discussed how and why they work.

However, that is not enough to take a model to production. Model development is an iterative process, and the model training step is followed by validation and updating steps:

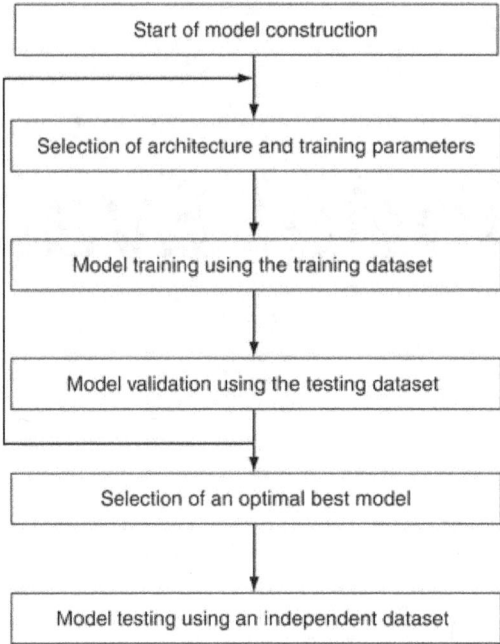

Figure 6.1: Machine learning model development process

This chapter will explain the peripheral steps in the process shown in the preceding flowchart; we will discuss how to select the appropriate hyperparameters and how to perform model validation using the appropriate error metrics. Improving a model's performance happens by iteratively performing these two tasks.

But why is it important to evaluate your model? Say you've trained your model and provided some hyperparameters, made predictions, and found its accuracy. That's the gist of it, but how do you make sure that your model is performing to the best of its ability? We need to ensure that the performance measure that you've come up with is actually representative of the model and that it will indeed perform well on an unseen test dataset.

The essential part about making sure that the model is the best version of itself comes after the initial training: the process of evaluating and improving the performance of the model. This chapter will take you through the essential techniques required when it comes to this.

In this chapter, we will first discuss why model evaluation is important, and introduce several evaluation metrics for both regression tasks and classification tasks that can be used to quantify the predictive performance of a model. This will be followed by a discussion on hold-out datasets and k-fold cross-validation and why it is imperative to have a test set that is independent of the validation set.

After this, we'll look at tactics we can use to boost the performance of the model. In the previous chapter, we talked about how having a model with a high bias or a high variance can result in suboptimal performance, and how building an ensemble of models can help us build a robust system that makes more accurate predictions without increasing the overall variance. We also mentioned the following as techniques to avoid overfitting our model to the training data:

- **To get more data**: A highly complex model can easily overfit to a small dataset but may not be able to as easily on a larger dataset.

- **Dimensionality reduction**: Reducing the number of features can help make the model less complex.

- **Regularization**: A new term is added to the cost function in order to adjust the coefficients (especially the high-degree coefficients in linear regression) toward a small value.

In this chapter, we'll introduce learning curves and validation curves as a way to see how variations in training and validation errors allow us to see whether the model needs more data, and where the appropriate level of complexity is. This will be followed by a section on hyperparameter tuning in an effort to boost performance, and a brief introduction to feature importance.

Exercise 49: Importing the Modules and Preparing Our Dataset

In this exercise, we will load the data and models that we trained as part of *Chapter 5, Ensemble Modeling*. We will use the stacked linear regression model from *Activity 14: Stacking with Standalone and Ensemble Algorithms*, and the random forest classification model to predict the survival of passengers from *Exercise 45: Building the Ensemble Model Using Random Forest*:

1. Import the relevant libraries:

    ```
    import pandas as pd
    import numpy as np
    import pickle

    %matplotlib inline
    import matplotlib.pyplot as plt
    ```

2. Load the processed data files from *Chapter 5, Ensemble Modeling*. We will use pandas' **read_csv()** method to read in our prepared datasets, which we will use in the exercises in this chapter. First, we'll read the house price data:

    ```
    house_prices_reg = pd.read_csv('houseprices_regression.csv')
    house_prices_reg.head()
    ```

    We'll see the following output:

	0	1	2	3	4	5	6	7	8	9	...	275	276	277	278	279	280	281	282	283	y
0	0.0	0.0	0.0	1.0	0.0	0.0	1.0	1.0	0.0	0.0	...	0.0	0.0	0.0	6.0	2006.0	99679.361798	112279.02	87500.0	123600.0	88000
1	0.0	0.0	0.0	1.0	0.0	0.0	1.0	1.0	0.0	0.0	...	0.0	0.0	0.0	12.0	2009.0	215512.586019	213242.84	185128.0	201000.0	222000
2	0.0	0.0	0.0	1.0	0.0	0.0	1.0	0.0	0.0	0.0	...	0.0	0.0	0.0	5.0	2009.0	190792.974301	204017.96	195725.0	160200.0	181000
3	0.0	0.0	0.0	0.0	1.0	0.0	1.0	0.0	0.0	0.0	...	0.0	0.0	0.0	5.0	2009.0	109232.674230	122006.03	92100.0	98500.0	86000
4	0.0	0.0	0.0	1.0	0.0	0.0	1.0	0.0	0.0	0.0	...	0.0	0.0	0.0	6.0	2009.0	194048.748934	188090.20	162021.8	194700.0	178000

    5 rows × 285 columns

    Figure 6.2: First five rows of house_prices

    Next, we'll read in the Titanic data:

    ```
    titanic_clf = pd.read_csv('titanic_classification.csv')
    titanic_clf.head()
    ```

We'll see the following output:

	Pclass	Sex	Age	SibSp	Parch	Fare	Emb_C	Emb_Q	Emb_S	Survived
0	3	0	22.0	1	0	7.2500	0	0	1	0
1	1	0	38.0	1	0	71.2833	1	0	0	1
2	3	0	26.0	0	0	7.9250	0	0	1	1
3	1	0	35.0	1	0	53.1000	0	0	1	1
4	3	0	35.0	0	0	8.0500	0	0	1	0

Figure 6.3: First five rows of Titanic

3. Next, load the model files that we will use for the exercises in this chapter by using the **pickle** library to load them from a binary file:

```
with open('../Saved Models/titanic_regression.pkl', 'rb') as f:
    reg = pickle.load(f)

with open('../Saved Models/random_forest_clf.pkl', 'rb') as f:
    rf = pickle.load(f)
```

Let's begin.

Evaluation Metrics

Evaluating a machine learning model is an essential part of any project: once we have allowed our model to learn from the training data, the next step is to measure the performance of the model. We need to find a metric that can not only tell us how accurate the predictions made by the model are, but also allow us to compare the performance of a number of models so that we can select the one best suited for our use case.

Defining a metric is usually one of the first things we should do when defining our problem statement and before we begin the EDA, since it's a good idea to plan ahead and think about how we intend to evaluate the performance of any model we build and how to judge whether it is performing optimally or not. Eventually, calculating the performance evaluation metric will fit into the machine learning pipeline.

Needless to say, evaluation metrics will be different for regression tasks and classification tasks, since the output values in the former are continuous while the outputs in the latter are categorical. In this section, we'll look at the different metrics we can use to quantify the predictive performance of a model.

Regression

For an input variable, X, a regression model gives us a predicted value, $\hat{y}$, that can take on a range of values. The ideal scenario would be to have the model predict $\hat{y}$ values that are as close as possible to the actual value of y. Therefore, the smaller the difference between the two, the better the model performs. Regression metrics mostly involve looking at the numerical difference between the predicted value and actual value (that is, the residual or error value) for each data point, and subsequently aggregating these differences in some way.

Let's look at the following plot, which plots the actual and predicted values for every point X:

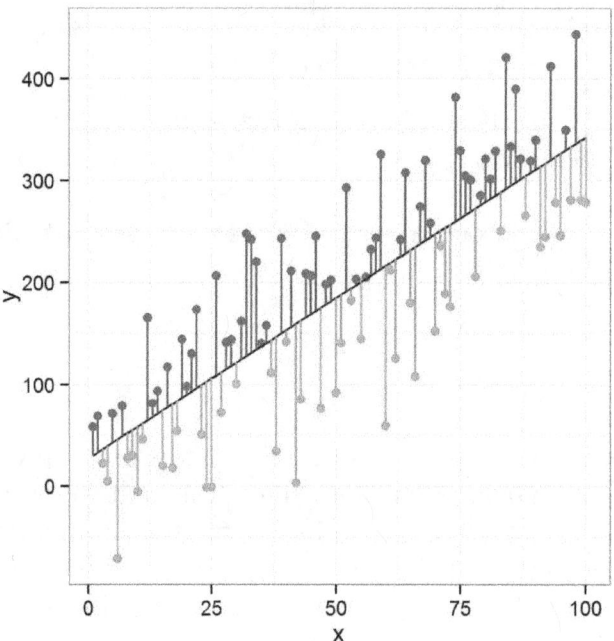

Figure 6.4: Residuals between actual and predicted outputs in a linear regression problem

However, we can't just find the mean value of $(\hat{y} - y)$ over all data points, since there could be data points that have a prediction error that is positive or negative, and the aggregate would ultimately end up canceling out a lot of the errors and severely overestimate the performance of the model.

Instead, we can consider the absolute error for each data point and find the **Mean Absolute Error** (**MAE**), which is given by the following formula:

$$MAE = \frac{1}{n}\sum_{i=1}^{n}|y^i - \hat{y}^i|$$

Figure 6.5: Mean Absolute Error

Here, y^i and $\hat{y}^i$ are the actual and predicted values, respectively, for the ith data point.

MAE is a **linear scoring function**, which means that it gives each residual an equal weight when it aggregates the errors. The MAE can take on any value from zero to infinity and is indifferent to the direction (positive or negative) of errors. Since these are error metrics, a lower value (as close to zero as possible) is usually desirable.

In order to not let the direction of the error affect the performance estimate, we can also take the square of the error terms. Taking the mean of the squared errors gives us the **Mean Squared Error** (**MSE**):

$$MSE = \frac{1}{n}\sum_{i=1}^{n}(y^i - \hat{y}^i)^2$$

Figure 6.6: Mean Squared Error

While the MAE has the same units as the target variable, y, the units for the MSE will be the squared unit of y, which may make the MSE slightly less interpretable while judging the model in real-world terms. However, if we take the square root of the MSE, we get the **Root Mean Squared Error** (**RMSE**):

$$RMSE = \sqrt{MSE} = \sqrt{\frac{1}{n}\sum_{i=1}^{n}(y^i - \hat{y}^i)^2}$$

Figure 6.7: Root Mean Squared Error

Since the errors are squared before they are averaged, having even a few error values that are high can cause the RMSE value to significantly increase. This means that the RMSE is more useful than MAE for judging models in which we want to penalize large errors.

Since MAE and RMSE have the same units as the target variable, it can be hard to judge whether a particular value of the MAE or RMSE is good or bad, since there is no scale to refer to. A metric that is commonly used to overcome this problem is the **R² Score**, or the **R-Squared Score**:

$$R^2 = 1 - \frac{MSE(model)}{MSE(base\ model)}$$

Figure 6.8: R-Squared score

The R² score has a lower limit of -∞ and an upper limit of 1. The base model predicts the target variable to be equal to the mean of the target values in the training dataset, that is, where $\hat{y}^i$ is equal to $\bar{y}$ for all values of i. Keeping this in mind, a negative value of R² would be one where the trained model makes a prediction that is worse than the mean, and a value close to 1 would be achieved if the MSE of the model is close to zero.

Exercise 50: Regression Metrics

In this exercise, we will use the same model and processed dataset that we trained in *Activity 14: Stacking with Standalone and Ensemble Algorithms* in *Chapter 5, Ensemble Modeling*, to calculate regression metrics. We will use scikit-learn's implementation of MAE and MSE:

1. Import the metric functions:

    ```
    from sklearn.metrics import mean_absolute_error, mean_squared_error, r2_score
    from math import sqrt
    ```

2. Use the loaded model to predict the output on the given data. We will use the same features as we did in *Activity 14: Stacking with Standalone and Ensemble Algorithms* in *Chapter 5, Ensemble Modeling*, and use the model to make a prediction on the loaded dataset. The column we saved as y is the target variable and we will create X and y accordingly:

    ```
    X = house_prices_reg.drop(columns=['y'])
    y = house_prices_reg['y'].values
    
    y_pred = reg.predict(X)
    ```

3. Calculate the MAE, RMSE, and R² scores. Let's print the values of the MAE and the RMSE from the predicted values. Also print the R² score for the model:

   ```
   print('Mean Absolute Error = {}'.format(mean_absolute_error(y, y_pred)))
   print('Root Mean Squared Error = {}'.format(sqrt(mean_squared_error(y, y_pred))))
   print('R Squared Score = {}'.format(r2_score(y, y_pred)))
   ```

   The output will be as follows:

   ```
   Mean Absolute Error = 12567.358027367643
   Root Mean Squared Error = 19256.557656417794
   R Squared Score = 0.9384546350842587
   ```

   Figure 6.9: Scores

We can see that the RMSE is much higher than the MAE. This shows that there are some data points where the residuals are particularly high, which is being highlighted by the larger RMSE value. But the R² score is very close to 1, indicating that the model actually has close to ideal performance compared to a base model, which would predict a mean value.

Classification

For an input variable, X, a classification task gives us a predicted value, $\hat{y}$, which can take on a limited set of values (two in the case of binary classification problems). Since the ideal scenario would be to predict a class for each data point that is the same as the actual class, there is no measure of how *close* or *far* the predicted class is from the actual class. Therefore, to judge the model's performance, it would be as simple as determining whether or not the model predicted the class correctly.

Judging a classification model's performance can be done in two ways: using numerical metrics, or by plotting a curve and looking at the shape of the curve. Let's explore both of these in greater detail.

Numerical Metrics

The simplest and most basic way to judge the performance of the model is to calculate the proportion of the correct predictions to the total number of predictions, which gives us the **accuracy**:

$$Accuracy = \frac{No.\,correctly\,predicted}{Total\,no.\,of\,predictions}$$

Figure 6.10: Accuracy

Although the accuracy metric is appropriate no matter the number of classes, the next few metrics are discussed keeping in mind a binary classification problem. Additionally, accuracy may not be the best metric to judge the performance of a classification task in many cases.

Let's look at an example of fraud detection: say the problem statement is to detect whether a particular email is fraudulent or not. Our dataset in this case is highly skewed (or imbalanced, that is, there are many more data points belonging to one class compared to the other class), with 100 out of 10,000 emails (1% of the total) having been classified as fraudulent (having class 1). Say we build two models:

- The first model simply predicts each email as not being fraud, that is, each of the 10,000 emails is classified with the class 0. In this case, 9,900 of the 10,000 were classified correctly, which means the model has 99% accuracy.

- The second model predicts the 100 fraud emails as being fraud, but also predicts another 100 emails incorrectly as fraud. In this case as well, 100 data points were misclassified out of 10,000, and the model has an accuracy of 99%.

How do we compare these two models? The purpose of building a fraud detection model is to allow us to know *how well the fraud was detected*: it matters more that the fraudulent emails were correctly classified than if non-fraud emails were classified as fraudulent. Although both the models were equally high in accuracy, the second was actually more effective than the first.

Since this cannot be captured using accuracy, we need the **confusion matrix**, a table with four different combinations of predicted and actual values that essentially gives us a summary of the prediction results of a classification problem:

		Predicted	
		0	1
Actual	0	True negatives	False positives
	1	False negatives	True positives

Figure 6.11: Confusion matrix

Here's what the terms used in the matrix mean:

- **True positives** and **true negatives**: These are the counts of the correctly predicted data points in the positive and negative classes respectively.

- **False positives**: These are also known as **Type 1 errors** and refer to the count of the data points that actually belong to the negative class but were predicted to be positive. Continuing from the previous example, a false positive case would be if a normal email is classified as a fraudulent email.

- **False negatives**: These are also known as **Type 2 errors** and refer to the count of the data points that actually belong to the positive class but were predicted to be negative. An example of a false negative case would be if a fraudulent email was classified as not being one.

Two extremely important metrics can be derived from a confusion matrix: **precision** and **recall**.

$$Precision = \frac{True\ positives}{Total\ predicted\ positives} = \frac{True\ positives}{True\ positives\ +\ False\ positives}$$

Figure 6.12: Precision

$$Recall = \frac{True\ positives}{Total\ actual\ positives} = \frac{True\ positives}{True\ positives\ +\ False\ negatives}$$

Figure 6.13: Recall

While precision tells us how many of the actual positives were correctly predicted to be positive (from the results the model says are relevant, how many are actually relevant?), recall tells us how many of the predicted positives were actually positive (from the real relevant results, how many are included in the model's list of relevant results?). These two metrics are especially useful when there is an imbalance between the two classes.

There is usually a trade-off between the precision and recall of a model: if you have to recall all the relevant results, the model will generate more results that are not accurate, hence lowering the precision. On the other hand, having a higher percentage of relevant results from the generated results would involve including as few results as possible. In most cases, you would give a higher priority to either the precision or the recall, and this entirely depends on the problem statement. For example, since it matters more that all the fraudulent emails are correctly classified, recall would be an important metric that would need to be maximized.

The next question that arises is how we take both precision and recall to evaluate our model using a single number instead of balancing two separate metrics. The **F_1 score** combines the two into a single number that can be used as a fair judge of the model and is equal to the harmonic mean of precision and recall:

$$F_1\ Score = 2 \times \frac{Precision \times Recall}{Precision\ +\ Recall}$$

Figure 6.14: F_1 Score

The value of the F_1 score will always lie between 0 (if either precision or recall is zero) and 1 (if both precision and recall are 1). The higher the score, the better the model's performance is said to be. The F_1 score gives equal weight to both measures and is a specific example of the general F_β metric, where β can be adjusted to give more weight to either recall or precision using the following formula:

$$F_\beta \text{ Score} = (1 + \beta^2) \times \frac{\text{Precision} \times \text{Recall}}{(\beta^2 \times \text{Precision}) + \text{Recall}}$$

Figure 6.15: F beta score

A value of $\beta < 1$ focuses more on precision, while taking $\beta > 1$ focuses more on recall. The F_1 score takes $\beta = 1$ to give both equal weight.

Curve Plots

Sometimes, instead of predicting the class, we have the class probabilities at our disposal. Say, in a binary classification task, the class probabilities of both the positive (class 1) and negative (class 0) classes will always add up to unity (or 1), which means that if we take the classification probability as equal to the probability of class 1 and apply a threshold, we can essentially use it as a cut-off value to either round up (to 1) or down (to 0), which will give the output class.

Usually, by varying the threshold, we can get data points that have classification probabilities closer to 0.5 from one class to another. For example, with a threshold of 0.5, a data point having a probability of 0.4 would be assigned class 0 and a data point having probability 0.6 would be assigned class 1. But if we change the threshold to 0.35 or 0.65, both those data points would be classified as 1 or 0.

As it turns out, varying the probability changes the precision and recall values and this can be captured by plotting the **precision-recall curve**. The plot has precision on the Y axis and recall on the X axis, and for a range of thresholds starting from 0 to 1 plots each (recall, precision) point. Connecting these points gives us the curve. The following graph shows an example:

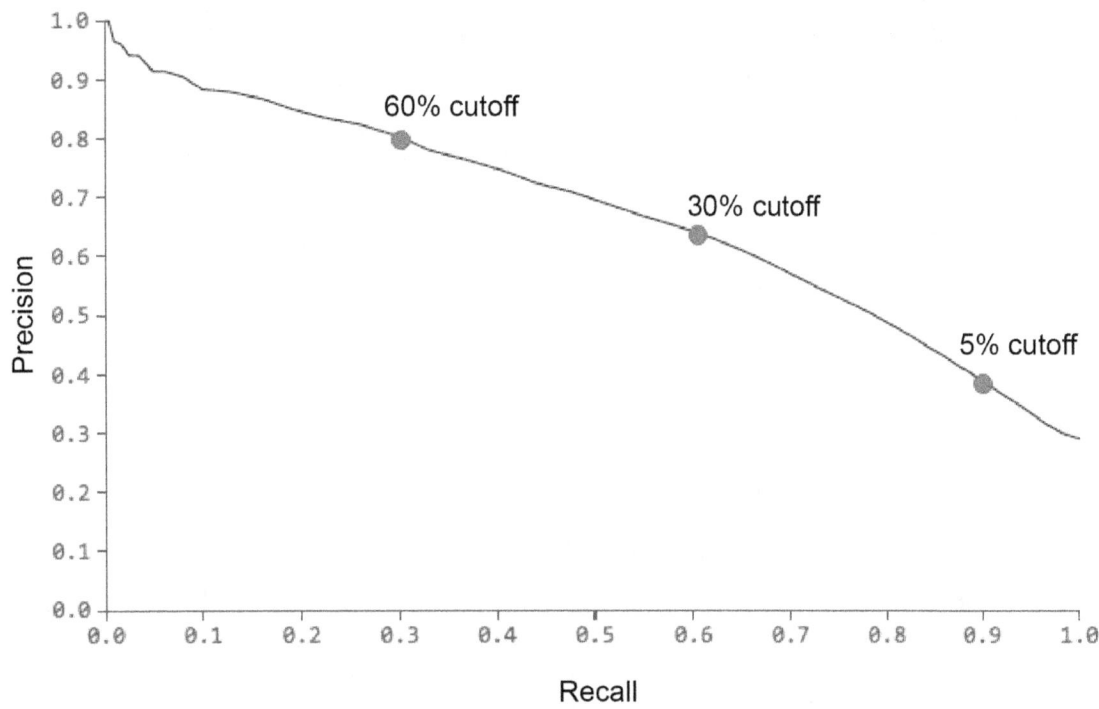

Figure 6.16: Precision-recall curve

We know that in an ideal case, the values of precision and recall will be unity. This means that upon increasing the threshold from 0 to 1, the precision would stay constant at 1, but the recall would increase from 0 to 1 as more and more (relevant) data points would be classified correctly. Thus, in an ideal case, the precision-recall curve would essentially just be a square and the **area under the curve** (**AUC**) would be equal to one.

Thus, we can see that, as with the F^1 score, the AUC is another metric derived from the precision and recall behavior that uses a combination of their values to evaluate the performance of the model. We want the model to achieve an AUC as high and close to 1 as possible.

278 | Model Evaluation

The other main visualization technique for showing the performance of a classification model is the **Receiver Operating Characteristic** (**ROC**) curve. The ROC curve plots the relationship between the **True Positive Rate** (**TPR**) on the Y axis and the **False Positive Rate** (**FPR**) on the X axis across a varying classification probability threshold. TPR is exactly the same as the recall (and is also known as the **sensitivity** of the model), and FPR is an equal complement of the **specificity** (that is, 1 - FPR = *Sensitivity*); both can be derived from the confusion matrix using these formulae:

$$TPR = \frac{True\ positives}{Total\ actual\ positives} = \frac{True\ positives}{True\ positives + False\ negatives}$$

Figure 6.17: True positive rate

$$FPR = \frac{False\ positives}{Total\ actual\ negatives} = \frac{True\ positives}{False\ positives + True\ negatives}$$

Figure 6.18: False positive rate

The following diagram shows an example of an ROC curve, plotted in the same way as the precision-recall curve: by varying the probability threshold such that each point on the curve represents a (TPR, FPR) data point corresponding to a specific probability threshold.

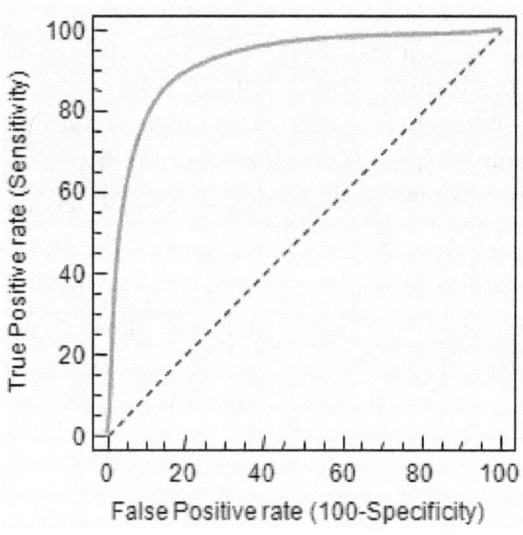

Figure 6.19: ROC curve

ROC curves are more useful when the classes are fairly balanced, since they tend to present an overly optimistic picture of the model on datasets with a class imbalance via their use of true negatives in the false positive rate in the ROC curve (which is not present in the precision-recall curve).

Exercise 51: Classification Metrics

In this exercise, we will use the random forest model we trained in *Chapter 5, Ensemble Modeling*, and use its predictions to generate the confusion matrix and calculate the precision, recall, and F_1 scores, as a way of rating our model. We will use scikit-learn's implementations to calculate these metrics:

1. Import the relevant libraries and functions:

    ```
    from sklearn.metrics import (accuracy_score, confusion_matrix, precision_score,
                                 recall_score, f1_score)
    ```

2. Use the model to predict classes for all data points. We will use the same features as we did earlier and use the random forest classifier to make a prediction on the loaded dataset. Every classifier in scikit-learn has a `.predict_proba()` function, which we will use here along with the standard `.predict()` function to give us the class probabilities and the classes respectively:

    ```
    X = titanic_clf.iloc[:, :-1]
    y = titanic_clf.iloc[:, -1]

    y_pred = rf.predict(X)
    y_pred_probs = rf.predict_proba(X)
    ```

3. Calculate the accuracy:

    ```
    print('Accuracy Score = {}'.format(accuracy_score(y, y_pred)))
    ```

    The output will be as follows:

    ```
    Accuracy Score = 0.6251402918069585
    ```

    Figure 6.20: Accuracy score

4. Print the confusion matrix:

    ```
    print(confusion_matrix(y_pred=y_pred, y_true=y))
    ```

    The output will be as follows:

    ```
    [[548   1]
     [333   9]]
    ```

    Figure 6.21: Confusion matrix

Here, we can see that the model seems to have a high number of false negatives, which means that we can expect the recall value for this model to be extremely low. Similarly, since the count of the false positives is just one, we can expect the model to have high precision.

5. Calculate the precision and recall:

```
print('Precision Score = {}'.format(precision_score(y, y_pred)))
print('Recall Score = {}'.format(recall_score(y, y_pred)))
```

The output will be as follows:

```
Precision Score = 0.9
Recall Score = 0.02631578947368421
```

Figure 6.22: Precision and recall scores

6. Calculate the F_1 score:

```
print('F1 Score = {}'.format(f1_score(y, y_pred)))
```

The output will be as follows:

```
F1 Score = 0.05113636363636364
```

Figure 6.23: F1 score

We can see that, since the recall is extremely low, this is affecting the F_1 score as well, making it close to zero.

Now that we have talked about the metrics we can use to measure the predictive performance of the model, let's talk about validation strategies, in which we will use a metric to evaluate the performance of the model in different cases and situations.

Splitting the Dataset

A common mistake made when determining how well a model is performing is to calculate the prediction error on the data that the model was trained on and conclude that a model performs really well on the basis of a high prediction accuracy on the training dataset.

This means that we are trying to test the model on data that the model has already *seen*, that is, the model has already learned the behavior of the training data because it was exposed to it–if asked to predict the behavior of the training data again, it would undoubtedly perform well. And the better the performance on the training data, the higher the chances that the model knows the data *too well*, so much so that it has even learned the noise and behavior of outliers in the data.

Now, high training accuracy results in a model having high variance, as we saw in the previous chapter. In order to get an unbiased estimate of the model's performance, we need to find its prediction accuracy on data it has not already been exposed to during training. This is where the hold-out dataset comes into the picture.

Hold-out Data

The **hold-out dataset** refers to a sample of the dataset that has been held back from training the model on and is essentially *unseen* by the model. The hold-out data points will likely contain outliers and noisy data points that behave differently from those in the training dataset, given that noise is random. Thus, calculating the performance on the hold-out dataset would allow us to validate whether the model is overfitting or not, as well as giving us an unbiased view of the model's performance.

We began our previous chapter by splitting the Titanic dataset into training and validation sets. What is this validation dataset, and how is it different from a test dataset? We often see the terms validation set and test set used interchangeably—although they both characterize a hold-out dataset, there are some differences in purpose:

- **Validation data**: After the model learns from the training data, its performance is evaluated on the validation dataset. However, in order to get the model to perform the best it can, we need to fine-tune the model and iteratively evaluate the updated model's performance repeatedly, and this is done on the validation dataset. The fine-tuned version of the model that performs best on the validation dataset is usually chosen to be the final model.

    The model, thus, is exposed to the validation dataset multiple times, at each iteration of improvement, although does not essentially *learn* from the data. It can be said that the validation set does affect the model, although indirectly.

- **Test data**: The final model that was chosen is now evaluated on the test dataset. The performance measured on this dataset will be an unbiased measure that is reported as the final performance metric of the model. This final evaluation is done once the model has been completely trained on the combined training and validation datasets. There is no training or updating of the model performed after this metric has been calculated.

    This means that the model is exposed to the test dataset only once, when calculating the final performance metric.

It should be kept in mind that the validation dataset should never be used to evaluate the final performance of the model: our estimate of the true performance of a model will be positively biased if the model has seen and been modified subsequently in an effort to specifically improve the performance on the validation set.

Having a single hold-out validation dataset does have some limitations, however:

- Since the model is only validated once in each iteration of improvement, it might be difficult to capture the uncertainty in prediction using this single evaluation.
- Dividing the data into training and validation sets decreases the size of the data upon which the model is trained, and this can lead to the model having high variance.
- The final model may *overfit* to this validation set since it was tuned in order to maximize performance on this dataset.

These challenges can be overcome if we use a validation technique called K-fold cross-validation instead of using a single validation dataset.

K-Fold Cross-Validation

K-fold cross-validation is a validation technique that helps us get an unbiased estimate of the model's performance by essentially rotating the validation set in k folds. This is how it works:

1. First, we choose the value of k and divide the data into k subsets.
2. Then, we set aside the first subset as the validation set and use the remaining data to train the model.
3. We measure the performance of the model on the validation subset.
4. Then, we set aside the second subset as the validation subset and repeat the process.
5. Once we have done this k times, we aggregate the performance metric values over all the folds and present the final metric.

The following figure explains this visually:

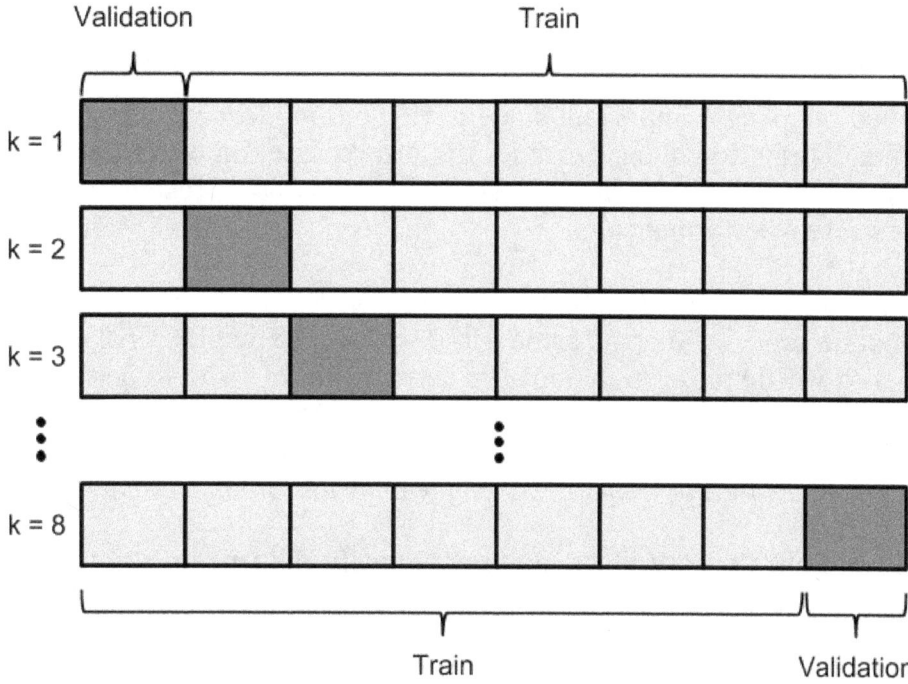

Figure 6.24: K-fold cross-validation

Although this method of validation is more computationally expensive, the benefits outweigh the costs. This approach makes sure that the model is validated on each example in the training dataset exactly once and that the performance estimate we achieve in the end is not biased in favor of a validation dataset, especially in the case of small datasets. A special case is **leave-one-out** cross-validation, where the value of k is equal to the number of data points.

Sampling

Now that we've looked at the strategies for splitting the dataset for training and validating the model, let's discuss how to allocate data points to these splits. There are two ways we can sample the data into the splits, and these are as follows:

- **Random sampling**: This is as simple as allocating random samples from the overall dataset into the training, validation, and/or test datasets. Randomly splitting the data only works when all the data points are independent of each other. For example, random splitting would not be the way to go if the data was in the form of a time-series, since the data points are ordered, and each depends on the previous one. Randomly splitting the data would destroy that order and not take into account this dependence.

- **Stratified sampling**: This is a way to ensure that each subset has the same distribution of values of the target variable as the original dataset. For example, if the original dataset has two classes in the ratio 3:7, stratified sampling ensures that each subset will also contain the two classes in the ratio 3:7.

  Stratified sampling is important since testing our model on a dataset with a different distribution of target values from the dataset on which the model was trained can give us a performance estimate that is not representative of the model's actual performance.

The size of the train, validation, and test samples also plays an important role in the model evaluation process. Keeping aside a large dataset to test the final performance of the model on will help us get an unbiased estimate of the model's performance and reduce the variance in prediction, but if the test set is so large that it compromises the model's ability to train due to a lack of training data, this will severely affect the model as well. This is a consideration that is especially relevant for smaller datasets.

Exercise 52: K-Fold Cross-Validation with Stratified Sampling

In this exercise, we'll implement K-fold cross-validation with stratified sampling on scikit-learn's random forest classifier. The **StratifiedKFold** class in scikit-learn implements a combination of the cross-validation and sampling together in one class, and we will use this in our exercise:

1. Import the relevant classes. We will import scikit-learn's **StratifiedKFold** class, which is a variation of **KFold** that returns stratified folds, along with the **RandomForestClassifier**:

   ```
   from sklearn.model_selection import StratifiedKFold
   from sklearn.ensemble import RandomForestClassifier
   ```

2. Prepare data for training and initialize the k-fold object. Here, we will use five folds to evaluate the model, and hence will give the **n_splits** parameter a value of **5**:

   ```
   X = titanic_clf.iloc[:, :-1].values
   y = titanic_clf.iloc[:, -1].values
   
   skf = StratifiedKFold(n_splits=5)
   ```

3. Train a classifier for each fold and record the score. The functioning of the **StratifiedKFold** class is similar to the **KFold** class that we used in the previous chapter, in *Exercise 48: Building a Stacked Model*: for each of the five folds, we will train on other four folds and predict on the fifth fold, and find the accuracy score for the predictions on the fifth fold. As we saw in the last chapter, the **skf.split()** function takes the dataset to split as input and returns an iterator comprising the index values used to subdivide the training data for training and validation for each row:

```
scores = []

for train_index, val_index in skf.split(X, y):
    X_train, X_val = X[train_index], X[val_index]
    y_train, y_val = y[train_index], y[val_index]

    rf_skf = RandomForestClassifier(**rf.get_params())

    rf_skf.fit(X_train, y_train)
    y_pred = rf_skf.predict(X_val)

    scores.append(accuracy_score(y_val, y_pred))

print(scores)
```

The output will be as follows:

```
[0.6145251396648045,
 0.6983240223463687,
 0.7471910112359551,
 0.7808988764044944,
 0.711864406779661]
```

Figure 6.25: Scores using random forest classifier

4. Print the aggregated accuracy score:

```
print('Mean Accuracy Score = {}'.format(np.mean(scores)))
```

The output will be as follows:

```
Mean Accuracy Score = 0.7105606912862568
```

Figure 6.26: Mean accuracy score

Performance Improvement Tactics

Performance improvement for supervised machine learning models is an iterative process, and a continuous cycle of updating and evaluation is usually required to get the perfect model. While the previous sections in this chapter dealt with the evaluation strategies, this section will talk about model updating: we will discuss some ways we can determine what our model needs to give it that performance boost, and how to make that change in our model.

Variation in Train and Test Error

In the previous chapter, we introduced the concepts of underfitting and overfitting, and mentioned a few ways to overcome them, later introducing ensemble models. But we didn't talk about how to identify whether our model was underfitting or overfitting to the training data.

It's usually useful to look at the learning and validation curves.

Learning Curve

The learning curve shows the variation in the training and validation error with the training data increasing in size. By looking at the shape of the curves, we can get a good idea of whether or not more data will benefit the modeling and possibly improve the model's performance.

Let's look at the following figure: the dotted curve represents the validation error and the solid curve represents the training error. The plot on the left shows the two curves converging to an error value that is quite high. This means that the model has a high bias and adding more data isn't likely to affect the model performance. So instead of wasting time and money collecting more data, all we need to do is increase model complexity.

On the other hand, the plot on the right shows a high difference between the training and test errors, even with an increasing number of data points in the training set. The wide gap indicates a high variance in the system, which means the model is overfitting. In this case, adding more data points will probably help the model generalize better:

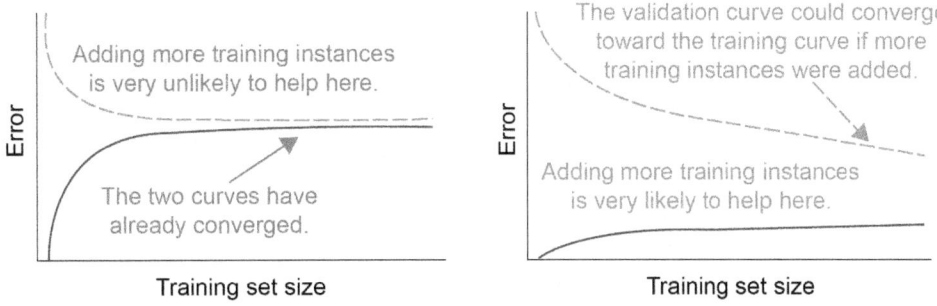

Figure 6.27: Learning curve for increasing data size

But how will we recognize the perfect learning curve? When we have a model with low bias and low variance, we will see a curve like the one shown in the following figure. It shows a low training error (low bias) as well as a low gap between the validation and training curves (low variance) as they converge. In practice, the best possible learning curves we can see are those that converge to the value of some irreducible error value (which exists due to noise and outliers in the dataset):

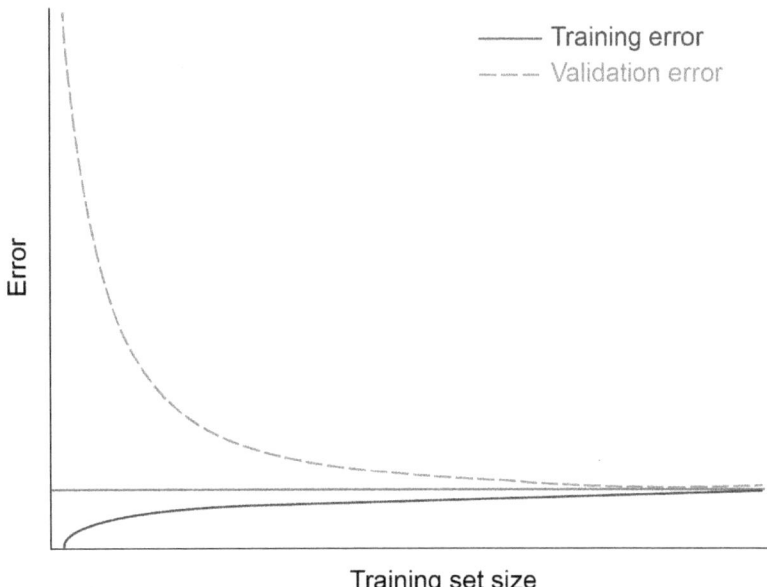

Figure 6.28: Variation in training and validation error with an increasing training data size for a low bias and variance model

Validation Curve

As we have discussed previously, the goal of a machine learning model is to be able to generalize to unseen data. Validation curves allow us to find the ideal point between an underfitted and an overfitted model where the model would generalize well. In the previous chapter, we talked a bit about how model complexity affects prediction performance: we said that as we move from an overly simplistic to an overly complex model, we go from having an underfitted model with high bias and low variance to an overfitted model with a low bias and high variance.

A validation curve shows the variation in training and validation error with a varying value of a model parameter that has some degree of control over the model's complexity–this could be the degree of the polynomial in linear regression, or the depth of a decision tree classifier.

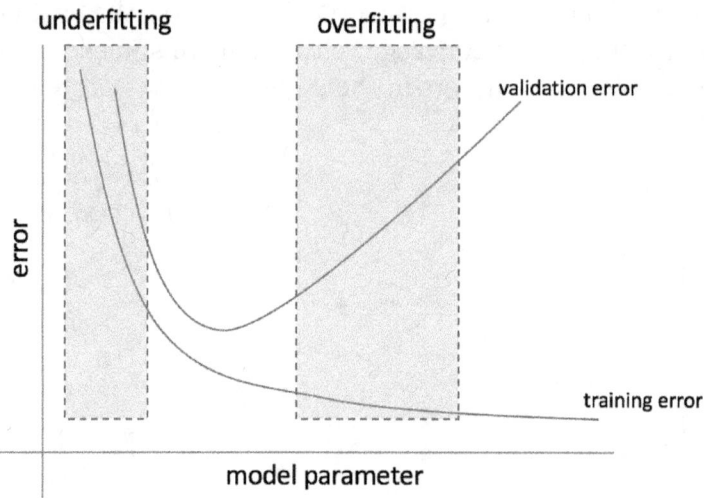

Figure 6.29: Variation in training and validation with increasing model complexity

The preceding figure shows how the validation and training error will vary with model complexity (of which the model parameter is an indicator). We can also see how the point in between the shaded regions is where the total error would be at a minimum, at the sweet spot between underfitting and overfitting. Finding this point will help us find the ideal value of the model's parameters that will help build a model with low bias as well as low variance.

Hyperparameter Tuning

We've talked about hyperparameter tuning several times before this; now let's discuss why it's so important. First, it should be noted that model parameters are different from model hyperparameters: while the former are internal to the model and are learned from the data, the latter define the architecture of the model itself.

Some examples of hyperparameters are as follows:

- The degree of polynomial features to be used for a linear regressor
- The maximum depth allowed for a decision tree classifier
- The number of trees to be included in a random forest classifier
- The learning rate used for the gradient descent algorithm

The design choices that define the architecture of the model can make a huge difference in how well the model performs. Usually, the default values for the hyperparameters work, but getting the perfect combination of values for the hyperparameters can really give the predictive power of the model a boost as the default values may be completely inappropriate for the problem we are trying to model. In the following figure, we see how varying the values of two hyperparameters can cause such a difference in the model score:

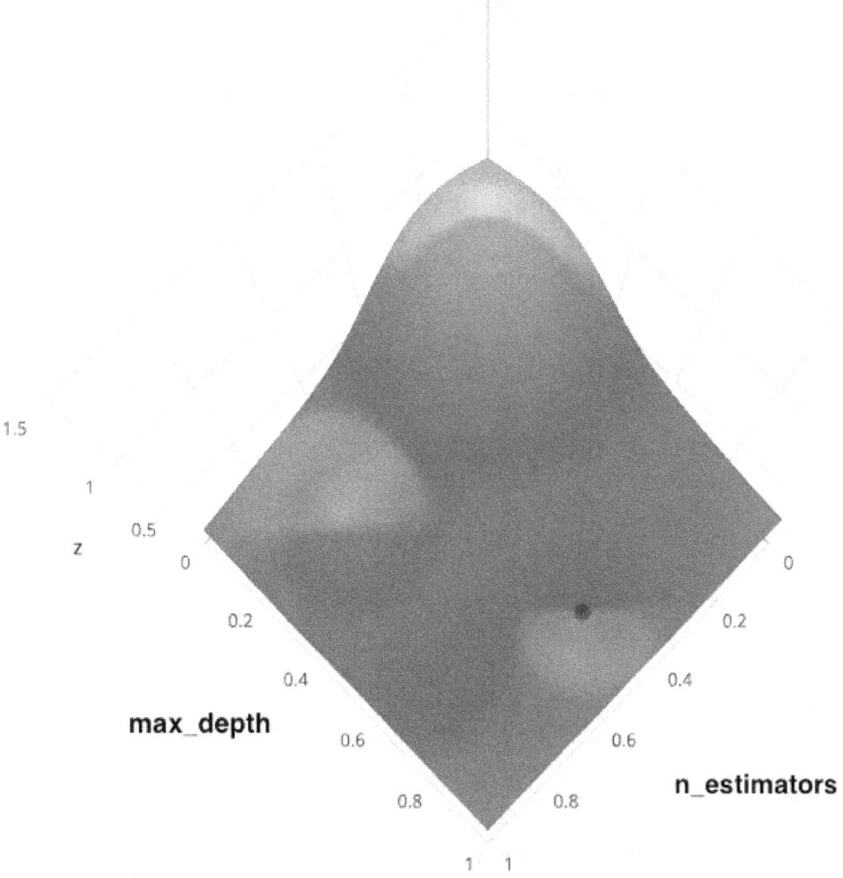

Figure 6.30: Variation in model score (Z axis) across values of two model parameters (the X and Y axes)

Finding that perfect combination by exploring a range of possible values is what is referred to as **hyperparameter tuning**. Since there is no loss function we can use to maximize the model performance, tuning the hyperparameters generally just involves experimenting with different combinations and choosing the one that performs best during validation.

There are a few ways in which we can go about tuning our model's hyperparameters:

- **Hand-tuning**: When we manually choose the values of our hyperparameters, this is known as hand-tuning. It is usually inefficient, since solving a high-dimensional optimization problem by hand can not only be slow, but also would not allow the model to reach its peak performance as we probably wouldn't try out every single combination of hyperparameter values.

- **Grid search**: Grid search involves training and evaluating a model for each combination of the hyperparameter values provided and selecting the combination that produces the best performing model. Since this involves performing an exhaustive sampling of the hyperparameter space, it is quite computationally expensive and hence inefficient.

- **Random search**: While the first method was deemed inefficient because too few combinations were tried, the second one was deemed so because too many combinations were tried. Random search aims to solve this by selecting a random subset of hyperparameter combinations from the grid (specified previously), and training and evaluating a model only for those. Alternatively, we can also provide a statistical distribution for each hyperparameter from which the values can be randomly sampled.

  The logic behind random search was proved by Bergstra and Bengio: if at least 5% of the points on the grid yield a close-to-optimal solution, then random search with 60 trials will find that region with a high probability.

  > **Note**
  >
  > You can read the paper by Bergstra and Bengio at http://www.jmlr.org/papers/v13/bergstra12a.html.

- **Bayesian optimization**: The previous two methods involved independently experimenting with combinations of hyperparameter values and recording the model performance for each. However, Bayesian optimization iterates over experiments sequentially and allows us to use the results of a previous experiment to improve the sampling method for the next experiment.

Exercise 53: Hyperparameter Tuning with Random Search

Using scikit-learn's **RandomizedSearchCV** method, we can define a grid of hyperparameter ranges and randomly sample from the grid, performing K-fold cross-validation with each combination of values. In this exercise, we'll perform hyperparameter tuning with the random search method:

1. Import the class for random search:

   ```
   from sklearn.model_selection import RandomizedSearchCV
   ```

2. Prepare data for training and initialize the classifier. Here, we will initialize our random forest classifier without passing any arguments, since this is just a base object that will be instantiated for each grid point on which to perform the random search:

   ```
   X = titanic_clf.iloc[:, :-1].values
   y = titanic_clf.iloc[:, -1].values

   rf_rand = RandomForestClassifier()
   ```

3. Specify the parameters to sample from. Here, we will list down the different values for each hyperparameter that we would like to have in the grid:

   ```
   param_dist = {"n_estimators": list(range(10,210,10)),
                 "max_depth": list(range(3,20)),
                 "max_features": list(range(1, 10)),
                 "min_samples_split": list(range(2, 11)),
                 "bootstrap": [True, False],
                 "criterion": ["gini", "entropy"]}
   ```

4. Run a randomized search. We initialize the random search object with the total number of trials we want to run, the parameter values dictionary, the scoring function, and the number of folds in the K-fold cross-validation. Then, we call the **.fit()** function to perform the search:

   ```
   n_iter_search = 60
   random_search = RandomizedSearchCV(rf_rand, param_distributions=param_dist, scoring='accuracy',
                                       n_iter=n_iter_search, cv=5)
   random_search.fit(X, y)
   ```

5. Print scores and hyperparameters for the top five models. Convert the **results** dictionary into a pandas DataFrame and sort the values by **rank_test_score**. Then, for the first five rows, print the rank, mean validation score, and the hyperparameters:

```
results = pd.DataFrame(random_search.cv_results_).sort_values('rank_test_score')
for i, row in results.head().iterrows():
    print("Model rank: {}".format(row.rank_test_score))
    print("Mean validation score: {:.3f} (std: {:.3f})".format(row.mean_test_score, row.std_test_score))
    print("Model Hyperparameters: {}\n".format(row.params))
```

The output will be as follows:

```
Model rank: 1
Mean validation score: 0.724 (std: 0.045)
Model Hyperparameters: {'n_estimators': 70, 'min_samples_split': 8, 'max_features': 2, 'max_depth': 10, 'criterion': 'gini', 'bootstrap': True}

Model rank: 2
Mean validation score: 0.719 (std: 0.051)
Model Hyperparameters: {'n_estimators': 180, 'min_samples_split': 7, 'max_features': 7, 'max_depth': 8, 'criterion': 'gini', 'bootstrap': True}

Model rank: 2
Mean validation score: 0.719 (std: 0.060)
Model Hyperparameters: {'n_estimators': 160, 'min_samples_split': 7, 'max_features': 6, 'max_depth': 7, 'criterion': 'gini', 'bootstrap': True}

Model rank: 4
Mean validation score: 0.718 (std: 0.046)
Model Hyperparameters: {'n_estimators': 200, 'min_samples_split': 5, 'max_features': 1, 'max_depth': 8, 'criterion': 'gini', 'bootstrap': False}

Model rank: 5
Mean validation score: 0.717 (std: 0.055)
Model Hyperparameters: {'n_estimators': 10, 'min_samples_split': 3, 'max_features': 2, 'max_depth': 6, 'criterion': 'gini', 'bootstrap': True}
```

Figure 6.31: Top five models' scores and hyperparameters

We can see that the model that performs best has only 70 trees, compared to the 160+ trees in the models ranked 2 to 4. Also, the model ranked 5 only has 10 trees and still has a performance comparable to that of the more complex models.

Feature Importance

While it is essential to focus on model performance, it's also important to understand how the features in our model contribute to the prediction:

- We need to be able to explain the model and how different variables affect the prediction to the relevant stakeholders who might demand insight into why our model is successful.

- The data might be biased and training a model on this data could hurt the model's performance and result in biased model evaluation, in which case the ability to interpret the model by finding the important features and analyzing them will help debug the performance of the model.

- In addition to the previous point, it must be noted that some model biases might just be socially or legally unacceptable. For example, if a model works well because it implicitly places high importance on a feature based on ethnicity, this might cause issues.

Besides these points, finding feature importance can also help in feature selection. If the data has high dimensionality and the trained model has high variance, removing features that have low importance is one way to achieve lowered variance through dimensionality reduction.

Exercise 54: Feature Importance Using Random Forest

In this exercise, we will find the feature importance from the random forest model we loaded earlier:

1. Find feature importance. Let's find the feature importance and save it in a pandas DataFrame with index equal to the column names, and sort this DataFrame in descending order:

    ```
    feat_imps = pd.DataFrame({'importance': rf.feature_importances_},
    index=titanic_clf.columns[:-1])
    feat_imps.sort_values(by='importance', ascending=False, inplace=True)
    ```

2. Plot the feature importance as a bar plot:

    ```
    feat_imps.plot(kind='bar', figsize=(10,7))

    plt.legend()
    plt.show()
    ```

The output will be as follows:

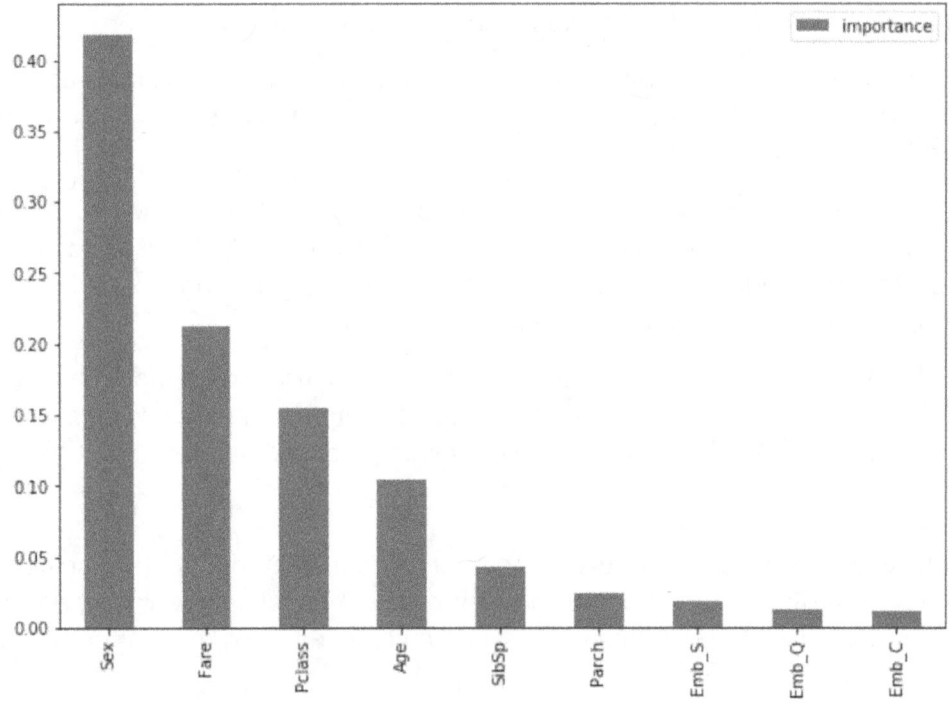

Figure 6.32: Histogram of features

Here, we can see that the **Sex**, **Fare**, and **Pclass** features seem to have the highest importance, that is, they have the most effect on the target variable.

Activity 15: Final Test Project

In this activity, we'll use the IBM HR Analytics Employee Attrition & Performance dataset (available at https://www.kaggle.com/pavansubhasht/ibm-hr-analytics-attrition-dataset, and the accompanying source code at https://github.com/TrainingByPackt/Supervised-Learning-with-Python) to solve a classification problem wherein we have to predict whether or not an employee will leave the company given the features. In the employee attrition problem, we want to maximize our recall, that is, we want to be able to identify all employees that will leave, even at the cost of predicting that a good employee will leave: this will help HR take the appropriate action for these employees so that they don't leave.

Each row in the dataset represents a single employee, and the target variable we have here is **Attrition**, which has two values: **1** and **0**, representing a *Yes* and *No* with respect to whether the corresponding employee left. We will use a gradient boosting classifier from scikit-learn to train the model. This activity is meant as a final project that will help consolidate the practical aspects of the concepts learned in this book, and particularly in this chapter.

We will find the most optimal set of hyperparameters for the model by using random search with cross-validation. Then, we will build the final classifier using the gradient boosting algorithm on a portion of the dataset and evaluate its performance using the classification metrics we have learned about on the remaining portion of the dataset. We will use the mean absolute error as the evaluation metric for this activity.

The steps to be performed are as follows:

1. Import the relevant libraries.
2. Read the **attrition_train.csv** dataset.
3. Read the **categorical_variable_values.json** file, which has details of categorical variables.
4. Process the dataset to convert all features to numerical values.
5. Choose a base model and define the range of hyperparameter values corresponding to the model to be searched over for hyperparameter tuning.
6. Define the parameters with which to initialize the **RandomizedSearchCV** object and use K-fold cross-validation to find the best model hyperparameters.
7. Split the dataset into training and validation sets and train a new model using the final hyperparameters on the training dataset.
8. Calculate the accuracy, precision, and recall for predictions on the validation set, and print the confusion matrix.
9. Experiment with varying thresholds to find the optimal point with high recall. Plot the precision-recall curve.
10. Finalize a threshold that will be used for predictions on the test dataset.
11. Read and process the test dataset to convert all features to numerical values.

12. Predict the final values on the test dataset.

> **Note**
> The solution for this activity can be found on page 373.

Summary

This chapter discussed why model evaluation is important in supervised machine learning and looked at several important metrics that are used to evaluate regression and classification tasks. We saw that while regression models were fairly straightforward to evaluate, the performance of classification models could be measured in a number of ways, depending on what we want the model to prioritize. Besides numerical metrics, we also looked at how to plot precision-recall and ROC curves to better interpret and evaluate model performance.

After this, we talked about why evaluating a model by calculating the prediction error on the data that the model was trained on was a bad idea, and how testing a model on data that it has already *seen* would lead to the model having a high variance. With this, we introduced the concept of having a hold-out dataset and why K-fold cross-validation is a useful strategy to have, along with sampling techniques that ensure that the model training and evaluation process remains unbiased.

The last section on performance improvement tactics started with a discussion on learning and validation curves, and how they can be interpreted to drive the model development process towards a better-performing model. This was followed by a section on hyperparameter tuning as an effort to boost performance, and a brief introduction to feature importance.

Appendix

About

This section is included to assist the students to perform the activities in the book.
It includes detailed steps that are to be performed by the students to achieve the objectives of the activities.

Chapter 1: Python Machine Learning Toolkit

Activity 1: pandas Functions

Solution

1. Open a new Jupyter notebook.

2. Use pandas to load the Titanic dataset:

   ```
   import pandas as pd
   ```

   ```
   df = pd.read_csv('titanic.csv')
   ```

   Use the **head()** function on the dataset as follows:

   ```
   # Have a look at the first 5 sample of the data
   df.head()
   ```

   The output will be as follows:

	Unnamed: 0	Cabin	Embarked	Fare	Pclass	Ticket	Age	Name	Parch	Sex	SibSp	Survived
0	0	NaN	S	7.2500	3	A/5 21171	22.0	Braund, Mr. Owen Harris	0	male	1	0.0
1	1	C85	C	71.2833	1	PC 17599	38.0	Cumings, Mrs. John Bradley (Florence Briggs Th...	0	female	1	1.0
2	2	NaN	S	7.9250	3	STON/O2. 3101282	26.0	Heikkinen, Miss. Laina	0	female	0	1.0
3	3	C123	S	53.1000	1	113803	35.0	Futrelle, Mrs. Jacques Heath (Lily May Peel)	0	female	1	1.0
4	4	NaN	S	8.0500	3	373450	35.0	Allen, Mr. William Henry	0	male	0	0.0

Figure 1.65: First five rows

Use the **describe** function as follows:

```
df.describe(include='all')
```

The output will be as follows:

	Unnamed: 0	Cabin	Embarked	Fare	Pclass	Ticket	Age	Name	Parch	Sex	SibSp
count	1309.000000	295	1307	1308.000000	1309.000000	1309	1046.000000	1309	1309.000000	1309	1309.00
unique	NaN	186	3	NaN	NaN	929	NaN	1307	NaN	2	NaN
top	NaN	C23 C25 C27	S	NaN	NaN	CA. 2343	NaN	Kelly, Mr. James	NaN	male	NaN
freq	NaN	6	914	NaN	NaN	11	NaN	2	NaN	843	NaN
mean	654.000000	NaN	NaN	33.295479	2.294882	NaN	29.881138	NaN	0.385027	NaN	0.49885
std	378.020061	NaN	NaN	51.758668	0.837836	NaN	14.413493	NaN	0.865560	NaN	1.04165
min	0.000000	NaN	NaN	0.000000	1.000000	NaN	0.170000	NaN	0.000000	NaN	0.00000
25%	327.000000	NaN	NaN	7.895800	2.000000	NaN	21.000000	NaN	0.000000	NaN	0.00000
50%	654.000000	NaN	NaN	14.454200	3.000000	NaN	28.000000	NaN	0.000000	NaN	0.00000
75%	981.000000	NaN	NaN	31.275000	3.000000	NaN	39.000000	NaN	0.000000	NaN	1.00000
max	1308.000000	NaN	NaN	512.329200	3.000000	NaN	80.000000	NaN	9.000000	NaN	8.00000

Figure 1.66: Output of describe()

3. We don't need the **Unnamed: 0** column. We can remove the column without using the **del** command, as follows:

```
df = df[df.columns[1:]] # Use the columns
df.head()
```

The output will be as follows:

	Cabin	Embarked	Fare	Pclass	Ticket	Age	Name	Parch	Sex	SibSp	Survived
0	NaN	S	7.2500	3	A/5 21171	22.0	Braund, Mr. Owen Harris	0	male	1	0.0
1	C85	C	71.2833	1	PC 17599	38.0	Cumings, Mrs. John Bradley (Florence Briggs Th...	0	female	1	1.0
2	NaN	S	7.9250	3	STON/O2. 3101282	26.0	Heikkinen, Miss. Laina	0	female	0	1.0
3	C123	S	53.1000	1	113803	35.0	Futrelle, Mrs. Jacques Heath (Lily May Peel)	0	female	1	1.0
4	NaN	S	8.0500	3	373450	35.0	Allen, Mr. William Henry	0	male	0	0.0

Figure 1.67: First five rows after deleting the Unnamed: 0 column

4. Compute the mean, standard deviation, minimum, and maximum values for the columns of the DataFrame without using **describe**:

```
df.mean()

Fare        33.295479
Pclass       2.294882
Age         29.881138
Parch        0.385027
SibSp        0.498854
Survived     0.383838
dtype: float64
```

```
df.std()

Fare        51.758668
Pclass       0.837836
Age         14.413493
Parch        0.865560
SibSp        1.041658
Survived     0.486592
dtype: float64
```

```
df.min()

Fare        0.00
Pclass      1.00
Age         0.17
Parch       0.00
SibSp       0.00
Survived    0.00
dtype: float64
```

```
df.max()
```

```
Fare        512.3292
Pclass        3.0000
Age          80.0000
Parch         9.0000
SibSp         8.0000
Survived      1.0000
dtype: float64
```

5. What about the 33, 66, and 99% quartiles? Use the **quantile** method as follows:

    ```
    df.quantile(0.33)
    ```

    ```
    Fare        8.559325
    Pclass      2.000000
    Age        23.000000
    Parch       0.000000
    SibSp       0.000000
    Survived    0.000000
    Name: 0.33, dtype: float64
    ```

    ```
    df.quantile(0.66)
    ```

    ```
    Fare       26.0
    Pclass      3.0
    Age        34.0
    Parch       0.0
    SibSp       0.0
    Survived    1.0
    Name: 0.66, dtype: float64
    ```

    ```
    df.quantile(0.99)
    ```

    ```
    Fare        262.375
    Pclass        3.000
    Age          65.000
    Parch         4.000
    SibSp         5.000
    Survived      1.000
    Name: 0.99, dtype: float64
    ```

6. How many passengers were from each class? Let's see, using the **groupby** method:

   ```
   class_groups = df.groupby('Pclass')
   for name, index in class_groups:
       print(f'Class: {name}: {len(index)}')
   ```

   Class: 1: 323
   Class: 2: 277
   Class: 3: 709

7. How many passengers were from each class? You can find the answer by using selecting/indexing methods to count the members of each class:

   ```
   for clsGrp in df.Pclass.unique():
       num_class = len(df[df.Pclass == clsGrp])
       print(f'Class {clsGrp}: {num_class}')
   ```

   Class 3: 709
   Class 1: 323
   Class 2: 277

   The answers to *Step 6* and *Step 7* do match.

8. Determine who the eldest passenger in third class was:

   ```
   third_class = df.loc[(df.Pclass == 3)]

   third_class.loc[(third_class.Age == third_class.Age.max())]
   ```

   The output will be as follows:

	Cabin	Embarked	Fare	Pclass	Ticket	Age	Name	Parch	Sex	SibSp	Survived
851	NaN	S	7.775	3	347060	74.0	Svensson, Mr. Johan	0	male	0	0.0

   Figure 1.68: Eldest passenger in third class

9. For a number of machine learning problems, it is very common to scale the numerical values between 0 and 1. Use the **agg** method with Lambda functions to scale the **Fare** and **Age** columns between 0 and 1:

   ```
   fare_max = df.Fare.max()
   age_max = df.Age.max()

   df.agg({
       'Fare': lambda x: x / fare_max,
       'Age': lambda x: x / age_max,
   }).head()
   ```

   The output will be as follows:

	Fare	Age
0	0.014151	0.2750
1	0.139136	0.4750
2	0.015469	0.3250
3	0.103644	0.4375
4	0.015713	0.4375

   Figure 1.69: Scaling numerical values between 0 and 1

10. There is one individual in the dataset without a listed **Fare** value:

    ```
    df_nan_fare = df.loc[(df.Fare.isna())]
    df_nan_fare
    ```

    This is the output:

	Cabin	Embarked	Fare	Pclass	Ticket	Age	Name	Parch	Sex	SibSp	Survived
1043	NaN	S	NaN	3	3701	60.5	Storey, Mr. Thomas	0	male	0	NaN

    Figure 1.70: Individual without a listed Fare value

Replace the NaN values of this row in the main DataFrame with the mean **Fare** value for those corresponding with the same class and **Embarked** location using the **groupby** method:

```
embarked_class_groups = df.groupby(['Embarked', 'Pclass'])

indices = embarked_class_groups.groups[(df_nan_fare.Embarked.values[0],
df_nan_fare.Pclass.values[0])]
mean_fare = df.iloc[indices].Fare.mean()
df.loc[(df.index == 1043), 'Fare'] = mean_fare
df.iloc[1043]
```

The output will be as follows:

```
Cabin                          NaN
Embarked                         S
Fare                       14.4354
Pclass                           3
Ticket                        3701
Age                           60.5
Name             Storey, Mr. Thomas
Parch                            0
Sex                           male
SibSp                            0
Survived                       NaN
Name: 1043, dtype: object
```

Chapter 2: Exploratory Data Analysis and Visualization

Activity 2: Summary Statistics and Missing Values

Solution

The steps to complete this activity are as follows:

1. Read the data. Use pandas' `.read_csv` method to read the CSV file into a pandas DataFrame:

   ```
   data = pd.read_csv('house_prices.csv')
   ```

2. Use pandas' `.info()` and `.describe()` methods to view the summary statistics of the dataset:

   ```
   data.info()
   data.describe().T
   ```

   The output of `info()` will be:

   ```
   <class 'pandas.core.frame.DataFrame'>
   RangeIndex: 1460 entries, 0 to 1459
   Data columns (total 81 columns):
   Id              1460 non-null int64
   MSSubClass      1460 non-null int64
   MSZoning        1460 non-null object
   LotFrontage     1201 non-null float64
   LotArea         1460 non-null int64
   Street          1460 non-null object
   Alley           91 non-null object
   LotShape        1460 non-null object
   LandContour     1460 non-null object
   Utilities       1460 non-null object
   LotConfig       1460 non-null object
   LandSlope       1460 non-null object
   Neighborhood    1460 non-null object
   Condition1      1460 non-null object
   Condition2      1460 non-null object
   ```

   Figure 2.39: The output of the info() method

The output of `describe()` will be:

	count	mean	std	min	25%	50%	75%	max
Id	1460.0	730.500000	421.610009	1.0	365.75	730.5	1095.25	1460.0
MSSubClass	1460.0	56.897260	42.300571	20.0	20.00	50.0	70.00	190.0
LotFrontage	1201.0	70.049958	24.284752	21.0	59.00	69.0	80.00	313.0
LotArea	1460.0	10516.828082	9981.264932	1300.0	7553.50	9478.5	11601.50	215245.0
OverallQual	1460.0	6.099315	1.382997	1.0	5.00	6.0	7.00	10.0
OverallCond	1460.0	5.575342	1.112799	1.0	5.00	5.0	6.00	9.0
YearBuilt	1460.0	1971.267808	30.202904	1872.0	1954.00	1973.0	2000.00	2010.0
YearRemodAdd	1460.0	1984.865753	20.645407	1950.0	1967.00	1994.0	2004.00	2010.0
MasVnrArea	1452.0	103.685262	181.066207	0.0	0.00	0.0	166.00	1600.0

Figure 2.40: The output of the describe() method

3. Find the total count and total percentage of missing values in each column of the DataFrame and display them for columns having at least one null value, in descending order of missing percentages.

   As we did in *Exercise 12: Visualizing Missing Values*, we will use the `.isnull()` function on the DataFrame to get a mask, find the count of null values in each column by using the `.sum()` function over the mask DataFrame and the fraction of null values by using `.mean()` over the mask DataFrame and multiply by 100 to convert it to a percentage. Then, we use `pd.concat()` to combine the total and percentage of null values into a single DataFrame and sort the rows by percentage of missing values:

```
mask = data.isnull()
total = mask.sum()
percent = 100*mask.mean()

missing_data = pd.concat([total, percent], axis=1,join='outer',
            keys=['count_missing', 'perc_missing'])
missing_data.sort_values(by='perc_missing', ascending=False, inplace=True)

missing_data[missing_data.count_missing > 0]
```

The output will be:

	count_missing	perc_missing
PoolQC	1453	99.520548
MiscFeature	1406	96.301370
Alley	1369	93.767123
Fence	1179	80.753425
FireplaceQu	690	47.260274
LotFrontage	259	17.739726
GarageYrBlt	81	5.547945
GarageCond	81	5.547945
GarageType	81	5.547945
GarageFinish	81	5.547945
GarageQual	81	5.547945

Figure 2.41: Total count and percentage of missing values in each column

4. Plot the nullity matrix and nullity correlation heatmap. First, we find the list of column names for those having at least one null value. Then, we use the **missingno** library to plot the nullity matrix (as we did in *Exercise 12: Visualizing Missing Values*) for a sample of 500 points, and the nullity correlation heatmap for the data in those columns:

```
nullable_columns = data.columns[mask.any()].tolist()
msno.matrix(data[nullable_columns].sample(500))
plt.show()

msno.heatmap(data[nullable_columns], figsize=(18,18))
plt.show()
```

The nullity matrix will look like this:

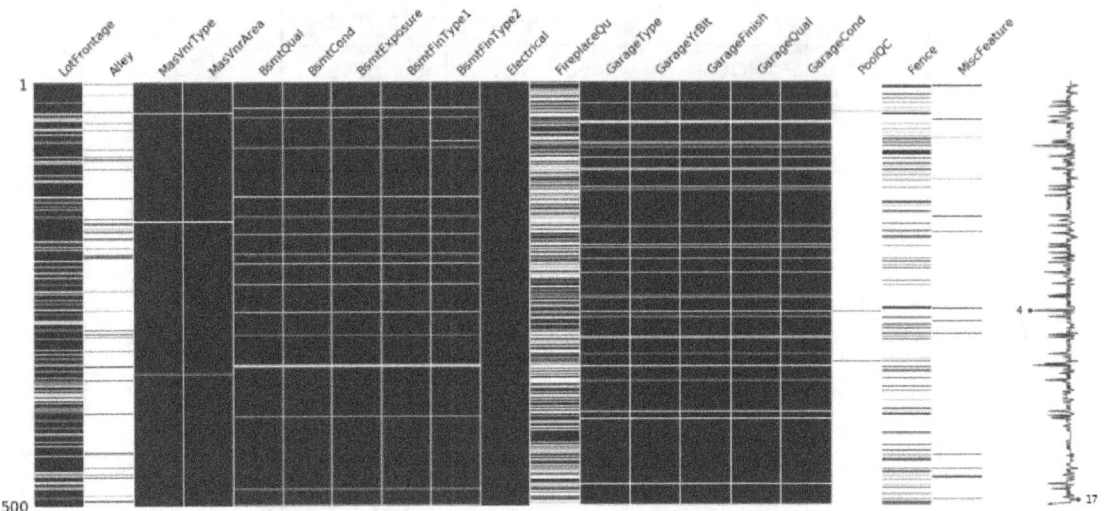

Figure 2.42: Nullity matrix

The nullity correlation heatmap will look like this:

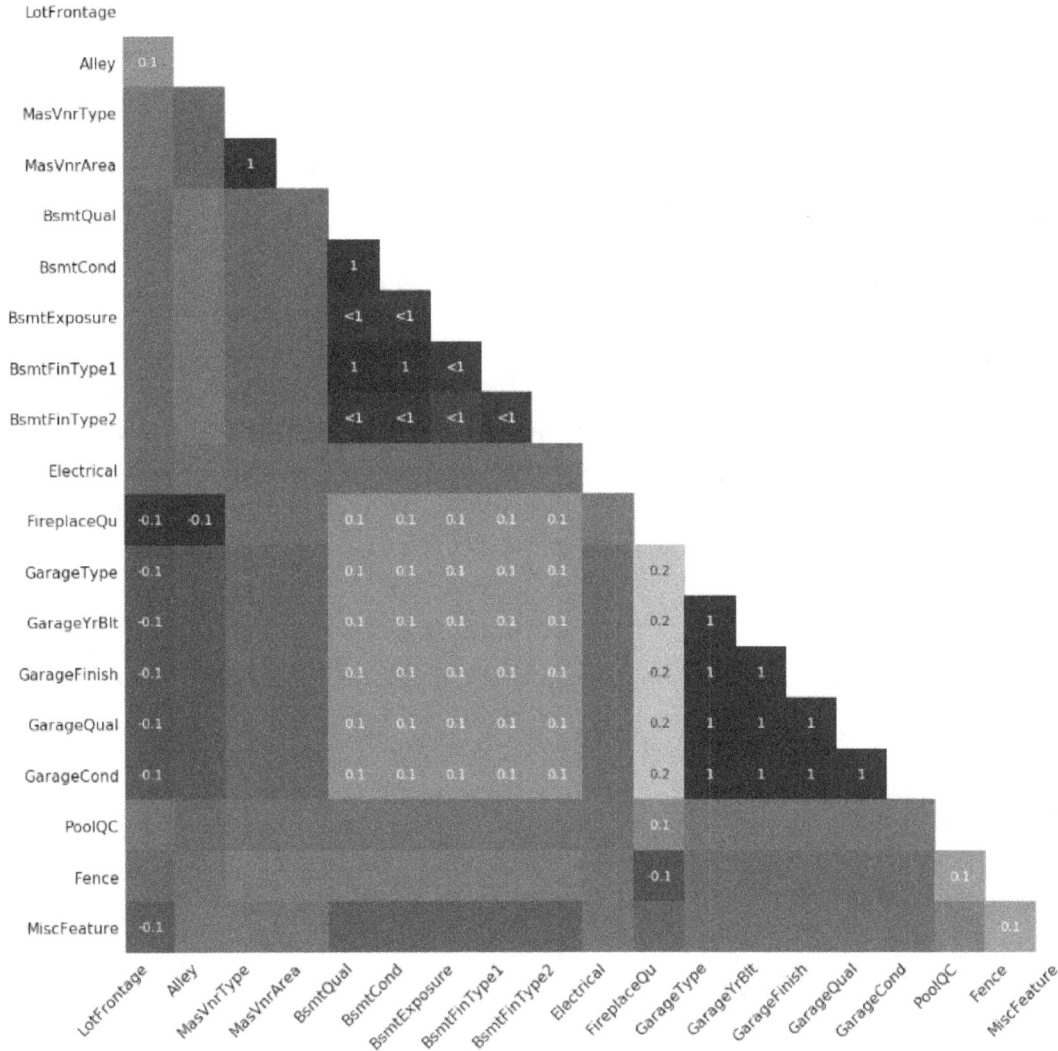

Figure 2.43: Nullity correlation heatmap

5. Delete the columns having more than 80% of values missing. Use the `.loc` operator on the DataFrame we created in *Step 3* to select only those columns that had less than 80% of values missing:

   ```
   data = data.loc[:,missing_data[missing_data.perc_missing < 80].index]
   ```

6. Replace null values in the **FireplaceQu** column with NA values. Use the `.fillna()` method to replace null values with the **NA** string:

   ```
   data['FireplaceQu'] = data['FireplaceQu'].fillna('NA')
   ```

Activity 3: Visually Representing the Distribution of Values

Solution

1. Plot a histogram using Matplotlib for the target variable, **SalePrice**. First, we initialize the figure using the `plt.figure` command and set the figure size. Then, we use Matplotlib's `.hist()` function as our primary plotting function, to which we pass the **SalePrice** series object for plotting the histogram. Lastly, we specify the axes labels and show the plot:

   ```
   plt.figure(figsize=(8,6))

   plt.hist(data.SalePrice, bins=range(0,800000,50000))

   plt.ylabel('Number of data points')
   plt.xlabel('SalePrice')
   plt.show()
   ```

The output will be as follows:

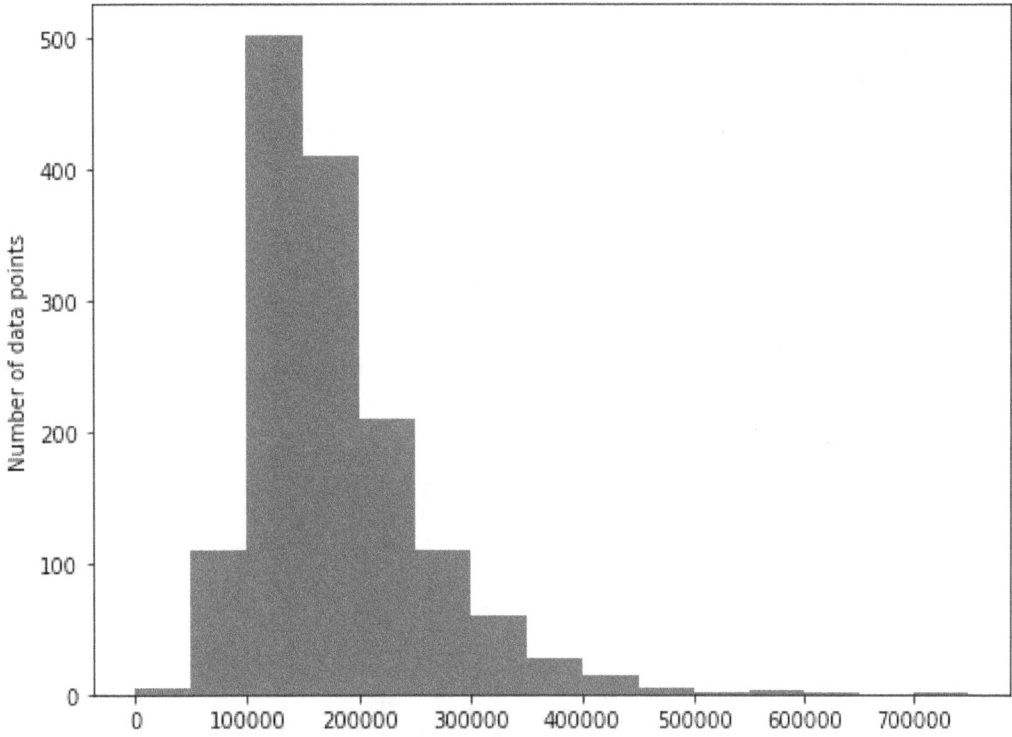

Figure 2.44: Histogram for the target variable

2. Find the number of unique values within each column having the object type. Create a new DataFrame called **object_variables** by using the **.select_dtypes** function on the original DataFrame to select those columns with the **numpy.object** data type. Then, find the number of unique values for each column in this DataFrame by using the **.nunique()** function, and sort the resultant series:

   ```
   object_variables = data.select_dtypes(include=[np.object])
   object_variables.nunique().sort_values()
   ```

   The output will be:

   ```
   CentralAir      2
   Street          2
   Utilities       2
   GarageFinish    3
   LandSlope       3
   PavedDrive      3
   LotShape        4
   LandContour     4
   KitchenQual     4
   MasVnrType      4
   ```

   Figure 2.45: Number of unique values within each column having the object type

3. Create a DataFrame representing the number of occurrences for each categorical value in the **HouseStyle** column. Use the **.value_counts()** function to calculate the frequencies of each value in decreasing order in the form of a pandas series, then reset the index to give us a DataFrame and sort the values by the index:

   ```
   counts = data.HouseStyle.value_counts(dropna=False)
   counts.reset_index().sort_values(by='index')
   ```

The output will be:

	index	HouseStyle
2	1.5Fin	154
5	1.5Unf	14
0	1Story	726
7	2.5Fin	8
6	2.5Unf	11
1	2Story	445
4	SFoyer	37
3	SLvl	65

Figure 2.46: Number of occurrences for each categorical value in the HouseStyle column

4. Plot a pie chart representing these counts. As in *Step 1*, we initialize the image using **plt.figure()** and use the **plt.title()** and **plt.show()** methods to set the figure title and display it respectively. The primary plotting function used is **plt.pie()**, to which we pass the series we created in the previous step:

```
plt.figure(figsize=(10,10))
plt.pie(counts, labels=counts.index)
plt.title('Pie chart showing counts for\nHouseStyle categories')
plt.show()
```

The output will be as follows:

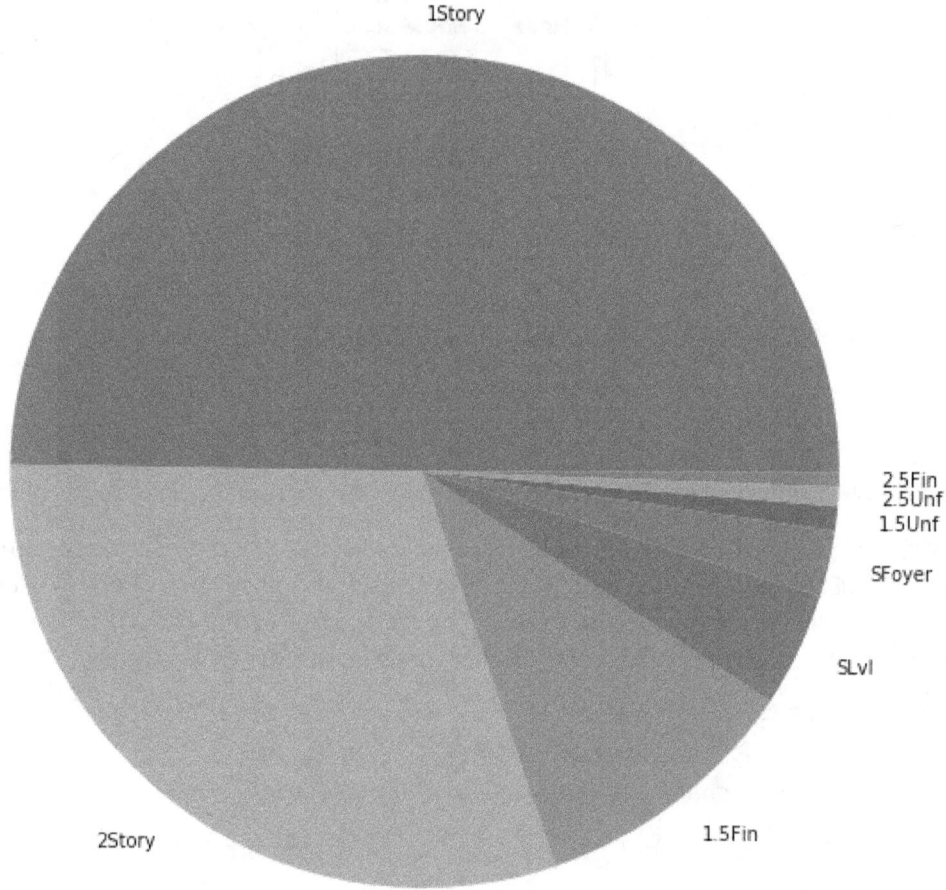

Figure 2.47: Pie chart representing the counts

5. Find the number of unique values within each column having the number type. As done in *Step 2*, now select columns having the **numpy.number** data type and find the number of unique values in each column using **.nunique()**. Sort the resultant series in descending order:

   ```
   numeric_variables = data.select_dtypes(include=[np.number])
   numeric_variables.nunique().sort_values(ascending=False)
   ```

   The output will be as follows:

   ```
   Id              1460
   LotArea         1073
   GrLivArea        861
   BsmtUnfSF        780
   1stFlrSF         753
   TotalBsmtSF      721
   SalePrice        663
   BsmtFinSF1       637
   GarageArea       441
   2ndFlrSF         417
   MasVnrArea       327
   WoodDeckSF       274
   OpenPorchSF      202
   BsmtFinSF2       144
   ```

   Figure 2.48: Number of unique values within each column having the number type

6. Plot a histogram using Seaborn for the **LotArea** variable. Use Seaborn's **.distplot()** function as the primary plotting function, to which the **LotArea** series in the DataFrame needs to be passed (without any null values; use **.dropna()** on the series to remove them). To improve the plot view, also set the **bins** parameter and specify the X axis limits using **plt.xlim()**:

   ```
   plt.figure(figsize=(10,7))
   sns.distplot(data.LotArea.dropna(), , bins=range(0,100000,1000))
   plt.xlim(0,100000)
   plt.show()
   ```

The output will be as follows:

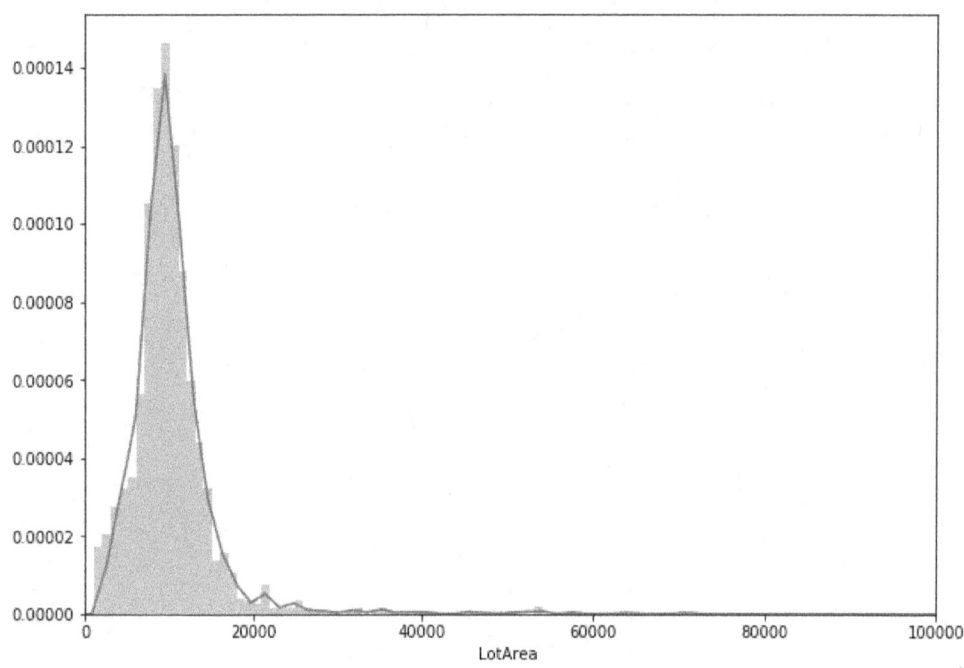

Figure 2.49: Histogram for the LotArea variable

7. Calculate the skew and kurtosis values for the values in each column:

   ```
   data.skew().sort_values()
   data.kurt()
   ```

   The output for skew values will be:

   ```
   GarageYrBlt     -0.649415
   YearBuilt       -0.613461
   YearRemodAdd    -0.503562
   GarageCars      -0.342549
   Id               0.000000
   FullBath         0.036562
   YrSold           0.096269
   GarageArea       0.179981
   BedroomAbvGr     0.211790
   MoSold           0.212053
   OverallQual      0.216944
   BsmtFullBath     0.596067
   ```

   Figure 2.50: Skew values for each column

The output for kurtosis values will be:

```
LotFrontage      17.452867
GarageYrBlt      -0.418341
MasVnrArea       10.082417
Id               -1.200000
Fireplaces       -0.217237
KitchenAbvGr     21.532404
BedroomAbvGr      2.230875
HalfBath         -1.076927
FullBath         -0.857043
BsmtHalfBath     16.396642
TotRmsAbvGrd      0.880762
GarageCars        0.220998
```

Figure 2.51: Kurtosis values for each column

Activity 4: Relationships Within the Data

Solution

1. Plot the correlation heatmap for the dataset. As we did in *Exercise 23: Correlation Heatmap*, plot the heatmap using Seaborn's **.heatmap()** function and pass the feature correlation matrix (as determined by using pandas' **.corr()** function on the DataFrame). Additionally, set the color map to **RdBu** using the **cmap** parameter and the minimum and maximum values on the color scale to **-1** and **1** using the **vmin** and **vmax** parameters respectively:

    ```
    plt.figure(figsize = (12,10))
    sns.heatmap(data.corr(), square=True, cmap="RdBu", vmin=-1, vmax=1)
    plt.show()
    ```

The output will be:

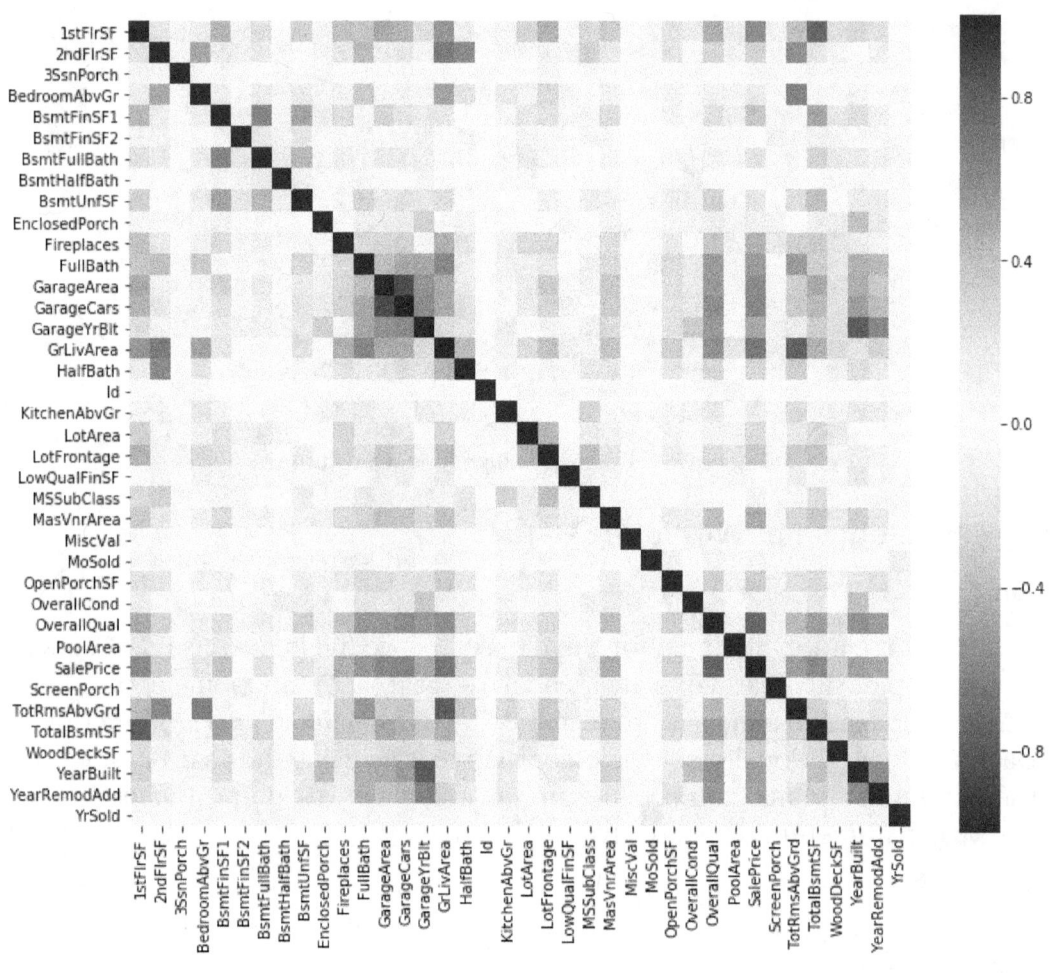

Figure 2.52: Heatmap for the dataset

2. Plot a more compact heatmap having annotations for correlation values using the following subset of features:

```
feature_subset = [
    'GarageArea',
'GarageCars','GarageCond','GarageFinish','GarageQual','GarageType',
    'GarageYrBlt','GrLivArea','LotArea','MasVnrArea','SalePrice'
]
```

Now do the same as in the previous step, this time selecting only the above columns in the dataset, and adding an **annot** parameter with the **True** value to the primary plotting function, all else remaining the same:

```
plt.figure(figsize = (12,10))
sns.heatmap(data[feature_subset].corr(), square=True, annot=True,
cmap="RdBu", vmin=-1, vmax=1)
plt.show()
```

The output will be as follows:

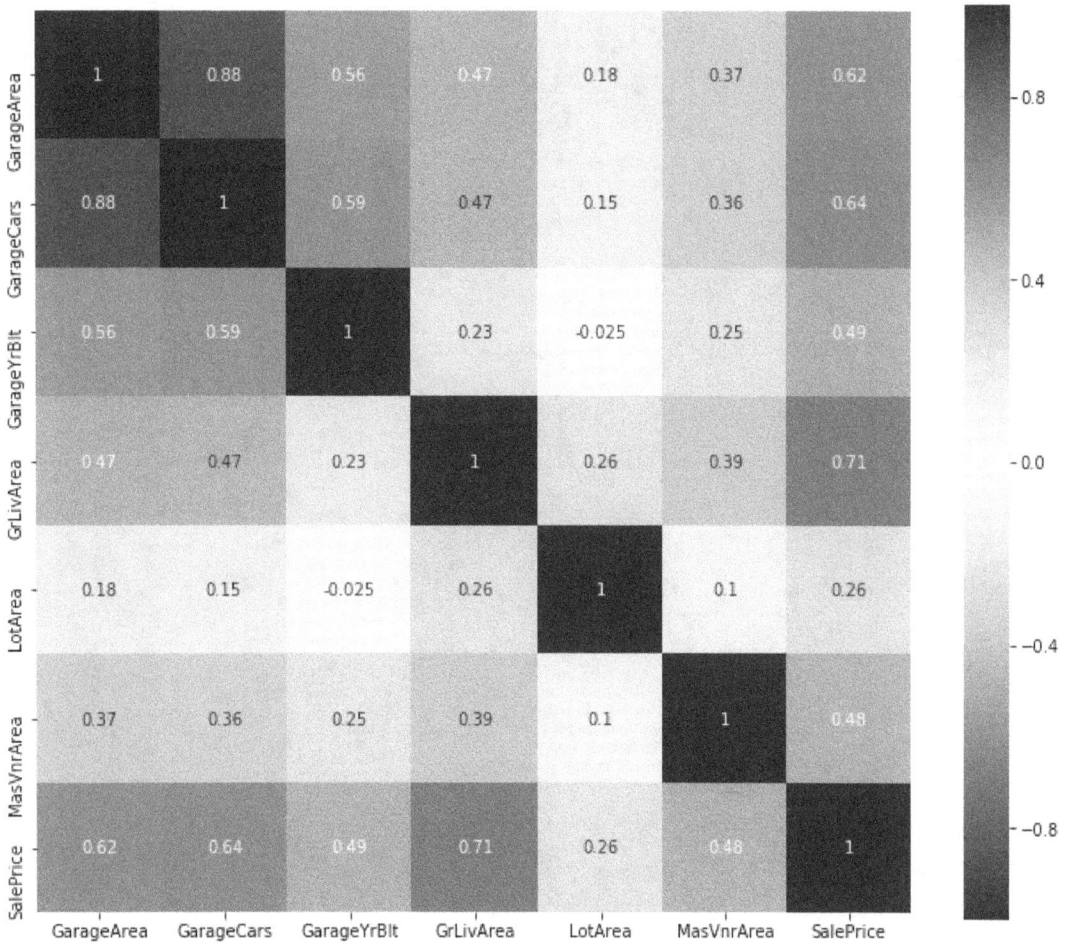

Figure 2.53: Heatmap with annotations for correlation values

322 | Appendix

3. Display the pairplot for the same subset of features, with the KDE plot on the diagonals and scatter plot elsewhere. Use Seaborn's **.pairplot()** function to plot the pairplot for the non-null values in the selected columns of the DataFrame. To make the diagonal plots KDE plots, pass **kde** to the **diag_kind** parameter and to set all other plots as scatter plots, pass **scatter** to the **kind** parameter:

   ```
   sns.pairplot(data[feature_subset].dropna(), kind ='scatter', diag_kind='kde')
   plt.show()
   ```

   The output will be:

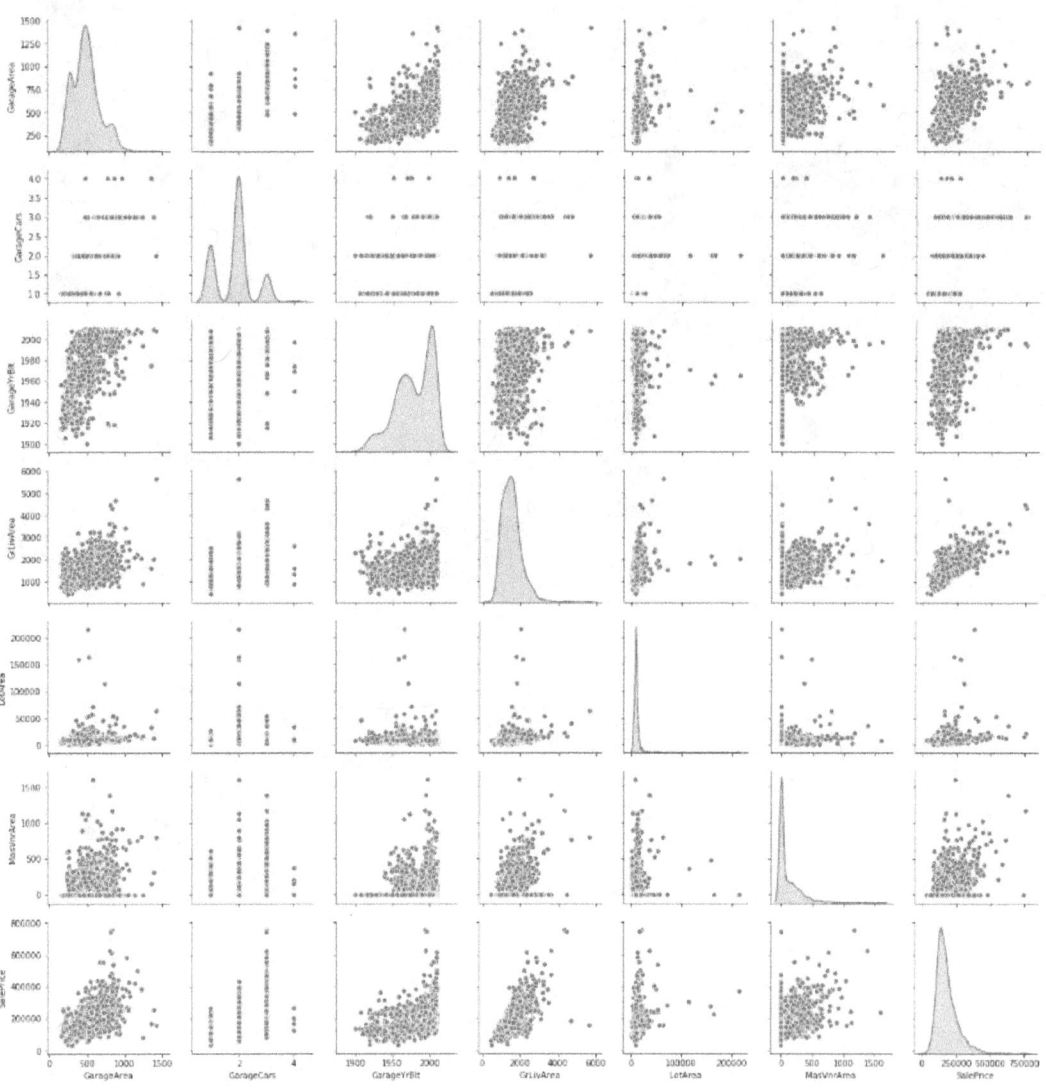

Figure 2.54: Pairplot for the same subset of features

4. Create a boxplot to show the variation in **SalePrice** for each category of **Garage-Cars**. The primary plotting function used here will be Seaborn's .**boxplot()** function, to which we pass the DataFrame along with parameters **x** and **y**, the former is the categorical variable and the latter is the continuous variable over which we want to see the variation within each category, that is, **GarageCars** and **SalePrice** respectively:

```
plt.figure(figsize=(10, 10))
sns.boxplot(x='GarageCars', y="SalePrice", data=data)
plt.show()
```

The output will be as follows:

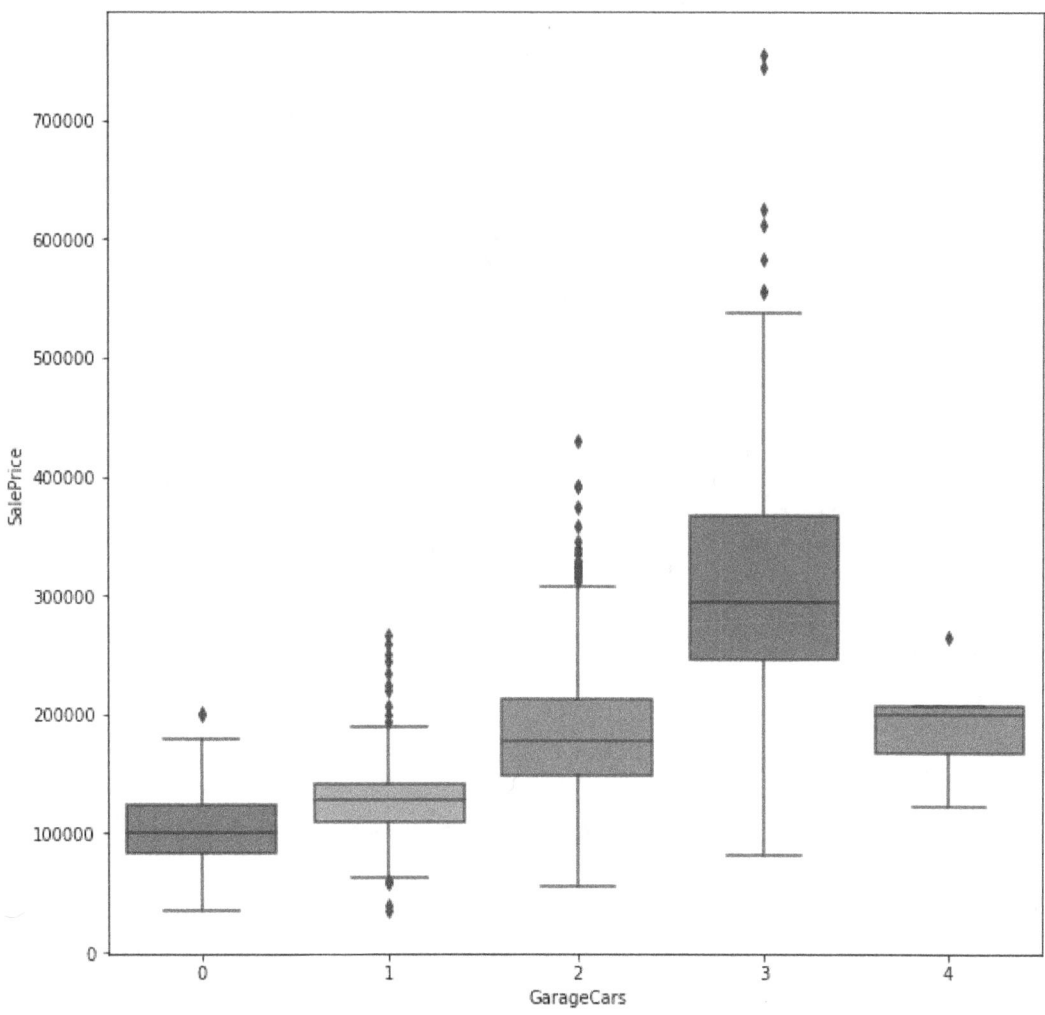

Figure 2.55: Boxplot showing variation in SalePrice for each category of GarageCars

5. Plot a line graph using Seaborn to show the variation in **SalePrice** for older and more recently built flats. Here, we will plot a line plot using Seaborn's `.lineplot()` function. Since we want to see the variation in **SalePrice**, we take this as the *y* variable, and as the variation is across a period of time, we take **YearBuilt** as the *x* variable. Keeping this in mind, we pass the respective series as values to the **y** and **x** parameters for the primary plotting function. We also pass a `ci=None` parameter to hide the standard deviation indicator around the line in the plot:

    ```
    plt.figure(figsize=(10,7))
    sns.lineplot(x=data.YearBuilt, y=data.SalePrice, ci=None)
    plt.show()
    ```

    The output will be as follows:

    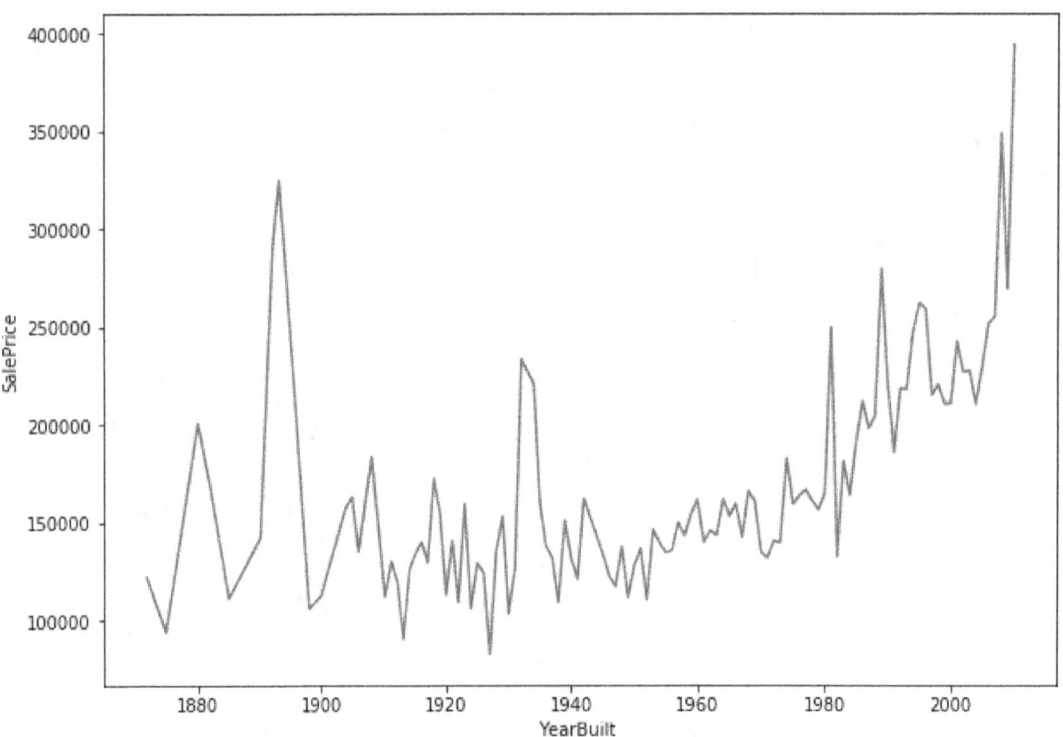

    Figure 2.56: Line graph showing the variation in SalePrice for older and more recently built flats

Chapter 3: Regression Analysis

Activity 5: Plotting Data with a Moving Average

Solution

1. Load the dataset into a pandas DataFrame from the CSV file:

   ```
   df = pd.read_csv('austin_weather.csv')
   df.head()
   ```

   The output will show the initial five rows of the **austin_weather.csv** file:

	Date	TempHighF	TempAvgF	TempLowF	DewPointHighF	DewPointAvgF	DewPointLowF	HumidityHighPercent
0	2013-12-21	74	60	45	67	49	43	93
1	2013-12-22	56	48	39	43	36	28	93
2	2013-12-23	58	45	32	31	27	23	76
3	2013-12-24	61	46	31	36	28	21	89
4	2013-12-25	58	50	41	44	40	36	86

   Figure 3.74: The first five rows of the Austin weather data

2. Since we only need the **Date** and **TempAvgF** columns, we'll remove all others from the dataset:

   ```
   df = df[['Date', 'TempAvgF']]
   df.head()
   ```

   The output will be:

	Date	TempAvgF
0	2013-12-21	60
1	2013-12-22	48
2	2013-12-23	45
3	2013-12-24	46
4	2013-12-25	50

   Figure 3.75: Date and TempAvgF columns of the Austin weather data

3. Initially, we are only interested in the first year's data, so we need to extract that information only. Create a column in the DataFrame for the year value, extract the year value as an integer from the strings in the **Date** column, and assign these values to the **Year** column. Note that temperatures are recorded daily:

   ```
   df['Year'] = [int(dt[:4]) for dt in df.Date]
   df.head()
   ```

   The output will be:

	Date	TempAvgF	Year
0	2013-12-21	60	2013
1	2013-12-22	48	2013
2	2013-12-23	45	2013
3	2013-12-24	46	2013
4	2013-12-25	50	2013

   Figure 3.76: Extracting the year

4. Repeat this process to extract the month values and store the values as integers in a **Month** column:

   ```
   df['Month'] = [int(dt[5:7]) for dt in df.Date]
   df.head()
   ```

   The output will be:

	Date	TempAvgF	Year	Month
0	2013-12-21	60	2013	12
1	2013-12-22	48	2013	12
2	2013-12-23	45	2013	12
3	2013-12-24	46	2013	12
4	2013-12-25	50	2013	12

   Figure 3.77: Extracting the month

5. Copy the first year's worth of data to a DataFrame:

   ```
   df_first_year = df[:365]
   df_first_year.head()
   ```

The output will be as follows:

	Date	TempAvgF	Year	Month
0	2013-12-21	60	2013	12
1	2013-12-22	48	2013	12
2	2013-12-23	45	2013	12
3	2013-12-24	46	2013	12
4	2013-12-25	50	2013	12

Figure 3.78: Copied data to new DataFrame

6. Compute a 20-day moving average filter:

```
window = 20
rolling = df_first_year.TempAvgF.rolling(window).mean();
rolling.head(n=20)
```

The output will be:

```
0     NaN
1     NaN
2     NaN
3     NaN
4     NaN
5     NaN
6     NaN
7     NaN
8     NaN
9     NaN
10    NaN
11    NaN
12    NaN
13    NaN
14    NaN
15    NaN
16    NaN
17    NaN
18    NaN
19    47.75
Name: TempAvgF, dtype: float64
```

7. Plot the raw data and the moving average signal, with the *x* axis as the day number in the year:

   ```
   fig = plt.figure(figsize=(10, 7))
   ax = fig.add_axes([1, 1, 1, 1]);
   
   # Temp measurements
   ax.scatter(range(1, 366), df_first_year.TempAvgF, label='Raw Data');
   ax.plot(range(1, 366), rolling, c='r', label=f'{window} day moving average');
   
   ax.set_title('Daily Mean Temperature Measurements')
   ax.set_xlabel('Day')
   ax.set_ylabel('Temperature (degF)')
   ax.set_xticks(range(1, 366), 10)
   ax.legend();
   ```

   The output will be as follows:

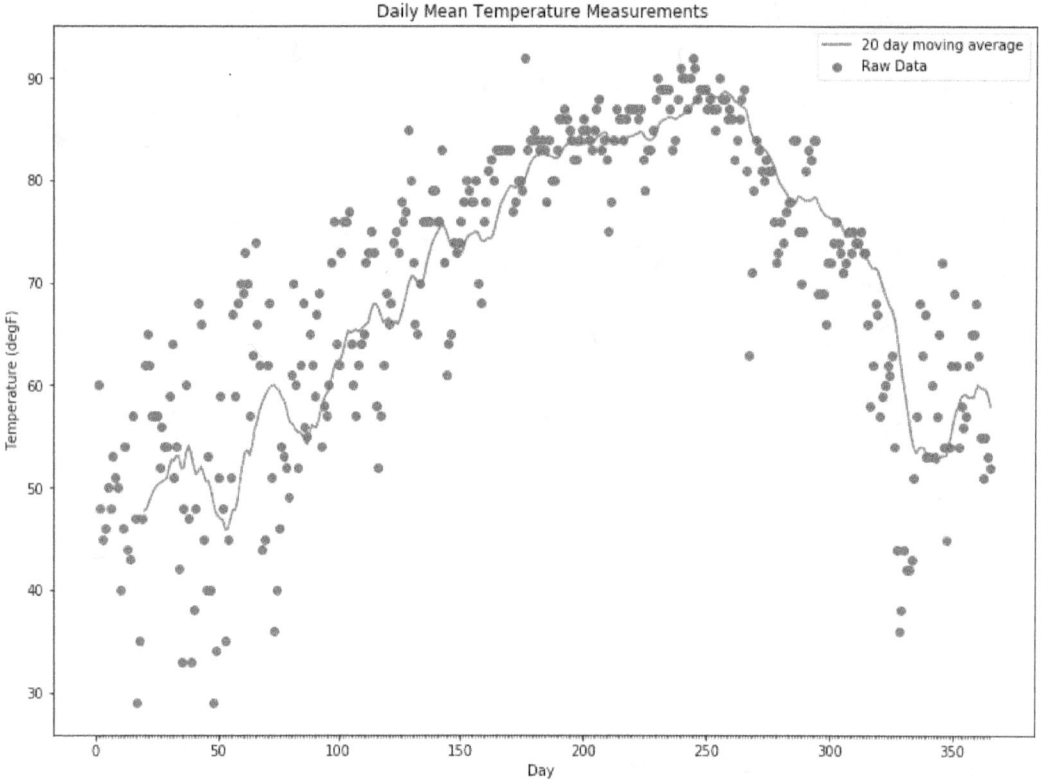

Figure 3.79: Scatter plot of temperature throughout the year

Activity 6: Linear Regression Using the Least Squares Method

Solution

1. Visualize the measurements:

   ```
   df.head()
   ```

   The output will be as follows:

	Date	TempAvgF	Year	Month
0	2013-12-21	60	2013	12
1	2013-12-22	48	2013	12
2	2013-12-23	45	2013	12
3	2013-12-24	46	2013	12
4	2013-12-25	50	2013	12

   Figure 3.80: First five rows of activity2_measurements.csv dataset

2. Visualize the rolling average values:

   ```
   rolling.head(n=30)
   ```

The output will be as follows:

12	NaN
13	NaN
14	NaN
15	NaN
16	NaN
17	NaN
18	NaN
19	47.75
20	48.00
21	48.70
22	49.30
23	49.85
24	50.20
25	50.40
26	50.55
27	50.70
28	50.90
29	51.85

Figure 3.81: Rolling head average

3. Create a linear regression model using the default parameters; that is, calculate a y intercept for the model and do not normalize the data:

```
model = LinearRegression()
model
```

The output will be as follows:

```
LinearRegression(copy_X=True, fit_intercept=True, n_jobs=None,
         normalize=False)
```

4. Now fit the model, where the input data is the day number for the year (1 to 365) and the output is the average temperature. To make later calculations easier, insert a column (**DayOfYear**) that corresponds with the day of the year for that measurement:

```
df_first_year.loc[:,'DayOfYear'] = [i + 1 for i in df_first_year.index]
df_first_year.head()
```

The output will be as follows:

	Date	TempAvgF	Year	Month	DayOfYear
0	2013-12-21	60	2013	12	1
1	2013-12-22	48	2013	12	2
2	2013-12-23	45	2013	12	3
3	2013-12-24	46	2013	12	4
4	2013-12-25	50	2013	12	5

Figure 3.82: Adding day of year column

5. Fit the model with the **DayOfYear** values as the input and **df_first_year.TempAvgF** as the output:

   ```
   # Note the year values need to be provided as an N x 1 array
   model.fit(df_first_year.DayOfYear.values.reshape((-1, 1)), df_first_year.TempAvgF)
   ```

   The output will be as follows:

   ```
   LinearRegression(copy_X=True, fit_intercept=True, n_jobs=None,
            normalize=False)
   ```

6. Print the parameters of the model:

   ```
   print(f'm = {model.coef_[0]}')
   print(f'c = {model.intercept_}')

   print('\nModel Definition')
   print(f'y = {model.coef_[0]:0.4}x + {model.intercept_:0.4f}')
   ```

   The output will be:

   ```
   m = 0.04909173467448788
   c = 60.28196597922625

   Model Definition
   y = 0.04909x + 60.2820
   ```

7. We can calculate the trendline values by using the first, middle, and last values (days in years) in the linear equation:

   ```
   trend_x = np.array([
       1,
       182.5,
       365
   ])

   trend_y = model.predict(trend_x.reshape((-1, 1)))
   trend_y
   ```

   The output will be as follows:

   ```
   array([60.33105771, 69.24120756, 78.20044914])
   ```

8. Plot these values with the trendline:

   ```
   fig = plt.figure(figsize=(10, 7))
   ax = fig.add_axes([1, 1, 1, 1]);

   # Temp measurements
   ax.scatter(df_first_year.DayOfYear, df_first_year.TempAvgF, label='Raw Data');
   ax.plot(df_first_year.DayOfYear, rolling, c='r', label=f'{window} day moving average');
   ax.plot(trend_x, trend_y, c='k', label='Model: Predicted trendline')

   ax.set_title('Daily Mean Temperature Measurements')
   ax.set_xlabel('Day')
   ax.set_ylabel('Temperature (degF)')
   ax.set_xticks(range(1, 366), 10)
   ax.legend();
   ```

The output will be as follows:

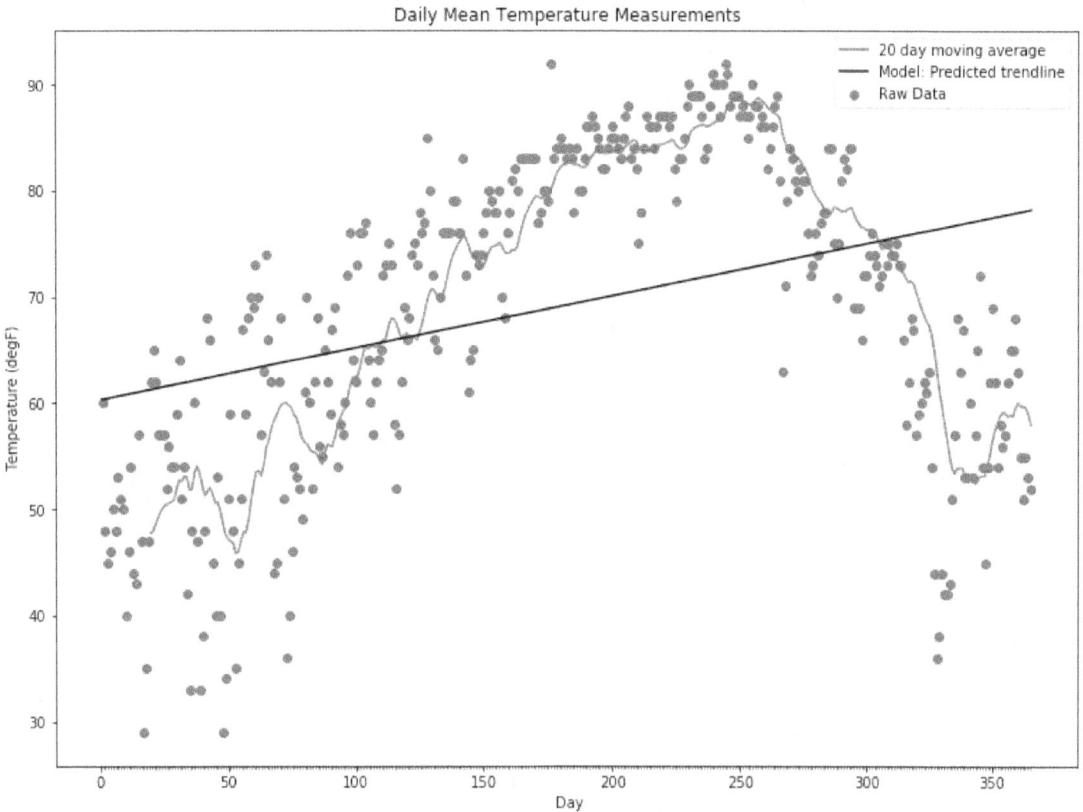

Figure 3.83: Scatterplot of temperature thought the year with the predicted trendline

9. Evaluate the performance of the model. How well does the model fit the data? Calculate the r^2 score to find out:

```
# Note the year values need to be provided as an N x 1 array
r2 = model.score(df_first_year.DayOfYear.values.reshape((-1, 1)), df_first_year.TempAvgF)
print(f'r2 score = {r2:0.4f}')
```

The output will be:

```
r2 score = 0.1222
```

Activity 7: Dummy Variables

Solution

1. Plot the raw data (**df**) and moving average (**rolling**):

   ```
   fig = plt.figure(figsize=(10, 7))
   ax = fig.add_axes([1, 1, 1, 1]);

   # Temp measurements
   ax.scatter(df_first_year.DayOfYear, df_first_year.TempAvgF, label='Raw
   Data');
   ax.plot(df_first_year.DayOfYear, rolling, c='r', label=f'{window} day
   moving average');

   ax.set_title('Daily Mean Temperature Measurements')
   ax.set_xlabel('Day')
   ax.set_ylabel('Temperature (degF)')
   ax.set_xticks(range(1, 366), 10)
   ax.legend();
   ```

   The output will be:

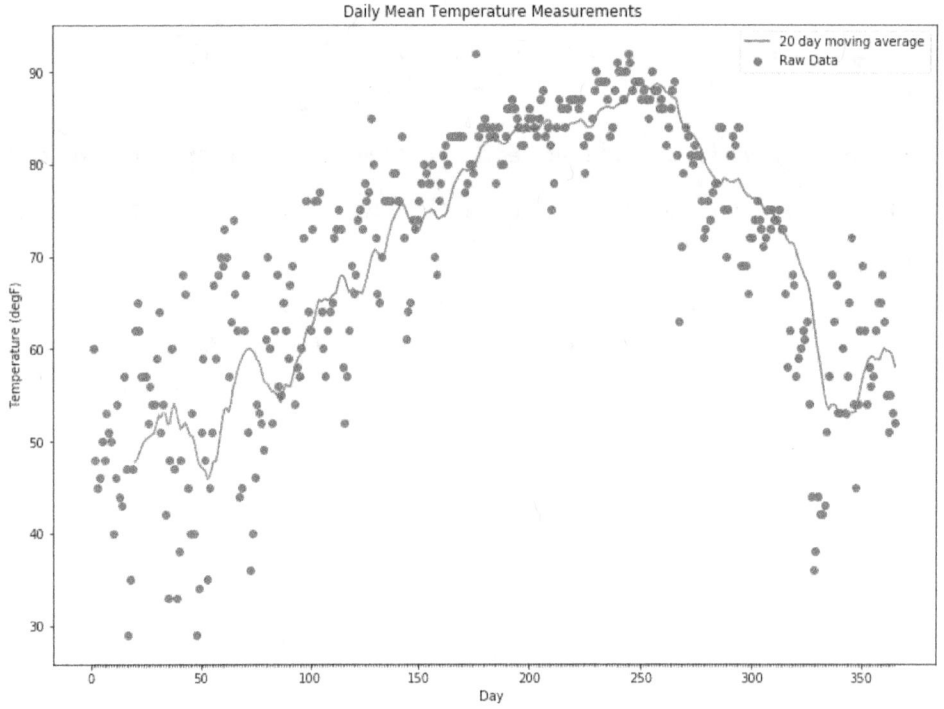

Figure 3.84: Scatterplot of Temperature throughout the year

2. Looking at the preceding plot, there seems to be an inflection point around day 250. Create a dummy variable to introduce this feature into the linear model:

   ```
   df_first_year.loc[:,'inflection'] = [1 * int(i < 250) for i in df_first_year.DayOfYear]
   ```

3. Check the first and last samples to confirm that the dummy variable is correct. Check the first five samples:

   ```
   df_first_year.head()
   ```

   The output will be as follows:

	Date	TempAvgF	Year	Month	DayOfYear	inflection	DayOfYear2
0	2013-12-21	60	2013	12	1	1	0.002740
1	2013-12-22	48	2013	12	2	1	0.005479
2	2013-12-23	45	2013	12	3	1	0.008219
3	2013-12-24	46	2013	12	4	1	0.010959
4	2013-12-25	50	2013	12	5	1	0.013698

   Figure 3.85: First five columns

Then, check the last five samples:

   ```
   df_first_year.tail()
   ```

   The output will be:

	Date	TempAvgF	Year	Month	DayOfYear	inflection	DayOfYear2
360	2014-12-16	55	2014	12	361	0	0.835499
361	2014-12-17	51	2014	12	362	0	0.837002
362	2014-12-18	55	2014	12	363	0	0.838498
363	2014-12-19	53	2014	12	364	0	0.839988
364	2014-12-20	52	2014	12	365	0	0.841471

   Figure 3.86: Last five columns

4. Use a least squares linear regression model and fit the model to the `DayOfYear` values and the dummy variable to predict `TempAvgF`:

   ```
   # Note the year values need to be provided as an N x 1 array
   model = LinearRegression()
   model.fit(df_first_year[['DayOfYear', 'inflection']], df_first_year.TempAvgF)
   ```

   The output will be as follows:

   ```
   LinearRegression(copy_X=True, fit_intercept=True, n_jobs=None,
            normalize=False)
   ```

5. Compute the r^2 score:

   ```
   # Note the year values need to be provided as an N x 1 array
   r2 = model.score(df_first_year[['DayOfYear', 'inflection']], df_first_year.TempAvgF)
   print(f'r2 score = {r2:0.4f}')
   ```

   The output will be as follows:

   ```
   r2 score = 0.3631
   ```

6. Using the `DayOfYear` values, create a set of predictions using the model to construct a trendline:

   ```
   trend_y = model.predict(df_first_year[['DayOfYear', 'inflection']].values)
   trend_y
   ```

   The output will be:

   ```
   array([51.60311133, 51.74622654, 51.88934175, 52.03245696, 52.17557217,
          52.31868739, 52.4618026 , 52.60491781, 52.74803302, 52.89114823,
          53.03426345, 53.17737866, 53.32049387, 53.46360908, 53.60672429,
          53.7498395 , 53.89295472, 54.03606993, 54.17918514, 54.32230035,
          54.46541556, 54.60853078, 54.75164599, 54.8947612 , 55.03787641,
          ...
          ...
          73.88056649, 74.0236817 , 74.16679692, 74.30991213, 74.45302734,
          74.59614255, 74.73925776, 74.88237297, 75.02548819, 75.1686034 ,
          75.31171861, 75.45483382, 75.59794903, 75.74106425, 75.88417946,
          76.02729467, 76.17040988, 76.31352509, 76.4566403 , 76.59975552,
          76.74287073, 76.88598594, 77.02910115, 77.17221636, 77.31533157])
   ```

7. Plot the trendline against the data and the moving average:

   ```
   fig = plt.figure(figsize=(10, 7))
   ax = fig.add_axes([1, 1, 1, 1]);
   
   # Temp measurements
   ax.scatter(df_first_year.DayOfYear, df_first_year.TempAvgF, label='Raw Data');
   ax.plot(df_first_year.DayOfYear, rolling, c='r', label=f'{window} day moving average');
   ax.plot(df_first_year.DayOfYear, trend_y, c='k', label='Model: Predicted trendline')
   
   ax.set_title('Daily Mean Temperature Measurements')
   ax.set_xlabel('Day')
   ax.set_ylabel('Temperature (degF)')
   ax.set_xticks(range(1, 366), 10)
   ax.legend();
   ```

   The output will be as follows:

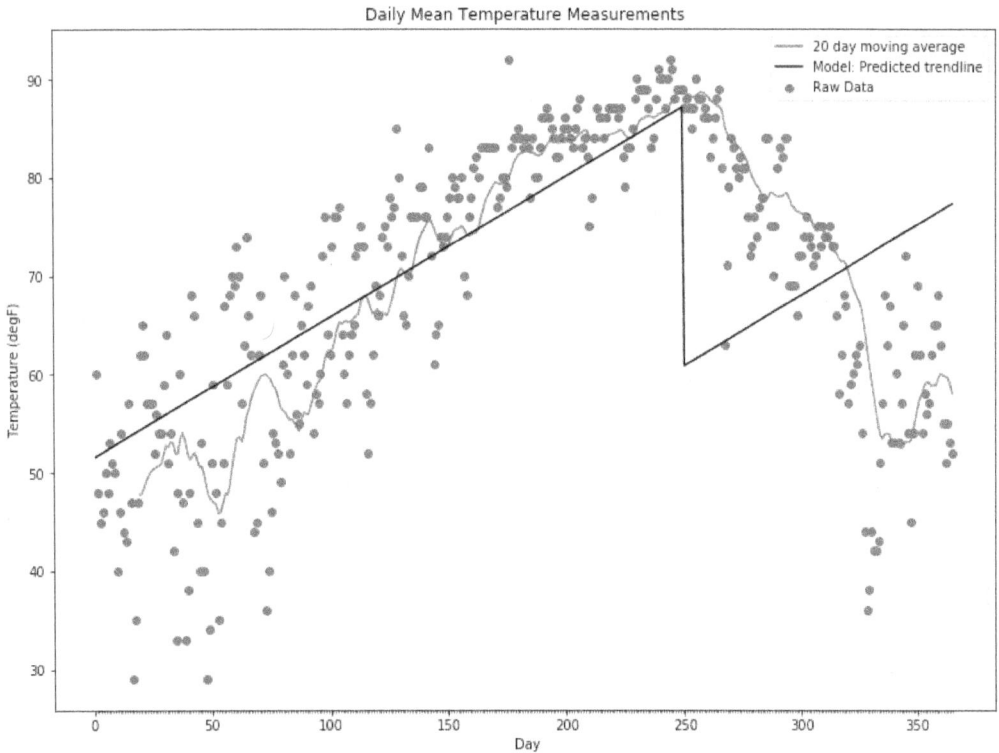

Figure 3.87: Predicted trendline

Activity 8: Other Model Types with Linear Regression

Solution

1. Use a sine curve function as the basis of the model:

    ```
    # Using a sine curve
    df_first_year['DayOfYear2'] = np.sin(df_first_year['DayOfYear'] / df_first_year['DayOfYear'].max())
    df_first_year.head()
    ```

    The output will be as follows:

	Date	TempAvgF	Year	Month	DayOfYear	inflection	DayOfYear2
0	2013-12-21	60	2013	12	1	1	0.002740
1	2013-12-22	48	2013	12	2	1	0.005479
2	2013-12-23	45	2013	12	3	1	0.008219
3	2013-12-24	46	2013	12	4	1	0.010959
4	2013-12-25	50	2013	12	5	1	0.013698

    Figure 3.88: First five rows

2. Fit the model:

    ```
    # Note the year values need to be provided as an N x 1 array
    model = LinearRegression()
    model.fit(df_first_year[['DayOfYear2', 'DayOfYear']], df_first_year.TempAvgF)
    ```

    The output will be as follows:

    ```
    LinearRegression(copy_X=True, fit_intercept=True, n_jobs=None,
             normalize=False)
    ```

3. Print the parameters of the model:

    ```
    print(f'a = {model.coef_[0]}')
    print(f'm = {model.coef_[1]}')
    print(f'c = {model.intercept_}')

    print('\nModel Definition')
    print(f'y = {model.coef_[0]:0.4}x^2 + {model.coef_[1]:0.4}x + {model.intercept_:0.4f}')
    ```

The output will be as follows:

```
a = 634.322313570282
m = -1.4371290614190075
c = 39.93286585807408

Model Definition
y = 634.3x^2 + -1.437x + 39.9329
```

4. Compute the r^2 value to measure the performance:

```
# Note the year values need to be provided as an N x 1 array
r2 = model.score(df_first_year[['DayOfYear2', 'DayOfYear']], df_first_year.TempAvgF)
print(f'r2 score = {r2:0.4f}')
```

The output will be:

```
r2 score = 0.7047
```

5. Construct the trendline values:

```
trend_y = model.predict(df_first_year[['DayOfYear2', 'DayOfYear']].values)
trend_y
```

The output will be:

```
array([40.23360397, 40.53432905, 40.83502803, 41.13568788, 41.43629555,
       41.736838  , 42.03730219, 42.33767507, 42.6379436 , 42.93809474,
       43.23811546, 43.5379927 , 43.83771344, 44.13726463, 44.43663324,
       44.73580624, 45.03477059, 45.33351327, 45.63202123, 45.93028146,
       46.22828093, 46.52600661, 46.82344549, 47.12058453, 47.41741073,
       ...
       ...
       59.96306563, 59.55705293, 59.14720371, 58.73351024, 58.31596484,
       57.89455987, 57.46928769, 57.04014072, 56.60711138, 56.17019215,
       55.7293755 , 55.28465397, 54.83602011, 54.38346649, 53.92698572,
       53.46657045, 53.00221334, 52.53390709, 52.06164442, 51.58541811,
       51.10522093, 50.62104569, 50.13288526, 49.6407325 , 49.14458033])
```

6. Plot the trendline with the raw data and the moving average:

   ```
   fig = plt.figure(figsize=(10, 7))
   ax = fig.add_axes([1, 1, 1, 1]);

   # Temp measurements
   ax.scatter(df_first_year.DayOfYear, df_first_year.TempAvgF, label='Raw Data');
   ax.plot(df_first_year.DayOfYear, rolling, c='r', label=f'{window} day moving average');
   ax.plot(df_first_year.DayOfYear, trend_y, c='k', label='Model: Predicted trendline')

   ax.set_title('Daily Mean Temperature Measurements')
   ax.set_xlabel('Day')
   ax.set_ylabel('Temperature (degF)')
   ax.set_xticks(range(1, 366), 10)
   ax.legend();
   ```

The output will be as follows:

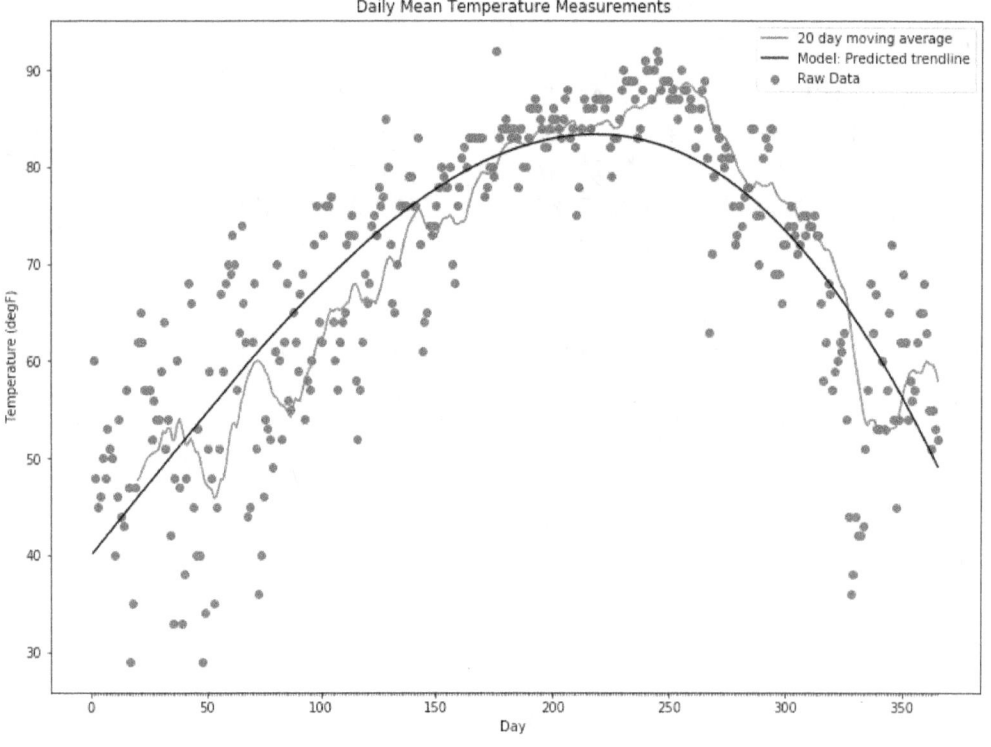

Figure 3.89: Predicted trendline

Activity 9: Gradient Descent

Solution

1. Create a generic gradient descent model and normalize the day of year values as between 0 and 1:

   ```
   grad_model = SGDRegressor(max_iter=None, tol=1e-3)
   _x = df_first_year.DayOfYear / df_first_year.DayOfYear.max()
   ```

2. Fit the model:

   ```
   grad_model.fit(_x.values.reshape((-1, 1)), df_first_year.TempAvgF)
   ```

   The output will be as follows:

   ```
   SGDRegressor(alpha=0.0001, average=False, early_stopping=False, epsilon=0.1,
         eta0=0.01, fit_intercept=True, l1_ratio=0.15,
         learning_rate='invscaling', loss='squared_loss', max_iter=None,
         n_iter=None, n_iter_no_change=5, penalty='l2', power_t=0.25,
         random_state=None, shuffle=True, tol=None, validation_fraction=0.1,
         verbose=0, warm_start=False)
   ```

3. Print the details of the model:

   ```
   print(f'm = {grad_model.coef_[0]}')
   print(f'c = {grad_model.intercept_[0]}')

   print('\nModel Definition')
   print(f'y = {grad_model.coef_[0]:0.4}x + {grad_model.intercept_[0]:0.4f}')
   ```

   The output will be as follows:

   ```
   m = 26.406162532140563
   c = 55.07470859678077

   Model Definition
   y = 26.41x + 55.0747
   ```

4. Prepare the *x* (`_trend_x`) trendline values by dividing them by the maximum. Predict **y_trend_values** using the gradient descent model:

   ```
   _trend_x = trend_x / trend_x.max()
   trend_y = grad_model.predict(_trend_x.reshape((-1, 1)))
   trend_y
   ```

   The output will be as follows:

   ```
   array([55.14705425, 68.27778986, 81.48087113])
   ```

5. Plot the data and the moving average with the trendline:

   ```python
   fig = plt.figure(figsize=(10, 7))
   ax = fig.add_axes([1, 1, 1, 1]);

   # Temp measurements
   ax.scatter(df_first_year.DayOfYear, df_first_year.TempAvgF, label='Raw Data');
   ax.plot(df_first_year.DayOfYear, rolling, c='r', label=f'{window} day moving average');
   ax.plot(trend_x, trend_y, c='k', linestyle='--', label='Model: Predicted trendline')

   ax.set_title('Daily Mean Temperature Measurements')
   ax.set_xlabel('Day')
   ax.set_ylabel('Temperature (degF)')
   ax.set_xticks(range(1, 366), 10)
   ax.legend();
   ```

The output will be as follows:

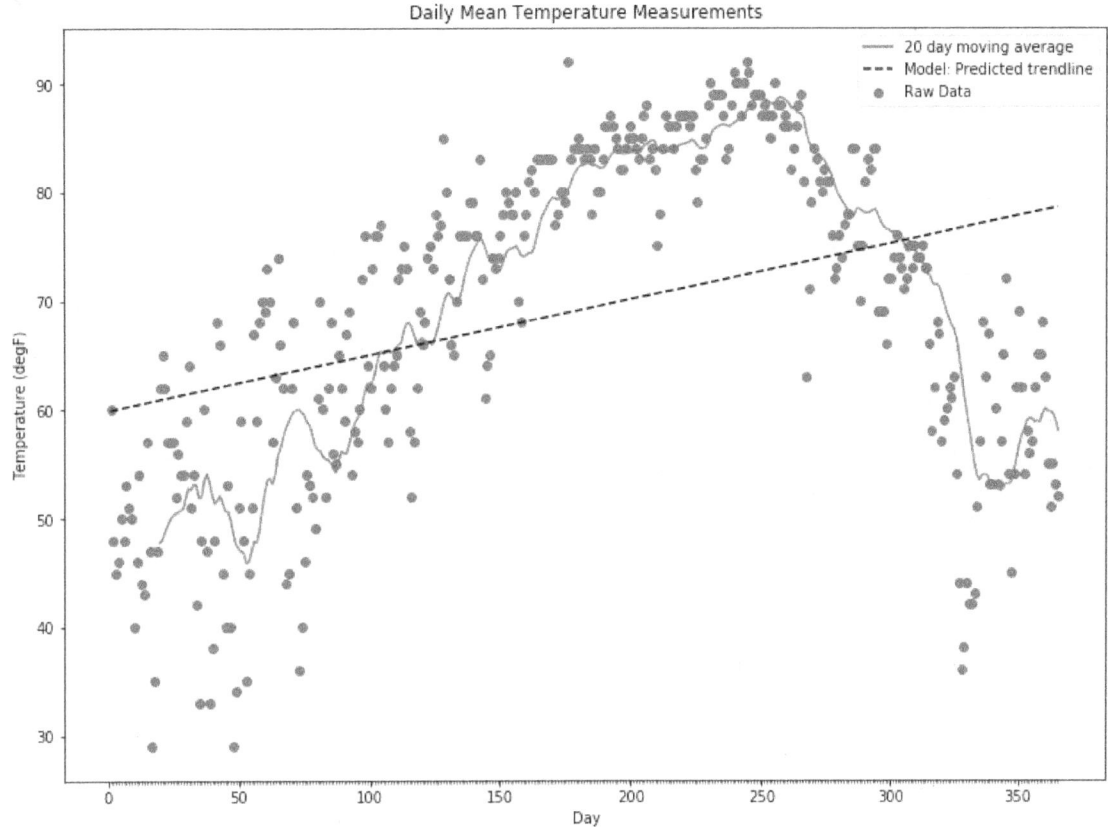

Figure 3.90: Gradient descent predicted trendline

Activity 10: Autoregressors

Solution

1. Plot the complete set of average temperature values (**df.TempAvgF**) with years on the *x* axis:

   ```
   plt.figure(figsize=(10, 7))
   plt.plot(df.TempAvgF.values);
   yrs = [yr for yr in df.Year.unique()]
   plt.xticks(np.arange(0, len(df), len(df) // len(yrs)), yrs);
   plt.title('Austin Texas Average Daily Temperature');
   plt.xlabel('Year');
   plt.ylabel('Temperature (F)');
   ```

   The output will be:

   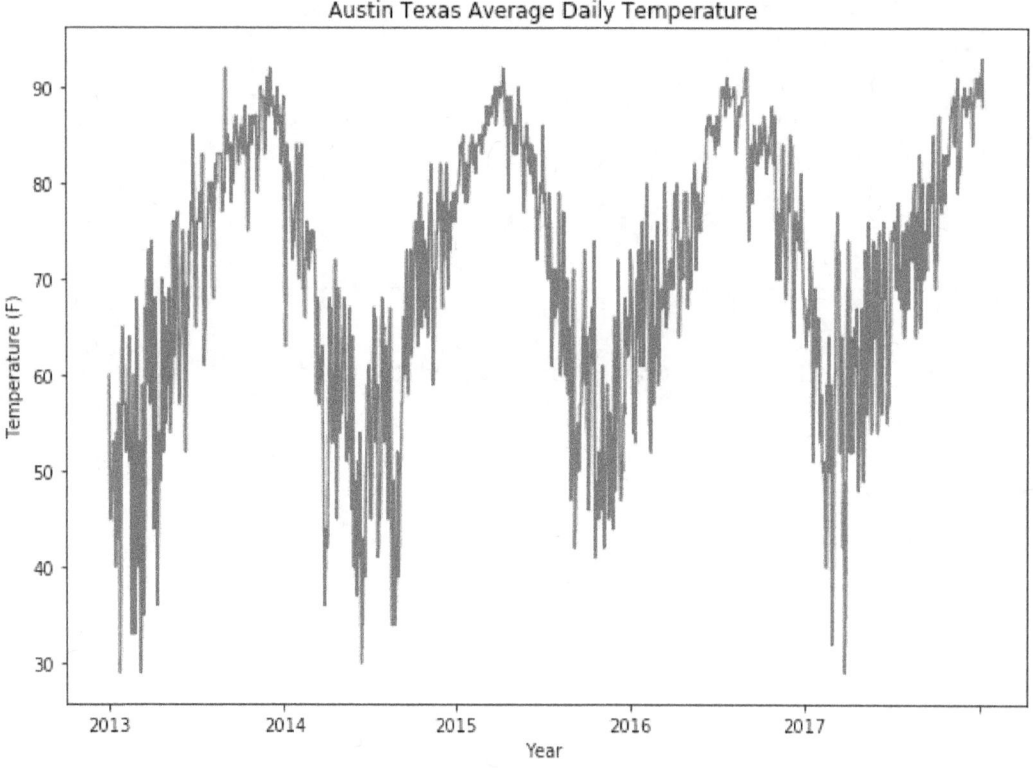

   Figure 3.91: Plot of temperature through the year

2. Create a 20-day lag and plot the lagged data on the original dataset:

```
plt.figure(figsize=(10, 7))
plt.plot(df.TempAvgF.values, label='Original Dataset');
plt.plot(df.TempAvgF.shift(20), c='r', linestyle='--',
    label='Lag 20');
yrs = [yr for yr in df.Year.unique()]
plt.xticks(np.arange(0, len(df), len(df) // len(yrs)), yrs);
plt.title('Austin Texas Average Daily Temperature');
plt.xlabel('Year');
plt.ylabel('Temperature (F)');
plt.legend();
```

The output will be:

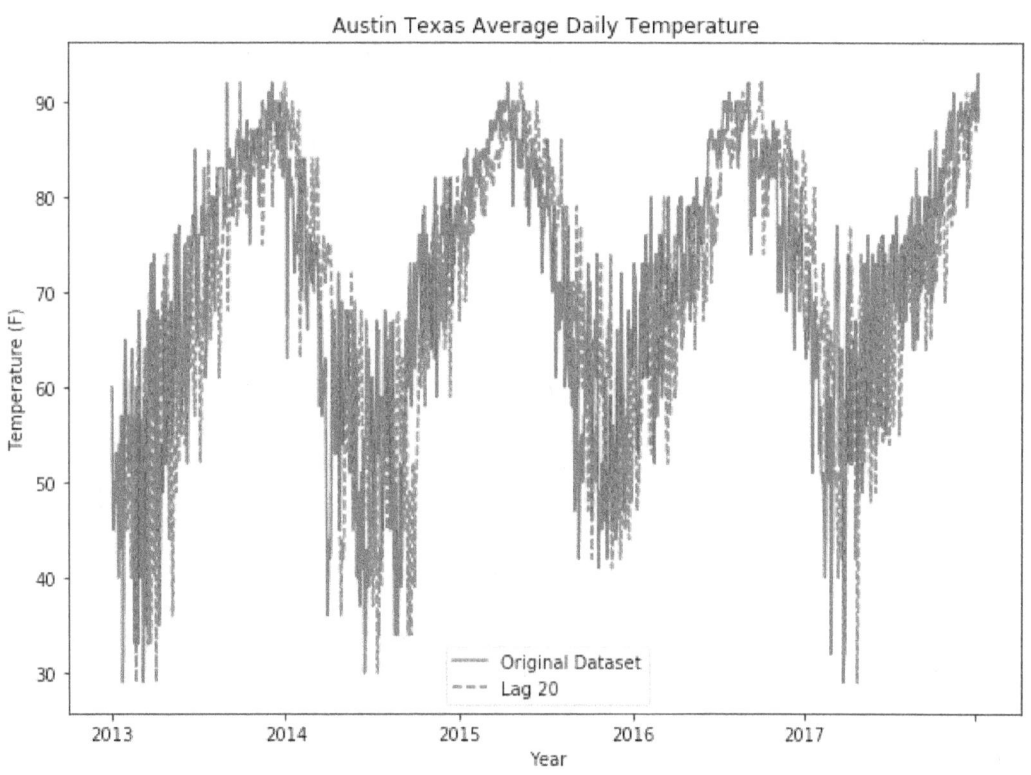

Figure 3.92: Plot of temperature through the years with a 20-day lag

3. Construct an autocorrelation plot to see whether the average temperature can be used with an autoregressor. Where is the lag acceptable and where is it not for an autoregressor?

```
plt.figure(figsize=(10, 7))
pd.plotting.autocorrelation_plot(df.TempAvgF);
```

We'll get the following output:

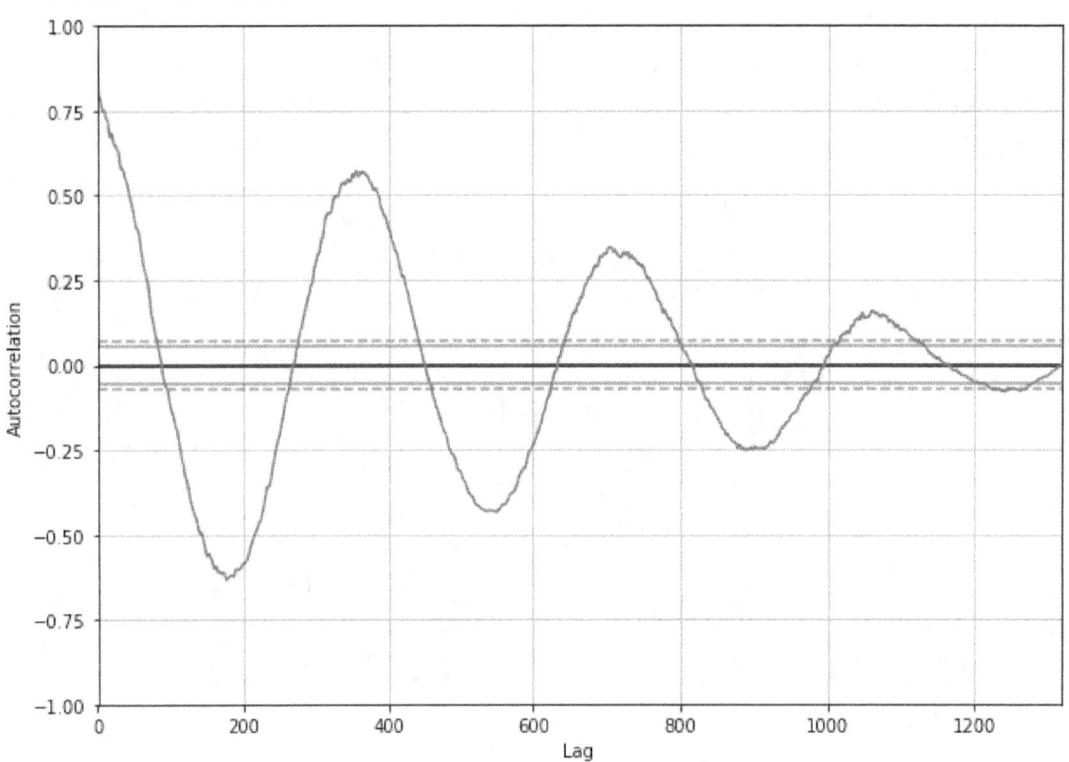

Figure 3.93: Plot of autocorrelation versus lag

The lag is acceptable only when the autocorrelation line lies outside the 99% confidence bounds, as represented by the dashed lines.

4. Chose an acceptable lag and an unacceptable lag and construct lag plots using these values for acceptable lag:

   ```
   plt.figure(figsize=(10,7))
   ax = pd.plotting.lag_plot(df.TempAvgF, lag=5);
   ```

   We'll get the following output:

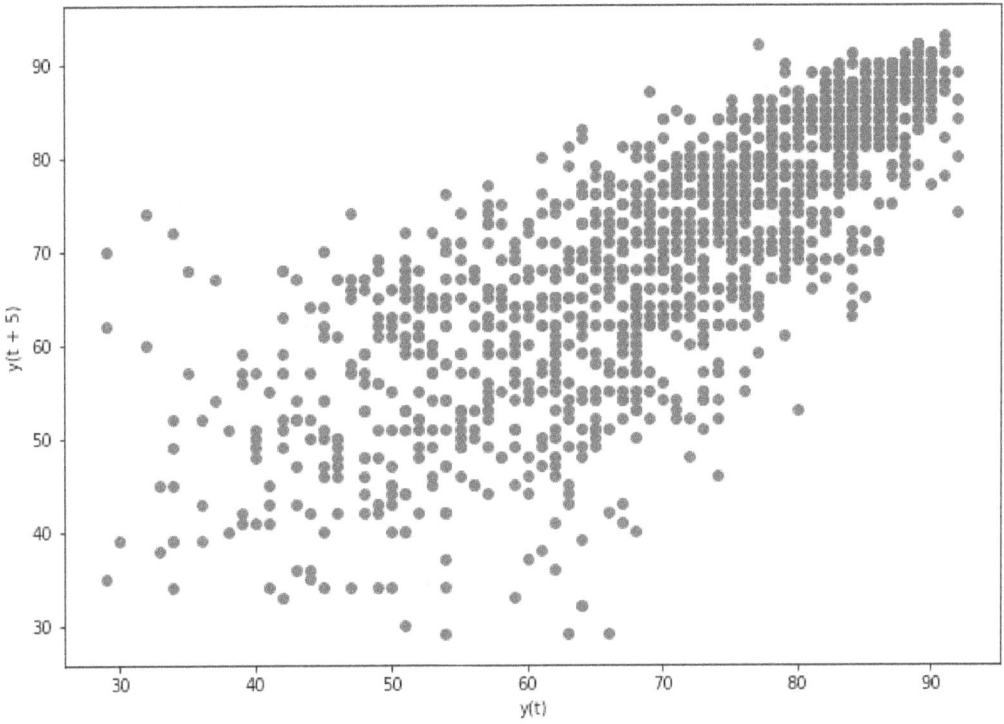

Figure 3.94: Plot of acceptable lag

Use these values for unacceptable lag:

```
plt.figure(figsize=(10,7))
ax = pd.plotting.lag_plot(df.TempAvgF, lag=1000);
```

We'll get the following output:

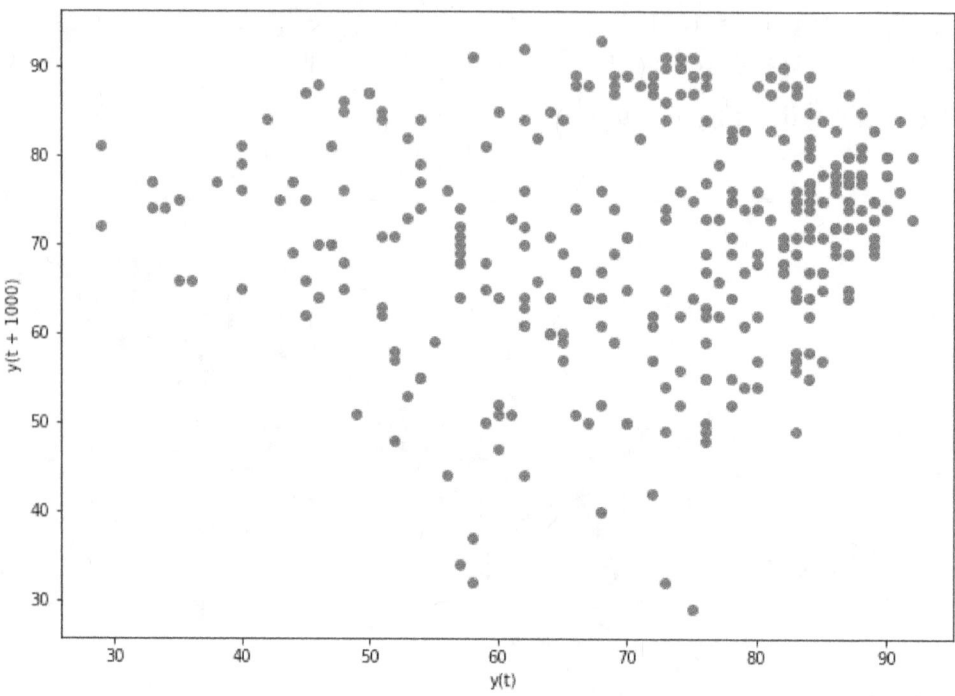

Figure 3.95: Plot of unacceptable lag

5. Create an autoregressor model, note the selected lag, calculate the R^2 value, and plot the autoregressor model with the original plot. The model is to project past the available data by 1,000 samples:

```
from statsmodels.tsa.ar_model import AR
model = AR(df.TempAvgF)
```

6. Fit the model to the data:

```
model_fit = model.fit()
print('Lag: %s' % model_fit.k_ar)
print('Coefficients: %s' % model_fit.params)
```

The output will be:

```
Lag: 23
Coefficients: const         1.909395
L1.TempAvgF      0.912076
L2.TempAvgF     -0.334043
L3.TempAvgF      0.157353
L4.TempAvgF      0.025721
L5.TempAvgF      0.041342
L6.TempAvgF      0.030831
L7.TempAvgF     -0.021230
L8.TempAvgF      0.020324
L9.TempAvgF      0.025147
L10.TempAvgF     0.059739
L11.TempAvgF    -0.017337
L12.TempAvgF     0.043553
L13.TempAvgF    -0.027795
L14.TempAvgF     0.053547
L15.TempAvgF     0.013070
L16.TempAvgF    -0.033157
L17.TempAvgF    -0.000072
L18.TempAvgF    -0.026307
L19.TempAvgF     0.025258
L20.TempAvgF     0.038341
L21.TempAvgF     0.007885
L22.TempAvgF    -0.008889
L23.TempAvgF    -0.011080
dtype: float64
```

7. Create a set of predictions for 1,000 days after the last sample:

```
predictions = model_fit.predict(start=model_fit.k_ar, end=len(df) + 1000)
predictions[:10].values
```

The output will be:

```
array([54.81171857, 56.89097085, 56.41891585, 50.98627626, 56.11843512,
       53.20665111, 55.13941554, 58.4679288 , 61.92497136, 49.46049801])
```

8. Plot the predictions, as well as the original dataset:

```
plt.figure(figsize=(10, 7))
plt.plot(df.TempAvgF.values, label='Original Dataset');
plt.plot(predictions, c='g', linestyle=':', label='Predictions');
yrs = [yr for yr in df.Year.unique()]
plt.xticks(np.arange(0, len(df), len(df) // len(yrs)), yrs);
plt.title('Austin Texas Average Daily Temperature');
plt.xlabel('Year');
plt.ylabel('Temperature (F)');
plt.legend();
```

The output will be:

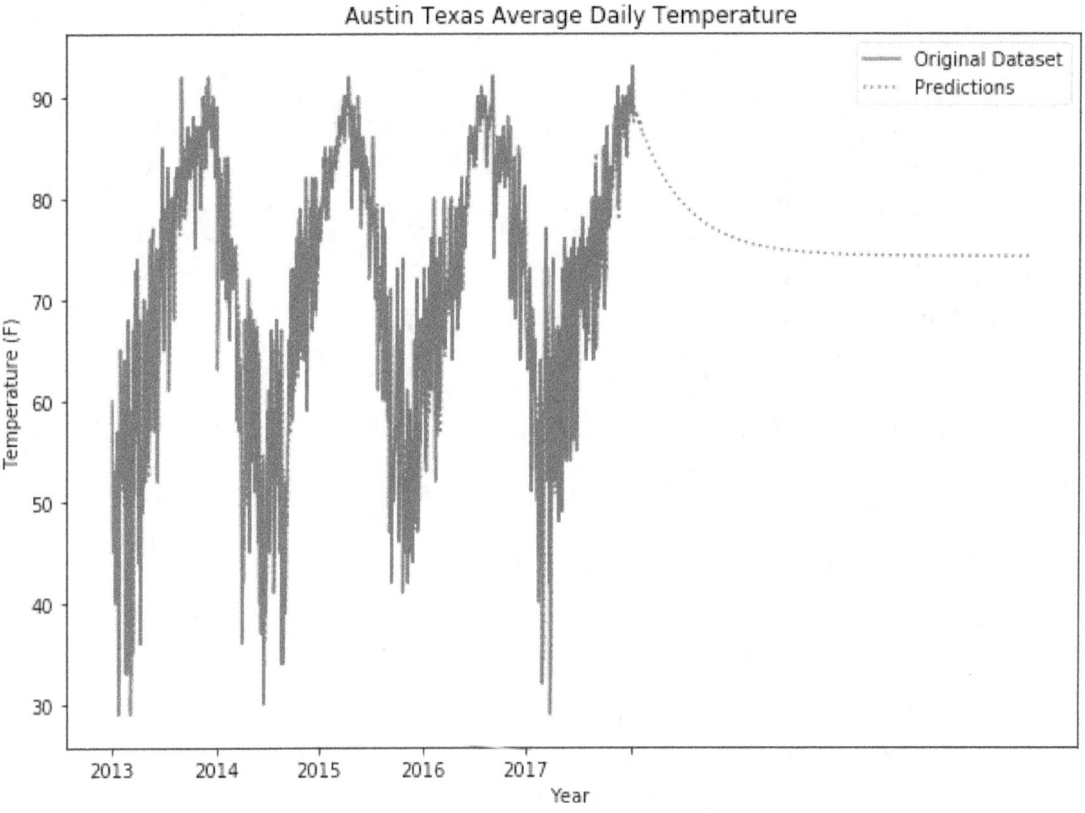

Figure 3.96: Plot of temperature through the years

9. Enhance the view to look for differences by showing the 100th to 200th samples:

```
plt.figure(figsize=(10, 7))
plt.plot(df.TempAvgF.values, label='Original Dataset');
plt.plot(predictions, c='g', linestyle=':', label='Predictions');
yrs = [yr for yr in df.Year.unique()]
plt.xticks(np.arange(0, len(df), len(df) // len(yrs)), yrs);
plt.title('Austin Texas Average Daily Temperature');
plt.xlabel('Year');
plt.ylabel('Temperature (F)');
plt.xlim([100, 200])
plt.legend();
```

We'll get the following output:

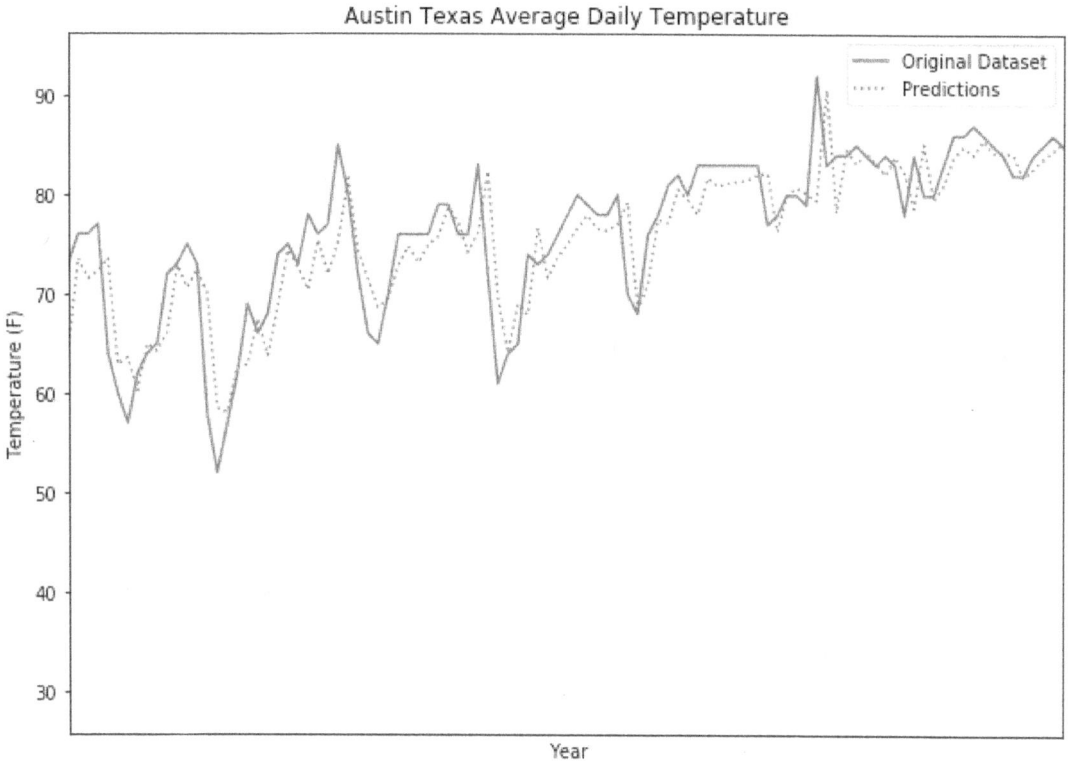

Figure 3.97: Plot of predictions with the original dataset

Chapter 4: Classification

Activity 11: Linear Regression Classifier – Two-Class Classifier

Solution

1. Import the required dependencies:

    ```
    import struct
    import numpy as np
    import gzip
    import urllib.request
    import matplotlib.pyplot as plt
    from array import array
    from sklearn.linear_model import LinearRegression
    ```

2. Load the MNIST data into memory:

    ```
    with gzip.open('train-images-idx3-ubyte.gz', 'rb') as f:
        magic, size, rows, cols = struct.unpack(">IIII", f.read(16))

        img = np.array(array("B", f.read())).reshape((size, rows, cols))


    with gzip.open('train-labels-idx1-ubyte.gz', 'rb') as f:
        magic, size = struct.unpack(">II", f.read(8))
        labels = np.array(array("B", f.read()))


    with gzip.open('t10k-images-idx3-ubyte.gz', 'rb') as f:
        magic, size, rows, cols = struct.unpack(">IIII", f.read(16))

        img_test = np.array(array("B", f.read())).reshape((size, rows, cols))


    with gzip.open('t10k-labels-idx1-ubyte.gz', 'rb') as f:
        magic, size = struct.unpack(">II", f.read(8))
        labels_test = np.array(array("B", f.read()))
    ```

3. Visualize a sample of the data:

   ```
   for i in range(10):
       plt.subplot(2, 5, i + 1)
       plt.imshow(img[i], cmap='gray');
       plt.title(f'{labels[i]}');
       plt.axis('off')
   ```

   We'll get the following output:

   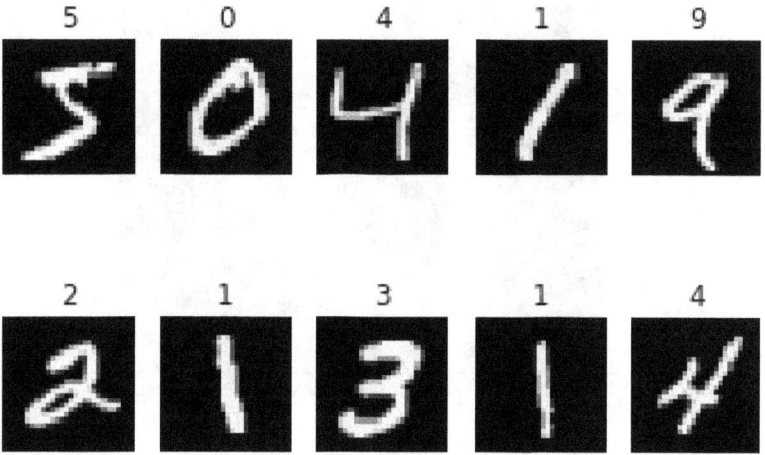

   Figure 4.76: Sample data

4. Construct a linear classifier model to classify the digits zero and one. The model we are going to create is to determine whether the samples are either the digits zero or one. To do this, we first need to select only those samples:

   ```
   samples_0_1 = np.where((labels == 0) | (labels == 1))[0]
   images_0_1 = img[samples_0_1]
   labels_0_1 = labels[samples_0_1]

   samples_0_1_test = np.where((labels_test == 0) | (labels_test == 1))
   images_0_1_test = img_test[samples_0_1_test].reshape((-1, rows * cols))
   labels_0_1_test = labels_test[samples_0_1_test]
   ```

5. Visualize the selected information. Here's the code for zero:

   ```
   sample_0 = np.where((labels == 0))[0][0]
   plt.imshow(img[sample_0], cmap='gray');
   ```

   The output will be as follows:

   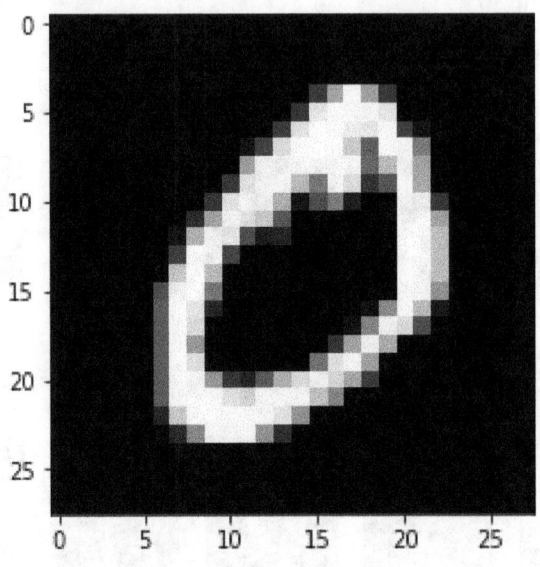

   Figure 4.77: First sample data

   Here's the code for one:

   ```
   sample_1 = np.where((labels == 1))[0][0]
   plt.imshow(img[sample_1], cmap='gray');
   ```

The output will be:

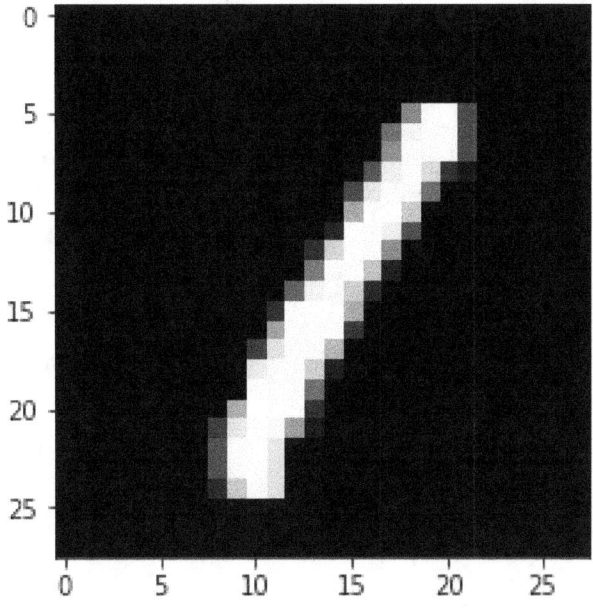

Figure 4.78: Second sample data

6. In order to provide the image information to the model, we must first flatten the data out so that each image is 1 x 784 pixels in shape:

    ```
    images_0_1 = images_0_1.reshape((-1, rows * cols))
    images_0_1.shape
    ```

    The output will be:

    ```
    (12665, 784)
    ```

7. Let's construct the model; use the **LinearRegression** API and call the **fit** function:

    ```
    model = LinearRegression()
    model.fit(X=images_0_1, y=labels_0_1)
    ```

    The output will be:

    ```
    LinearRegression(copy_X=True, fit_intercept=True, n_jobs=None,
             normalize=False)
    ```

8. Determine the R² score against the training set:

   ```
   model.score(X=images_0_1, y=labels_0_1)
   ```

   The output will be:

   ```
   0.9705320567708795
   ```

9. Determine the label predictions for each of the training samples, using a threshold of 0.5. Values greater than 0.5 classify as one; values less than or equal to 0.5 classify as zero:

   ```
   y_pred = model.predict(images_0_1) > 0.5
   y_pred = y_pred.astype(int)
   y_pred
   ```

   The output will be:

   ```
   array([0, 1, 1, ..., 1, 0, 1])
   ```

10. Compute the classification accuracy of the predicted training values versus the ground truth:

    ```
    np.sum(y_pred == labels_0_1) / len(labels_0_1)
    ```

    The output will be:

    ```
    0.9947887879984209
    ```

11. Compare the performance against the test set:

    ```
    y_pred = model.predict(images_0_1_test) > 0.5
    y_pred = y_pred.astype(int)
    np.sum(y_pred == labels_0_1_test) / len(labels_0_1_test)
    ```

    The output will be:

    ```
    0.9938534278959811
    ```

Activity 12: Iris Classification Using Logistic Regression

Solution

1. Import the required packages. For this activity, we will require the pandas package for loading the data, the Matplotlib package for plotting, and scikit-learn for creating the logistic regression model. Import all the required packages and relevant modules for these tasks:

    ```
    import pandas as pd
    import matplotlib.pyplot as plt
    from sklearn.linear_model import LogisticRegression
    ```

2. Load the Iris dataset using pandas and examine the first five rows:

    ```
    df = pd.read_csv('iris-data.csv')
    df.head()
    ```

    The output will be:

	Sepal Length	Sepal Width	Petal Length	Petal Width	Species
0	5.1	3.5	1.4	0.2	Iris-setosa
1	4.9	3.0	1.4	0.2	Iris-setosa
2	4.7	3.2	1.3	0.2	Iris-setosa
3	4.6	3.1	1.5	0.2	Iris-setosa
4	5.0	3.6	1.4	0.2	Iris-setosa

    Figure 4.79: The first five rows of the Iris dataset

3. The next step is feature engineering. We need to select the most appropriate features that will provide the most powerful classification model. Plot a number of different features versus the allocated species classifications, for example, sepal length versus petal length and species. Visually inspect the plots and look for any patterns that could indicate separation between each of the species:

    ```
    markers = {
        'Iris-setosa': {'marker': 'x'},
        'Iris-versicolor': {'marker': '*'},
        'Iris-virginica': {'marker': 'o'},
    }
    plt.figure(figsize=(10, 7))
    for name, group in df.groupby('Species'):
        plt.scatter(group['Sepal Width'], group['Petal Length'],
    ```

```
                label=name,
                marker=markers[name]['marker'],
            )

plt.title('Species Classification Sepal Width vs Petal Length');
plt.xlabel('Sepal Width (mm)');
plt.ylabel('Petal Length (mm)');
plt.legend();
```

The output will be:

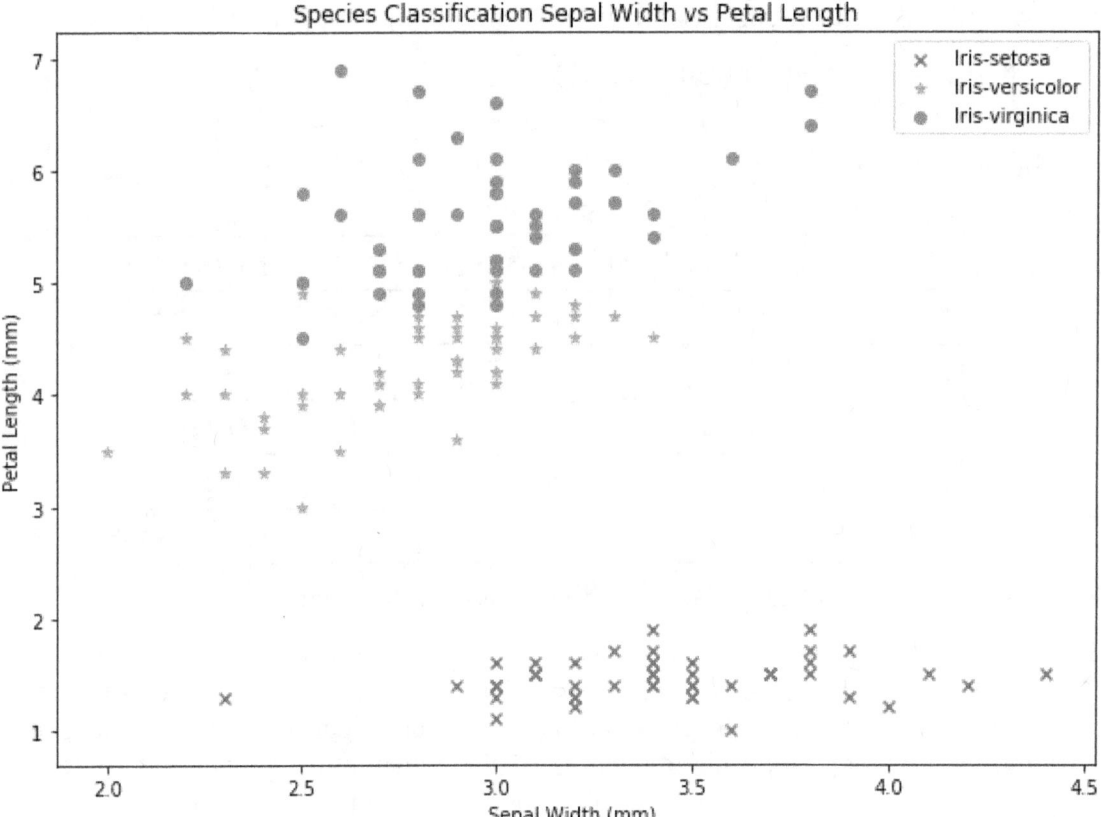

Figure 4.80: Species classification plot

4. Select the features by writing the column names in the following list:

   ```
   selected_features = [
       'Sepal Width', # List features here
       'Petal Length'
   ]
   ```

5. Before we can construct the model, we must first convert the **species** values into labels that can be used within the model. Replace the **Iris-setosa** species string with the value **0**, the **Iris-versicolor** species string with the value **1**, and the **Iris-virginica** species string with the value **2**:

   ```
   species = [
       'Iris-setosa', # 0
       'Iris-versicolor', # 1
       'Iris-virginica', # 2
   ]
   output = [species.index(spec) for spec in df.Species]
   ```

6. Create the model using the **selected_features** and the assigned **species** labels:

   ```
   model = LogisticRegression(multi_class='auto', solver='lbfgs')
   model.fit(df[selected_features], output)
   ```

   The output will be:

   ```
   LogisticRegression(C=1.0, class_weight=None, dual=False, fit_intercept=True,
               intercept_scaling=1, max_iter=100, multi_class='auto',
               n_jobs=None, penalty='l2', random_state=None, solver='lbfgs',
               tol=0.0001, verbose=0, warm_start=False)
   ```

7. Compute the accuracy of the model against the training set:

   ```
   model.score(df[selected_features], output)
   ```

   The output will be:

   ```
   0.9533333333333334
   ```

8. Construct another model using your second choice **selected_features** and compare the performance:

   ```
   selected_features = [
       'Sepal Length', # List features here
       'Petal Width'
   ]
   model.fit(df[selected_features], output)
   model.score(df[selected_features], output)
   ```

   The output will be:

   ```
   0.96
   ```

9. Construct another model using all available information and compare the performance:

   ```
   selected_features = [
       'Sepal Length', # List features here
       'Sepal Width'
   ]
   model.fit(df[selected_features], output)
   model.score(df[selected_features], output)
   ```

   The output will be:

   ```
   0.82
   ```

Activity 13: K-NN Multiclass Classifier

Solution

1. Import the following packages:

   ```
   import struct
   import numpy as np
   import gzip
   import urllib.request
   import matplotlib.pyplot as plt
   from array import array
   from sklearn.neighbors import KNeighborsClassifier as KNN
   ```

2. Load the MNIST data into memory.

   Training images:
   ```
   with gzip.open('train-images-idx3-ubyte.gz', 'rb') as f:
       magic, size, rows, cols = struct.unpack(">IIII", f.read(16))

       img = np.array(array("B", f.read())).reshape((size, rows, cols))
   ```
   Training labels:
   ```
   with gzip.open('train-labels-idx1-ubyte.gz', 'rb') as f:
       magic, size = struct.unpack(">II", f.read(8))
       labels = np.array(array("B", f.read()))
   ```
   Test images:
   ```
   with gzip.open('t10k-images-idx3-ubyte.gz', 'rb') as f:
       magic, size, rows, cols = struct.unpack(">IIII", f.read(16))

       img_test = np.array(array("B", f.read())).reshape((size, rows, cols))
   ```
   Test labels:
   ```
   with gzip.open('t10k-labels-idx1-ubyte.gz', 'rb') as f:
       magic, size = struct.unpack(">II", f.read(8))
       labels_test = np.array(array("B", f.read()))
   ```

3. Visualize a sample of the data:
   ```
   for i in range(10):
       plt.subplot(2, 5, i + 1)
       plt.imshow(img[i], cmap='gray');
       plt.title(f'{labels[i]}');
       plt.axis('off')
   ```

The output will be:

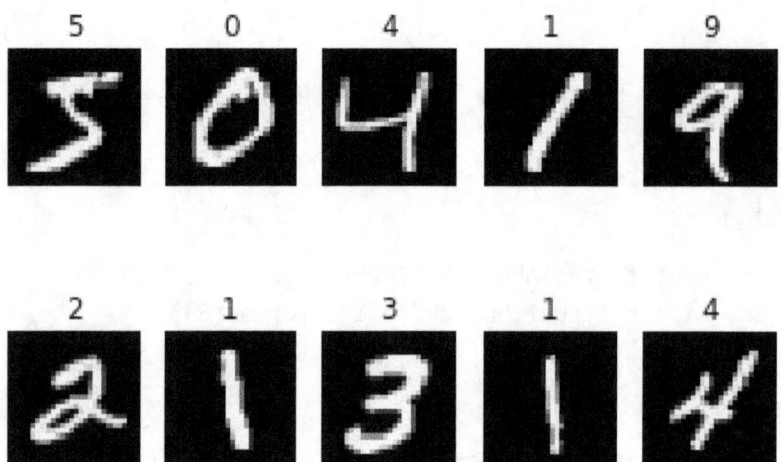

Figure 4.81: Sample images

4. Construct a K-NN classifier, with three nearest neighbors to classify the MNIST dataset. Again, to save processing power, randomly sample 5,000 images for use in training:

```
selection = np.random.choice(len(img), 5000)
selected_images = img[selection]
selected_labels = labels[selection]
```

5. In order to provide the image information to the model, we must first flatten the data out so that each image is 1 x 784 pixels in shape:

```
selected_images = selected_images.reshape((-1, rows * cols))
selected_images.shape
```

The output will be:

```
(5000, 784)
```

6. Build the three-neighbor KNN model and fit the data to the model. Note that, in this activity, we are providing 784 features or dimensions to the model, not simply 2:

```
model = KNN(n_neighbors=3)
model.fit(X=selected_images, y=selected_labels)
```

The output will be:

```
KNeighborsClassifier(algorithm='auto', leaf_size=30, metric='minkowski',
        metric_params=None, n_jobs=None, n_neighbors=3, p=2,
        weights='uniform')
```

7. Determine the score against the training set:

    ```
    model.score(X=selected_images, y=selected_labels)
    ```

    The output will be:

    ```
    0.9692
    ```

8. Display the first two predictions for the model against the training data:

    ```
    model.predict(selected_images)[:2]

    plt.subplot(1, 2, 1)
    plt.imshow(selected_images[0].reshape((28, 28)), cmap='gray');
    plt.axis('off');
    plt.subplot(1, 2, 2)
    plt.imshow(selected_images[1].reshape((28, 28)), cmap='gray');
    plt.axis('off');
    ```

    The output will be as follows:

    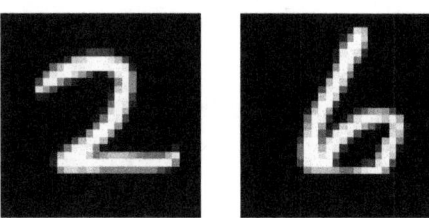

    Figure 4.82: First predicted values

9. Compare the performance against the test set:

    ```
    model.score(X=img_test.reshape((-1, rows * cols)), y=labels_test)
    ```

    The output will be:

    ```
    0.9376
    ```

Chapter 5: Ensemble Modeling

Activity 14: Stacking with Standalone and Ensemble Algorithms

Solution

1. Import the relevant libraries:

   ```
   import pandas as pd
   import numpy as np
   import seaborn as sns

   %matplotlib inline
   import matplotlib.pyplot as plt

   from sklearn.model_selection import train_test_split
   from sklearn.metrics import mean_absolute_error
   from sklearn.model_selection import KFold

   from sklearn.linear_model import LinearRegression
   from sklearn.tree import DecisionTreeRegressor
   from sklearn.neighbors import KNeighborsRegressor
   from sklearn.ensemble import GradientBoostingRegressor, RandomForestRegressor
   ```

2. Read the data and print the first five rows:

   ```
   data = pd.read_csv('house_prices.csv')
   data.head()
   ```

   The output will be as follows:

	Id	MSSubClass	MSZoning	LotFrontage	LotArea	Street	Alley	LotShape	LandContour	Utilities	...	PoolArea
0	1	60	RL	65.0	8450	Pave	NaN	Reg	Lvl	AllPub	...	0
1	2	20	RL	80.0	9600	Pave	NaN	Reg	Lvl	AllPub	...	0
2	3	60	RL	68.0	11250	Pave	NaN	IR1	Lvl	AllPub	...	0
3	4	70	RL	60.0	9550	Pave	NaN	IR1	Lvl	AllPub	...	0
4	5	60	RL	84.0	14260	Pave	NaN	IR1	Lvl	AllPub	...	0

   Figure 5.19: The first 5 rows

3. Preprocess the dataset to remove null values and one-hot encode categorical variables to prepare the data for modeling.

   First, we remove all columns where more than 10% of the values are null. To do this, calculate the fraction of missing values by using the `.isnull()` method to get a mask DataFrame and apply the `.mean()` method to get the fraction of null values in each column. Multiply the result by 100 to get the series as percentage values.

   Then, find the subset of the series having a percentage value lower than 10 and save the index (which will give us the column names) as a list. Print the list to see the columns we get:

   ```
   perc_missing = data.isnull().mean()*100
   cols = perc_missing[perc_missing < 10].index.tolist()
   cols
   ```

   The output will be:

   ```
   ['Id',
    'MSSubClass',
    'MSZoning',
    'LotArea',
    'Street',
    'LotShape',
    'LandContour',
    'Utilities',
    'LotConfig',
    'LandSlope',
    'Neighborhood',
   ```

   Figure 5.20: Output of preprocessing the dataset

   As the first column is **id**, we will exclude this column as well, since it will not add any value to the model.

   We will subset the data to include all columns in the **col** list except the first element, which is **id**:

   ```
   data = data.loc[:, cols[1:]]
   ```

For the categorical variables, we replace null values with a string, **NA**, and one-hot encode the columns using pandas' **.get_dummies()** method, while for the numerical variables we will replace the null values with **-1**. Then, we combine the numerical and categorical columns to get the final DataFrame:

```
data_obj = pd.get_dummies(data.select_dtypes(include=[np.object]).
fillna('NA'))
data_num = data.select_dtypes(include=[np.number]).fillna(-1)

data_final = pd.concat([data_obj, data_num], axis=1)
```

4. Divide the dataset into train and validation DataFrames.

   We use scikit-learn's **train_test_split()** method to divide the final DataFrame into training and validation sets in the ratio 4:1. We further split each of the two sets into their respective **x** and **y** values to represent the features and target variable respectively:

   ```
   train, val = train, val = train_test_split(data_final, test_size=0.2,
   random_state=11)

   x_train = train.drop(columns=['SalePrice'])
   y_train = train['SalePrice'].values

   x_val = val.drop(columns=['SalePrice'])
   y_val = val['SalePrice'].values
   ```

5. Initialize dictionaries in which to store train and validation MAE values. We will create two dictionaries, in which we will store the MAE values on the train and validation datasets:

   ```
   train_mae_values, val_mae_values = {}, {}
   ```

6. Train a decision tree model and save the scores. We will use scikit-learn's **DecisionTreeRegressor** class to train a regression model using a single decision tree:

   ```
   # Decision Tree

   dt_params = {
       'criterion': 'mae',
       'min_samples_leaf': 10,
       'random_state': 11
   }

   dt = DecisionTreeRegressor(**dt_params)
   ```

```
dt.fit(x_train, y_train)
dt_preds_train = dt.predict(x_train)
dt_preds_val = dt.predict(x_val)

train_mae_values['dt'] = mean_absolute_error(y_true=y_train, y_pred=dt_
preds_train)
val_mae_values['dt'] = mean_absolute_error(y_true=y_val, y_pred=dt_preds_
val)
```

7. Train a k-nearest neighbors model and save the scores. We will use scikit-learn's **kNeighborsRegressor** class to train a regression model with $k=5$:

   ```
   # k-Nearest Neighbors
   
   knn_params = {
       'n_neighbors': 5
   }
   
   knn = KNeighborsRegressor(**knn_params)
   
   knn.fit(x_train, y_train)
   knn_preds_train = knn.predict(x_train)
   knn_preds_val = knn.predict(x_val)
   
   train_mae_values['knn'] = mean_absolute_error(y_true=y_train, y_pred=knn_
   preds_train)
   val_mae_values['knn'] = mean_absolute_error(y_true=y_val, y_pred=knn_
   preds_val)
   ```

8. Train a Random Forest model and save the scores. We will use scikit-learn's **RandomForestRegressor** class to train a regression model using bagging:

   ```
   # Random Forest
   
   rf_params = {
       'n_estimators': 50,
       'criterion': 'mae',
       'max_features': 'sqrt',
       'min_samples_leaf': 10,
       'random_state': 11,
       'n_jobs': -1
   }
   ```

```
    rf = RandomForestRegressor(**rf_params)

    rf.fit(x_train, y_train)
    rf_preds_train = rf.predict(x_train)
    rf_preds_val = rf.predict(x_val)

    train_mae_values['rf'] = mean_absolute_error(y_true=y_train, y_pred=rf_
    preds_train)
    val_mae_values['rf'] = mean_absolute_error(y_true=y_val, y_pred=rf_preds_
    val)
```

9. Train a gradient boosting model and save the scores. We will use scikit-learn's **GradientBoostingRegressor** class to train a boosted regression model:

    ```
    # Gradient Boosting

    gbr_params = {
        'n_estimators': 50,
        'criterion': 'mae',
        'max_features': 'sqrt',
        'max_depth': 3,
        'min_samples_leaf': 5,
        'random_state': 11
    }

    gbr = GradientBoostingRegressor(**gbr_params)

    gbr.fit(x_train, y_train)
    gbr_preds_train = gbr.predict(x_train)
    gbr_preds_val = gbr.predict(x_val)

    train_mae_values['gbr'] = mean_absolute_error(y_true=y_train, y_pred=gbr_
    preds_train)
    val_mae_values['gbr'] = mean_absolute_error(y_true=y_val, y_pred=gbr_
    preds_val)
    ```

10. Prepare the training and validation datasets with the four meta estimators having the same hyperparameters that were used in the previous steps. We will create a **num_base_predictors** variable that represents the number of base estimators we have in the stacked model to help calculate the shape of the datasets for training and validation. This step can be coded almost identically to the exercise in the chapter, with a different number (and type) of base estimators.

11. First, we create a new training set with additional columns for predictions from base predictors, in the same way as was done previously:

    ```
    num_base_predictors = len(train_mae_values) # 4

    x_train_with_metapreds = np.zeros((x_train.shape[0], x_train.shape[1]+num_base_predictors))
    x_train_with_metapreds[:, :-num_base_predictors] = x_train
    x_train_with_metapreds[:, -num_base_predictors:] = -1
    ```

    Then, we train the base models using the k-fold strategy. We save the predictions in each iteration in a list, and iterate over the list to assign the predictions to the columns in that fold:

    ```
    kf = KFold(n_splits=5, random_state=11)

    for train_indices, val_indices in kf.split(x_train):
        kfold_x_train, kfold_x_val = x_train.iloc[train_indices], x_train.iloc[val_indices]
        kfold_y_train, kfold_y_val = y_train[train_indices], y_train[val_indices]

        predictions = []

        dt = DecisionTreeRegressor(**dt_params)
        dt.fit(kfold_x_train, kfold_y_train)
        predictions.append(dt.predict(kfold_x_val))

        knn = KNeighborsRegressor(**knn_params)
        knn.fit(kfold_x_train, kfold_y_train)
        predictions.append(knn.predict(kfold_x_val))

        gbr = GradientBoostingRegressor(**gbr_params)
        rf.fit(kfold_x_train, kfold_y_train)
        predictions.append(rf.predict(kfold_x_val))

        gbr = GradientBoostingRegressor(**gbr_params)
        gbr.fit(kfold_x_train, kfold_y_train)
        predictions.append(gbr.predict(kfold_x_val))

        for i, preds in enumerate(predictions):
            x_train_with_metapreds[val_indices, -(i+1)] = preds
    ```

After that, we create a new validation set with additional columns for predictions from base predictors:

```
x_val_with_metapreds = np.zeros((x_val.shape[0], x_val.shape[1]+num_base_
predictors))
x_val_with_metapreds[:, :-num_base_predictors] = x_val
x_val_with_metapreds[:, -num_base_predictors:] = -1
```

12. Lastly, we fit the base models on the complete training set to get meta features for the validation set:

```
predictions = []

dt = DecisionTreeRegressor(**dt_params)
dt.fit(x_train, y_train)
predictions.append(dt.predict(x_val))

knn = KNeighborsRegressor(**knn_params)
knn.fit(x_train, y_train)
predictions.append(knn.predict(x_val))

gbr = GradientBoostingRegressor(**gbr_params)
rf.fit(x_train, y_train)
predictions.append(rf.predict(x_val))

gbr = GradientBoostingRegressor(**gbr_params)
gbr.fit(x_train, y_train)
predictions.append(gbr.predict(x_val))

for i, preds in enumerate(predictions):
    x_val_with_metapreds[:, -(i+1)] = preds
```

13. Train a linear regression model as the stacked model. To train the stacked model, we train the logistic regression model on all the columns of the training dataset, plus the meta predictions from the base estimators. We then use the final predictions to calculate the MAE values, which we store in the same **train_mae_values** and **val_mae_values** dictionaries:

```
lr = LinearRegression(normalize=False)
lr.fit(x_train_with_metapreds, y_train)
lr_preds_train = lr.predict(x_train_with_metapreds)
lr_preds_val = lr.predict(x_val_with_metapreds)

train_mae_values['lr'] = mean_absolute_error(y_true=y_train, y_pred=lr_preds_train)
val_mae_values['lr'] = mean_absolute_error(y_true=y_val, y_pred=lr_preds_val)
```

14. Visualize the train and validation errors for each individual model and the stacked model. Then, we will convert the dictionaries into two series and combine them to form two columns of a Pandas DataFrame:

```
mae_scores = pd.concat([pd.Series(train_mae_values, name='train'),
                        pd.Series(val_mae_values, name='val')],
                       axis=1)
mae_scores
```

The output will be as follows:

	train	val
dt	16222.572774	25274.595890
gbr	16207.692537	20078.417487
knn	23669.883219	29642.142466
lr	12567.358027	17661.226920
rf	19484.653579	23023.638425

Figure 5.21: The train and validation errors for each individual model and the stacked model

15. We then plot a bar chart from this DataFrame to visualize the MAE values for the train and validation sets using each model:

    ```
    mae_scores.plot(kind='bar', figsize=(10,7))
    plt.ylabel('MAE')
    plt.xlabel('Model')
    plt.show()
    ```

    The output will be as follows:

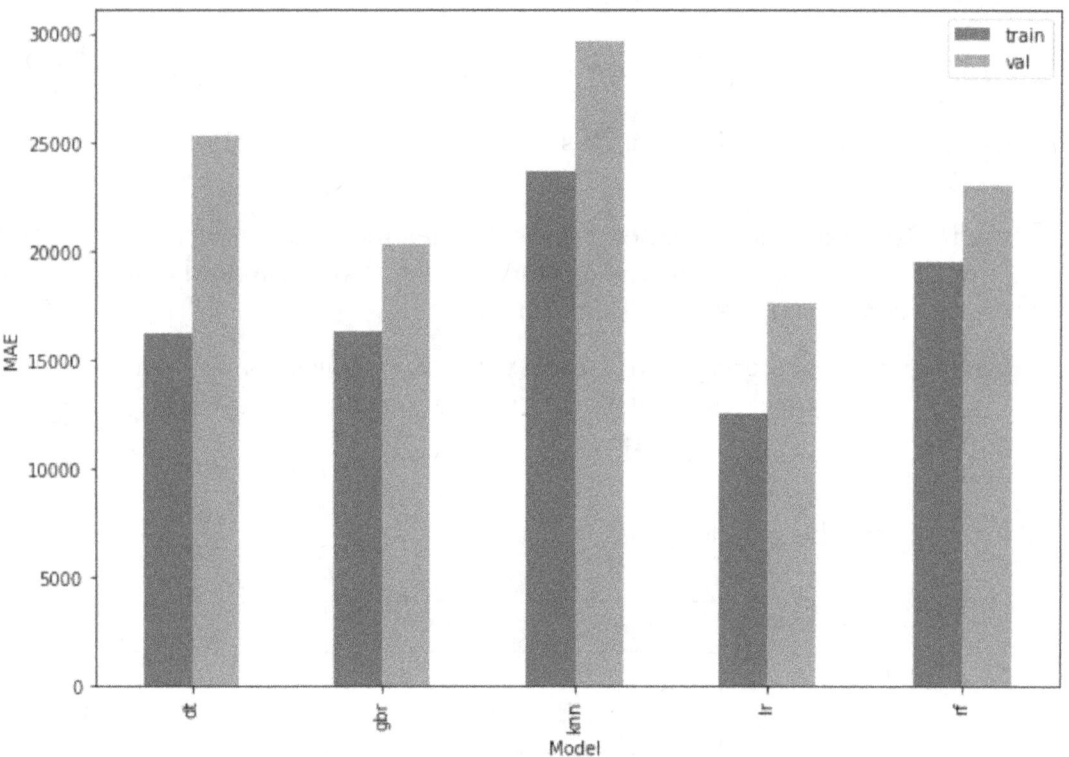

Figure 5.22: Bar chart visualizing the MAE values

As we can see in the plot, the linear regression stacked model has the lowest value of mean absolute error on both training and validation datasets, even compared to the other ensemble models (Random Forest and gradient boosted regressor).

Chapter 6: Model Evaluation

Activity 15: Final Test Project

Solution

1. Import the relevant libraries:

   ```
   import pandas as pd
   import numpy as np
   import json

   %matplotlib inline
   import matplotlib.pyplot as plt

   from sklearn.preprocessing import OneHotEncoder
   from sklearn.model_selection import RandomizedSearchCV, train_test_split
   from sklearn.ensemble import GradientBoostingClassifier
   from sklearn.metrics import (accuracy_score, precision_score, recall_score, confusion_matrix, precision_recall_curve)
   ```

2. Read the **attrition_train.csv** dataset. Read the CSV file into a DataFrame and print the **.info()** of the DataFrame:

   ```
   data = pd.read_csv('attrition_train.csv')
   data.info()
   ```

   The output will be as follows:

   ```
   <class 'pandas.core.frame.DataFrame'>
   RangeIndex: 1176 entries, 0 to 1175
   Data columns (total 31 columns):
   Age                      1176 non-null int64
   Attrition                1176 non-null int64
   BusinessTravel           1176 non-null object
   DailyRate                1176 non-null int64
   Department               1176 non-null object
   DistanceFromHome         1176 non-null int64
   Education                1176 non-null int64
   EducationField           1176 non-null object
   EnvironmentSatisfaction  1176 non-null int64
   Gender                   1176 non-null int64
   HourlyRate               1176 non-null int64
   ```

   Figure 6.33: Output of info()

3. Read the JSON file with the details of the categorical variables. The JSON file contains a dictionary, where the keys are the column names of the categorical features and the corresponding values are the list of categories in the feature. This file will help us one-hot encode the categorical features into numerical features. Use the `json` library to load the file object into a dictionary, and print the dictionary:

   ```
   with open('categorical_variable_values.json', 'r') as f:
       cat_values_dict = json.load(f)
   cat_values_dict
   ```

   The output will be as follows:

   ```
   {'BusinessTravel': ['Travel_Rarely', 'Non-Travel', 'Travel_Frequently'],
    'Department': ['Research & Development', 'Sales', 'Human Resources'],
    'MaritalStatus': ['Married', 'Divorced', 'Single'],
    'EducationField': ['Other',
     'Technical Degree',
     'Life Sciences',
     'Marketing',
     'Medical',
     'Human Resources'],
    'JobRole': ['Research Director',
     'Laboratory Technician',
     'Healthcare Representative',
     'Sales Executive',
     'Research Scientist',
     'Manufacturing Director',
     'Sales Representative',
     'Manager',
     'Human Resources']}
   ```

   Figure 6.34: The JSON file

4. Process the dataset to convert all features to numerical values. First, find the number of columns that will stay in their original form (that is, numerical features) and that need to be one-hot encoded (that is, the categorical features). **data.shape[1]** gives us the number of columns in **data**, and we subtract **len(cat_values_dict)** from it to get the number of numerical columns. To find the number of categorical columns, we simply count the total number of categories across all categorical variables from the **cat_values_dict** dictionary:

   ```
   num_orig_cols = data.shape[1] - len(cat_values_dict)
   num_enc_cols = sum([len(cats) for cats in cat_values_dict.values()])
   print(num_orig_cols, num_enc_cols)
   ```

The output will be:

```
26 24
```

Create a NumPy array of zeros as a placeholder, with a shape equal to the total number of columns, as determined previously, minus one (because the **Attrition** target variable is also included here). For the numerical columns, we then create a mask that selects the numerical columns from the DataFrame and assigns them to the first **num_orig_cols-1** columns in the array, **X**:

```
X = np.zeros(shape=(data.shape[0], num_orig_cols+num_enc_cols-1))

mask = [(each not in cat_values_dict and each != 'Attrition') for each in data.columns]
X[:, :num_orig_cols-1] = data.loc[:, data.columns[mask]]
```

Next, we initialize the **OneHotEncoder** class from scikit-learn with a list containing the list of values in each categorical column. Then, we transform the categorical columns to one-hot encoded columns and assign them to the remaining columns in **X**, and save the values of the target variable in the **y** variable:

```
cat_cols = list(cat_values_dict.keys())
cat_values = [cat_values_dict[col] for col in data[cat_cols].columns]

ohe = OneHotEncoder(categories=cat_values, sparse=False, )

X[:, num_orig_cols-1:] = ohe.fit_transform(X=data[cat_cols])
y = data.Attrition.values

print(X.shape)
print(y.shape)
```

The output will be:

```
(1176, 49)
(1176,)
```

5. Choose a base model and define the range of hyperparameter values corresponding to the model to be searched over for hyperparameter tuning. Let's use a gradient boosted classifier as our model. We then define ranges of values for all hyperparameters we want to tune in the form of a dictionary:

```
meta_gbc = GradientBoostingClassifier()

param_dist = {
    'n_estimators': list(range(10, 210, 10)),
```

```
        'criterion': ['mae', 'mse'],
        'max_features': ['sqrt', 'log2', 0.25, 0.3, 0.5, 0.8, None],
        'max_depth': list(range(1, 10)),
        'min_samples_leaf': list(range(1, 10))
}
```

6. Define the parameters with which to initialize the **RandomizedSearchCV** object and use K-fold cross-validation to find the best model hyperparameters. Define the parameters required for random search, including **cv** as **5**, indicating that the hyperparameters should be chosen by evaluating the performance using 5-fold cross-validation. Then, initialize the **RandomizedSearchCV** object and use the **.fit()** method to begin the optimization:

```
rand_search_params = {
        'param_distributions': param_dist,
        'scoring': 'accuracy',
        'n_iter': 100,
        'cv': 5,
        'return_train_score': True,
        'n_jobs': -1,
        'random_state': 11
}
random_search = RandomizedSearchCV(meta_gbc, **rand_search_params)
random_search.fit(X, y)
```

The output will be as follows:

```
RandomizedSearchCV(cv=5, error_score='raise-deprecating',
          estimator=GradientBoostingClassifier(criterion='friedman_mse', init=None,
              learning_rate=0.1, loss='deviance', max_depth=3,
              max_features=None, max_leaf_nodes=None,
              min_impurity_decrease=0.0, min_impurity_split=None,
              min_samples_leaf=1, min_sampl...    subsample=1.0, tol=0.0001, validation_fraction=0.1,
              verbose=0, warm_start=False),
          fit_params=None, iid='warn', n_iter=100, n_jobs=-1,
          param_distributions={'n_estimators': [10, 20, 30, 40, 50, 60, 70, 80, 90, 100, 110, 120, 130, 140, 150, 160, 170, 180, 190, 200], 'criterion': ['mae', 'mse'], 'max_features': ['sqrt', 'log2', 0.25, 0.3, 0.5, 0.8, None], 'max_depth': [1, 2, 3, 4, 5, 6, 7, 8, 9], 'min_samples_leaf': [1, 2, 3, 4, 5, 6, 7, 8, 9]},
          pre_dispatch='2*n_jobs', random_state=11, refit=True,
          return_train_score=True, scoring='accuracy', verbose=0)
```

Figure 6.35: Output of the optimization process

Once the tuning is complete, find the position (iteration number) at which the highest mean test score was obtained. Find the corresponding hyperparameters and save them to a dictionary:

```
idx = np.argmax(random_search.cv_results_['mean_test_score'])
final_params = random_search.cv_results_['params'][idx]
final_params
```

The output will be:

```
{'n_estimators': 150,
 'min_samples_leaf': 9,
 'max_features': 0.3,
 'max_depth': 9,
 'criterion': 'mse'}
```

Figure 6.36: The hyperparameters dictionary

7. Split the dataset into training and validation sets and train a new model using the final hyperparameters on the training dataset. Use scikit-learn's **train_test_split()** method to split **X** and **y** into train and test components, with test comprising 15% of the dataset:

```
train_X, val_X, train_y, val_y = train_test_split(X, y, test_size=0.15, random_state=11)
print(train_X.shape, train_y.shape, val_X.shape, val_y.shape)
```

The output will be:

```
((999, 49), (999,), (177, 49), (177,))
```

Train the gradient boosted classification model using the final hyperparameters and make predictions on the training and validation sets. Also calculate the probability on the validation set:

```
gbc = GradientBoostingClassifier(**final_params)
gbc.fit(train_X, train_y)

preds_train = gbc.predict(train_X)
preds_val = gbc.predict(val_X)
pred_probs_val = np.array([each[1] for each in gbc.predict_proba(val_X)])
```

8. Calculate the accuracy, precision, and recall for predictions on the validation set, and print the confusion matrix:

    ```
    print('train accuracy_score = {}'.format(accuracy_score(y_true=train_y, y_pred=preds_train)))
    print('validation accuracy_score = {}'.format(accuracy_score(y_true=val_y, y_pred=preds_val)))

    print('confusion_matrix: \n{}'.format(confusion_matrix(y_true=val_y, y_pred=preds_val)))
    print('precision_score = {}'.format(precision_score(y_true=val_y, y_pred=preds_val)))
    print('recall_score = {}'.format(recall_score(y_true=val_y, y_pred=preds_val)))
    ```

    The output will be as follows:

    ```
    train accuracy_score = 1.0
    validation accuracy_score = 0.864406779661017
    confusion_matrix:
    [[146   0]
     [ 24   7]]
    precision_score = 1.0
    recall_score = 0.22580645161290322
    ```

    Figure 6.37: Accuracy, precision, recall, and the confusion matrix

9. Experiment with varying thresholds to find the optimal point with high recall.

    Plot the precision-recall curve:

    ```
    plt.figure(figsize=(10,7))

    precision, recall, thresholds = precision_recall_curve(val_y, pred_probs_val)
    plt.plot(recall, precision)

    plt.xlabel('Recall')
    plt.ylabel('Precision')
    plt.show()
    ```

The output will be as follows:

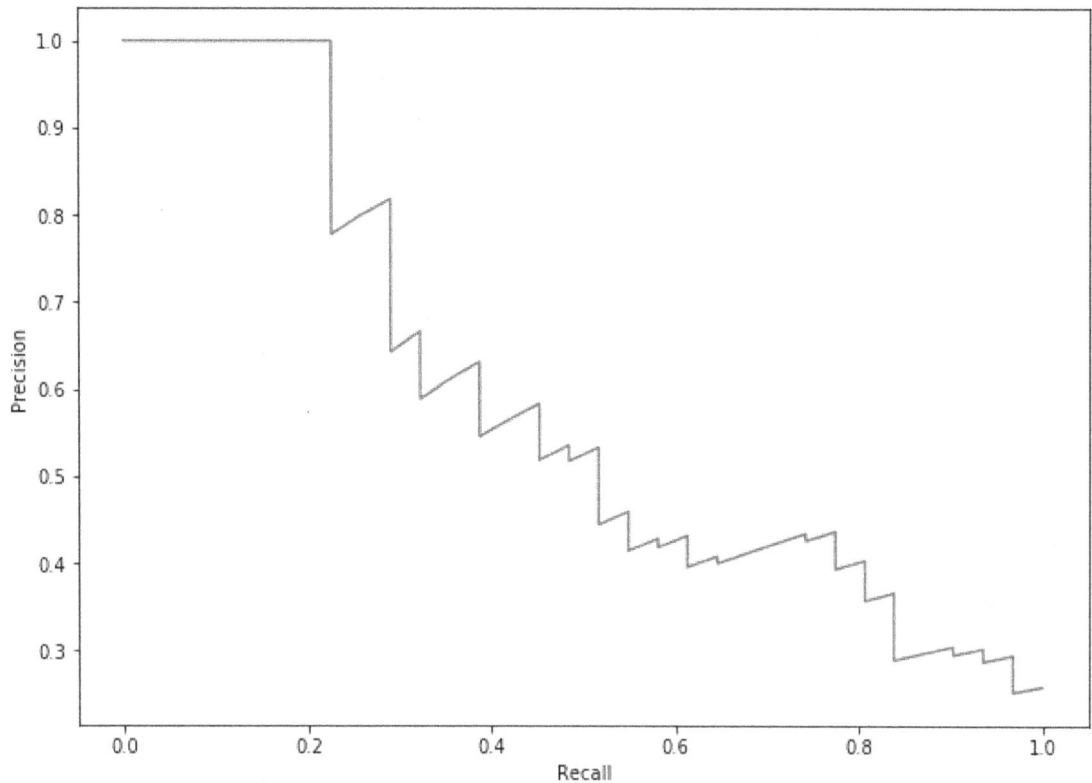

Figure 6.38: The precision-recall curve

Plot the variation in precision and recall with increasing threshold values:

```
PR_variation_df = pd.DataFrame({'precision': precision, 'recall': recall},
index=list(thresholds)+[1])

PR_variation_df.plot(figsize=(10,7))
plt.xlabel('Threshold')
plt.ylabel('P/R values')
plt.show()
```

The output will be as follows:

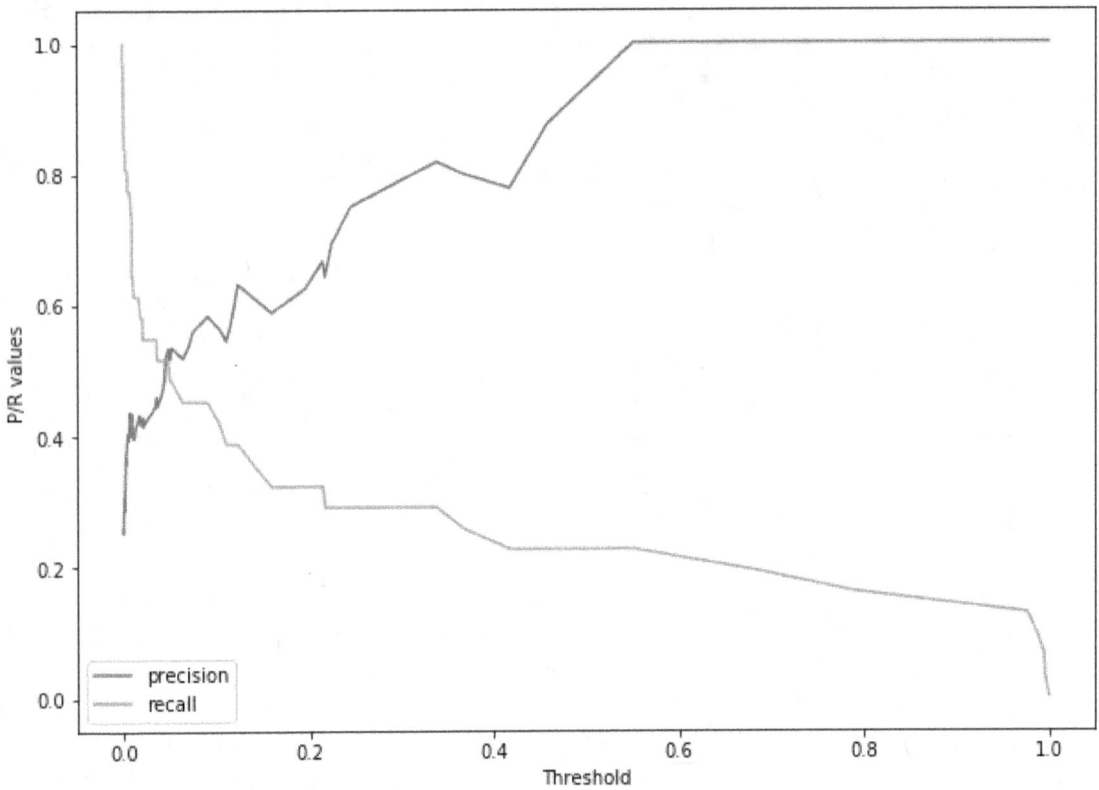

Figure 6.39: Variation in precision and recall with increasing threshold values

10. Finalize a threshold that will be used for predictions on the test dataset. Let's finalize a value, say, 0.3. This value is entirely dependent on what you feel would be optimal based on your exploration in the previous step:

```
final_threshold = 0.3
```

11. Read and process the test dataset to convert all features to numerical values. This will be done in a manner similar to that in *step 4*, with the only difference that we don't need to account for the target variable column, as the dataset does not contain it:

    ```
    test = pd.read_csv('attrition_test.csv')
    test.info()


    num_orig_cols = test.shape[1] - len(cat_values_dict)
    num_enc_cols = sum([len(cats) for cats in cat_values_dict.values()])
    print(num_orig_cols, num_enc_cols)


    test_X = np.zeros(shape=(test.shape[0], num_orig_cols+num_enc_cols))

    mask = [(each not in cat_values_dict) for each in test.columns]
    test_X[:, :num_orig_cols] = test.loc[:, test.columns[mask]]

    cat_cols = list(cat_values_dict.keys())
    cat_values = [cat_values_dict[col] for col in test[cat_cols].columns]

    ohe = OneHotEncoder(categories=cat_values, sparse=False, )

    test_X[:, num_orig_cols:] = ohe.fit_transform(X=test[cat_cols])
    print(test_X.shape)
    ```

12. Predict the final values on the test dataset and save them to a file. Use the final threshold value determined in *step 10* to find the classes for each value in the training set. Then, write the final predictions to the **final_predictions.csv** file:

    ```
    pred_probs_test = np.array([each[1] for each in gbc.predict_proba(test_X)])
    preds_test = (pred_probs_test > final_threshold).astype(int)

    with open('final_predictions.csv', 'w') as f:
        f.writelines([str(val)+'\n' for val in preds_test])
    ```

The output will be a CSV file, as follows:

```
1   0
2   0
3   0
4   0
5   0
6   0
7   0
8   0
9   0
10  0
11  1
12  1
13  0
14  0
15  0
16  0
```

Figure 6.40: The CSV file

Index

About

All major keywords used in this book are captured alphabetically in this section. Each one is accompanied by the page number of where they appear.

A

adaboost: 250, 253
adaptive: 233, 249-251, 253, 255, 263
adjustment:141
aggregate: 36, 42, 270, 282
algebra: 19, 143
algorithm: 2-6, 67, 139, 141, 172, 175, 199, 214-215, 217, 231, 234, 237, 240-241, 246-249, 253, 289, 295
algorithms: 3, 6, 19, 105, 151, 199, 214, 234, 242, 261, 263, 268, 272
anaconda: 8-9, 16-19, 167
arange: 160, 162, 169-170, 208
arrays: 119, 209, 257
asymmetry:83
asymptote:147

B

bagged:263
bagging: 233-234, 240-248, 263
bayesian:290
biased: 282-283, 293
bigquery:54
binary: 96, 236-237, 249, 269, 273-274, 276
binned:82
boolean:62
boosted: 248-249
boosting: 231, 233-234, 240-241, 248-251, 253-255, 261-263, 295
bootstrap: 240-244, 247, 249, 254, 291
boxplot: 99, 104

C

cluster:202
clustering: 6, 19, 175, 198
concat: 63, 236
converge:287

D

database: 5, 54-55, 108, 155, 261
data-dense:62
dataframe: 23-24, 27, 31-35, 37, 39, 41, 44, 46-48, 54-55, 57, 59, 62-63, 65, 67, 69-71, 73, 77-78, 80, 85-87, 89, 97, 99, 102, 113, 116, 125-126, 177, 206, 216-217, 236, 292-293
dataframes: 24, 34, 62, 261
datapoints:244
datatypes:77
dayofyear: 124, 131
dictionary: 24, 36, 39-40, 54, 57, 71-72, 291-292
distplot:83
dropna: 41, 67, 79, 83
dtypes: 54, 77-78
dummies:236

E

edgecolor: 201, 203, 210, 212
ensemble: 2, 46, 67, 130, 214, 228, 231, 233-234, 240-250, 253-257, 261, 263, 266-268, 272, 279, 284, 286
enumerate:207

epochs: 145-147
euclidean:199

F

facecolor: 201, 203, 210
fillna: 43-45, 67-68
fourier:19

G

gaussian: 67, 82
gradient: 107, 111, 117-118, 139-145, 148, 150-154, 172, 233, 253-255, 261-263, 289, 295
graphviz:230
greedy: 246, 253
groupby: 35, 40, 44-45, 47-48, 71, 97, 101, 113, 177, 179, 201, 203, 210, 218, 220-221, 224, 226

H

high-bias:240

I

imputation: 67-70
imshow: 187-188, 193
ipython: 1, 7
isnull: 62-63, 70, 72, 89, 96
iteration: 36, 207, 248-249, 281-282

J

jupyter: 1, 7-11, 13-14, 16, 18-19, 22-23, 34, 47-48, 54, 75, 143, 168, 216

K

k-closest: 6
kernel: 11-12, 14-15, 84, 94
k-fold: 258, 267, 282-284, 291, 295-296
k-nearest: 6, 67, 175, 198-199, 257, 261-262
kurtosis: 83, 85-87

L

liblinear: 189
linearsvc: 257-259
linspace: 83, 127-128, 135, 148, 179, 181
logistic: 150, 175, 182-185, 189-192, 195, 197-200, 231, 257, 260

M

markdown: 1, 16-18
matlab: 19
matplotlib: 19-20, 54, 75, 87, 89, 97, 112, 116, 124, 131, 138, 153, 155, 171, 185, 196-197, 200, 206, 213, 228, 235, 268
median: 56, 67, 69, 96, 154-157
missingno: 54, 63, 65-66, 105
multiclass: 191-192, 198, 200, 213

N

neural: 2, 109, 150, 176, 182
non-linear: 67, 182, 199, 231
nullity: 62-63, 65-66, 73

O

outliers: 53, 82-83, 86, 96, 234, 239, 249, 253, 280-281, 287

P

pandas: 1, 19-20, 22-24, 31, 34, 37, 41, 45, 47-48, 54, 57, 62, 67-68, 73-74, 79, 85, 89, 99, 102, 105, 112, 116, 124, 131, 138, 153, 155, 161, 163, 171, 177, 197, 200, 206, 216-218, 228, 235-236, 268, 292-293
pickle: 20, 268-269
plateau: 125
pydata: 19-20, 23-24, 31, 47
pyplot: 54, 112, 116, 124, 131, 138, 153, 155, 171, 185, 196-197, 200, 206, 213, 228, 235, 268

Q

quantile: 47
quantize: 88
quartiles: 47, 56, 96

R

regression: 2, 19, 73-74, 87, 103, 105, 107-108, 111, 117-119, 122, 124-125, 130-133, 137-139, 143, 150, 153-158, 161, 172, 175-178, 182, 184-185, 189-192, 195-200, 228, 231, 234, 238-240, 242, 244, 253, 257, 260-262, 265-270, 272, 288, 296
reshape: 119-120, 123, 133, 144, 151, 156-157, 178-180, 186-187, 189, 191-195, 205, 210

S

seaborn: 19-20, 54, 83, 87, 90, 94, 102, 104
skewness: 82-83
sklearn: 54, 119, 124, 131, 138, 148, 151, 153, 155, 185, 192, 196-197, 200, 206, 213, 228, 230, 235, 244, 247, 250, 254, 257, 272, 279, 284, 291
statsmodel: 167
stratified: 284

U

univariate: 53, 105

W

wrapper: 54, 118

www.ingramcontent.com/pod-product-compliance
Lightning Source LLC
LaVergne TN
LVHW081512050326
832903LV00025B/1458